ULRICHUS VELENUS

(OLDŘICH VELENSKÝ)

AND HIS TREATISE AGAINST THE PAPACY

STUDIES
IN MEDIEVAL AND
REFORMATION THOUGHT

EDITED BY

HEIKO A. OBERMAN, Tübingen

IN COOPERATION WITH

E. JANE DEMPSEY DOUGLASS, Claremont, California
LEIF GRANE, Copenhagen
GUILLAUME H. M. POSTHUMUS MEYJES, Leiden
ANTON G. WEILER, Nijmegen

VOLUME XIX

A. J. LAMPING

ULRICHUS VELENUS

LEIDEN
E. J. BRILL
1976

ULRICHUS VELENUS

(Oldřich Velenský)

AND HIS TREATISE AGAINST THE PAPACY

BY

A. J. LAMPING

LEIDEN
E. J. BRILL
1976

ISBN 90 04 0 4397 7

In libellum quendam, qui emissus est,
quod Petrus Romam non venerit.
Nemo sacris poterit libris convincere Petrum
Perlusstrasse locum, Martia Roma, tuum.
At si non Romae plausu circoque frequenti,
Edocuit plureis ordine pontifices.
Non igitur Petrus, sed Simon in urbe reliquit
Tot successores nomine reque malos.

Voor Aafke

CONTENTS

CONTENTS

PREFACE

The study of a treatise from the beginning of the sixteenth century would perhaps seem to transport one to quite another world, but one soon finds that much that was characteristic of that time can be paralleled today. The men of the sixteenth century were also searching for a new form of pastorate and a new interpretation of the faith proclaimed by the Bible, since they also had to find answers to the problems posed by their time. We shall not of course be able to experience everything exactly as they did and their solutions will not usually be ours, but acquaintance with the tensions of that time helps us to set our own circumstances in perspective. The main "lesson of history" is that the church has gone through many periods of great difficulty and that this is part of her very nature: we must search for ways to make the Gospel comprehensible and applicable in all the varying political and social changes we are confronted with. This is not to say that our own concerns are only of relative importance —anyone who experiences day-to-day existence in all its intensity could never subscribe to such a notion—but it certainly encourages us to play our part in the church on its way through history.

This study was a doctoral thesis in the theological faculty of the University of Leiden. My supervisor was Professor G. H. M. Posthumus Meyjes, to whom I should like to express my gratitude for his interest and careful attention to detail. Dr. M. Bohatcová and Dr. J. Brambora of Prague were very helpful—especially in drawing my attention to sources that would have been very diffiicult to discover at such a distance from Czechoslovakia.

December 1975   A. J. LAMPING

INTRODUCTION

On the 24th November 1520, a little book of very modest size was published by the printer Sylvan Otmar of Augsburg. Although it contained barely sixty pages, it unleashed a violent debate among theologians within a few years of its appearance. It was at the time generally regarded, both by those who supported its arguments and by those who opposed them, as a direct attack against the established Church and even now its influence is still felt in the sphere of Church polemics. This is hardly surprising, since the author postulated that the Apostle Peter never went to Rome and was consequently not martyred there.

As is common in publications of this period, the title of this treatise was in fact a summary of its contents: *In hoc libello gravissimis certissimisque et in sacra scriptura fundatis racionibus variis probatur: Apostolum Petrum Rhomam non venisse neque illic passum, proinde satis frivole et temere Rhomanus Pontifex se Petri successorem iactat et nominat, etc.* The author's name does not appear on the title page, but, at the beginning of the foreword, one Ulrichus Velenus Minhoniensis greets his readers.

There are several reasons why this treatise attracted so much attention so soon after its publication.[1] The most important was its timing —it appeared just when papal primacy had become a burning question. In the previous year, a heated debate had taken place between the Catholic theologian Eck and Luther in Leipzig and, in this debate, Luther had denied *daß der Primat eine Institution des göttlichen Rechtes sei.*[2] A few weeks after the appearance of Velenus' treatise, on the 10th December 1520, Luther had set fire, at the gate of the city of Wittenberg, to the papal bull *Exsurge Domine*, thus demonstrating his repudiation of the powers of the pope. Velenus' clear aim, in publishing his treatise, was to undermine the historical foundation of the papacy, that is, the tradition that Peter had been the bishop of Rome. The document was therefore of great contemporary relevance.

Because it aroused so much interest, several reprints and new

---

[1] An example of this is the verse that precedes this introduction. Michael Hummelberger sent it on 5 February 1522 to Thomas Blarer, the burgomaster of Constance and—as a theologian—a follower of Luther. It refers to Velenus' treatise. (Cod. Mscr. 6, Simleriana, Zürich).

[2] Christa Tecklenburg Johns: *Luthers Konzilsidee in ihrer historischen Bedingtheit und ihrem reformatorischen Neuansatz* (Berlin, 1966), p. 140.

editions appeared within a very short space of time. The dating of these other editions raises a number of problems.[3] A Latin edition was produced by Andreas Cratander at Basle. This probably appeared at the same time as Sylvan Otmar's edition, but it may have been published at an earlier date. There were also two German translations, one of which was printed at Augsburg.

The additional editions undoubtedly made it possible for many more people to read the treatise. The popularity of the work was also increased by its extremely clear arrangement. The author develops his argument gradually in the first part by dividing it into eighteen statements or *persuasiones*, each of which forms a complete subdivision within the framework of the total argument. In the second part, he attempts to answer seven fallacious arguments or *cavilli* which might be used to dispute the *persuasiones* contained in the first part of his treatise. By arranging the text in this way, the author keeps the refutation of the counter-arguments separate from his own affirmations, with the result that there is no interruption in his presentation of the argument as a whole.

The treatise is moreover introduced by a passionately worded foreword, in which the author states his own position within the whole spectrum of the argument against papal primacy: the historical basis of the pope's exercise of power in the world has, he claims, already been proved by Lorenzo Valla to be quite false. Luther, he goes on, has disproved the theological defence of papal authority in his disputation with Eck at Leipzig. All that remains now, Velenus argues, is for the point of departure and the basis of the whole idea of papal primacy—Peter's stay in Rome as a bishop—to be proved wrong. The author sets himself the task of doing precisely this.

Interest in the treatise lessened with the passage of time, as the reformers found more important tasks to undertake, but in the middle of the sixteenth century it revived and Flacius Illyricus brought out a new German edition in 1551. An Italian translation, which was probably also by Flacius, appeared in 1566.

The book was reprinted several times in the seventeenth century. In 1618, Melchior Goldast included the whole text, with the exception of the foreword, in his *Monarchiae S. Romani Imperii III*. In 1666, the Lutheran theologian Johann Konrad Dannhauer published an *editio recognita*.

---

[3] See Appendix: "A Survey of the Editions of the *Petrum Romam non venisse*" Nos. 1–4 inclusive.

We may conclude from the fact that the work was reprinted a century and a half after it had first been published that there was a continued interest in its contents. Even clearer proof of this is found in the numerous debates that took place in ecclesiastical circles about Peter's stay as a bishop in Rome after the publication of Velenus' treatise, which featured quite prominently in the arguments.

After the fierce polemics in which Velenus' contemporaries, notably Luther on the one hand and John Fisher and Cochlaeus on the other, had engaged, there was a renewal of controversy towards the end of of the sixteenth century, when the Jesuit theologian Robert Bellarmine[4] reacted powerfully to the renewed impulse provided by Flacius Illyricus.

The controversy continued in the seventeenth century, but then it was concerned only with some of Velenus' arguments. This is because most Protestant theologians had by this time come to accept the tradition that Peter had died in Rome and at the same time the thesis that he was the first bishop of the *Romana Ecclesia*. On the other hand, however, they rejected the tradition that he had been a bishop there for twenty-five years. It was only in the Netherlands that a number of theologians continued to defend Velenus' treatise *Petrum Romam non venisse*[5] as a whole.

At the beginning of the eighteenth century, Friedrich Spanheim[6] once again mentioned and critically assessed all of Velenus' arguments, but his treatise contains only an indirect reference to Velenus' name. From then onwards, the subject once more ceased to interest theologians, at least for some time. This situation continued until 1827, when G. Veesenmeyer discovered a copy of Velenus' book in the city library at Ulm and devoted an article to it.[7] In this article, he provided a short review of the polemics in which Luther, Cochlaeus and Fisher had engaged.

Attention was once again drawn to the theme in 1866, when F. C. Baur added an appendix to the second edition of his book, *Paulus, der Apostel Jesu Christi*. In this appendix, *Zur Literatur der*

---

[4] *Disputationes de controversia christianae fidei adversus huius temporis haereticos* (1586).

[5] This short form of the title of Velenus' treatise will be used throughout in this book.

[6] *Dissertatio de ficta profectione Petri apostoli in urbem Romam deque non una traditionis origine* (1679 and 1703).

[7] *Von des Ulrich Velenus Schrift, daß Petrus nie nach Rom gekommen sey, und den Schriften dagegen .In Sammlung von Aufsätzen zur Erläuterung der Kirchen-, Literatur-, Münz- und Sittengeschichte.*

Petrus-Sage, the author began by giving a brief account of Flacius' view and then went on to review the whole controversy. What is more, it is clear from Baur's survey that the man who in fact initiated the dispute concerning the tradition of Peter in Rome, that is, Velenus, was no longer known at the time and that Baur regarded Flacius Illyricus as the originator of the controversy.

From then onwards, Velenus' ideas went their own way almost unnoticed[8] until the modern age. In the present century, both F. Heiler, in his work *Altkirchliche Autonomie und päpstlicher Zentralismus*,[9] and O. Cullmann in his book on Peter have come down on the side of the Catholic tradition of Peter in Rome. This century has also witnessed the debate between H. Lietzmann[10] and K. Heussi[11]—a controversy initiated by Adolf Harnack's statement that Peter's death as a martyr in Rome was disputed *einst aus tendenziös-protestantischen, dann aus tendenziös-kritischen Vorurteilen*.[12]

With the passage of time, however, the arguments tended more and more to be based on evidence derived from the history of the Church's liturgy and from recently discovered archaeological data. In particular, the question of the reliability of the discovery of Peter's tomb in Rome was raised, but it is, of course, not possible to attribute polemics in this sphere to the continued effect of Velenus' *Petrum Romam non venisse*. It would therefore seem that the influence of his treatise on a theological debate that had lasted for centuries had in fact ceased.

Anyone reading this work, which first appeared in 1520, at the present time, however, is bound to be struck by the original way in which the author develops his theme, although it cannot be denied that most of his arguments have been superseded by later knowledge. In the chapters that follow, I propose to deal in turn with the content of the treatise (Chapter I), the author himself (Chapter II), his back-

---

[1] A survey has been provided by Oscar Cullman: *Petrus. Jünger—Apostel—Märtyrer* (II, 1960), p. 72–82 inclusive. He mentions E. Gibbon, J. G. Eichhorn, F. Schleiermacher, W. M. L. de Wette and appears to have made the acquaintance of Velenus (whom he calls Venelus) and his treatise only via Goldast's collection.

[9] 1941.

[10] *Petrus und Paulus in Rom* (I, 1915; II, 1927).

[11] *War Petrus in Rom?* (1936) and *Die römische Petrustradition in kritischer Sicht* (1955).

[12] *Die Chronologie der altchristlichen Literatur bis Eusebius*, II[1] (1897), p. 244. Four years later, Harnack's view was refuted in great detail by C. Erbes, in his article *Petrus nicht in Rom, sondern in Jerusalem gestorben* (ZKG, XXII, p. 1–47, 161–231). Velenus was, however, not named by this author, nor was his treatise and the arguments were to a great extent different.

grounds and sources (Chapter III), the reactions of his contemporaries (Chapter IV) and finally the continued effect of his treatise on later writers (Chapter V).

CHAPTER ONE

THE TREATISE[1]

In accordance with the custom of the times, the title of the treatise contains a detailed description of the contents: "Various important and reliable arguments, which are based on Scripture, are set out in this little book, showing that the Apostle Peter neither came to Rome nor suffered and that it is therefore quite worthless and audacious for the Roman Pontiff to suppose that he is and to call himself the successor of Peter, etc."

Aii   The treatise itself is preceded by two verses taken from Juvenal's Satires:[2] *Aude aliquid brevibus Gyaris, et carcere dignum | si vis esse aliquid probitas laudatur, et alget.* These lines prepare the reader for the fact that the subject to be discussed in the author's treatise will lead him into territory where he will be threatened with exile—the island of Gyaris—and imprisonment.[3]

The foreword, in which the author makes himself known to his readers as "Ulrichus Velenus Minhoniensis", opens with the thesis that, through the action of the Antichrist, an atrocious form of superstition has entered Christianity, namely the denial of Sacred Scripture. It is precisely with this denial of the Bible that the author is concerned throughout the whole of his treatise. In his foreword, the author has more to say about the Antichrist, "who is now present in the Roman Church". The same Antichrist burned Girolamo Savonarola with fire in Florence.[4] In England, he had Wyclif's bones scattered over the ocean. It was also the Antichrist who had the leading *magistri* of the

Aiii   University of Prague, John Hus and Jerome of Prague, called by a

---

[1] The indications of the signature which are given in the margin in this chapter are those of the Latin edition published by Otmar.

[2] I, 73–74.

[3] In Otmar's German edition, a very free paraphrase of this quotation from Juvenal is given: *Wer yetzund herfür kommen wil | der müß sich nit dunken zü vil | Das er thu das sey henckens wertt | oder das man strafft mit dem schwert | Es hat kain not, all erberkait | tregt yetzt nit für ains domens brait*

[4] Velenus here uses the same words *(Florentiae tertium vulcano tradidit)* as Thomas Přelouč, Lukáš of Prague's secretary, used in the eye-witness account that he wrote in 1502. (See A. Molnár: *Voyage d'Italie*, Comviat. 1962[1]).

ruse to the Council of Constance and had them burnt there. From "our own times", the author also mentions John Reuchlin and Pico della Mirandola, whom the Antichrist "treated unjustly" and Doctor Martin Luther, whom he "ensnared with his rage", as well as Ulrich von Hutten. Above all, the author stresses, it should not be forgotten how he allowed the blood of so many Bohemians to flow.

Everywhere, however, the author says, there is a search for true piety and fortunately there are signs of renewal in the Church. But the Antichrist refuses to be expelled. He has already been on the rampage for many centuries, "this three-headed Cerberus from the underworld, who wears the threefold crown as a symbol". Two of his heads have, however, already been cut off. He lost the first in the duel with Lorenzo Valla, who had proved that the bull in which it was stated that Pope Sylvester had received Rome and the whole of Italy and the regions of the West as a gift from the Emperor Constantine was a forgery. In our own times, the author continues, his second head has been cut off by Martin Luther "by depriving him of the primacy; he has, after all, proved that the decretals were simply fictitious".

The beast, however, behaves as though it does not feel its wounds. It still lifts up its third head, thus affirming that it is the successor of Peter. Its reason for acting in this way is to re-establish the primacy of Aiv the pope of Rome. "And, because I can see no one who will cut off this last head, I will do it with God's help. My armour I take from Sacred Scripture. And in this I shall—and I declare this according to my conscience—use neither ruse nor deceit. I quote Scripture according to its 'true meaning'".[5]

This foreword, in which Velenus outlines his aim and his method, is followed by the eighteen *persuasiones* or statements. The first of these begins with the affirmation that "in all the books that have come my way concerning Peter's coming to Rome and his death there as a martyr, I have been able to find nothing but contradictions". Orosius,[6] for example, says that Peter arrived in Rome at the beginning of Claudius' reign. Others, however, maintain, on the authority of Jerome,[7] that this took place during the second year of Claudius' reign. Others again—including the author of the treatise *Fasciculus Temporum*[8]—say that Peter came to Rome in the fourth year of the Em-

---

[5] *Germanum intellectum.*

[6] *Historiarum adversus paganos libri VII*, lib. VII, c. VI (MPL 31–446).

[7] *De viris illustribus*, c. I (MPL 23–828).

[8] The text here reads: *Liber ille, qui temporum historias, ceu fasciculo quodam com-*

peror's reign. Velenus next refers to the book that describes the lives of the saints "and that is usually called *Passionale*".[9] The opinion expressed in this book is different from those given in all the other works that Velenus has so far mentioned, since it is stated in it that Peter came to Rome one[10] year after Christ's death, that is, in the thirteenth year of Claudius' reign.

The same confusion is also found, Velenus says, in the books in which the years are counted "from the beginning of the world" or *ab urbe condita*, as is the case[11] in the *Enneades* of Anthonius Sabellicus[12] or Platina's *Historia pontificum*,[13] which "makes use of the data provided by Orosius". These contradictions make Peter's coming to Rome very uncertain and give rise to doubts as to whether he was ever in Rome.

What is more, the author insists, this tradition of Peter in Rome is also in conflict with Paul's letters and Luke's Act of the Apostles, but for centuries no one dared to protest against the tradition. It even was very near "the Roman tyrants had included it among the articles of faith, so that what cannot be proved has still to be believed".[14]

If there is, then, no indication at all in Sacred Scripture by which Peter's stay in Rome can be vouchsafed and if the evidence provided by the historians is so confused and contradictory, it is surely not foolish to suppose that Peter was never in Rome. If he had been, then —at least according to Aristotle—all the statements made by the historians ought to agree with each other. And if he was the bishop of Rome, then his successor ought to be named without hesitation. But here too there is confusion—some say he was followed by Linus, but

---

prehendit (German edition: *das büchlin Fasciculus Temporum genannt*). What is meant here is a treatise by Werner Rolewincka (1474). (See Potthast: *Wegweiser durch die Geschichtswerke der europäischen Mittelalters*, 1862).

[9] ± 1300, written by unknown authors.

[10] This error occurs in both Latin editions: *anno post passione Christi*. This is corrected in the German edition: *Sant Peter sey gen Rom kommen zwainzig jar nach dem tod Christi, welches nach der rechnung felt in das dreyzehend jar Claudii*.

[11] Velenus may, however, also have been thinking of Flavius Josephus, about whom Jerome (*De viris illustribus*, c. XIII) wrote: *scripsit libros ab exordia mundi* (MPL 23–852).

[12] German text: *das grosse historienbüch Anthonii Sabellici* (first edition 1497, Venice).

[13] *Historia B. Platinae de vitis pontificum romanorum* (1479).

[14] If it is correct (see p. 91 ff.) that Velenus was thinking of Marsilio of Padua's *Defensor pacis, Dictio II*, here, what may be meant by these *fidei articulos* is Boniface VIII's bull *(Unam sanctam catholicam ecclesiam)*, from which Marsilio quotes: *Porro subesse Romano pontifici omnem humanam creaturam, declaramus, dicimus, et diffinimus omnino esse de necessitate salutis*.

many others[15] insist that the second bishop of Rome was Clement, whereas others again say that Clement was the third.[16] It is in any case clear, Velenus says, that, even though these data are provided by very holy men, they must of necessity be disputed. Here Velenus quotes Augustine:[17] *hoc genus literarum an auctoritate Canonum distinguendum est* and Thomas Aquinas, who said[18] that "neither theologians nor the Church herself are obliged to believe those things which cannot be traced back to Scripture and which are dubious because they are contradictory."

Bii

In the second and third *persuasiones*, the contradictory nature of the data concerning the date of Peter's arrival in Rome is discussed at greater length: "Those who say that Peter arrived in Rome in the first, second or fourth year of Claudius' reign are contradicted by those who say that Peter was firstly five (or, according to others, seven) years in the East, then occupied the bishop's chair in Antioch for seven years and finally spent some time in Pontus, Galatia, Bithynia and the districts of Asia. If this last fact is correct, then he can only have come to Rome after fourteen or fifteen years, that is, in the seventh or eighth year of Claudius' reign. If we accept Jerome's statement that the assembly of the apostles at Jerusalem, at which Peter was present, took place eighteen years after the ascension—which is in accordance with what Luke says in his book of the Acts of the Apostles—then Peter's coming to Rome must be dated a few years later, that is, in the ninth or eleventh year of Claudius' reign. If he was the Bishop of Rome for twenty-five years after this, then he must have been put to death as a martyr not by Nero, but by Vespasian, but no one has as yet made this claim."

---

[15] *De viris illustribus* (cp. XV): *Clemens ... quartus post Petrum Romae episcopus, si quidem secundus Linus fuit, tametsi plerique Latinorum secundum post apostolum putent fuisse Clementem* (MPL 23–854).

[16] The lists of the popes go back to the *Liber Pontificalis*. The earliest editorial work on this book presumably dates back to the beginning of the sixth century. The main source is the *Catalogus Liberianus* (354), which in turn goes back to Hippolytus. The confusion referred to by Velenus is discernible in these three sources. Hippolytus has: *Petrus, Linus, Anencletus, Clemens, Euaristus*; the *Cat. Lib.* has: *Petrus, Linus, Clemens, Cletus, Anaclitus*; the *Liber Pontif.* has: *Petrus, Linus, Cletus, Clemens, Anenclitus*. (See also *Gestorum Romanorum Pontificum*, I—*Liber Pontificalis*, ed. T. Mommsen, 1898, and A. Brackman: *Liber pontificalis*, RE³, 1902, pp. 439–446).

[17] *De doctrina christiana*, II, cp. 8 (MPL 34 - 12).

[18] *Quodlibetum*, XII, q. 17, a. 26: *Expositores autem in aliis quae non sunt fidei, multa ex suo sensu dixerunt, et ideo in his poterant errare. Tamen dicta expositorum necessitatem non inducunt, quod necesse sit eis credere, sed solum Scriptura canonica, quae in veteri et in novo testamento est.*

It is therefore clear, Velenus continues, that Peter could not have come to Rome in the ninth year of Claudius' reign. This also emerges from what Tranquillus has written, namely: "Claudius expelled the Jews from Rome because, incited by Christ, they had risen in revolt",[19]

Biii a situation differently described in the letters of the Apostle Paul. The behaviour of the Jews had also roused the Emperor to action against the Christians and he had driven them too out of the city. That is why Aquila, a Jew, had fled, together with his wife Priscilla, from Rome to Corinth. "I do not need to dwell here", Velenus says, "on the fact that Stapulensis[20] approaches the matter from a different point of view and changes the words that the Apostle uses both in his letter to Timothy and in that to the Romans and says: *salutat vos Priscilla et Acyla*. I prefer to follow so many learned exegetes who preserve the earlier reading, in which Erasmus also makes no change in this instance".[21]

What is certain, Velenus concludes, is that Peter could not have come to Rome in the ninth year of Claudius' reign, because all the Christians had, in that year, been expelled from the city together with the Jews.[22] If he arrived after that time and stayed in the city for twenty-five years, then his death must be attributed to Vespasian. This is the only possible conclusion, but it is not credible.

In his fourth *persuasio*, Velenus sets out to demonstrate that Peter also did not come to Rome in the twentieth year after Christ's death. After all, Velenus points out, Paul says in his letter to the Galatians

Biv that he saw Peter in Jerusalem three years after his conversion and then saw him again in the same city fourteen years later. It is therefore certain that Peter stayed in Jerusalem and the surrounding districts during those seventeen years and did not go to Rome. After a while, Paul again met Peter, this time in Antioch and punished him severely there. A certain period of time must have gone by between this punishment and their previous encounter in Jerusalem. What is more, Paul was not converted immediately after Christ's ascension—he was

---

[19] C. Suetonius Tranquillus (± 95–± 135): *De vita Caesarum libri VIII* (*Vita Claudii* 25, 4: *Judaeos impulsore Christo assidue tumultuantes Roma expulit*).

[20] *Sancti Pauli Epistolae XIV ex vulgata editione adiecta intelligentia ex graeco, cum commentariis Jac. Fabri Stapulensis* (Paris, 1512).

[21] *Novum Instrumentum* (1516), revised in 1518: *Novum Testamentum*. In Cratander's edition, Velenus gives Erasmus' name throughout in capital letters (perhaps as homage ?)

[22] According to Orosius: *Adversus paganos* VII, 6, 15 (MPL 31–469). The statement by Suetonius mentioned above is quoted in this place.

still opposing the Christian faith when Stephen was stoned to death. "You see", Velenus points out, "that, between Christ's ascension and Peter's punishment at Antioch, twenty years may easily have elapsed, during which time Peter was certainly not in Rome". But even after that time he was not in Rome, "since, if I were to concede that Peter had come to Rome in that twentieth year, this coming would have taken place in the thirteenth year of Claudius' reign. If we were then to add to this the twenty-five years that he is said to have governed the Church of Rome, then he must have died at the time of Vespasian and that, as I have already said, is impossible". Velenus then concludes this *persuasio* with the statement: "It would be wrong to accuse this benevolent prince of the murder of Peter".

C   In the fifth and sixth *persuasiones*, Velenus takes Paul's letter to the Romans as his point of departure. According to Origen,[23] this epistle must have been written after the two letters to the Corinthians and, according to Athanasius, it follows the first letter to the Thessalonians. When Paul was in Corinth for the third time, Velenus continues, he wrote his letter to the Romans, in which he greets many of the brethren by name and especially the leaders of the community such as Narcissus, Junias, Andronicus, Priscilla and Aquila. If, then, Paul had supposed that Peter was at that time in Rome, Velenus asks, surely he would have deigned to greet him as well and have treated him with great honour? The reason why he is not named in the letter, however, is simply that he was not in Rome then. The same conclusion can be drawn from what is said by Ambrose, who had read in all kinds of old books, namely that Narcissus was at that time the presbyter of Rome.[24]

Velenus then goes on to elaborate the concept presbyter. "We must know", he writes, "that the early church did not recognise *pontifices*, *patriarchae*, *cardinales* and *archiepiscopi*. There were only two *ecclesiasticos ordines:* presbyters or bishops and deacons. This conclusion can be drawn from Paul's letters, in which he writes about 'the saints with their bishops and deacons' (Philippians) and 'presbyters' (Timothy and Titus), and also from the Acts of the Apostles, which speaks of the 'presbyters' of Ephesus. Moreover, writing to the presbyters in the diaspora of Pontus, Galatia, Cappadocia, Asia and Bithynia, Peter calls

Cii himself an 'elder' (at that time knowing nothing of the proud name *summorum pontificum*). Narcissus was therefore a presbyter or an elder

---

[23] *Commentariorum in epistolam S. Pauli ad Romanos praefatio* (MPG 14–458).

[24] *Commentaria in epistolam ad Romanos*, cp. XVI: *Narcissus hic illo tempore presbyter dicitur fuisse, sicut legitur in aliis codicibus* (MPL 17–109).

or a bishop—all these words mean the same thing—of the Church of Rome and was responsible not only for the city, but also for the surrounding districts. With him were Andronicus and Junias, two of the seventy-two apostles, as Origen believed.[25] If Priscilla and Aquila, who were very zealous in Rome, are added to this, then I am at a loss to know what kind of work there was for *Petro veterano* to do there. The truth, however, is that he was not in Rome and Paul therefore does not greet him in his letter to the Romans." Velenus thus concludes that Peter was not in Rome up to the time of Nero's reign and asks: if he was in the city for twenty-five years afterwards, by whom was he killed?

The point of departure for the seventh *persuasio* is the letter to the Galatians, in which Paul states that he had the task of preaching among the uncircumcised, whereas Peter had to work among the circumcised. That, at least, was the arrangement made at the synod of Jerusalem. Why, then, should Peter have gone to Rome, "the mother of the pagan world", and, what is more, even many years before Paul arrived there, according to tradition, while he did not concern himself at all with the Jews? This fact is clear from the Acts of the Apostles, in which Luke says that the Jews told Paul that they knew nothing of "this new sect" (that is, the Christian faith). On the one hand, then, it was not Peter's task to go to Rome and, on the other, if he nonetheless had gone there, what did he do in the city if the Jews knew nothing of the Christian faith? "Anyone who wants to", Velenus concludes, "can now see how credible it is that Peter should have been in Rome".

Ciii

The next four *persuasiones* deal with the two years during which Paul was held prisoner in Rome. He wrote to the Galatians and the Ephesians from prison, Velenus says, but there is no evidence in these letters that he had Peter with him as a colleague, "although it was always Paul's practice to greet the faithful in the name of his colleagues".

Civ

There is, Velenus claims, an indication that Peter was not in Rome at that time in the letter sent to the Philippians. In this letter, Paul writes that certain Christians were proclaiming the gospel with the impure intention of harming him. Their hope was to stir up Nero, who hated all Christians, to punish Paul. But, if Peter had been in Rome for years at this time, then it is remarkable that the proclamation of the Christian message should have shocked the Romans so much that

---

[25] *Comment. in epist. ad Rom.*, Lib. X (MPG 14–682): *fortassis ex illis septuaginta duobus qui et ipsi apostoli nominati sunt.*

they wanted to bring about Paul's destruction. "Had Peter therefore
been idle all those years?" Velenus asks "And, what is more, the anger
of the people must have been directed against Peter, since he was the
head of the Church".

The epistle to the Colossians, which ends with the words: "Aristarchus my fellow-prisoner greets you, and Mark the cousin of Barnabas
... and Jesus who is called Justus. There are the only men of the
circumcision among my fellow-workers for the kingdom of God, and
they have been a comfort to me" is even clearer in this respect. "What,
then, was Peter doing? Did he keep quiet like an *emeritus miles*?"
Velenus asks. "Was he too not a fellow-worker in Christ's kingdom?
D   ... To think that of Peter is atrocious. So, Peter, you were not in
Rome at that time."

Finally, there is a very informative letter of this period, namely the
one written by Paul to Philemon in Colossus about the latter's slave
Onesimus, "At the beginning of this letter," Velenus says, "he greets
Philemon, his wife Apphia, the Bishop of Colossus, Archippus, and
—because he was more easily able to act as an intermediary—he also
names Timothy. Why, then, did Paul leave out the name of Peter in
this greeting? Philemon would have more ready to grant forgiveness
if he had been impressed by the authority of such a great preacher of
the gospel". Velenus goes on to say: "I think it is shameful that this
letter of Paul's has been buried under the dust for so many centuries,
concealed in a hiding-place and ignored by everyone. If it had been
read, fewer errors would have arisen in the Church. What can show
more clearly that Peter was not in Rome than this letter from Rome?".

"When Paul had been in prison for two years and many in Rome
had been converted to faith in Christ", the twelfth *persuasio* begins,
"Nero finally set him free. Paul himself testifies to this, writing to
Timothy: 'I was rescued from the lion's mouth'. This captivity took
place during the first five years of Nero's reign, while the Emperor
was still benevolent (so benevolent indeed that he had scruples about
signing a death sentence) and, in that benevolent frame of mind, he
released Paul." In the last nine years of his reign, however, Nero
became more cruel ("although this history", Velenus says, "is uncertain, since, according to Josephus,[26] many authors have written
Dii   the history of Nero, either obscuring the truth out of flattery or prac-
tising deceit out of hatred"). During that period of tyranny, Paul was,

---

[26] *Antiquitates Iudaicae* (93/94).

after ten years, once again put in chains and had a more difficult time than ever before. This was when he wrote his second letter to Timothy, recalling in it his earlier captivity: "At my first defence no one took my part; all deserted me". Velenus concludes by asking: "Where was Peter then?" and answers his question: "Not in Rome, or he would not have deserted Paul, when the latter had to defend himself. It is therefore a thousand times more tolerable to believe that Peter was not in Rome than to cause shame to such an excellent apostle by saying that he left Paul in the lurch".

The thirteenth *persuasio* returns to Paul's first period of captivity in Rome, in connection with the passage in Luke's Acts of the Apostles, according to which, when Paul came near to Rome, the brethren came as far as the Forum of Appius to meet him and Paul, after resting for three days, entered into discussions with the Jews. "And so Luke describes all these things in order," Velenus writes, "but does not mention Peter at all. Did he, then, not speak to Peter during those two years?" Luke's description, however, is concerned with Paul's first period spent in Rome during the fourth year of Nero's reign. That is why, Velenus insists—and here he makes a short detour before returning quickly to the main highway of his argument—Jerome[27] was right when he described the vision of Paul and Thecla and the fable of the baptising of the lion[28] as *apochriphas scriptoras*, because, if they were not apocryphal, the apostle's constant companion would certainly have mentioned them. Velenus concludes: "I would also add this: the report that Peter came to Rome in the second year of Claudius' reign and was bishop there for twenty-five years is not only apocryphal, but also false, since Luke does not mention it at all in his careful historical account".

Diii

The conclusion in the fourteenth *persuasio* is, that Peter could not have arrived in Rome even in the last year of Nero's reign, "since Paul, freed from the hands of Nero, resolved to go to Spain and the East, as Lyra[29] and some others claim". Velenus continues: "When, ten years later, he fell once more into Nero's hands and saw death

---

[27] *De viris illustribus*, cp. VII (MPL 23–840), an almost literal quotation.

[28] Πράξεις Παύλου και Θέκλης cp. 24 (*Act. Ap. Apocr.* I, 260–261), according to Tertullian (*De baptismo*, cp. 17), written by a presbyter in Asia Minor. Thecla is reputed to have been a disciple of Paul's.

[29] ± 1270–± 1350; *Postillae perpetuae in Vetus et Novum Testamentum*. The probable reason for Velenus' following Nicholas of Lyra here—in contrast to his rejection of Lyra in many other places—is that Faber Stapulensis also presupposed that Paul made a journey to Spain.

approaching, he wrote to Timothy, asking him to come to Rome
with Mark, because, apart from Luke, not a single colleague was still
with him. How, then," Velenus asks, "can the whole Roman band
claim that Peter was in Rome without a break from the second year
of Claudius' reign until the end of Nero's? But the words of Sacred
Scripture convince me more than the tyrants, who twist the words of
Christ and Paul". In the same letter (2 Tim.), Velenus concludes, Paul
writes that Onesiphorus searched for him and finally found him. That
long search would not have been necessary if Peter had been in Rome
and Onesiphorus had been kept informed by him. One final argument
is that Peter is not named among the greetings in this letter.

Div   The fifteenth *persuasio* deals with the correspondence between Seneca
and Paul. Velenus was of the opinion that this correspondence "was
written when Paul was taken prisoner for the second time by Nero".[30]
He gives three reasons for this dating of the exchange of letters:
"Firstly, because Nero was at that time bloodthirsty and cruel and
this cannot be said of the first five years of his reign. Secondly, because
the letters that Paul had written during his first period of captivity had
reached Seneca at once and he had derived great benefit from them.
Thirdly, because, in one of his letters to Paul, Seneca recalls the fire
that Nero had started in Rome and this took place at the end of the
Emperor's reign." In the whole of this correspondence, Peter is not
mentioned at all. He was not known to Seneca, who would undoubtedly have praised him highly if he, Peter, had done what Paul
was clearly not able to do because he was in prison, namely introduce
him to the circle of those who believed in Christ. Paul would also
have referred Seneca to Peter, in order that he could hear the message
from the man who was able to transmit the Christian faith better than
anyone else. It is clear, then, Velenus concludes, from this correspondence that Peter was not in Rome at the end of Nero's reign.

In his sixteenth *persuasio*, "so that no one should be overwhelmed
by the Roman curia, which goes against so many prominent witnesses",
the author of *Petrum Romam non venisse* proposes to consider "how their
E   *authores* agree about the joint martyrdom of Peter and Paul". The
whole Roman Church sings, in the ceremonies in their honour, the
antiphon *Gloriosi principes terrae, quomodo in vita sua dilexerunt se, ita et in*

---

[30] This correspondence is mentioned by Jerome in his *De viris illustribus*, cp. XII
(MPL 23–850). The text probably originated not much before the year 400. Faber
includes the correspondence in his commentary on Paul's letters. Erasmus did not
accept it as authentic.

morte non sunt separati.[31] "What is said here, however," Velenus writes, "about their suffering (martyrdom) on the same day is pertinently refuted by Linus, who uses many different arguments which I cannot quote here because they are so extensive. I will, however, refer the reader to the Passion narratives which are found in the recently discovered work written by Linus and published in Latin by Jacob Stapulensis".[32] In this work,[33] we are told that Peter was hanged upside down on a cross at a place called Naumachia. Linus does not, however, mention where Paul lost his life. The fact that he names various officials, executioners and spectators as witnesses of the death of both Christians, however, proves that he does not mean that both suffered a martyr's death at the same place.

Dionysius,[34] on the other hand—not Paul's disciple, Velenus points out, but "some loose fellow"—was of a different opinion. According to him, when they were led off to death and separated from each other, Paul said to Peter: *Pax tecum, fundamentum ecclesiarum et pastor ovium et agnorum Christi.*

There is also no agreement, Velenus claims, about the tradition that they were both put to death because of an edict promulgated by Nero. After all, although Nero is generally held responsible, Linus maintains that it was Agrippa who had Peter put to death, because he was incensed about the conversion of his concubine as the result of Peter's admonitions and Nero knew nothing of this order to have Peter crucified.[35] There are therefore many different and mutually contradictory fabrications and there is a complete absence of certainty.

In this context, it is wonderful to note that Josephus, who was taken to Rome by Vespasian and there described the history of the Jewish war,[36] mentions Nero's victims (in his *Antiquitates*), but has nothing at all to say about Peter and Paul. Yet he was well disposed

---

[31] Roman breviary: *Pars aestiva ,Die 3 Julii, infra octavam SS Petri et Pauli App. Ad Laudes. Ad Bened .Ant.* (Earliest quotations in the *Antiphonale* of Ivrea, Kapitt. bibl. 106, 11th century; Bamberg lit. 23, 12th century).

[32] In Faber's edition of Paul, we find: *Lini episcopi de passione Petri tradita Ecclesiis orientalium et deinde in latinum conversa liber primus* (and: ...*conversa liber secundus*).

[33] *Martyrium beati Petri apostoli a Lino episcopo conscriptum*, cp. X (*Act. Ap. Apocr.* I, 11, 12).

[34] Dionysius the Areopagite (who called himself a disciple of Paul's). A Greek treatise dating back to the sixth century and translated by John Scotus Eriugena (± 890) into Latin. Faber produced an edition in 1498. Valla and Erasmus did not accept it as authentic. (See Renaudet: *Préréforme et humanisme.*)

[35] *Martyrium beati Petri apostoli a Lino episcopo conscriptum*, cp. II, III (*Act. Ap. Apocr.* I, 2).

[36] Published by Faber in an abridged form (1510).

towards Christians, since he recalls with reverence John the Baptist[37] and the Apostle James,[38] the brother of Jesus Christ and presbyter at Jerusalem.[39] "On the basis of all these data," Velenus says, "I believe that we must assume that the end of Peter's life took place in Jerusalem, together with James. After all, Josephus writes that others were also killed with James during the time that Annas was high priest".

Eii

What is more, there is another reason why "ratio" objects to the view that Peter was put to death together with Paul—Peter was the oldest of all the apostles and, in comparison with him, Paul was still a young man when he was called. "Could Peter, then, still have been alive," Velenus asks, "when Paul was an old man? Who would allow himself to judge in this dark maze? There are too few certainties to hold on to and thus to find one's way out of the maze".

Having demonstrated that Peter could not have died in Rome and having expressed the supposition that his martyrdom in fact took place in Jerusalem, Velenus proposes to elaborate this supposition further in his seventeenth *persuasio*. Before doing this, however, he defends his thesis that "no evidence can be found in Scripture that can be used to show that Paul suffered in Rome under Nero". When the Apostle fell for the second time into Nero's hands, he wrote to Timothy: *tempus resolutionis meae instat*.[40] This was a reference to his decrepit body, not to his martyrdom, [41] because, when he wrote this, he was already an old man (and, moreover, this is not the view of others, but his own statement, because he had already written, ten years before this in his letter to Philemon,[42] that he was old). This is why he asked Timothy to come to him before his death, which he was expecting to take place very soon. After all, enlightened by the Holy Spirit, he had predicted his liberation from prison; this is why he had written:[43] "The Lord will rescue me from all evil and save me for his heavenly kingdom", the last words *(regnum coeleste)* often meaning the Church in Sacred Scripture. In this, Paul was not deceived, since, "according to the testimony of many", he was released a second time by Nero. Shortly after this, he is believed to have died.

---

[37] *Antiquitates*, lib. XVIII.

[38] *ibid*. lib. XX.

[39] A paraphrase of *De viris illustribus*, cp. XIII (MPL 23–852).

[40] 2 Tim. 4. 6.

[41] A refutation of Nicholas of Lyra's postil, which refers to martyrdom in this text.

[42] Philem. 9.

[43] 2 Tim. 4. 18.

"In order not to dwell any longer on this point", however, Velenus now chooses to provide arguments supporting the thesis that Peter and Paul suffered martyrdom in Jerusalem. The first of these arguments is taken from Matt. 23. 34, in which Christ —at least according to the

Eiii text of the Vulgate—says: "I send you *prophetas et sapientes et scribas* and you will kill and crucify them". Christ did not say this, Velenus claims, about the prophets of the *legis veteris*, but about the apostles, as John Chrysostom explains in his homily on Matthew's gospel.[44] Jerome's exegesis of this passage is:[45] ...*alios prophetas, alios sapientes, alios scribas, ex quibus lapiditus est Stephanus, Paulus occisus, crucifixus Petrus.* "With these words", Velenus says, "Jerome also testifies to the fact that, apart from Stephen, Peter and Paul suffered as well in Jerusalem".

The interpretation provided by Nicholas of Lyra[46] is in the same vein: *Ex eis occidetis, sicut Iacobum fratrem Ioannis, et Stephanum et multos alios. Et crucifigetis ut Petrum et Andream fratrem eius, et multos alios, flagellabitis sicut Paulum et Sylam* ... "Who can raise any objections to this powerful testimony?", Velenus asks. "Who dares to accuse not only Jerome, Chrysostom and Nicholas of Lyra, but also Christ himself of deceit? In the gospel of Luke, after all, Christ says: 'Do not fear those who kill the body; fear him who, after you have been killed, has power to cast you into gehenna'. Here Jesus is saying that his apostles were to be put to death in Jerusalem and not in Rome and by the scribes and pharisees and not by the Roman emperors (although I do not deny that some of them were killed outside Jerusalem)."

In the eighteenth *persuasio*, the author of the *Petrum Roman non venisse* discusses the question as to "how such a false conviction could have entered the Church". Those things that are laid down as articles of faith are still fresh in our memories, Velenus says, even though nothing is said about them in the books written by historians and they are diametrically opposed to the *Christi dogmata*. If this is the case

Eiv in our own confused times, he goes on, what may not have been invented by the flatterers of the Roman curia concerning Peter's arrival, suffering and pontificate in Rome. "Do you believe that the Church, which was founded by a poor Christ and spread by poor apostles, ought to have so much wealth? And that one man ought to rule over everyone in it? Who has ever declared that? Today, however, it is solemnly asserted that the highest authority over the *rei publicae*

---

[44] *Homilia* LXXIV (MPG 58–679).

[45] *Commentar. in Evang. Matthaei*, lib. IV, cp. XXIII (MPL 26–189).

[46] Postil on Matt. 23. 34.

christianae is invested in one man. And if anyone refuse to nod assent, the whole Christian people is called to arms against him. One is therefore induced to accept the pope as the head of the universal Catholic Church, despite the fact that this is contrary to all written evidence, to the words of Christ himself and to the rite and example of the early Church". It was possible for the people to believe in the mendacious bulls concerning the Emperor Constantine's donation to Sylvester and in the same way they could be led downhill with the stories about Peter. After all, it is always possible to find witnesses for the most shameful lies.

F   In the second part of his book, Velenus reviews seven *cavilli* or fallacious arguments which might be used by the Roman Church to dispute his *persuasiones*. Each *cavillus* is followed by a *responsio* or refutation.

In the first of these *cavilli*, the Postil of Lyra is quoted as evidence that Paul must have made his second journey to Jerusalem in the fourteenth year after his conversion to faith in Christ and not in the seventeenth year, since the first three years, at the end of which Paul also went to Jerusalem, have to be included in the total number of fourteen years. Velenus' reply to this supposed Roman *cavillus* is that Nicholas of Lyra's argument is refuted by many reliable authors, "but, since it is not necessary to send a trained army to fight against a great number of inexperienced troops, it should be sufficient to put one Jerome, who again and again mentions these seventeen years, into the field against so many Lyras".[47]

In the second *cavillus*, the word Babylon in the first epistle of Peter[48] is discussed and the argument, which is largely based on evidence drawn from Jerome,[49] is put forward that Babylon is used here *figuraliter* for Rome. The "Roman" conclusion, then, is that Peter wrote this letter from Rome.

Fii   Velenus' *responsio* is that, according to the *cosmographi*, there were two cities of Babylon. "One was in Assyria and was built by the son of Medus (or, if we are to believe Herodotus, by Semiramis). The other is known as the Egyptian Babylon. It is mentioned by Stephen, Strabo[50] and Ptolomy[51] and also by the more recent scholars Ludovi-

---

[47] For example, in his exegesis of the epistle to the Galatians (MPL 26–398/410).
[48] 1 Pet. 5. 13.
[49] *De virus illustribus*, cp. VIII (MPL 23–843).
[50] ± 60–± 20 B. C. Wrote a geographical work about Palestine. He also mentions the Stephen referred to here.
[51] Claudius Ptolomaeus (± 100–± 140), who wrote Γεωγραφικὴ ὁρήγησις.

cus Caelius in his *Antiquitates*[52] and Raphael Volateranus in his *Geographia*.[53] Strabo shows that it was situated closer to Arabia than to Egypt, which is why it is called Chayro in the Arabic language".

It is feasible that Peter wrote his letter from Babylon or "Chayro", because he proclaimed the name of Christ in Judaea and the surrounding districts. If, however, Rome is nonetheless persistently regarded as Babylon, what God said about the latter through the prophet Jeremiah should not be forgotten: "Go out of the midst of her, my people! Let every man save his life from the fierce anger of the Lord" and in the New Testament through the words of John: "The woman, arrayed in purple ... Come out of her, my people, lest you take part in her sins". Velenus therefore concludes: "You see the consequence of this *figurate interpretatio*—that everyone is permitted to defect from the Roman curia without fear of punishment. Of what, then, will we Bohemians be accused? Oh, that everyone should follow

Fiii   our example and defect from that Babylon!"

The argument used in the third *cavillus* is this: when Paul came to Rome, the brethren came as far as the Forum of Appius to meet him. Through whose activity, then, would they have believed in Christ, if Peter had not been in Rome?

To counter this argument, Velenus quotes Orosius,[54] who wrote that the Christians went out immediately after Jesus' death to preach and that there was soon a great number of believers in Rome. Tiberius, who would himself have liked to accept faith in God, was in conflict with the Roman Senate about it. From the time of his rule until that of Nero, the Christian religion was safe in Rome. The author of the *Petrum Romam non venisse* thus concludes: "No one need therefore be surprised by the fact that there were so many of the brethren in Rome who were able to go to meet Paul when he came to Rome. There was no lack of presbyters, such as Narcissus, Andronicus, Junias and others, with the consequence that they had no need at all of the presence of Peter". They were, however, advised by Paul, first by letter and then by word of mouth.

Fiv   In the fourth *cavillus*, it is argued that the greatest certainty can be provided by the disciples of the apostles and by those who were alive soon after the apostolic period and that it is precisely these who handed down the tradition that Peter and Paul suffered martyrdom in

---

[52] *Antiquarum lectionum commentarii* (Paris, 1517).
[53] *Commentariorum urbanorum libri XXXVI* (Paris, 1511).
[54] *Historiarum adversus paganos*, lib. VII, cp. IV (MPL, 31–460).

Rome. Among these men are Linus, who is mentioned in Paul's letter to Timothy, Dionysius the Areopagite, who is named by Luke in the Acts of the Apostles, and Hegesippus,[55] who came to Rome at the time of Anicetus and still remembered[56] the martyrdom of Peter and Paul.

To this *cavillus* Velenus replies that it is well known that not only the apostles' disciples, but also the apostles themselves knew that all kinds of things were said in their name which were contrary to the truth and to Christian ideas. In the name of Paul, for example, a letter was written to the Thessalonians which can easily be proved false as pseudo-apostolic. "And Jerome writes[57] that the vision of Paul and Thecla and the fable of the baptism of the lion were written by a presbyter in Asia", Velenus continues. "Later, as Tertullian has pointed out,[58] this author admitted that he did it out of love for Paul. The same applies to the books written by Clement, whom the Apostle mentions in his letter to the Colossians.[59] His writings are tainted by many heretical errors, among them Eunomius' heresy".[60] Velenus also quotes in this context "the writings of a certain Dionysius, the Bishop of Alexandria"[61] as "so falsified that the Arian heresy could appeal to them as an authority". Velenus goes on: "Rufinus[62] also says in his *Apologia pro Origene* that the audacity of the heretics was so great that they were not even able to keep their unclean hands away from the sacred words of the gospel". Anyone who wishes to know more about this, the author of our treatise assures us, will be completely informed if he reads the books written by Tertullian against Marcion.[63]

G   This is why Origen wrote:[64] "It is necessary for us to consider

---

[55] Wrote five books ὑπόμνηματα (ca. 180), of which nothing has been directly preserved. Velenus gives here an almost word for word quotation from the *De viris illustribus*, cp. XXII.

[56] *Meminit passionis Petri et Pauli*, a translation of ὑπόμνηματα.

[57] *De viris illustribus*, cp. VII (MPL 23–840).

[58] *De baptismo*, cp. XVII (MPL 1–1219): *quasi titulo Pauli de suo cumulans, convictum atque confessum id se amore Pauli fecisse*. This datum, however, is mentioned by Jerome (*De viris illustribus*, cp. VII).

[59] Velenus' quotation from *De viris illustribus*, cp. XV, here is wrong. Jerome says: ... *de quo apostolus Paulus ad Philippenses scribens* (MPL 23–854). The text referred to is Phil. 4. 3.

[60] ± 395, one of the Arian leaders, the Bishop of Cysicus.

[61] ± 250, author, among other things, of Paschal letters.

[62] Tyrannius Rufinus (± 345–410) defended Origin against Jerome, among other things by translating Origen's major work Περὶ ἀπχων into Latin (*De principiis*). This is the treatise to which Velenus is referring here (MPG 11–45/195).

[63] *Libri V adversus Marcion* (MPL 2–239/524).

[64] *Sermo XXVI* on Matthew.

everything very carefully so that we should not believe all the mysterious things that they have described in the name of the saints". As far as Dionysius is concerned, there can be no doubt that the Passion narrative of Peter and Paul is wrongly attributed to him. Both Lorenzo Valla and Erasmus of Rotterdam, after all, say in their *libros annotationibus*[65] that these treatises which are circulating in his name are false.

What is more, Velenus stresses, the Passion narratives of Peter and Paul which have been made popular in the name of Linus are tainted with deceit. "I am therefore of the opinion that some *graeculum mendacem*[66]—a *leno*[67] rather than a Linus—falsified these stories. It must have been someone who had sniffed at Paul's letter to Timothy, but not understood it, since he has completely twisted the meaning of the stories. But Linus, who was with Paul when he wrote his letter to Timothy, was not so foolish as to have forgotten everything and to have written the opposite."

Gii

"I am of the same opinion regarding Hegesippus. How is it possible for someone, who came to Rome at a much later period, to narrate the true history? He did not experience any thing of what happened himself. At the time of those stories of the martyrdom of Peter and Paul, he was not in Rome. It is certain, then, that someone thought up this fable many years after Hegesippus".

Velenus returns to the Passion narratives of Linus in the fifth *cavillus*, quoting especially the description of the meeting between Jesus and Peter at the city gate of Rome. "Peter asked there: *Quo vadis, Domine*? and Christ replied: 'I am coming to Rome to be crucified again. Whereupon Peter said: 'Lord, I will turn round and follow you. After these words, the Lord rose up to heaven.[68] And so that this should be firmly believed, a chapel has been built at the place where these words were spoken."

Velenus regards this as a "profane deception", because "Peter himself said to the Jews:[69] 'heaven must receive Jesus until the time for establishing all things'. Why, then, should Christ be given back to the

---

[65] *Laurentii Vallensis in lat. N.T. interpretationem ex collatione graecorum exemplarium Adnotationes*, published by Erasmus (Paris, 1505).

[66] Assuming that Faber Stapulensis translated these books from Greek (Μαρτύριον Πετρου) into Latin.

[67] A pimp or procurer.

[68] *Martyrium beati Petri apostoli a Lino episcopo conscriptum*, cp. VI (*Act. Ap. Apocr.* I, 7, 8).

[69] Acts 3. 21.

earth before this establishment of all things, which will not take place until the day of judgement?".

H   This is why, our author says, no one has ever believed that Christ has *personaliter* come down to appear on earth in one way or another to the saints. He has, on the other hand, always remained in heaven to speak to them from there. The saints so addressed have included Stephen, Paul and Peter. "Why, then," he asks, "should we want to ascribe so flagrant a lie to a disciple of the Apostle?" As far as the chapel is concerned, it is a lie to say that it was ever built. No church was ever built during the first few centuries in Rome or its surrounding districts, because at that time Christians were in the habit of meeting in caves.

The sixth *cavillus* is based on the supposition that Mark wrote his gospel in Rome on the grounds of what he had heard from Peter. There are quotations in this *cavillus* from Clement's books with *informationes*[70] and from Jerome's *De viris illustribus*.[71] It is this Mark about whom Peter speaks in his letter,[72] when he says: "My son Mark sends you greetings".

Hii   After writing his gospel, Mark left Rome for Egypt, founding a church in Alexandria and dying in the ninth year of the reign of the Emperor Nero. Philo wrote a book about his work in Alexandria.[73]

After having established that "the books circulating under the name of Clement are, on the one hand, forgeries and, on the other, wrongly attributed to him", Velenus, in his *responsio*, outlines a different theory concerning this Mark. There are, he points out, two men in the New Testament with the name of Mark. The first of these is John Mark, who originally accompanied Paul and Barnabas on their journeys,[74] but later returned to Antioch. Later, he went to Cyprus with Barnabas. When the latter was put to death as a martyr on Cyprus, however, Mark fled to Egypt. It is about this Mark that Philo the Jew had written and it was also this man to whom Peter was referring in his letter from *Chayro, hoc est Babylone*. "And it is credible that this Mark should have been known to Peter because Alexandria was not far

---

[70] The writings referring to here are the Pseudo-Clementines; these were written in the third century. In 1504, Faber published an edition of these *Clementine Recognitions* in Paris, in his *Recognitiones Petri Apostoli*.

[71] Cp. VIII (MPL 23–843/844).

[72] 1 Pet. 5. 13.

[73] This information is taken from Jerome's *De viris illustribus*, cp. VIII (MPL 23–843).

[74] Acts 13.

from Chayro". Many legends have been told about him, including the one that he wrote a gospel in Rome on the basis of information provided by Peter. "This, however," Velenus insists, "is clearly wrong, since it is nowhere to be found in any of the canonical books that this Mark was ever in Rome with Peter. The mendacity is clear from the disparity between the writers. Jerome, for instance, maintains, on the authority of Clement, that Mark wrote the gospel at the request of the brethren.[75] Others, however, such as Platina, claim that Peter, who was urged to do it prompted by the requests made by the Romans, had order Mark, whom he regarded as well suited to the task, to write the gospel."

All the authors, however, agree that Mark died and was buried at Alexandria in the eighth year of Nero's reign. "It is precisely for this reason," Velenus points out, "that they went astray. They believed that there was no other Mark among the apostles' disciples, with the result that they attributed everything to this one". There was, however, another Mark-Mark Aristarchus, a fellow-worker of Paul's mentioned by name at the end of the latter's epistle to Philemon: "Mark Aristarchus, Demas and Luke, my fellow-workers, greet you".

Hiii   Velenus continues: "Later, when Paul, as an old man, wrote to Timothy from prison, he remembered this Mark: 'Do your best to come to me soon... Luke alone is with me. Get Mark and bring him with you; for he is very useful in serving me... When you come, bring the cloak that I left with Carpus at Troas, also the books and above all the parchments'.[76] Jacobus Stapulensis, who was no insignificant exegete of the story of the apostles, has given us this very fair explanation:[77] 'The Apostle had Luke with him and asked for Mark and for the parchments which had been left behind with Carpus. But why did he do that? Simply because he wanted to bequeath them to Luke and Mark, who had been chosen by the Holy Spirit as sacred authors, so that should place the gospel on record'." Velenus therefore concludes his *responsio* by saying: "And what is said in these words is that Mark Aristarchus, not John Mark, wrote the gospel (and he may still have been alive after Nero's reign, because the Apostle asked for him in his second letter to Timothy, roundabout the thirteenth year of Nero's reign)."

According to the seventh and last *cavillus*, Philo of Alexandria

---

[75] Quoted from the *De viris illustribus*, cp. VIII.
[76] 2 Tim. 4. 11, 13.
[77] *Sancti Pauli Epistolae XIV* (Paris, 1512).

reported to his fellow Jews in Rome during the reign of Caligula and later when Claudius was emperor. On this occasion, Velenus says in his *cavillus*, Philo discussed many matters with the Apostle Peter "and formed such a close friendship with him that, insofar as it was possible for him to do so, he praised the Christians in his books and spoke about them in terms of great respect".

Velenus' *responsio* to this *cavillus* is very brief: "This nonsense can only be dismissed with scorn. How could the Jew Philo have met Peter in Rome during the reign of the Emperor Claudius, when Peter (as we have already demonstrated with many arguments) could not have been in Rome at that time? If, then, there is any reason at all to assume that Philo praised the Christians because of his friendship with Peter, I am of the opinion that he must have met him in Judaea, where he was working until the end of his life". It is, however, not surprising, the author of our treatise adds, that "someone from such a stubborn people" should speak in the highest terms about Christ, since even legions of demons were constrained to preach Christ!

Hiv   With these words, Velenus concludes his treatise, expressing the hope that "by bringing to light the faults and errors of the Babylon of the West" he would "by grace obtain the imperishable crown".

CHAPTER TWO

THE AUTHOR

1. *The Search for the Author's Identity*

Until fifty years ago, the real identity of the author concealed behind the name Ulrichus Velenus Minhoniensis was not known. When G. Veesenmeyer devoted an article[1] to the treatise *Petrum Romam non venisse* in 1827, the book had ceased to be the object of discussion in specialised books and articles for more than a century. With regard to the author of the treatise, Veesenmeyer wrote in his article: *Ob der Name, Velenus, erdichtet sey, kann ich nicht sagen. Mir scheint es wenigstens, und ich gestehe, daß ich nicht weiß, was ich aus dem Minhoniensis machen soll.* A little later, in 1856, Emil Weller suggested in his *Wörterbuch der Pseudonumen*[2] that Velenus was a pseudonym for "Joh. Heinr. Boeckler". A search through C. G. Jöcher's *Allgemeines Gelehrten Lexikon*[3] yields no trace of a Johann Heinrich Boeckler who might possibly be considered as the author behind the name. The Church historian Boeckler who is mentioned in Jöcher's work lived from 1611 until 1672 and the other two Boecklers with the same Christian names included in the lexicon also lived after 1600. In Volume IV of the same work, Velenus is said to be *ein erdichteter Name eines Gelehrten im 16. Seculo.*

In 1874, the French abbot Pierre Martin wrote an article[4] in connection with the treatise *Petrum Roman non venisse*—with which he was familiar only from the reproduction of the text provided by Melchior Goldast in his *Monarchiae S. Romani Imperii* of 1618—in which he had to admit: *Nous n'avons pu trouver aucun détail biographique sur cet écrivain.*

In 1889, a good suggestion was made by E. L. Enders:[5] *...Ulrichus Velenus Minhoniensis, der sonst unbekannt ist (wäre Minhouiensis zu lesen, so wüßten wir seinen Geburtsort: Minichow, Mnichow, Dorf im Kr. Eger in*

---

[1] *Sammlung von Aufsätzen zur Erläuterung der Kirchen-, Literatur-, Münz- und Sittengeschichte* (Ulm, 1827), p. 138ff.

[2] Leipzig, 1856, p. 152.

[3] 1751.

[4] *Saint Pierre. Sa venue et son martyre à Rome*, in *Revue des questions historiques* (Paris, 1874).

[5] *Luthers Briefwechsel*, III (Stuttgart, 1889), p. 83.

Böhmen).[6] This suggestion was accepted by Otto Clemen, who included it in two of his articles, published in 1900 and 1906.[7] In the *Nederlandsche Bibliographie* of Nijhoff and Kronenberg (1923), Velenus is called, without any commentary, a pseudonym.[8]

In 1925, the Czech Church historian F. M. Bartoš published the results of his search for the identity of the author of the treatise *Petrum Romam non venisse* in an article, which has unfortunately not been translated, entitled: "Zapadlé dílko bratrské vědy".[9] In 1930, he published another report of his findings in an article in a collection of commemorative essays published by the Hus Faculty in Prague.[10] Bartoš concluded that Ulrichus Velenus Minhoniensis must have been the Bohemian scholar and printer Oldřich Velenský of Mnichov.

Having been put on the trail by Bartoš, others went on with the search. Velenský was well known to those acquainted with the history of the Bohemian Brethren as a printer of books (although the data published by these experts about his work are very few in number[11]). In the "National Bibliography of Books Printed in Czech and Slovak up to 1800",[12] there are nine titles of editions printed by Velenský,[13] including no less than six titles translated by Velenský himself from Latin into Czech.

What is more, Velenský's name had already been mentioned in 1922 in a book published outside the zone where Czech is spoken. In his *Geschichte der Böhmischen Brüder*, J. T. Müller provided a survey of the writings of Lukáš of Prague, in which, at the end of treatise 34,[14]

---

[6] Mnichov is at the same time also the Czech word for Munich. The name is therefore no doubt derived from a settlement of monks.

[7] *Zentralblatt für Bibliothekswesen*, XVII (1900), p. 586 ff and *Flugschriften aus den ersten Jahren der Reformation*, III-5 (1906), p. 187 ff.

[8] p. 751, No. 2112.

[9] A literal translation reads: "A forgotten work from the science of the (Bohemian) brethren". The article was published in the series *Věstníku Král. Čes. Spolec Nauk* (The "Royal Bohemian Society for Sciences") and is usually referred to as *Věstník KČSN ιῤ i*, 1925, č 2 (1–28) (Prague, 1926).

[10] *Kolem Husova díla o církvi*, in *Sborník k.l. desítiletí Husovy fakulty* (1930), pp. 13–20. In 1946, Bartoš wrote a short popular article about Velenský in his book *Bojovníco a mučedncí*, pp. 83–85.

[11] In his *Geschichte des Buchdrucks in Böhmen und Mähren* (1928), Josef Volf, for example, gives only his name; he does not mention any of the books that he printed.

[12] *Knihopis českých a slovenských tisku od doby nejstarši až do konce XVIII. století*, ed. Z. V. Tobolka and F. Horák (Prague, 1925–1967).

[13] For printing presses in Bohemia at the time of the Brethren, see Mirjam Bohatcová: *Počatky publikační činnosti jednoty bratrské* (Prague, 1962).

[14] Herrnhut, 1922, I, p. 546.

he included a quotation:[15] *Gedruckt in Weißwasser im Verlag von Ulrich Velenský von Mnichow, i.J.d. H. 1521, am Donnerstag vor St. Mathias.*

That Velenský had been active not only as a translator, but also as an author was a new datum revealed by Bartoš' investigations and not corrected by others after him. On the contrary, all those who have since written about Velenský[16] agree that Bartoš' brief reconstructed biography is historically reliable. What is more, this biography has also been taken over in a concise form in the "Nationaι Bibliography of Czech and Slovak Books",[17] although several hypotheses, which will later be seen to be untenable, have been added.

Bartoš published his findings in the Czech language and this has clearly been an obstacle to the dissemination of this fairly recently acquired knowledge among a wider circle of interested scholars. The only scholar to have taken stock of it quickly was Otto Clemen, who referred, in the Weimar edition of 1930, in his notes on a letter from Luther to Spalatinus (dated 3 February 1521)—in which Velenský's treatise is mentioned—to Bartoš' articles and gave a few biographical data about Velenský himself.

In 1940, W. Bienert wrote an article on the Petrine tradition[18] in which he included Bartoš' data and R. Bäumer published a detailed study in 1962[19] of the debate among Velenský's contemporaries, similarly with recourse to the investigation conducted by Bartoš. In other cases, however, the name Ulrichus Velenus Minhoniensis continued to be regarded as a pseudonym—an example of this is the entry in the authoritative *General Catalogue of Printed Books* (1964).

An illustration of the extent to which the language barrier has affected research into our author's work and identity can be found in the remarkable fact that Czech scholars have, on the one hand, been well informed about all the books printed by Velenský in his own country, because they have had access to the early Bohemian sources. They have therefore been in a position to begin compiling a biography.

---

[15] Müller's translation.

[16] Rudolf Říčan: *Die Böhmischen Brüder* (Berlin and Prague, 1958); J. B. Čapek: an article in *Jednota Bratrská 1457–1957* (Prague, 1957); A. Molnár: various articles in *Communio Viatorum* (1958, 1962, 1964); Emil Pražak: *Oldřich Velenský a cesta českého humanismu k světovosti* (Prague, 1966).

[17] Vol. 2/VIII, 236–250; Book No. 16. 494.

[18] *Luther über die Petrus-in-Rom-Tradition*, in *Theologische Jahrbücher*, 8 (Halle, 1940), p. 36 ff.

[19] *Die Auseinandersetzungen über die römische Petrustradition in den ersten Jahrzehnten der Reformationszeit*, in *Römische Quartalschrift für christliche Altertumskunde und für Kirchengeschichte*, Vol. 57, 1962, pp. 20–57.

On the other hand, however, the treatise *Petrum Romam non venisse*, which was published abroad, has not been known to them or at best hardly known. Even scholars such as Bartoš and Mirjam Bohatcová[20] were only familiar with the various editions through the publications of Otto Clemen to which we have already referred.

Scholars in Western Europe have been similarly affected by the language barrier. All the editions of *Petrum Romam non venisse* have been known to a small group, but these scholars have been unaware of the author's activities in Bohemia as a printer and translator. Unlike their colleagues in Czechoslovakia, therefore, they have not been in a position to reconstruct a biography of Velenský.

As Bartoš wrote in his article of 1925: "The Germans were acquainted with the book, but not with the author; we, on the other hand, were familiar with a printer, but did not know that he had written this book". It is this mutual lack of information that has given rise to the lacuna in the official biography in the "National Bibliography of Czech and Slovak Books", a gap which, as we shall see has been filled in with an incorrect hypothesis. The correct data which should in fact have been used to fill in this gap in Velenský's biography are, after all, to be found in the very treatise which has not been known in Czechoslovakia because it was not originally printed there, namely *Petrum Romam non venisse*.

Finally, we must mention an article about Velenský published in 1966 in *Česka Literatura*[21] by the Czech scholar Emil Pražak and entitled "Oldřich Velenský a cesta českého humanismu k světovosti".[22] By using the data collected by Bartoš, Pražak was able to throw light on the figure of Velenský from two points of view—the Czech and the Western European. He also gave emphasis to another aspect that Bartoš had not considered in his article—the part played by Velenský in the Bohemian humanism of his period and above all his influence on the development of the Czech language. Unfortunately, Pražak's article is written from an altogether too one-sided, Marxistic point of view, with the result that all that is seriously considered is what the scholar Velenský, with his humanistic training, thought of the revolutionary movements of his own times. His theological reflections and themes are either not discussed at all or else explained

---

[20] See note 13.

[21] 1966, Vol. 14, p. 443–458.

[22] A literal translation reads: "Velenský and the way of Bohemian humanism to world fame".

historically conditioned forms expressing the then current struggle to change human society.

2. *Problems of Interpretation*

Pražak's method of approaching the subject leads to another and wider problem of interpretation, which can be expressed in the following way: A period during which Bohemian opposition to the Church of Rome was interpreted as a purely religious struggle and also as a precursor of the Reformation or else even as an original attempt to reform Christianity was followed by a period during which the Hussite movement was regarded as an expression of Bohemian nationalism. This in turn resulted in (or was combined with) the view which emerged in the nineteen-fifties, namely that the Hussites and the later Bohemian Brethren had, in accordance with their own intentions, to be seen as men struggling to achieve a classless society.[23] The most radical conclusion to which this view led was that all the religious themes exploited by men were nothing but historically conditioned means which had of necessity to be used to express deeper revolutionary tendencies in society. As one Czech scholar has expressed it: *verständlich ist, daß jede antifeudale Bewegung eine religiöse Form haben mußte, und daß die Kämpfe einzig und allein unter religiösen Losungen ausgetragen werden konnten.*[24] According to this radical view, then, the Antichrist is seen as the one who oppresses the people at the lowest level of society and the early Church is regarded as a communist ideal.

During the first of these periods of interpretation, which was characterised by an exclusive concern with religious themes, scholars conducted exhaustive and detailed research into sources. This took place just before and roundabout the turn of the present century. A. Gindely and J. Goll[25] edited and published many texts concerned with the Bohemian Brethren that had fallen into oblivion. On the basis of these sources, these and other scholars on the one hand revealed the influences exerted by the religious movements of the

---

[23] See Peter Brock: *The Political and Social Doctrines of the Unity of Czech Brethren* (The Hague, 1957) and Josef Macek: *Die Hussitenbewegung in Böhmen* (Prague, 1958, 2nd edn.).

[24] Josef Macek, *op. cit.*, p. 21.

[25] A. Gindely, *Geschichte der Böhmischen Brüder* (Prague, 1861); reprint of the second edition, Osnabrück, 1968. J. Goll: *Quellen und Untersuchungen zur Geschichte der Böhmischen Brüder* (Prague, 1878).

preceding period on the struggle in the Church in Bohemia. (They were above all convinced that there were direct links between the Waldensians and the Unitas Fratrum.) On the other hand, they at the same time stressed the original nature of many of the Hussites' ideas. According to the interpretation of the scholars working at this period, then, the Bohemian movement was situated in a direct causal relationship with the late mediaeval historical process in the development of ideas in Europe. These scholars did not, however, recognise primarily a social motivation in this process.

Müller, the historian from Herrnhut took this view as his point of departure, but drew attention to the fact that the religious principles which played such an important part in the struggle in the Church in Bohemia had social consequences—the radical Hussites and the Brethren of the first generation applied the "law of Christ" to life itself in rules of conduct which aimed at the renewal of society.

The dominant figures in the writing of the history of Hussitism from the nineteen-twenties onwards have been F. M. Bartoš and A. Molnár, both of whom also regarded the Hussite movement as initially a purely religious reformation, but recognised that these movement of reform was able to take place because of dissatisfaction with the situation in society as a whole. The oppressed people were aware that resistance to the Church of Rome provided a practical opportunity for liberation from the Church's hierarchy, the members of which were closely linked with the oppressors. Purification of the Church was experienced, in other words, as and could therefore grow into purification of society.

After the Second World War, the third pattern of interpretation, which is strongly marked by the political climate in modern Czechoslovakia, began to emerge. In the introduction to his book *Das hussitische Denken im Lichte seiner Quellen*,[26] Robert Kalivoda provides a detailed survey of the Marxist studies of the Hussite movement. His point of departure is, after all, *daß es verständlich ist, daß die tatsächlich wissenschaftliche Darstellung der hussitischen Ideologie erst durch Anwendung der marxistischen dialektischen Methode möglich ist.*[27] Kalivoda mentions as a pioneer in the employment of this method K. Konrad, in whose work, *Husitska revoluce*, attention is drawn to the fact *daß es die Entwicklung der Ware-Geld-Wirtschaft war, die im 14. und 15. Jahrhundert die allgemeine Krise des Feudalismus hervorgerufen hat.* Applying this thesis to the

---

[26] Berlin, 1969.
[27] *op. cit.*, p. 29.

Bohemia of those days, the same author is able to say *daß die hussitische Revolution, durch sozial-ökonomische und Klassenwidersprüche des Feudalismus hervorgerufen ist ... und daß sie ihrem Charakter nach schon eine frühe Form der bürgerlichen Revolution war.*[28]

Another recent author, Josef Macek, in the book for which he was awarded the State prize in Czechoslovakia in 1952 *(Husitské revoluční hnutí)*,[29] even went so far as to describe the Hussite movement as *der gewaltigste Klassenkampf in der Epoche des Feudalismus bis zum 15. Jahrhundert.* Macek developed the Marxist revolutionary interpretation of Hussitism in the following way:[30] *Die hussitische revolutionäre Bewegung ist—als Bauernkrieg im Sinne der Definition von Marx und Engels—ihrer historischen Stellung nach eine Vorstufe zur bürgerlichen Revolution. Zum ersten Male in der Geschichte der Menschheit wurde die Forderung nach einer völligen Säkularisation erfüllt, die Stellung der Kirche schwer erschüttert und dadurch den späteren revolutionären Bewegungen ein erfolgreicher Angriff gegen den Feudalismus ermöglicht.*

Before we consider whether these and similar problems of interpretation also play any part in defining Velenský's place in Bohemian society, however, we must look a little more closely at the political and religious situation in fifteenth century Bohemia.

3. *Bohemia in the Fifteenth Century*

The history of Bohemia in the fifteenth century and at the beginning of the sixteenth has been discussed in great detail by J. T. Müller in the first volume of the *Geschichte der Böhmischen Brüder*.[31] We have no need to go into such detail here. All that is necessary for our purposes is to provide a broad outline of the background to Velenský's life and work in the Bohemia of the period.

After the death of John Hus and Jerome of Prague in 1415, the country was disturbed by party struggles. These conflicts had existed even before the Council of Constance and can to a very great extent be traced back to a struggle between the Germans, who exerted a powerful influence at the Bohemian court and over the leaders of the Church, and the Slavic Bohemians, who had come to occupy a sub-

---

[28] *op. cit.*, p. 30.
[29] German edition: *Die hussitische Revolutionäre Bewegung* (Berlin, 1958), p. 170.
[30] *op. cit.*, p. 176.
[31] Herrnhut, 1922. A later work on this period is R. Říčan: *Die Böhmischen Brüder* (Berlin and Prague, 1958).

ordinate position in the country despite the fact that they were the original inhabitants. German was the official language and—especially in Prague—the language used by those who belonged to the upper social level of the population. Official decisions were published in Latin and German and very rarely in Czech.[32]

The Decree of Kuttenberg (Kudna Horá) in 1409, however, led to a considerable reduction of the German influence at the Charles University of Prague and the consequent departure of most of the German teaching staff for Leipzig. This resulted in an apparent settlement of the conflict in favour of the Bohemians, but it did not mean a complete disappearance of the controversy. The most important reason for this is that the emperor, Sigismund (who was also King of Bohemia), and his son-in-law and successor, Albrecht II of Habsburg, continued to represent the German influence. As soon as Sigismund used armed force to combat the (Slavic) Hussite movement, this was almost unquestioningly regarded as an attempt on the part of the German rulers to suppress the Bohemian population. A "Prague manifesto" dated 3 April 1420 even went so far as to speak of "our natural enemies, the Germans".[33] It cannot be denied that there are many points of contact here with the interpretation of the Hussite movement as a nationalist tendency. Howard Kaminsky,[34] one of the leading American specialists in early Hussitism, is more subtle and cautious in his language and speaks of "proto-nationalism" and a combination of "slavonicism, national messianism and anti-Germanism".

It is, however, without any doubt possible to defend the position that the religious conflict, for which the way had been prepared for a long time before the appearance of John Hus,[35] but which broke out after his death at the stake, was subjected to very powerful impulses by nationalist feelings aroused by the German rulers. What is more, nationalist considerations continued to play an important part in the conflicts in religion and the Church throughout the whole of this century.

The real importance of nationalism in the Hussite movement will become clear when we begin to look for the reasons why the death

---

[32] J. Jakoubek and A. Novák: *Geschichte der Čechischen Litteratur* (Leipzig, 1913), p. 33ff.

[33] Quoted in H. Kaminsky: *Master Nicholas of Dresden: The Old Color and the New* (Philadelphia, 1965), p. 6.

[34] *op. cit.*, p. 5.

[35] See Chapter III: "Backgrounds and Sources".

of Hus was able to cause the population of Bohemia to revolt against
the Church of Rome. Some scholars are of the opinion that Hus provided very little basis in his preaching and writing for such a radical
break with Rome. Müller, for example, claimed:[36] *In Bezug auf die
meisten Lehrpunkte ist er vollständig auf den Boden der katholischen Kirche
geblieben*. He came into conflict with Rome above all because he agreed
with two of Wyclif's important ideas—the doctrine of the authority of
Scripture and the predestination of believers. Hus' influence on the
Bohemian people, however, has to be explained on the basis of his
practical Church politics and his struggle against the Catholic hierarchy. This appealed to nationalist feelings in Bohemia and it was above
all his death as a martyr that made him a national figure. As Müller
has said,[37] *Darüber verblaßte Wyclifs Name im Gedächtnis der Nachwelt
und die böhmische Wycllfiten wurden Hussiten.*

Basing his arguments on the same conviction as the Protestant
historian Müller, the Belgian Benedictine Paul de Vooght has tried to
rehabilitate Hus and to correct his condemnation by the Council of
Constance. According to de Vooght, Hus believed that he had remained within the tradition of the Catholic Church and that he had
done no more than point to abuses in the hierarchy.[38] De Vooght has
also pointed out that Hus did not challenge the doctrine of transub-
stantiation[39] and that he also continued to regard the Mass, offered by
unworthy priests, as sacramentally valid.[40]

Ernst Werner,[41] on the other hand, has opposed de Vooght's view
and has, with the aid of a number of quotations from Hus' works,
shown that he on several occasions did not confine his criticism of the
papacy simply to a protest against abuses, but challenged the primacy
of the pope as such. *Es will unter solchen Umständen wenig besagen*, Werner
says,[42] *wenn de Vooght Hus bescheinigt, er habe das Papsttum nicht a limine
abgelehnt, sondern in ihm eine nützliche, wenn auch reformbedürftige Institution gesehen.* Werner points out: *Entscheidend blieb, daß Hus den Papst als
Haupt der katholischen Kirche entthronte.* Werner is also of the opinion
that it is not possible to say, as Müller does, on the one hand that Hus

---

[36] *op. cit.*, p. 12.
[37] *ibid.*
[38] P. de Vooght: *L'hérésie de Jean Huss* (Louvain, 1960), p. 473.
[39] P. de Vooght: *Hussiana* (Louvain, 1960), p. 278.
[40] *ibid.*
[41] Ernst Werner: *Der Kirchenbegriff bei Jan Hus, Jakoubek von Mies, Jan Zelivský
und den linken Taboriten* (Berlin, 1967).
[42] *ibid.*, p. 15/16; cf. P. de Vooght, *Hussiana*, p. 61.

in Bezug auf die meisten Lehrpunkte vollständig auf den Boden der katholischen Kirche geblieben ist and, on the other, that he took over Wyclif's ideas about the predestination of believers. This latter view, Werner insists, brought him into sharp conflict with the Church:[43] *Er rührte damit an die Existenzgrundlagen des Papsttums und der gesamten römisch-katholischen Kirche. Das konstanzer Konzil konnte nicht zustimmen, daß die heilige Universalkirche nur aus einer Versammlung von Prädestinierten bestand, denn dann hätte die reale Kirche als hierarchische Organisation ihre Verankerung verloren...* It is interesting to note that, in this question, Werner's opinion is disputed by his fellow-Marxist Kalivoda, whose point of departure is simply *die Tatsache, daß in der eigentlichen dogmatisch-theologischen Sphäre Hus nicht von der kirchlichen Orthodoxie abgewichen ist.*[44] In this, Kalivoda is clearly on de Vooght's side!

There is, then, complete disagreement about the question of Hus' orthodoxy and these differences of opinion can moreover be observed cutting across the various groups of interpretation. Despite this, however, there is general acceptance of the fact that the response of the Bohemian people to Hus' preaching must be explained on the basis of nationalist feelings. What is more, although these nationalist feelings have themselves been explained in different ways—on the one hand, for example, as the result of the conflict between the German ruling class and the Slavs and, on the other, as "an early form of the bourgeois revolution" against the feudalism of the Church's hierarchy—there is general agreement, in this question at least, that nationalism acted as a stimulus in the religious conflict.

All the same, despite this measure of agreement about the explanation for the break with the Catholic Church, it would be wrong to conclude that the Bohemian people were united in their views about the Church and politics because of their nationalist feelings. From the very beginning of the struggle, the Hussites had been divided into two distinct tendencies—a conservative movement, consisting mainly of magisters from Prague, noblemen and inhabitants of the cities, and a radical movement, consisting principally of inhabitants of the rural districts who had responded vigorously to Wyclif's criticism of the worldly Church. The first of these two Hussite movements was originally called by the name of "Pragers" (who later came to be known as Utraquists), while the second became known as the "Taborites" (so called after Mount Tabor, where they had their centre). It is

---

[43] *ibid.*, p. 22.
[44] *op. cit.*, p. 31.

also entirely in keeping with the Marxist interpretation that scholars such as Kalivoda and Werner should have regarded the Taborites as having continued in a pure form the "bourgeois revolution" and the Pragers as having reverted to feudalism.

In an attempt to form a single solid front against the Catholic Church and Emperor Sigismund, both parties concluded an agreement, the "Four Articles of Prague"[45]—in which they combined their views. These four articles insisted on the free proclamation of God's Word, the celebration of the Lord's Supper and communion, for the laity as well, under both forms, the Church's return to the original apostolic sobriety and the application of mortal sins to those occupying high positions in the Church and the world.

It proved impossible, however, to keep the two Hussite parties together by means of this joint declaration. (It was only for the sake of national interests and the world outside that the two parties subscribed to a joint statement of aims and separate texts were circulated by the Pragers and the Taborites from the very year when the Four Articles were first composed in 1420.[46] The Pragers soon came to regard the radical nature of the Taborites' demands as a threat to their own social and political interests and an armed conflict broke out. In 1434, the Taborites were defeated at Lipany by the Hussite—and Catholic!—nobles.

After so much bloodshed, Sigismund worked strenuously to achieve peace in his country and succeeded in having an agreement, the Compactates of Basle, drawn up at the Council of Basle, on the basis of the Articles of Prague. These Compactates were promulgated in 1436. Since this agreement was above all a compromise, it was possible for the moderate Hussites to predominate, with the consequence that the extremists had to be satisfied with a life led as far as possible in secrecy.

Among the moderates were first of all the Pragers, who had by now come to call themselves Utraquists. They had formed their own church, which was not dependent on Rome, but which was led by Archbishop Rokycana, who was self-elected and under whose guidance they worked for peace with and recognition by Rome. They had considerable influence at the University and, since many of the Bohemian noblemen belonged to the Utraquist Church, a majority of votes

---

[45] The full text will be found in Müller, *op. cit.* (Appendix I) and Kalivoda, *op. cit.*

[46] Texts in Kalivoda, *op. cit.*

in the Diet. Because of this, they were for many decades able to exert a powerful influence on politics and Church affairs. Another group of Bohemians who must also be included among the moderates were those Catholics who—frequently because they had studied in Italy— were deeply influenced by the ideals of the Renaissance and were also inclined to work to achieve a measure of independence in the Church.

The radical Hussite movement had, however, by no means disappeared. After the defeat at Lipany, the Taborites had no more part to play, but another radical form of Hussitism soon emerged, expressed not as an armed religious conflict, but as a non-violent protest against the Church and society, conducted according to the rules of the gospel. The leader of this new movement was Peter Chelčický,[47] who began to preach roundabout 1425 against the use of armed violence, the authority of the state and the worldliness of the Church and in favour of a renewal of spiritual life. He advocated a simple, pure way of life, the equality of all men and the consequent abolition of all offices and positions of authority in the Church together with the taking of oaths that inevitably accompanied the acceptance of these functions. A circle of believers soon gathered around this lay preacher who—strangely enough at the intercession of Rokycana—were given a place on the royal estate of Kunwald so that they could put into practice, in their own community, their chosen way of life lived according to the rules of the "law of Christ" (by which was meant the gospel and above all the Sermon on the Mount).

This movement was marked by a very rapid growth and other villages with similar communities sprang up on different estates, especially under the inspiring leadership of Chelčický's successor Řehoř (Gregory), a nephew of Bishop Rokycana. In the long run, this expansion inevitably led to the need for organised structures and persons occupying positions of authority within those structures. In 1467, priests were elected and ordained by a Waldensian bishop (so as to be able in this way to speak of a valid succession outside the secularised Catholic Church and the Utraquist Church) and a centralised government or "little council" was developed. It was from this time onward that the title "Bohemian Brethren" (Jednota bratrská[48] or Unitas Fratrum) came to be used.

---

[47] This is presumably the pseudonym of a member of the landed nobility, Petr Záhorka, who was born roundabout 1380. After 1424, this name disappears from the sources and a year later the name Peter Chelčický begins to make its appearance (See Peter Brock, *op. cit.*).

[48] The Czech word *jednota* can be translated as "community", on condition that

In the early years, the Brethren were in the main simple, often un-
lettered peasants, but the situation began to change after 1480, when
a group of students from Prague joined the community, among them
two men, Brother Lukáš and Vavřinec Krasonický, who very quickly
made a deep impression on the Unitas. Lukáš of Prague was able, in
his many writings, to give a theological substructure to the ideas
current among the Brethren and to justify them to the world outside.

Any outline of the conflicts in Bohemia in the fifteenth century
would be incomplete if we failed to mention the humanists who
originated in the first place in intellectual Catholic circles and later
also came from among the Utraquists, who were, despite the theological and scientific justification of the ideas circulating among the
Bohemian Brethren provided by Lukáš and Krasonický (with a few
exceptions[49]) strongly opposed to the Brethren. Above all, the Utraquists despised the Brethren for using the language of the people, for
their simple, peasant way of life and for their reserved attitude towards
the authorities. The Catholic humanists also frequently succeeded in
having very severe measures against the Brethren promulgated by the
king.

Finally, it is also necessary to review briefly the social conflict
which played a part in this controversy. The nobility, the middle
classes and the peasants all fought for their own interests, at the same
time making use of the religious conflicts of the period. The landed
nobility, who had gained most of all from a consolidation of relationships, belonged predominantly to the Utraquist Church. The humanists were found above all in the towns and the Brethren drew their
members principally from among the poor country people, who were
therefore able to be inspired by the ideal of a renewal of society which
was one of the great aims of the Unitas Fratrum.

It would, however, be an oversimplification of the situation and
therefore unjustified to regard these tensions within society as the
only reason for the conflict and, on this basis, to trace the causes of the
religious struggle in Bohemia back to an early expression of class
warfare. On the one hand, Marxist terminology of this kind cannot
adequately be applied to the climate of thought and the way of life
of fifteenth century man, for whom religion was an integral part of
his existence and, on the other, it cannot do justice to the impulses

---

equal value is given both to the organisational aspect and to the spiritual content
in it (as in the Latin word *unitas*).

[49] See Chapter III, 1: the popular humanists.

produced by taking the teaching of the gospel seriously and applying that teaching to the renewal of human society. In his defence of the Marxist method, K. Konrad said:[50] *Die Fragen der hussitische Revolution sind lebendige Fragen. Die wissenschaftliche Untersuchung des Hussitentums ist deshalb keine rein akademische, sondern vor allem eine politische Aufgabe.* In making this claim, however, Konrad overlooked the fact that these "living questions" were expressed by men living in the fifteenth century and that, in any study of these questions, the spiritual and mental climate of the period has to be taken into account. That climate was above all totally different from that of the twentieth century, when man is able to think in a secularised way about religion and the Church. What is more, Konrad has quite failed to consider the possibility of a renewal of society inspired by the gospel.

The image of the Bohemian Brethren which emerges from a balanced study of history, then, has more light and shade. There was clearly an interaction between the call of the gospel to improve society on the one hand and the recognition of that call by the victims of injustice in society. There would have been no impulse in Bohemia to renew society without that appeal made by the teaching of the gospel and, conversely, without the faults in society the appeal of the gospel would never have aroused such a response. Any attempt to eliminate one of these two elements in this mutual interaction is bound to result in an interpretation of the history of the period which does violence to the real events and ideas.

Velenský, then, was born and grew up in a Bohemia which was sharply divided both in religion and socially and this background must have conditioned his thought and his work.

4. *Velenský's Scientific Training*

Very little is known about Oldřich Velenský's life and that is almost exclusively based on his own few statements in the treatises published by him. There are almost no biographical data on him in the writings of his contemporaries. We can only reconstruct a brief description of his life if we conduct a careful investigation into contemporary sources on the basis of the data supplied by Velenský himself—his writings, after all, contain direct and indirect references to certain events, persons or publications and certain conclusions can be drawn

---

[50] Kalivoda, *op. cit.*, p. 29.

from these data with regard to Velenský's involvement in them. It is, of course, inevitable that, in any research based on so few data, all that we can do in the case of certain periods in Velenský's life is to form hypotheses, many of which will be quite acceptable, but never completely certain.

We may be quite sure, however, that Oldřich's family belonged to the lower landed gentry, whose property in Mnichov had to be sold at the time that his grandparents were alive because of financial difficulties. Enders[51] had therefore clearly been searching in the right direction when he concluded that the name Minhoniensis pointed to the Bohemian village of Minichov as the author's place of origin. He was not correct, however, in his attempt to define the position of this village more accurately *im Kr. Eger*, a region bordering on Bavaria and now known by its Czech name of Chebsko. According to the results of research into archives quoted by Bartoš[52] and from which the data concerning Velenský's family have been derived, the estate of Mnichov was situated near Nový Zamék and Česka Lípa (about fifty miles north of Prague). The Velenský family is named as owning this estate as early as the fourteenth century. The property was handed over to other owners in 1450, however, and soon afterwards sold once again.

It is nonetheless clear from all kinds of data in his later life that the young Oldřich was not without means. In the first place, as a student at the University of Prague, he was, unlike some of the young men of his own age, not designated in the University registers as a "pauper". According to the *Monumenta Historica Universitatis Carolo-Ferdinandeae Pragensis*,[53] a certain "Walericus Mnichowiensis" gained his baccalaureate and was third of a group of twenty-two examinees and "Udalricus Mnichowiensis" was admitted as a baccalariatus after the annual assembly of the Faculty of Arts on 9 October 1515, when Joannes Presticemus was dean. If we assume that, in a normal course of study, the University student of that period would gain his baccalaureate roundabout his twentieth year we may conclude that Velenský was born in or about 1495.

There is a lack of data concerning the next four years. Velenský's name does not occur in the registers of the University of Prague

---

[51] See p. 27.
[52] *op. cit.*: A. Sedlaček (*Hrady*, XIV); F. Zuman *(Věstniku okresu belskeho)*; A. Sedlaček *(Ottuv Slovnik)*; A. Sedlaček *(Slovniku misto pisneho)*.
[53] *Liber Decanorum facultatis philosophicae universitatis Pragensis* (1367–1585), *Pars* II (Prague, 1832), pp. 256–258.

during this period, with the result that he could not therefore have prepared for his licentiate there. According to the concise biography in the Czech "National Bibliography",[54] he studied in Wittenberg, where he became acquainted with Luther and was influenced by the latter's theological ideas. There is, however, no sign of Velenský's name in the registers of the University of Wittenberg at this time. Mirjam Bohatcová, who has made a special study of the printing presses of the Bohemian Brethren[55] and looked for biographical data concerning Velenský while making that study, has therefore written,[56] as far as this period in Wittenberg is concerned, *daß es meines Wissens keine authentische Quellen gibt, obzwar es in der Literatur*[57] *immer von neuen wiederholt wird.*

According to F. M. Bartoš,[58] it is not possible to obtain any certain information about where Velenský was living and what he was doing between the autumn of 1515 and 1518, but "it is possible that he was in Paris, the centre of the Christian Renaissance at that time. It is at the very least surprising how much of the material used by him came from Paris". He then mentions Velenský's reference—in his reply to the second *cavillus*—to the work of the "recent scholars" Ludovicus Caelius and Raphael Volateranus. The first of these scholars had published his book *Antiquarum lectionum Commentarii. Reparavit Lod. Caelius Rhodiginus* in 1517 and the second had published his *Commentariorum urbanorum libri XXXVI* in 1511. Both works appeared in Paris.[59] What is more, as Bartoš points out, in his sixteenth *persuasio* Velenský speaks about the "Passion narratives which are found in the recently discovered work written by Linus and published in Latin by Jacobus Stapulensis". This shows that Velenský had read Stapulensis' great work, *Sancti Pauli Epistolae XIV*, which appeared in Paris in 1512 and was reprinted there in 1515.[60] The following sentence occurs in that book: *Lini episcopi de passione Petri tradita Ecclesiis orientalium et deinde in latinum conversa liber primus* (and *...conversa liber secundus*). The same book also plays an important part in Velenský's arguments. It is

---

[54] *op. cit.*; the biography will be found under No. 16. 494.

[55] *op. cit.*

[56] In a letter to me dated 14. January 1973.

[57] For example, Josef Volf, *op. cit.*

[58] *op. cit.*, p. 17.

[59] For this and the following references to titles, see A. Renaudet: *Préréforme et humanisme* (Paris, 1916, II, 1953).

[60] *Sancti Pauli Epistolae XIV ex vulgata editione, adiecta intelligentia ex graeco, cum commentariis Jac. Fabri Stapulensis.*

mentioned by Velenský (in his third *persuasio*) in connection with a problem of translation in the letters to the Romans and to Timothy and also includes—placed between the epistles to Philemon and the Hebrews—the correspondence between Seneca and Paul, quoted by Velenský in his fifteenth *persuasio*.

Bartoš also maintains that there is another reference to Paris as the place where Velenský was living at this time in the *Libros annotationibus* of Lorenzo Valla and Erasmus which Velenský mentions in his fourth *cavillus*. This, in Bartoš' opinion, must be the 1505 edition of Erasmus: *Laurentii Vallensis viri tam graecae quam latinae linguae peritissimi in latinam exemplarium adnotationes apprime utiles*, which was also printed in Paris, by Judocus Badius Ascensius (Josse Bade). Bartoš also regards it as remarkable that Velenský, on the authority of Valla and Erasmus, describes the writings of Dionysius the Areopagite as forgeries and (in his refutation of the fourth *cavillus*) says the same of the "books of Clement". Both collections of writings were published by Faber Stapulensis in Paris. In 1498, the *Theologia vivificans*[61] was published and, in 1504, the *Pro piorum recreatione*.[62]

Finally, Bartoš also mentions the fact that Velenský worked in Claudianus' printing press in 1518 and that he was "perhaps involved there in the translation and printing of the *Pastor of Hermas*, which, in all probability, took place in accordance with the *editio princeps* of 1512 by Faber".[63]

Pražak was convinced by Bartoš' suggestion and put forward other arguments in an attempt to make Velenský's possible period in Paris plausible. He wrote: [64]"If the examples already given are not sufficient, the following can also be mentioned: Erasmus' Latin edition of Lucian's treatise, containing the complaint to Saturn of a poor man against the rich,[65] a treatise which Velenský translated, had only been published twice before that time (1506 and 1514) and, what is more, both times in Paris. The dialogue *Julius* —which was also translated at a later date by Velenský—was written to satisfy the French point of

---

[61] *Theologia vivificans. Cibus solidus. Dionysii coelestis Hierarchia, divina Nomina, mystica Theologia, undecim Epistola.*

[62] *Pro piorum recreatione et hoc in opere contenta; Recognitiones Petri Apostoli. Complementum Epistolae Clementis.*

[63] Bartoš came to this hypothesis because (*op. cit.*, p. 17): "the language used points to Faber's edition and not to the earlier, Bohemian edition (1462)"

[64] *op. cit.*, p. 453.

[65] *Luciani viri quam disertissimi compluria opuscula longe festivissima ab Erasmo Roterodamo et Thoma Moro interpretibus optimis in latinorum linguam traducta* (1506, Paris, Josse Bade).

view and—if it was not the work of Erasmus—it was in any case certainly produced in France. Finally, in his foreword to his translation of Erasmus' *Enchiridion*, Velenský refers to a work by the Florentine humanist Peter Crinitus, the *De poetis latinis*, which was published three times in Paris (1508, 1510 and 1512).[66] All possibility of chance is precluded by these arguments and we are therefore bound to regard it as proved that Velenský was in Paris. What is more, none of the books mentioned appeared later than 1517, so that it is also possible to conclude that Velenský left France either in that year or at the beginning of the next".

Neither Bartoš nor Pražak, however, looked for evidence—or at least they do not mention that they looked for it—in the relevant Paris archives for sources in the period between 1515 and 1518. If they had done any research of this kind, the result would certainly have been negative, since the name Velenus or Velenský (or a corrupt form of it, because of the different linguistic zone) does not occur in those archives, at least according to my investigations.

Let us now briefly review the documents which have to be considered in any research into whether Velenský spent these years in Paris. The *Offices claustraux—XVIe siècle: Saint Germain des Prés* (Série L 778) and *Collège Cardinal Lemoine* (M 145) are in the keeping of the *Direction des Archives de France*. If Velenský stayed outside the University, but within Stapulensis' circle, it is possible that his name would be found in these sources. Neither of these two documents has as yet been provided with a detailed index, but the *Direction des Archives* finally came to the conclusion that *la tentative d'y retrouver une trace du séjour d'Ulrichus Velenus n'a obtenu qu'un résultat négatif.*[67] The registers of the *Faculté de théologie* (MM) are indexed, but they appear to contain data only for the period following 1540. The name Velenský does not, moreover, occur in the indices of Series J *(Trésor des Chartes)*, K *(Monuments historiques)*, L *(Monuments ecclésiastiques)*, M *(Mélanges)*, X *(Parlement de Paris)* and Y *(Chatelet de Paris)*.

In the library of the Sorbonne, there are two lists of names: the *Rotulus nominandorum* 1510–1517 *(Registre 62)*, a list which contains only the names of the students from the diocese of Paris and from Normandy registered between these years at the University, and the *Registre 91*, which contains the names of the students from the German

---

[66] J. Graesse: *Trésor de livres rares et précieux*, II (Dresden, 1861), p. 30.
[67] In a letter to me dated 5 January 1974.

natio and the English. The name Velenský does not appear in either of these lists.

Although this research into Paris archives has yielded no evidence which would allow us to say with certainty that Velenský spent some time in Paris, either as a registered student or as a member of Stapulensis' circle, the assumption made by Bartoš and Pražak can nonetheless be supported by other arguments. It is, in other words, possible to interpret a number of Velenský's statements on the basis of the *a priori* supposition that the author may have stayed in Paris. If that *a priori* assumption is not made, these statements would certainly not lead us to believe that Velenský ever went to Paris. The more importance is attached to Bartoš' hypothesis, however, the more force these arguments tend to have and the more clearly they point in the direction of an accumulation of convincing evidence. Having set out these reservations and outlined our reasons for hesitating to accept Bartoš' hypothesis, then, we may go on to make the following comments.

Velenský quotes (in his last *cavillus*) Flavius Josephus and it is possible that he may have found this text and the commentary on it in a work published in 1510 by Stapulensis and printed by Josse Bade—the *Aegesippi historiographi*.[68] This treatise contains an abbreviated version of Josephus' *De bello Judaico*—which is attributed to the Pseudo-Hegesippus—with a Christian tendency that is alien to Josephus. What is particularly striking is that this Christian tendency is also to be found in Velenský's version.

Another possible argument is Velenský's admiration of Ficino. (He translated and published one of Ficino's dialogues in 1520.) It can, of course, be argued—and A. Molnár does precisely this[69]—that Velenský became acquainted with Ficino's works because they had been brought into Bohemia by Lukáš of Prague when he returned from his Italian journey. Stapulensis' acknowledged *intimité spirituelle avec Marsil Ficine*,[70] to which he testifies in many of his works,[71] makes it reasonable, however, for us to assume that Velenský became interested

---

[68] *Aegesippi historiographi fidelissimi ac disertissimi et inter christianos antiquissimi historia. De bello iudaico sceptri sublatione Iudaeorum dispersione et antistite e graeca latina facta, cum eiusdem Anacephaleosi et rebellis congruentiarum cum Josephi libris; etiam de gestis Macchabeorum.*

[69] In his article *Voyage d'Italie* (Comviat, 1962 - 1).

[70] A. Renaudet: *Humanisme et renaissance* (1958), p. 201.

[71] For example, *Liber de triplici vita* (1492), *Mercurii Trismegisti liber de potestate et sapientia Dei per Marsilium Ficinum traductum* (1494).

in the writings of the Italian Platonist during the time he spent in Paris.

Pražak has used, as an argument for Velenský's having stayed in Paris, the anonymous dialogue *Julius*. This pamphlet was circulating in the French capital shortly after 1514 and causing a considerable stir there. If Velenský did in fact come to Paris in 1515, he must have experienced personally the sensational effect that this anti-papal treatise was having. It is therefore possible that he decided to translate it himself at some later period.

One further event can also be mentioned which may perhaps be used to support the hypothesis put forward by Bartoš and Pražak. In his treatise, Velenský speaks about the "unjust treatment of Reuchlin". The trial of Reuchlin and the case against his book *Augenspiegel* had opened under the Inquisitor van Hoochstraten in 1513. It dragged on for several years, during which Stapulensis was in close contact with Reuchlin. If we assume that Velenský came to Paris in the latter part of 1515 and stayed there till the end of 1517—and during that period moved among the circle of friends and acquaintances surrounding Stapulensis (after all, many of the examples that we have mentioned point to this)—then it is clear that Velenský may well have been a witness at this trial.

Taking all these facts into consideration, we are bound to acknowledge the correctness of Bartoš' assertion that "it is at the very least surprising how much of the material used by Velenský came from Paris". We are, however, bound to conclude that—however much this material points in the direction of an accumulation of evidence—it is unfortunately not possible to find any historical certainty in it. There was, moreover, such an intensive trade in books at the beginning of the sixteenth century that it would be quite wrong to conclude from Velenský's use of certain books that had recently been published in Paris that he must necessarily have been in Paris himself.

On the otherhand, however, it has to be admitted that it is not really possible to reconstruct an acceptable alternative. The statement in the Czech "National Bibliography" is, as we have seen, incorrect —Velenský was never registered as a student at Wittenberg. Furthermore, his name cannot be found in the registers of any other European University insofar as these lists of students are available for inspection. In the absence of any reasonable alternative, then, Bartoš' theory becomes more and more plausible.

It is also possible to base another theory on the fact that Velenský became known in 1519 as a printer of books. The assumption that has to be made in this hypothesis is that, in accordance with the practice of the period, Velenský spent some time with a printer and learned the trade with him after he had completed his studies. This assumption is made by the author of the entry in the Czech "National Bibliography", who says: "he became acquainted with the art of printing books in Nuremberg", in other words, after his studies at Wittenberg. The same suggestion is made by Jan Jakoubek in his *Dějiny Literaty české* II.[72] According to this author, Velenský spent several years in Nuremberg and learned the printing trade at Hölzel's press, on the advice of his (later) teacher Claudianus, who had also worked at the same printing press.

There is, however, not a single concrete datum that can be used in support of this hypothesis.[73] It is, on the other hand, not necessary to find any such support for this theory as an explanation for Velenský's skill as a printer, if Pražak was right to conclude from the data available for the year 1518–1519 that it was not until that time that Velenský learned the printing trade, when he was with Claudianus.

A more plausible assumption than that Velenský spent a period as an apprentice in Nuremberg is that he may have been trained at Basle at the press of Andreas Cratander, where his treatise *Petrum Romam non venisse* was published in 1520. Pražak was clearly thinking along those lines when he wrote[74] "that it must be assumed that Velenský spent some time, on the return journey from Paris to his Bohemian homeland, at the famous centre of printing on the frontier of France and Switzerland and that he established contacts there which led to the later publication of his treatise by Cratander". He has also pointed out that the dialogue Julius was published by Cratander in March 1518, in other words, roundabout the time when Velenský was on his way back from Paris to Bohemia. This would be another explanation for Velenský's familiarity with the pamphlet.[75]

In itself, this is certainly an attractive theory, but, like the previous hypothesis, it too cannot be proved. Research into the data on Cratan-

---

[72] Quoted by Pražak, *op. cit.*, p. 455.

[73] The very accurate lists of the names of printers and their collaborators in Jozef Benzing's books (for example, *Buchdrucklexikon des 16. Jahrhunderts*, Frankfurt a.M., 1951) contain no reference to Velenský.

[74] *op. cit.*, p. 453.

[75] W. K. Ferguson (*Erasmi opuscula*, 1933) p. 63, believed that Frobenius may have been the printer.

der's printing works[76] has shown that Cratander certainly employed
and housed various scientifically trained proof-readers—one of these was
Oecolampadius—but the name Velenský does not occur in these
sources. What is more, Velenský was not, at least according to the
records, registered as a student at the University of Basle.

In conclusion, we may therefore say that we cannot be certain as to
where Velenský lived and what he was doing during the period
between the latter part of 1515 and the summer of 1518. Wherever he
may have lived and worked during this time, however, what is certain
is that he was intensely interested in what had been recently published
in Paris and especially in the writings of Stapulensis and Erasmus. It is,
moreover, important to point out that, even though Velenský may
have been in Paris at this time, he can only have been influenced by
Erasmus' ideas by reading his writings and cannot have been in personal contact with him, since the Dutch scholar certainly did not visit
the French capital during the period in question.

At the same time, however, we may also conclude that Bartoš'
hypothesis is the most plausible, on the one hand because it is best
supported by many indications contained in Velenský's own work and,
on the other, because of the lack of any really acceptable alternative.
We may therefore fill in the gap in Velenský's biography by saying
that, after gaining his baccalaureate at the Faculty of Arts in the University of Prague, he let himself be trained in humanism for several
years afterwards by the leaders in this science as practised in Paris.[77]

5. *Velenský as a Printer*

We can speak with greater—although even here not with absolute—
certainty about the period following the summer of 1518. In the
opinion of most Czech historians,[78] it is highly probable that Velenský
went at that time to Mladá Boleslav (known in German as Jung-
Bunzlau) to work at the printing press of Nicholas Claudianus (Miku-
láš Klaudián), a doctor and a member of the Bohemian Brethren.
Claudianus had directed the printing of the Latin edition of Lukáš of
Prague's *Apologia sacrae scripturae* in 1511 at Hölzel's press in Nurem-

---

[76] Eugen A. Meier and others: *Andreas Cratander, ein Basler Drucker und Verleger der Reformationszeit* (Basle, 1966).

[77] For which he had no opportunity at the University of Prague with its
scholastic emphasis. (See Chapter III: "Backgrounds and Sources").

[78] Among others, R. Říčan: *Die Böhmischen Brüder* (1958); J. B. Čapek: *Jednota
Bratrská* (1957); F. M. Bartos, *op. cit.*

berg. (This was the book that came into Luther's hands during the controversy about indulgences, prompting him to read more about the Brethren later.[79]) Afterwards, at his own printing works at Mladá Boleslav, Claudianus brought out an edition of the New Testament. He also produced, among other things, a map of Bohemia. What Velenský above all shared with this man of many and diverse talents was a great admiration for Erasmus.

The Czech historians have based their hypothesis that Velenský went to work at Claudianus' press in 1518 in particular on their scientific investigation into the language and style of the editions produced by Claudianus at the time and their recognition of similar linguistic and stylistic features in Velenský's idiom. Pražak, for example, has shown[80] that the translation of the *Pastor of Hermas* that was published in June 1518 is characterised by a very exact reproduction in Czech of the classical Latin constructions, a linguistic practice which is typical of all Velenský's translations. Bartoš, who believes that Stapulensis' edition was Velenský's source for this particular translation, has also claimed that Velenský's linguistic usage and ideas can be recognised in the conclusion of this edition.[81] Both Pražak and Bartoš have therefore concluded either that Velenský was commissioned by Claudianus to do this translation or that he offered Claudianus his already completed translation.

Another argument put forward by Pražak is that the works printed at Mladá Boleslav during that year do not fit into the general style of books published by Claudianus. In July 1518, for example, a selection from Lactantius *(De vero dei cultu)* and another from Seneca *(De ira)* were published at the press. The first of these two works is an especially good example, since Velenský quotes from Lactantius' *De vero dei cultu* in the foreword that he wrote a year later for his translation of Erasmus' *Enchiridion*. Pražak has therefore concluded that he must have been especially concerned with this work.

Roundabout the middle of 1519, Oldřich Velenský took over Claudianus' printing press at Mladá Boleslav. This is the conclusion that can be drawn from the "testament" written by Claudianus in August 1521 in Leipzig,[82] in which he mentions a "transaction" that had taken

---

[79] See Bartoš: *Das Auftreten Luthers und die Unität der böhmischen Brüder*, ARG XXXI, 1934, pp. 103–120.

[80] *op. cit.*, p. 454.

[81] Bartoš: *Zapadlé dílko bratrské vědy* (1925), p. 17.

[82] Quoted by Bartoš, *op. cit.*, p. 18.

place between himself and Velenský a little time before the writing of the "testament". There is no explicit reference in the text to the taking over of the printing works, but the transaction must nonetheless refer to this, since no more works were published by Claudianus after the summer of 1519. What is more, the editions signed from that date onwards by Velenský as the printer are set in Claudianus' type. A new woodcut also appears on the title page of the books produced from that time onwards—Velenský's own sign, illustrating his printing press (*prelum Ulricianum*).

These editions, however, do not come from Mladá Boleslav, but from Bělá pod Bezdězem (in German known as Weißwasser). The reason for this must be that Velenský must have closed the business in Mladá Boleslav down as soon as he had taken it over from Claudianus and had the press and the type transferred to his new home. It was in Bělá that the first edition published by the printer Velenský appeared on 20 October 1519. One has the distinct impression that this first work was a purely commercial undertaking. It is a kind of "almanach",[83] which originally appeared in Latin in Nuremberg and was published by Velenský in Czech. The obvious assumption to make is that Claudianus provided him with this material, which he had from his period in Nuremberg, and that Velenský put it on the market from financial necessity (after purchasing the printing press).

This whole affair is characteristic of Velenský's position with regard to the Brethren. Most of the printing presses in Bohemia worked at this time[84] for the Unitas and were financed by the Brethren, who decided what books they should print. After Velenský had left Mladá Boleslav, the Brethren, in accordance with their system, set up a new press and appointed Jirik Štyrsa as manager. Velenský, however, now appeared on the scene as an independent printer with his own publishing programme and outside the control of the Brethren. Mladá Boleslav was the policy-making centre of the Unitas (Lukáš of Prague also lived and worked there) and it is reasonable to assume that Velenský believed that his independence as a publisher was threatened by the influence exerted by the leadership of the Brethren at Mladá Boleslav and therefore moved his press. This assumption, however, is not supported by any data and might, moreover, give rise to the

---

[83] *Prenostika*, Knihopis No. 14. 281.

[84] See M. Bohatcová, *op. cit.* The most important printing press belonging to the Unitas Fratrum was in Litomysl. From 1506 until 1532, this press was under the leadership of Pavel Olivetský.

further assumption that Velenský wanted to oppose the Brethren and none of the available data suggest this.

It is possible that Velenský moved his printing press from Mladá Boleslav to Bělá because the latter was situated on the estate of Jan Špetla, with whom—as we shall see later on—Velenský enjoyed good relationships and on whose estate he could carry out his work more safely at a time when the central authority was losing power and noblemen were in a position to protect forbidden groups.

The second work that Velenský printed and published at Bělá was his own translation of Erasmus' *Enchiridion militis christiani*. This was dated 17 December 1519 and entitled "The very comforting and useful book of Erasmus of Rotterdam concerning the Christian knight".[85] This work, which had been published for the first time in Antwerp in 1503, was not entirely unknown in Bohemia. In his book "On the six causes of errors" (1517), Lukáš of Prague had already included parts of Erasmus' work—the concluding chapters on "some special sins". Bartoš[86] believes that Velenský published the complete text of the Enchiridion in translation because Lukáš and Claudianus had urged him to do so "as a tribute to Erasmus for his favourable attitude towards Hus".[87] There can be no doubt that the pressure brought to bear on Velenský by his teachers in this respect must have been a powerful stimulus to him, but a reading of the comprehensive foreword to this edition brings to light a deeper reason for Velenský's decision to publish this particular work of Erasmus in translation. In this foreword, he says: "that this book is very useful and must be explained to many people who do not know it" in order to provide them with arguments for a firmly based criticism of the traditional Church. It is clear therefore that Velenský believed that the various themes discussed by Erasmus supported the criticism of the Roman Church made by the Utraquists and the Brethren. In this connection, one is reminded of Erasmus' rejection of the Roman practice of attaching great value to external religious forms, such as intercession to the saints, the veneration of relics, sprinkling with holy water and the unreflecting adoration of Christ's presence in the sacrament. These were expressions of faith which had to be regarded as superstitions if

---

[85] *Přeutěšená a mnoho prspěšná kniha Erazima Roterdamskeho o rytieři křesťanském,* Knihopis No. 2351.

[86] *Erasmus und die böhmische Reformation* (*Comviat,* 1958, 1/2).

[87] *Hus exustus est, non revictus* (May, 1518, in a letter defending his edition of the New Testament).

they were not accompanied by a deeply experienced union with Christ. All that really mattered were the fruits of the Spirit.

These were ideas which had been well known in Bohemia since the early days of the Hussites' attempts to reform the Church and they were especially associated with the radical renewals introduced by the Brethren at the beginning. In connection with the theme of the imitation of Christ, moreover, Erasmus had written that Christ's words had to be followed not only in the spirit, but also in practical living, being given form in ethical precepts on humility, mercy and voluntary poverty. The comparison between this type of writing and the rules of life formulated by the Brethren themselves as a practical application of the gospel teaching was very obvious indeed to readers in Bohemia.

The main theme of Erasmus' *Enchiridion* must also have inspired Velenský personally, since in this work the author above all calls on Christians to combat the "great enemy" with firm resolution in the certain knowledge that God will be with them. Whereas Erasmus does not personify this "great enemy" anywhere in his treatise, treating the combat as an inner struggle against evil in which the believer has to use the Bible as a weapon, Velenský does personify the enemy as the Antichrist who threatens the Church and the Christian people. The believer must fight against this Antichrist and the weapon with which he conquers in that struggle is the Bible.

The extent to which Velenský saw himself as this combatant armed with the Bible is clear from the foreword which he wrote later for his *Petrum Romam non venisse*, in which he followed Erasmus' example: "My armour is Scripture, which must be quoted in its *germanum intellectum*". What is more, however, the extent to which Velenský had developed his own interpretation is also clear from his attack against scholasticism in the context of what he says about the authority of the Bible: "All opinions are subject to one point of view, the law of Christ, whether they are proclaimed by Scotus or by Thomas. The whole Roman division arises if one man adheres to Doctor Scotus and the other to Thomas Aquinas and this leads to a struggle which often lasts until death." In this context, Velenský calls the scholastic theologians of his own times in Bohemia "unchaste".[88] A direct frontal attack against scholasticism cannot be regarded simply as Velenský's elaboration of the combat against the "great enemy" in the sense intended by Erasmus.

---

[88] If it is possible to translate the difficult Czech word *oplzlé* in this way.

Velenský is also providing his own interpretation when he desig-
nates the "great enemy" as the Antichrist. In this, he is clearly attacking
the intolerant attitude of the popes and he provides an almost identical
survey of the victims of the Antichrist as the one given in the foreword to his treatise *Petrum Romam non venisse*. Here too, he mentions
Wyclif, Hus, Jerome of Prague, the victims of the Hussite war, Ulrich
von Hutten, Pico della Mirandola, Savonarola and Luther and, in
addition, Erasmus, whose name is not to be found in the parallel
sentence in his treatise.

It is moreover clear that, although he found Erasmus' *Enchiridion*
valuable as an aid in the Church controversy in Bohemia, Velenský
also provided the treatise with a foreword in which he went his own
way. He even permitted himself to make a critical comment about the
"particular preacher": "It is true that Erasmus and Luther have
clarified and made known the truth about God, but they have overlooked the fact that another people, the Bohemians, received the
divine truth as a gift".

At the end of this foreword, we are introduced to the party conflicts
of in Bohemia at the time. Velenský appeals to the leading nobleman
of the Utraquist party, Jan Špetla of Janovice, to combat the "great
enemy" as a "true Christian knight" (the *miles christianus* of the *Enchiridion*). Jan Špetla had, after all, "publicly confessed the chalice of
the Lord in kingdom of Bohemia" and thus became a "leading defen-
dant of the truth".

As we have already said in passing above, this Jan Špetla was
Velenský's protector. The mention of his name is therefore clearly
intended as a tribute to the man. It can also be regarded, however, as
an indication that Velenský enjoyed good relationships with the
political leadership of the Utraquist party. (As we shall see later, Bartoš
was to draw certain conclusions from this with regard to Velenský's
later career.)

Velenský also added to his translation of Erasmus' work a detailed
appendix—thirty-six pages in length—although his intention here was
different from that in his foreword. Rudolf Říčan[89] has pointed out
that Velenský gives evidence in this commentary of his understanding
of the need to explain many of the arguments and images employed
by Erasmus to the simple Bohemian people before they could use the
book itself. For this reason, he provided a commentary on the exam-

---

[89] *Die tschechische Reformation und Erasmus* (*Comviat*, 1973, 3, p. 188).

ples taken from mythology and said a little about the Greek authors and philosophical schools. It was for the same reason that Velenský also defended the humanists' interest in early pagan civilisation. It is necessary to understand, he argues, the real intention of the myths, as Paul did whenever he quoted a Greek author. Velenský also gives several examples of humanists' criticisms of the traditional theology. One notable instance is that of Lorenzo Valla, who proved that Dionysius the Areopagite was not a discipel of Paul's.

Říčan is also of the opinion that these commentaries, which were inclined towards humanism, scandalised the simple believers in Bohemia—that they *manchem konservativen Leser anstössig waren und daß er deshalb im J. 1520 eine zweite Edition ohne diesen Anhang besorgt hat.*[90] This second edition,[91] however, was anonymous and scholars of undisputed authority[92] do not ascribe it to Velenský.

On 1 February 1520, Velenský produced a translation of a dialogue by Lucian at the press at Bělá with the title: "Useful letters of poor and rich people who accuse each other before Saturn, by the Greek sage Lucian".[93] Velenský's publication is taken from the Saturnalia and is the part in which Cronosolon, the priest of Cronus, provides regulations for the feasts of Saturn, prompted by a complaint made by a poor man that he has been neglected in favour of the rich.[94]

It is quite possible that Velenský chose to translate and publish this particular work by Lucian because its critical content was very much in keeping with the tendencies among the Bohemian Brethren to renew society. An example of this similarity is the question (Chap. 11) whether it is possible to defend the situation in which there are "rogues unbelievably rich and alone leading a comfortable life" and alongside them men who "know poverty and despair as companions". The answer given (Chap. 13) is that "every man must be treated equal, slave and freeman, poor and rich". This undoubtedly calls to mind the rules of life formulated by the Brethren in their early and radical years. The fact that it at the same time reflects a classical pagan view is no real objection, since Velenský explains in his appendix to the *Enchiridion*

---

[90] *op. cit.*, p. 189.

[91] No distinction is made between this edition and the edition of December 1519 in the Knihopis (No. 2351).

[92] See Mirjam Bohatcová, *op. cit.*

[93] *Kratochvolní spolu i požitečni listové a žaloby chudých a behatých před Saturnem*, Knihopis No. 4992.

[94] Complete text: *Lucian*, VI, translated by K. Kilburn (Loeb Library, London, 1959), pp. 105, 107.

that the profound intentions underlying the pagan forms are what have to be borne in mind.

The choice of this particular pagan work, however, points to Velenský's education in humanism and, whether or not this was received in Paris or Basle, it was certainly the result of Erasmus' influence. Erasmus' edition of Lucian appeared for the first time in Paris in 1506 and was reprinted in 1517. Another edition also appeared in Basle in 1517.[95] We may therefore assume that Velenský became acquainted with Erasmus' Latin translation of Lucian's works during the time that he was studying the science of humanism and that he decided to publish a Czech edition of this particular dialogue because it was so critical of society.

Shortly after publishing his translation of Lucian's dialogue, Velenský produced, on 24 February, a Czech version of the anonymous treatise *Julius exclusus:*[96] "The Apostle Peter's dialogue with Pope Julius II". It is not difficult to guess Velenský's reasons for publishing this text. It was originally intended as an anti-war tract and was, in the opinion of most of the scholars who have studied it, written from a strongly Gallican point of view, but it is at the same time so critical of the pope that it was an obviously suitable vehicle for the views current in Bohemia regarding the Antichrist. The unknown author of the treatise narrates how Pope Julius II appears at the gate of heaven, but the only key that he has with him is the key of his money-box. He knocks and Peter appears, but, unimpressed by what the pope says, refuses to admit him to heaven. Julius then proposes to lay siege to heaven with troops raised from among the souls of the soldiers who have died in the wars waged by the pope himself.

Parts of this text[97] betray a striking similarity to what Velenský was to write later in his *Petrum Romam non venisse*. It is therefore reasonable to assume that the *Julius exclusus* was an important source of inspiration for Velenský's later treatise on the pope. The anonymous writer says, for example, with regard to the pope's triple crown or tiara, that "no barbarian tyrant ever dared to wear it" (lines 34/35) and, with regard to the pope's appearance, that he looked" as though he had

---

[95] Allen, I, p. 414.

[96] *Spolurozmlúvanie s. Petra apoštola a najsvatějšieho Julia druhého papaže, a témuž při porodu daného anjela, buď zlého nebo dobrého, o moci cierkevní a též cierkve hlavě.* Knihopis No. 15. 625.

[97] Complete text in W. K. Ferguson: *Opuscula Erasmi*, The Hague, 1933, pp. 38–124. Ferguson also includes a detailed argument in favour of Erasmus' authorship.

just come out of hell" (line 89), so that there was good reason for changing the title *pontifex maximus* to *pestis maximus* (line 44). These statements would certainly seem to have served as models for Velenský's later descriptions of the pope as the Antichrist in his foreword to the *Petrum Romam non venisse*. In the same way, his ideas about the *ecclesia primitiva* which he elaborated in his *persuasiones* may also have been influenced by the views expressed in this anonymous text, in which the pope is criticised, for example, because the princes of the Church are "great lords who will not return to the good Church with the poverty of the apostles". He is urged to consider "the way in which the Church arose and was established—this took place by patience and by the blood of the martyrs" (line 1184).

James K. McConica[98] has disputed the opinion that the treatise expresses the Gallican point of view, basing his argument on statements in the spirit of such quotations as these. "It might be natural to see the *Julius Exclusus* as a French propaganda piece if some passages were isolated...", he says. "No one has yet pointed out, however, that ... the French are placed in a very favourable light... The first and dominant purpose of this work is evangelical ... The essential theme of the whole dialogue is not an assertion of a conciliarist or Gallican position as such, but the contrast between the contemporary papacy at its most secular and the spirit of the apostolic Church".[99] We cannot consider here whether McConica's summing up on this basis of the whole dialogue is correct or not,[100] but it can certainly be assumed, on the basis of similar statements in the *Petrum Romam non venisse*, that it was this aspect above all which appealed to Velenský.

Both Renaudet and Allen[101] have suggested that the author of the treatise *Julius exclusus* was Erasmus who, in their opinion, wrote the work in 1513 or 1514, with the full knowledge of Thomas More. Henri Hauser and Carl Stange, on the other hand,[102] believed that the author was Faustus Andrelinus of Forli, Erasmus' friend in Paris. In holding this opinion, they were following D. F. Strauß,[103] who had

---

[98] *Erasmus and the "Julius": a Humanist reflects on the Church*, in *The Pursuit of Holiness in Late Medieval and Renaissance Religion*, e.d C. Trinkaus and H. A. Oberman (Leiden, 1974), p. 444 ff.

[99] *op. cit.*, p. 454.

[100] A discussion of McConica's view can be found in the same collection (see note 98).

[101] Renaudet, *op. cit.*, p. 666; Allen, Letters 430, 502, 543.

[102] H. Hauser: *Le Julius est-il d'Érasme?* (1927); C. Stange: *Julius II, eine Legende* (1937).

[103] D. F. Strauß: *Ulrich von Hutten* (1858).

pointed out as early as 1858 that a 1518 edition of the *Julius exclusus* contained the initials "F.A.F.", followed by the words *Poete Regii*. Roland Bainton, however,[104] has drawn attention to the fact that Faustus Andrelinus was already dead by 1518, although he notes that the anonymous edition of March 1518, printed by Cratander, obviously appeared earlier, *denn die Ausgabe mit den Initialen stellt einen Fehler der anderen richtig*. Bainton also believes that Erasmus and Andrelinus co-operated in the publication: *Sowohl Erasmus wie Andrelini waren 1511 in Paris, und Andrelini mag ihm die vielen Einzelheiten der päpstlichen Politik gegenüber den Franzosen mitgeteilt haben.*

Despite this, however, Bainton still assumes that the real author of the satire on Julius' exclusion from heaven was Erasmus and puts forward a number of arguments in support of this. In the first place, there is a satirical poem on Julius preserved[105] in Erasmus' handwriting.[106] On the back of this manuscript is the name "Th. Morus Byth. Capad.", to whom Erasmus apparently gave the poem when he returned to England in 1511. One has the impression that this poem is a precursor of the later satirical dialogue.[107] In the second place, it is also clear from many letters—among others, letters written to Cardinal Riario[108] and to the Abbot Anton of Bergen[109]—that Erasmus was very critical of Pope Julius II: "Julius' trumpets plunged the whole world into war". At the very time, moreover, that Erasmus was making such negative statements about the pope—in 1512/1513—the first handwritten copy of the *Julius exclusus* began to circulate. Bainton has therefore concluded: *Die Wahrscheinlichkeit, daß Erasmus der Verfasser war, ist sehr groß.*

W. K. Ferguson[110] is even firmer in what he says about the authorship of the treatise: "Erasmus refused to acknowledge his respon-

---

[104] *Erasmus* (Göttingen, 1972), p. 101 ff.

[105] In *Fundation Custodia* (coll. F. Lugt), Institut Neerlandais, Paris.

[106] Text in W. K. Ferguson, *op. cit.*, p. 35, and C. Reedijk: *The Poems of Desiderius Erasmus* (Leiden, 1956), pp. 391–393.

[107] According to J. B. Pineau (*Revue de Littérature comparée*, V, 1935, p. 385 ff), W. K. Ferguson, *op. cit.*, and R. Bainton, *op. cit.* C. Reedijk, *op. cit.*, is not convinced by this argument and says that most parallels "seem to be based on anecdotes concerning the pope that we may assume to have been common knowledge at the time" (p. 392). He regards Erasmus, however, as the author of the Julius exclusus. In his *Érasme, Thierry Martens et le Iulius exclusus* (*Scrinium erasmianum* II, ed. J. Coppens, Leiden, 1969), he states, Erasmus was in Louvain in the same time—1518—Martens printed an edition of the dialogue.

[108] Allen, II, 333.

[109] Allen, I, 288.

[110] *op. cit.*, p. 42.

sibility for the dialogue, resorting when necessary to every form of equivocation short of literal mendacity. Yet despite the care with which he endeavoured to preserve his anonymity, there can be no doubt that he was the author of the Iulius". He has also pointed out that contemporary writers attributed the dialogue directly to Erasmus— Luther (in a letter dated 11 November 1517), Conrad Grebel (in a letter of 26 October 1518) and Christoph Scheurl (in letters dated 30 September 1517 and 5 January 1518). Since there is so much unanimity among Erasmus' contemporaries, we are bound to assume that Velenský probably also regarded Erasmus as the author of the *Julius exclusus*.

During the same year—although the precise date is not known— another translated dialogue, "Pasquillus and Cyrus",[111] came from Velenský's press. This edition would seem to have had the function of supplementing the *Julius exclusus*. If the two dialogues are considered in combination, it is clear that Velenský many have been protesting against the papacy as such and not against one particular pope. It may be important to stress this, since treatises of the type usually known as anti-papal have frequently been defended by loyal Catholics who objected to the rule or the way of life of one pope in particular. Erasmus therefore was sympathetic towards the dialogue *Julius exclusus*, even if he was not the author of it himself, because he accused Pope Julius II of having a warlike attitude. On the other hand, he defended the papacy itself when Luther called not the person, but the office of the pope into question in his writings.[112] In Bohemia, the leading humanist Hasištejn[113] was sharply critical of Pope Alexander, but he was firmly opposed to the Brethren as soon as they began to attack the institute of the papacy as such. Velenský, however, leaves us in no doubt about his attitude towards the papacy. In the very same year he published both a treatise directed against Julius II of the della Rovere family and a satire written from the standpoint of the della Rovere party against Julius' successor Leo X, who was a member of the Medici family. In doing this, he demonstrated his fundamental rejection of the papacy as such.

The content of the dialogue "A conversation between two persons, Pasquillus and Cyrus" is a discussion of contemporary events. Pas-

---

[111] *Rokovánie dvu osob, Paškvilla a Cyra*, Knihopis No. 14. 878.
[112] Allen, Letter 1183.
[113] Bohuslav Hasištejnský of Lobkovice (1460–1512), who was originally a Utraquist, but became a faithful Roman Catholic after studying in Italy.

quillus wants to leave Rome because the pope and the curia would give him no more prebends. In addition, he was aware of too many lies and too much deceit in the leadership of the Church. Julius II might have been able to build three churches if he had really spent the money that was intended for it on building churches. And Leo X, who needed money for his war against the Duke of Urbino, created thirty-one cardinals so that they would pay him 500 000 ducats. Cyrus is of the opinion that the pope and the cardinals will lead better lives now that their deceit has been exposed, but Pasquillus persists in his decision to leave Rome and resolves to go to Spain.

We cannot say with any certainty who the author of this dialogue was. It has been suggested that it was Ulrich von Hutten[114] and also that it may have been his friend Crotus. From 1517 onwards, the work appeared with the title *Pasquillus exul*, in all kinds of collections,[115] which, unlike Velenský's other sources, were not published in Paris. It is not known where or how Velenský became acquainted with this satire.

In 1520—and here too the precise date of publication is not known— Velenský published a treatise in two parts,[116] the first part containing a translation of Marsilio Ficino's "Acrimonious treatise on the truth, assigned to Cardinal Riario", the second containing "Twelve Christian corrections of the trial of Pico della Mirandola". Ficino's original text is to be found in his *De institutione principis*,[117] in which a conversation on the truthfulness of the ecclesiastical office is reproduced. In this dialogue, Raffaele Riario says: "Remember that we are ordinary men and that we do not differ from other men in any way". The writer, Ficino, replies: "A prince of the Church must excel in knowledge, truthfulness, wisdom, gentleness and incorruptibility... A prince of the Church must open his ears to the complaint of the poor... And the house of a prince of the Church must be a place of refuge for the innocent, a hope for the good and a seat of honour for the wretched. Then Christ will build his community on this *petra*".

The "Corrections of the Trial of Pico della Mirandola", which form the second part of Velenský's treatise, are taken from Pico's *Apologia*, which was written in 1487 as a defence against the pope's condemnation in 1486 of his book *Conclusiones*.

---

[114] Strauß, *op. cit.*, I, p. 310.

[115] *ibid.*, p. 312.

[116] *Spis vtipný, kterak Pravda k kardinálu Ryarovi přišla. Dvanáctera sprava boje křesťanskeho od Jana Piky hraběte Mirandulskeho*, Knihopis No. 2464.

[117] H. J. Hak: *Marsilio Ficino* (1934), p. 112; complete text in *Opera Omnia Marsilii Ficini* (Basle, Adam Petri, 1561).

Why did Velenský choose these works in particular for translation
and publication? Once again, we may assume that he was influenced
by Stapulensis, who was a great admirer of Pico and through whom
Velenský may have become acquainted with the *Apologia*. The same
may apply to Velenský's use of Ficino's treatise, since Stapulensis had
gone deeply into the works of this author during his Italian journeys
and had even published several of them.[118] We may, however, also
—and with greater reason—assume that Velenský came to know
Ficino's works through another channel. In 1500, this work in particular of Ficino's was translated into Czech, presumably by the
Bohemian humanist Řehoř Hrubý.[119] Pražak has compared the two
translations and has come to the conclusion[120] "that Velenský must
have had the earlier edition (Hrubý's) at hand and that he strove at all
costs to do a better translation". If this means, as Pražak affirms, that
Velenský's only intention was "to demonstrate a new stylistic ideal,
that of conveying the classical Latin constructions into the Czech
idiom", then we are bound to regard it as a one-sided conclusion. In
his other editions, Velenský had already shown far too clearly that
his main concern was that the content of the material that he chose to
translate would provide support for the Church struggle in Bohemia
for us to suppose that in this case his only intention was to achieve an
ideal of stylistic perfection. This conclusion is even more unjustified
in view of the fact that Ficino's work has a very clear connection with
Velenský's own ideas about the renewal of Church and society. A
more justifiable conclusion therefore is that Velenský knew Hrubý's
translation of Ficino's treatise and this fitted into the general framework of his intentions. The fact that he did not simply print Hrubý's
text, but retranslated the original himself undoubtedly has something
to do with his own ideal of stylistic perfection acquired from his
humanistic training. The choice of this particular work, however,
was based on his religious view of Church and society—something to
which Pražak is, as we have already seen, not alert.

On 5 May 1520, Velenský produced an edition of a translation of
Luther's work *Ein Sermon van dem hochwürdigen Sakrament des heiligen
wahren Leichnams Christi und von den Bruderschaften*,[121] which had appeared

---

[118] See Note 71.
[119] Pražak, *op. cit.*, p. 451.
[120] *ibid.*, p. 452.
[121] *O velebné svátosti svatého pravého těla Kristova a o bratrstvie řeč*, Knihopis No. 5121.
The German text: WA II, p. 738.

for the first time only six months previously, in December 1519. Velenský signed this works as its printer, but not—as he did in the case of his previous editions—as its translator. It is not easy to say whether or not we are bound to conclude from this that this translation was made by someone else. This treatise is seldom mentioned by Czech historians[122] and linguistic experts have not yet attempted to determine, on the basis of an analysis of the idiom used in the treatise, whether Velenský may have been the translator. Even on the basis of the content it is not really clear why he decided to publish this particular text. The second part—*Von den Bruderschaften*—does not deal with the Bohemian Brethren, nor does it even allude to them. Not a single name is mentioned in it, but it can be inferred from Luther's description that he was thinking of *Schwärmer*. He characterises these religious enthusiasts as groups of Christians living in isolation and believing that salvation was only to be found within their own circle and, despite their religious exclusivism, held quite dissolute orgies of eating and drinking.

The last two works produced at the printing press in Bělá were treatises by Lukáš of Prague. On 19 November 1520, Velenský published Lukáš' "On bowing down before and adoring the divine body and blood"[123] and, on 21 February 1521, his work "On the rebaptism of believers baptised by Roman Catholic priests".[124]

Velenský's publication of the two works by Lukáš as an independent printer who was not carrying out a commission for the Brethren points to his religious and spiritual connection with the Brethren, but we cannot conclude from this that he was a member of the Unitas. After publishing these two treatises, Velenský closed the press at Bělá and went to Moravia.

The treatise *Petrum Romam non venisse* appeared in November 1520, while the press at Bělá was still functioning. Nonetheless, it was printed and published outside Bohemia and, what is more, in Latin and in German. What reason could there have been for this? Velenský himself provides no answer to this question and we can only guess. We can, for instance, conjecture that, where his own work was at the same time his most public and sharp attack against the established Church, he allowed this treatise to appear outside his home country

---

[122] Even Bartoš does not mention this edition.

[123] *Sepsanie duodov. O klaněnie a klekánie před svátosti těla a krve Božie*, Knihopis No. 5036.

[124] *Spis dosti činící otázce protivnikuov, proč křest se opětuje*, Knihopis No. 5037.

for reasons of personal safety. (This suggestion was made to me by M. Bohatcová.[125]). In this context, we are bound to think of the political situation in Bohemia at the time. From 1516 onwards, following the death of King Vladislav, the central authority had begun to lose power and it had become to some extent possible to express opinions freely, especially in those parts of the country governed by Utraquist noblemen. Since Mladá Boleslav and Bělá were, moreover, villages on estates belonging to such nobles, it was possible for printing to be carried on there without disturbance. On the other hand, however, the Utraquists would not, because of their particular political interests, permit any sharp confrontation to come about with the king and the Church of Rome. The publication of a treatise such as the *Petrum Romam non venisse* would therefore certainly not have been tolerated.

Another question which arises in this context is whether Velenský purchased the printing press in Mladá Boleslav with the intention of publishing a select number of writings within the framework of his own theological views and his aims in the sphere of Church politics, selling the press again as soon as his publishing programme was completed. Or may he, on the other hand, not have bought and sold the press with this underlying intention, both the purchase and the sale being not planned in advance, but simply the result of fortuitous circumstances?[126]

Once again, we are unable to appeal to statements made by Velenský himself. It is, however, possible to defend the following thesis. Between 1515 and 1518, Velenský became acquainted with a number of texts which had a formative effect on him and reinforced his already latent[127] view of the papacy. As soon as he had decided to devote himself actively to the task of combatting the papacy which he had rejected, he recognised how effective the translation and publication of these treatises would be in his own country, where the struggle against the papacy had already been conducted for some years with a degree of success. To accomplish this task, Velenský needed a printing press. With that end in view, he trained as a printer at Claudianus' press at Mladá Boleslav and later took the press over himself. It is possible that he may have had this specific intention because the pattern of his list of publications is different from that of most other humanists

---

[125] In a letter to me dated 14 January 1973.
[126] See, for example, Josef Volf, *op. cit.*, p. 156: *Da es ihm offenbar an Absatz mangelte, gab er den Buchdruck auf.*
[127] See Chapter III: "Backgrounds and Sources".

who were printing books at that time. During his apprenticeship with Claudianus, he was obliged to concern himself with the publication of works by classical authors[128] and, although interest in such works had been revived by the study of humanism, they did not contribute directly to Velenský's specific aims in the sphere of Church politics. (His publication of Seneca's treatise is an example of this.) As soon as he became an independent printer and publisher, however, he produced no more of these classical treatises.

With the exception of his first commercial edition, the *Prenostika*, all the works that he published as an independent printer are clearly related to each other in their ideas. One has a strong impression therefore that Velenský worked according to a definite programme, in the sense that, by throwing light on various aspects of the problem of papal primacy, his different publications formed a preparation for his own treatise, the *Petrum Romam non venisse*. It is difficult to conclude from the data available whether or not he planned, at the very outset of this programme, to write a book attacking the papacy himself, but it is certainly a verifiable fact that there is a thread running through all his publications and leading to the *Petrum Romam non venisse*. Many examples can be given to illustrate this. Whereas, in his first edition, in the foreword that he wrote for Erasmus' *Enchiridon*, he raised the question of papal intolerance, in his own treatise he went further and launched a frontal attack against the papacy, accusing it of failing, and even using the same examples (and sometimes the same expressions!) as he used in his foreword to the *Enchiridion*. In the dialogues *Julius exclusus* and *Pasquillus*, the worldly nature of the papacy was criticised. In the *Petrum Romam non venisse*, however, a radical analysis was made of the causes of this process of secularisation, statements from the two dialogues that he had previously published acting as inspiration to the author. A deep longing for a more just way of life could be heard in the classical treatise of the pagan author Lucian and this same longing was also expressed in the Christian language of Marsilio Ficino's dialogue with Cardinal Riario. The same aspiration for a better society was later given a firm exegetical basis in Velenský's reflections, in his own *Petrum Romam non venisse*, about the *ecclesia primitiva*. (This idealised image of the early Church played an important part in all

---

[128] This was nonetheless a new element in Claudianus' list of publications. (It can be compared, for example, with the title of a book published by Claudianus a few months before Velenský's arrival on the "art of midwifery": *Zprávy o naučeni ženám těhotným a babám pupkořeznym*).

Velenský's other editions.) Finally, while the papacy had been either directly or indirectly criticised in all his previous publications, in his treatise *Petrum Romam non venisse* he disputed the very basis of the primacy of the pope by denying that Peter had ever stayed in Rome. It is clear, then, that the *Petrum Romam non venisse* was the conclusion and the culmination of Velenský's work.

This argument—that Velenský's list of publications followed a clearly directed programme—is, however, weakened by his publication of the edition of Luther in May 1520, which does not fit into this pattern, and of the two works by Lukáš of Prague, which appeared before the printing press closed down. A slight adjustment has there-fore to be made to this thesis. When he went back to his home country in 1518, Velenský took with him a number of works which he thought would provide him with support in the task of spreading his own ideas and which he therefore aimed to publish. In view of the short period of time between the different dates of publication, it may even be conjectured that he had already to a great extent completed the work of translation. These texts, then, must have been the *Enchiridion*, the dialogues *Julius exclusus* and *Pasquillus*, the section from Lucian's *Saturnalia* and probably also Ficino's *De institutione principis* and Pico's *Apologia*. These treatises, which came from the sphere of influence of Erasmus and Stapulensis, provide us on the one hand—if they are seen as a whole—with a survey of the field within which Velenský was later to conduct his arguments against the papacy—the latter, being in conflict with the *ecclesia primitiva*, was, Velenský was to insist, an ex-pression of the Antichrist, who could only be fought with the Bible—and, on the other hand, they also acted as sources, giving form to his later arguments. In this sense, it is possible to speak about a "pro-gramme" carried out by Velenský. Luther's treatise, which first appeared in December 1519, only came to Velenský's attention when he had already collected all the material mentioned above and was already employed in the task of publishing it. What is more, the two works written by Lukáš of Prague were not printed and published by Velenský until his own selection of texts had been completed. The simplest explanation for these editions is that Velenský was personally sympathetic towards these authors and that he was also prompted by commercial considerations and the need to make his press profitable.

It should also be borne in mind that the two treatises on the Lord's Supper, which were of obvious contemporary importance in Utraquist Bohemia, could act as a support in his attack against the papacy, since

the latter was above all the authority which defended communion under one kind only. Both these editions, then, may be regarded as supplementing Velenský's programme.

6. *Velenský's Other Activities*

While Oldřich Velenský was actively printing and publishing at his
press, he was probably also busy in another sphere—there are indications of efforts made by him to restore good relationships between
Erasmus and the Bohemian Brethren.

Erasmus had been informed about the situation in the Church in
Bohemia by the Catholic humanist Jan Šlechta, a former official at the
royal chancellery, *der schon damals alles kaufte, was aus der Feder Erasmus'
auf dem Markt erschien*.[129] On 10 October 1519[130] Šlechta had reviewed,
in a detailed but one-sided letter, the various opinions and tendencies
prevalent at the time, stressing above all the anti-papal ideas of the
"Picards" (by this he of course meant the Brethren, but his use of this
heavily weighted term shows that he also regarded them as fanatical
heretics). On 1 November[131] Erasmus replied, saying in his letter that
it was of course true that the pope made mistakes, but that he had
nonetheless to be obeyed. Appealing to Augustine, Erasmus insisted
on the validity of the sacraments even if the priests administering them
were unworthy. It was therefore wrong to regard the pope as the
Antichrist. The humanistic movements which called the pope the
Antichrist (and supported their claim with Donatistic arguments) were
also fundamentally mistaken.

The contents of Erasmus' letter came to the attention of the Bohemian Brethren, who assumed that he had misunderstood their teaching
because he had been incorrectly informed. They therefore decided to
send envoys to Erasmus. In the spring of 1520, Nicholas Claudianus
and Laurence Votik went to Antwerp, where Erasmus was staying
at the time, to offer him a copy of the *Apologia* of Lukáš of Prague and
to ask him to comment on it. Erasmus' reply, however, was evasive.
The Church authorities already held him in suspicion and he had
therefore to be cautious.[132]

---

[129] Bartoš: *Erasmus und die böhmische Reformation* (*ComViat*, 1958, 2/3, p. 118).

[130] Allen, Letter 1021. This is not Šlechta's first letter to Erasmus. He wrote,
for example, that he had received Erasmus' reply on 11 September after having
waited for a whole year for it. There must therefore have been an earlier letter
written some time around September 1518. It was, however, lost.

[131] Allen, Letter 1039.

[132] All that Erasmus himself said was that *duos Bohemos* had been with him, but

Erasmus' reaction caused disappointment in Bohemia and the Brethren looked for another opportunity to present their case to Erasmus. This chance arose when a powerful Moravian nobleman, Archleb of Boskovice, who was a patron of Lutheranism, but who also had access to Erasmus, used his influence over the latter. Probably in October of 1520, Archleb wrote quite a diplomatic letter,[133] pleading for the rights of the Bohemian Church. Bartoš suspects[134] that Velenský was the author of this letter, because there is a remarkable similarity between the terminology and arguments used in the letter on the one hand and Velenský's description of the Reformation in Bohemia in his foreword to his translation of Erasmus' *Enchiridion* on the other. (There is, for example, a very similar appreciation in both texts of Erasmus and Luther, but again with the comment that also *apud nos habemus qui ... solida scripturarum argumentatione resistant.*) Bartoš rejects the possibility that this similarity may have been purely coincidental on the grounds that there is evidence, in a later period of Velenský's life,[135] that Archleb was in contact with him.[136]

Erasmus' reply to this letter came four months later. It was dated 28 January and was sent from Louvain.[137] Once again, however, Erasmus reacted negatively, saying that, as a son of the Catholic Church, he wanted the Bohemian Church to be reunited with Rome. The pope, he insisted, should not be judged so severely, since he was not responsible for everything that took place in Rome. Even if Peter were still pope, he would have to overlook a great deal of which he would not be able to approve: *atque ut nunc sunt res humanae, si Petrus ipse Romae praesideret, cogeretur, opinor, ad quaedam coniuere quae nequaquam probaret in animo suo.* Erasmus therefore warned his readers against *libri Lutheri* which were in the hands of so many Bohemians and in which the pope was attacked by being called such names as *asinum, haereticum, antichristum, pestem orbis.*

---

that he was already informed about the matter because Šlechta had *diligenter* given him a report. The content of the conversation is known to us only through the treatise written by Joachim Camerarius (1500–1574): *Historia narratio de Fratrum Ortodoxorum ecclesiis in Bohemia, Moravia et Polonia.* (Allen, intr. to Letter 1117.)

[133] Allen, Letter 1154.

[134] *Zapadlé dílko bratrské vědy*, pp. 21, 22. (In his article *Erasmus und die böhmische Reformation, ComViat*, 1958, he repeats this supposition.)

[135] See p. 67.

[136] Bartoš' supposition would nonetheless seem to dispute. Archleb probably read the foreword to the *Enchiridion* and took arguments from it to use in his letter to Erasmus.

[137] Allen, Letter 1183.

It is not known how Velenský reacted to Erasmus' defence of the pope. The warning given by Erasmus, whom he had previously admired so much, against attacks on the pope and Erasmus' use of the title "Antichrist" as an example of such an attack must clearly have struck Velenský as a direct and personal rebuke, despite Erasmus' mention of Luther's books in his letter.

After the period that he spent as a printer in Bělá, Velenský lived for a number of years in Moravia. Practically nothing is know, however, about his stay there. He must have carried out scientific work, since his translation of the second volume of Luther's *Responsio* to Catharinus[138] was published on 15 March 1522 by Pavel Severinus in Prague. The theme of this work is the Antichrist, in the context of the vision in Daniel 8.

Archleb of Boskovice, the leading Lutheran in Moravia, played some part, the precise nature of which is not known, in the genesis of this work by Velenský. We do, however, know that a copy of Velenský's translation was sent to Archleb immediately after it had been published—it is for this reason that Bartoš has suspected[139] that this Moravian nobleman gave Velenský Luther's original Latin text and urged him to translate it. Archleb cannot possibly have financed this edition, since Velenský says in his foreword that the book was printed "at my expense for good people and for the increase of good ideas". This foreword is dated one day before the date of publication (14 March) and must therefore have been written in Severinus' press or at least in Prague.

This was, moreover, the second time that Velenský had been concerned with a work of Luther's—on this occasion as a translator and the first time, two years previously, as a printer. What is more, he obviously had a relationship with the leader of the Lutheran party in Moravia. These two facts, then, point at least to his having had relationships of some kind with the Lutherans and possibly even with Luther himself. In any case, we know that he offered his own treatise *Petrum Romam non venisse* to Luther, since the latter wrote, in a letter

---

[138] *Viklad o Antikristu na viděni Danielovo v osmé kapitole proroctvie jeho polóžené* (not mentioned in the Knihopis; M. Bohatcová has provided the description). Luther's Latin title was: *Ad librum eximii magistri nostri Ambrosii Catharini, defensoris Silvestri Prieratis acerrimi. Responsio Martini Lutheri. Cum exposita visione Danielis VIII de Antichristo.* (In 1524, Paul Speratus made a German translation with a title similar to Velenský's: *Offenbarung des Endchrists aus dem Propheten Daniel, wieder Catharinum.*)

[139] *Zapadlé dílko*, pp. 20/22.

dated 3 February 1521, and sent to Spalatinus:[140] *E Bohemia iuvenis eruditus ad me dedit libellum probare conatus S. Petrum nunquam venisse aut fuisse Romam.* What is, however, not possible to deduce from this sentence is whether Velenský personally offered his treatise to Luther or whether he sent it to him.

Ten years later, Velenský's name appears again. Jan Blahoslav, the historian of the Bohemian Brethren, who, half a century later, carried out detailed research into the archives in order to compose the *Acta Unitas Fratrum*,[141] wrote in 1571[142] that Velenský was living in 1530 in Nové Benátky with Bedři (Frederick) of Doni, where Jan Augusta was the governor of the corporation of the Brethren, *cuius hic fuit et auditor et antagonista.*

This brief mention of Velenský throws light on the situation, but at the same time gives rise to uncertainty. Frederick of Doni was one of the Utraquist noblemen who were inclined towards Lutheranism and who solemnly entered the Unitas Fratrum in 1530 in order to build a bridge between the Utraquist Church, the Brethren and Lutheranism. It was Frederick of Doni too who went in 1530 to the Imperial Diet of Augsburg as the representative of the Lutheran nobility of Bohemia[143] and whose son Borzivog stayed with Luther in Wittenberg in the winter of 1530–1531.[144] If Velenský lived with this man, this must mean that he moved in circles which aimed to unite the neo-Utraquists (who were inclined towards Lutheranism) with the earlier Brethren.

A similar conclusion may also be drawn from Blahoslav's remark that Jan Augusta was at that time the governor of the community of the Brethren in Nové Benátky. This Augusta was the most prominent representative of the group of men among the Brethren who were constantly calling on the Utraquist Church to purify itself, in the sense of recognising Luther's doctrine of grace, and who believed that the Brethren had to act as a bridge in this process. Říčan[145] said this of him: *Er meinte, die utraquistische Kirche könnte in der kleinen, aber vorbildlich organisierten Unität eine Stütze finden, wenn man die Annäherung*

---

[140] WA *(Briefwechsel)*, II, p. 375.

[141] A detailed survey of this collection of documents has been provided by Müller, *op. cit.*, pp. 578–604.

[142] *Grammatika česka* (ed. Hradil and Jiriček), p. 285 (quoted by Bartoš, *op. cit.*, and Říčan, *op. cit.*).

[143] Enders, *Luthers Briefwechsel*, IX, p. 104.

[144] O. Clemen: *Beiträge zur Lutherforschung*, ZKG 1916, p. 120.

[145] *Die Böhmischen Brüder*, p. 97.

oder sogar die Vereinigung der beiden Kirchen durchführen würde. If Velenský was an *auditor* of Jan Augusta, this must mean that he felt himself to be closely associated with the movement of reconciliation in Bohemia.

The uncertainty to which the quotation from Blahoslav's text gives rise is, of course, to be found in the fact that Velenský is said to be *et auditor et antagonista*. In what respect, then, could he have been an opponent of Jan Augusta? Certainly he could not have opposed him in any fundamental sense, or he would not have settled in the community of Nové Benátky and have lived with Frederick of Doni. The only possible reason for his opposing Augusta is that he objected to the latter's method, which led to the other party becoming irritated by the sharp tone of his writings and not to reconciliation. Velenský, on the other hand, preferred diplomatic consultation.[146] Blahoslav's reference therefore cannot provide us with any certainty as to whether Velenský was a member of the Brethren in that year (1530). What is more, the Czech scholars who have investigated this matter hold very divergent opinions. Bartoš[147] believed that he was a member of the Brethren. Molnár[148] calls him a member of the Unitas even during the time that he spent in Mladá Boleslav. Mirjam Bohatcová, on the other hand, is very sceptical regarding these statements.[149] Pražak denies that he was a member[150] and has drawn attention to the fact that Krasonický does not mention Velenský at all in his book "On the scholars" *(O učenich)*, which he wrote in the same year (1530) and in which he refers to scholars and prominent members of the Unitas. Finally, Čapek[151] says that Velenský "lived from 1531 onwards in Nové Benátky as a brother".

We hear about Oldřich Velenský once more in 1538, when a book written by him, "A treatise on how a man can flee from the plague",[152] was published in Prague. This treatise—which is only available in Prague—contains, according to Bartoš,[153] an exposure of various superstitious ideas concerning possible ways of protecting oneself against illness during times of plague and was "most probably based on a similar humanistic book". Bartoš does not elaborate on this com-

---

[146] This statement anticipates the final conclusion.

[147] *op. cit.*, p. 20.

[148] In *Voyage d'Italie (ComViat.* 1962 - 1).

[149] In the letter already quoted.

[150] *op. cit.*, p. 456.

[151] *Die Entwicklung und die Bedeutung der Unität auf dem Felde der Kultur* (in *Jednota Bratrská*, 1957).

[152] *Spis ž člověk muže před morem ujiti*, Knihopis No. 16. 494.

[153] *op. cit.*, p. 20, note 70.

ment and I have not had access to the text itself, with the result that
it has proved impossible to verify whether or not another work
formed the basis for Velenský's book. It is therefore no more than
speculative and a pure supposition that this last work by Velenský
may at the same time have been a last return to the period when he
was training under and influenced by Stapulensis, a time when he
also became acquainted with the work of Ficino, who also concerned
himself with the same theme. In 1479, Ficino wrote his *Consolio contra
la pestilenzia*,[154] in which he gave extremely practical hints to people
living during times of plague and epidemics.

In Bartoš' opinion, the contents of the treatise indicate that it was
written in 1531 and at the same time give the impression that it is un-
finished. Certain scholars[155] have therefore assumed that Velenský
died in 1531. Others[156] have not drawn this conclusion and are satisfied
with the simpler one that there is a complete absence of data regarding
Velenský after 1531. Pražak has pointed out[157] that a number of
Bohemian humanists of that period went abroad because they could
arouse no response in their homeland and has suggested this as a
possible explanation for the disappearance of Velenský's name after
1531. "It is reasonable to assume", he has written, "that he (Velenský)
went abroad, dying there before leaving any traces of his work".
This hypothesis, however, can be neither proved nor disputed.

The main question concerning those scholars who have carried out
research into Oldřich Velenský's life and work, however, is why he
suddenly withdrew from public life after a short period in which his
activities as a printer brought him into the full glare of publicity. Two
different answers have been given to this question. Bartoš has evolved
a theory based on the reference to several Bohemian leaders known to
us from the history of the period: "the opportunity for propaganda
which Velenský had as a printer of books was not effective enough
for him. He therefore exchanged this for a sharper weapon—political
activity, presumably in collaboration with Jan Špetla, the leader of the
Moravian landed nobility, or with Frederick of Doni, the less prominent statesman who was inclined towards Lutheranism and with
whom we met Velenský for the last time".[158] He must therefore have

---

[154] H. J. Hak, *op. cit.*
[155] Among others, Milada Blekastad in her dissertation on *Comenius* (1960),
p. 64.
[156] Among others, Molnár and Čapek.
[157] *op. cit.*, p. 457.
[158] *op. cit.*, p. 22.

striven, Bartoš believes, to achieve the ideal of reunion between the Utraquists and the Brethren within the framework of the Lutheran Reformation.

Pražak's search for an answer to this question has led him in a completely different direction.[159] "Velenský's silence after 1521 may have been caused by disillusionment about the consequences of Luther's break with Erasmus, the divergence between humanistic thought and the Reformation and also Luther's reaction to the movement to renew society, which was incomprehensible and shocking to a Utraquist[160] of Velenský's type." In a note, Pražak also adds: "Another reason may also be that Luther did not regard the treatise *(Petrum Romam non venisse)* as convincing".

Bearing in mind on the one hand the political leaders whose names occur in Velenský's biography—Jan Špetla of the Utraquists and Archleb of Boskovice and Frederick of Doni among the Lutheran group—and their relationship with Velenský and, on the other, the political situation in Bohemia at the time, we are bound to conclude that Bartoš' hypothesis is the most plausible.

A period of relative peace followed the cruel persecutions of the Brethren in the fourteen-sixties. A religious peace was concluded in 1485 and, under the terms of the treaty, the Utraquists and the Roman Catholics were regarded as subjects with equal rights. (This treaty was extended in 1512 for an unlimited period.) The Brethren, it is true, were excluded from the treaty, but they nonetheless benefited from the general religious peace in the country.

During Oldřich Velenský's time, however, this safety no longer existed. From 1500 onwards, renewed activity in persecution was stimulated by the Roman Catholic nobility, together with the humanists who had been educated in Italy. (The latter were opposed to a radical attitude in religious matters as well as to nationalism and to the propaganda in favour of the use of the language of the people among the Brethren.) The leaders in the campaign against the Brethren were Bohuslav Hasištejnský, a member of the humanistically trained Bohemian nobility, Augustine Käsebrod, who was connected with the royal chancellery, and Bishop John Filipec, who represented the Roman Catholic Church. After a royal command in 1503 to track down and punish the heretics—this could have been toned down by influential members of the landed nobility—the so-called St James'

---

[159] *op. cit.*, p. 457.
[160] It would have been more logical if he had written "Hussite humanist" here.

mandate was passed on 25 July 1508 by the Bohemian diet. This mandate forbade all gatherings of the Brethren and made the printing of their writings a punishable offence.

After the death of King Vladislav in 1516, this mandate became less threatening, because the power of the central authority began to decline and those members of the nobility who were favourably inclined towards the Brethren were able to take them under their protection on their land. In 1526, however, this period of safety also passed, because Ferdinand I, who took over the government of the country at that time, was spurred on by aggressive Roman Catholic leaders to make the provisions of the St James' mandate fully operative again.

In this context, it is also important to bear in mind the internal problem affecting the Brethren. The peasant revolt had broken out in Germany in 1525 and this had been suppressed with atrocious violence, among others by the Lutheran princes. This diminished the credibility of Lutheranism among the Bohemian Brethren, with their tradition of non-violence and the renewal of society and Lukáš of Prague therefore broke off relations with Wittenberg.

The breach between the Brethren and Luther was also widened by their different ways of understanding the doctrine of the Lord's Supper. The ubiquitarian doctrine was regarded by the Brethren as a veneration of earthly matter. Luther had provided an elucidation of his view in his treatise of 1523 *Vom anbeten des Sakraments des heyligen Leychnams Christi*, which was dedicated to *meinen lyben herrn und freunden den Brudern, genannt Waldenser, ynn Behemen und Mehren*,[161] but Lukáš continued to have objections. In the fifteen-thirties, however, there was a reaction to this breach in the form of a movement of reconciliation. The initiatives in this direction were taken by the Utraquist landed nobles who were inclined towards Lutheranism (the so-called neo-Utraquists). Their first step towards reunion was to work for a close association between the Brethren and the Utraquist Church. Taking action in 1530, they entered the Unitas together with a large group. Those who led in this process of reconciliation were Frederick of Doni and Archleb of Boskovice, but Jan Špetla—to whom Velenský had appealed in his foreword to the *Enchiridion*—also played a positive part in this process.

Bartoš' hypothesis seems all the more acceptable when seen against

---

[161] WA 11, pp 417–456.

the background of these historical data. Velenský could therefore
—according to Bartoš' thesis—continue to publish his books during
the period when the St James' mandate was—*de facto*—inoperative.
As soon as the conflicts once again became sharper, however, not
only with regard to the Roman Catholic Church, but also with regard
to Luther, Velenský found that he could work more efficiently when
he actively entered the arena of Church politics, placing himself at the
service of those whose aim was to unite the Utraquists and the Brethren
(thus forming a single front over and against the authorities and the
official Church) and to put them (once more) in touch with the Lutheran Reformation. As this was a task that had to be carried out in
secret, Velenský's name disappeared from public life.

Bartoš does not, it should be noted, say that Velenský stopped
working as a publicist because it became too dangerous for him in
view of the political situation. What he has concluded is that he
stopped because another kind of work seemed more meaningful to
him because of this change in the political situation. Bartoš' hypothesis does not at the same time exclude the other, previously mentioned assumption, namely that Velenský concluded his activity as a
printer as soon as his planned programme had come to an end.

Our reconstructed biography of Velenský is therefore bound to be
very sober, in view of the extreme scarcity of any historically certain
facts. Many questions about Velenský's life must remain open. In
particular, we can only frame hypotheses about those periods in his
life which might provide an answer to our questions about his spiritual
formation and his motives. The man who wrote a treatise that was for
centuries to cause such a stir in theological circles was to remain a
practically unknown figure in history.

CHAPTER THREE

BACKGROUNDS AND SOURCES

1. *A Provisional Determination of the Author's Position*

Writing about the treatise *Petrum Romam non venisse*, Amadeo Molnár[1] said that it was *ein schönes Beispiel eines gelungenen Anlaufes zur historischen Kritik*. This is a correct assessment. Clearly, it could be no more than an *Anlauf* because of the period in which it was written. Velenský inevitably had to draw his conclusions within the context of scientific knowledge at the time that he was living. He elaborated the data in such an original manner, however, that the treatise cannot simply be called a forerunner in historical criticism, but an undoubtedly "successful" forerunner in that sphere.

In this context, it is important to clarify the sense in which the word "original" is used here. As we shall see, Velenský did very little historical or exegetical research of his own into the subject, with the result that few new points of view emerge from his treatise. He made use of data which he had found in other writers' works, but he did this in such a systematic and clear way that these other author's results, arranged in the light of one single theme, achieved an entirely new effect in Velenský's work. This is all the more remarkable because this aspect of the treatise is really only of secondary importance, at least as far as Velenský's own intention in writing the work was concerned. His use of historical and textual criticism was, in other words, only important as an aid providing him with an objective basis for his argument that Peter could never have been in Rome and his consequent protest against the papacy in general. His knowledge on the one hand of Hussite theology and, on the other, of the humanistic ideas of his own times served therefore as a background to this protest and as sources for his historical research. These two elements at the same time provided the two bearings on which the whole argument of the treatise was based—the ideas underlying the Reformation in Bohemia which formed the intellectual climate in which the author grew up and the ideals of humanism with which he became acquainted as a student. Velenský's backgrounds and sources have therefore to be sought in these two fields.

---

[1] *Das Erziehungswesen der Brüder* (*ComViat.* 1964, 2).

It is clearly desirable to begin our investigation by providing a brief outline of humanism in Bohemia and indicating its relationship with the movement to reform the Church there. The details can be filled in afterwards.

Two different movements can be distinguished in humanism at the end of the fifteenth century. The first of these was closely linked with the Catholic aristocracy. These humanists were strongly orientated towards the earlier culture and did not feel drawn to the movements of renewal which were current in Bohemia. They wanted to preserve the link with the Church of Rome and vehemently resisted the social consequences of the Hussits' reform of the Church. According to one Marxist interpretation of this period, as we have seen, "the Hussite revolution was caused by socio-economic and class conflicts in feudalism". If this author was thinking only of the Catholic aristocracy in Bohemia and of the controversy brought about by their elitist attitude, then we are bound to regard his assessment of the situation as correct. The humanism of these aristocrats, however, had the least influence of all on the process of social and religious development in Bohemia at the end of the fifteenth century. The popular humanists, who, it is true, came from civilised and cultured circles, but who were, because of their deep commitment to the lower orders of society and to their interests, radically opposed to the aristocracy, exerted a much greater influence. For this reason, these humanists on the one hand encouraged nationalism and, because of this alone, Hussitism, which had separated itself from Rome, and, on the other, directed their energies to the education of those who had had little schooling in order to enable them to defend their own social interests more effectively. Their educational aim was given clear form in the publication in the language of the people of a number of treatises which were able to stimulate either a new attitude or the acquisition of new knowledge.

It hardly needs to be said that these popular humanists were not accepted by the members of the Utraquist Church, who wanted to consolidate relationships between Church and society. On the other hand, however, it is not true to say that they had good relationships with the Bohemian Brethren on the basis of a mutual recognition of aims. There is no evidence at all that the Brethren were powerfully influenced by them. There are two possible reasons for this. The first is that, at the time when popular humanism was in the ascendancy, that is, towards the end of the fifteenth century, the Brethren had already found their own special place and form and had already been training their own people for several decades, with the result that they did not regard the educational approach of the popular humanists as particularly meaningful for them. The second and probably more important reason is that the Brethren were to such an extent convinced of the need to put the aim of evangelical renewal first that they could not accept as an aim the ideal of popular education for the purpose of changing society, especially as the popular humanists showed how different their attitude was in the emphasis that they placed on the cultivation of the language of the people.

It is, of course, not possible to draw a clear dividing line between the two groups. It was a period during which Church and society overlapped to a great extent, with the result that a renewal of the Church at the same time implied a change in the structures of society. Just as the point of departure for the popular humanists was the social message of the gospel, so too did the Brethren draw conclusions for practical daily living from the law of Christ. Both groups regarded the use of the language of the people as a necessary means for achieving their aims. The difference between them is to be found in their deepest intentions, which resulted in their having different priorities.

This, then, is a very general outline of Bohemian humanism and we can now examine the situation in Bohemia at that time in greater detail. The first Bohemian humanists had been educated in Italy and were therefore orientated towards Italian culture generally. They were unconcerned with the problems in their own country and unable to understand the Bohemian movement of political and religious renewal. The leading representative of this humanist movement, Bohuslav Hasištejnský of Lobkovice (1460–1512), was, it is true, originally a Utraquist, but, after studying in Italy, he became a loyal Roman Catholic. Because of his purely literary interest in ancient civilisation and learning, he despised the Brethren, who were mostly uneducated. As Říčan has said, *die Schlichtheit der Brüder, ihre wirklich religiöse Verinnerlichung und ihre Volkstümlichkeit, ihre Pflege der Nationalsprache und ihre Verachtung der klassischen Sprachbildung stieß die Humanisten ab, in deren Augen sie eigenwillige Dummköpfe und Ketzer waren.*[2]

From 1495 onwards, however, humanism in Bohemia began to move in a different direction. Hasištejnský's friend and disciple, Viktorinus Kornel Všehrdý (ca. 1460–1520) broke with the Roman Catholic Church and, together with Řehoř Hrubý of Jeleni († 1514), left the

---

[2] R. Říčan, *Die Böhmischen Brüder* (Berlin, 1958), p. 69.

elitist group of humanists and became deeply committed to the nationalist cause. They encouraged the growth of a "popular humanism"[3],
the followers of which were committed to the struggle in Bohemia
against Rome and within which opposition both to scholasticism and
to the wordly nature of the Church at the time as well as the humanistic
ideal of the inner transformation of the individual played an important
part.

To begin with, they made overtures to the University of Prague, but
that *Hochburg des Utraquismus*,[4] where scholasticism reigned supreme and
recognition by Rome was still sought, viewed them with mistrust.
The only popular humanist to teach there, and then only for a few
years, was the young Václav Pisecký (1482–1511).

Their contribution to the struggle in Bohemia was nonetheless predominantly literary. Their humanism is called "popular" because they
published works in the language of the people—their translations of
contemporary works of world literature into Czech and their provision
of commentaries on the texts were attempts to supply the Bohemian
people with arguments to support their opposition to the established
Church. With this aim in mind, Hrubý translated Lorenzo Valla's *De
falso credita et ementita constantini donatione declamatio* roundabout 1513,
Marsilio Ficino's *De institutione principis* in 1500 and Erasmus' *Moriae
Encomium* in 1511.[5] Valla's treatise could provide Bohemians with
proof of the falsity of the Church's claims to worldly power, Ficino's
work in Hrubý's Czech version could provide them with a new insight
into the real dignity of the hierarchy and the *Moriae Encomium* with an
image of man renewed.

Although these popular humanists made an important material contribution to the revolution in Bohemia, they nonetheless continued to
place great emphasis on the formal literary level of their work. Having
chosen to express themselves in the language of the people, they
attempted in every way to cultivate the distinctive character of the
Czech language. In 1495, Všehrdý even formulated a method of
translation in which this aim would be achieved. According to him, so
that full justice should be done to the distinctively Czech idiom, "no
translator is obliged to translate word for word, so long as he repro-

---

[3] The term is J. B. Čapek's, *op. cit.*, p. 202/203.

[4] W. Weiszäker in the RGG article about the University of Prague.

[5] The same year that the first edition appeared in Paris. Because of this short
interval, Jakoubek and Novák *(Geschichte der Čechischen Litteratur)* dated Hrubý's
translation 1513.

duces faithfully and intelligibly the intention of the text translated".[6]

Our answer to the question as to whether Oldřich Velenský was influenced by this popular humanism must inevitably be in the negative as far as the purely formal literary aspect of his work is concerned. The very opposite is in fact true. In Velenský's opinion, the distinctive characteristics of the original treatise would have been lost if Všehrdý's method of translation had been followed and he therefore strove to reproduce all the features of the (Latin) original in his Czech translations. In order to achieve this aim, he used not the ordinary colloquial language of the people, but the syntax of the original Latin. He also tried to express in his translations into Czech the peculiarities of the original Latin style, thus allowing greater justice to be done to the intention underlying the original texts.[7] What is moreover quite remarkable is that Velenský's style eventually prevailed over that of the popular humanists, with the result that, half a century later, Latinisms were no longer regarded in Bohemia as examples of a foreign influence on the native language, but had become quite customary in the literature of the period. This enabled Jan Blahoslav, the archivist of the Unitas Fratrum who was also an outstanding linguistic expert, to write in 1571[8] that "Velenský's Czech is very fine and exemplary".

In this formal respect, then, Velenský is not representative of humanism in Bohemia. As far as the content of his writing is concerned, however, there are clear influences of the teachings spread by the popular humanists in their translations and commentaries. Two of these humanists who served him above all as examples are Václav Pisecký and Řehoř Hrubý. He copied almost literally a criticism of scholastic theology from a text[9] written by Pisecký in 1510 and dedicated to one Michael of Straže and included it, as we have seen in our section on Velenský as a printer, in his foreword to Erasmus' *Enchiridion:* "All opinions are subject to one point of view, the law of Christ, whether they are proclaimed by Scotus or by Thomas. The whole Roman division arises if one man adheres to Doctor Scotus and the other to Thomas Aquinas and this leads to a struggle which often lasts until death".

---

[6] Quoted in Pražak, *op. cit.*, p. 451.

[7] According to Pražak, *op. cit.* It was also because he recognised this specific technique of translation in the Claudianus edition of the Pastor of Hermas (1518) that Bartoš concluded (*op. cit.*, p. 17) that Velenský must have been the translator of this work and therefore that he was employed in Claudianus' press during that year.

[8] In his *Grammatika česka* (ed. Hradil and Jiriček, 1857), p. 285.

[9] *Listu Michalovi ze Straže*, quoted by Pražak, *op. cit.*, p. 449.

It is clear from this quotation that Pisecký regarded this struggle within scholasticism as a symptom of a division within the Church caused by the Antichrist. Scholasticism had therefore to be combatted by a return to the primitive Church, in which the "law of Christ" could still be heard in a pure form. This idea, which is above all characteristic of the pre-Hussite Reformation[10] and which continued to be influential in the struggle in the Bohemian Church, can also be found, as we have seen, in almost exactly the same form in Velenský's writings.

What is most striking, however, is Velenský's spiritual affinity with Hrubý. We have already mentioned that Velenský translated a work by Ficino which had also been published in the language of the people by this Bohemian humanist some twenty years previously *(De institutione principis)* and that Lorenzo Valla's treatise on the "Donation of Constantine"—which plays such an important part in Velenský's *Petrum Romam non venisse*—had already become well known in Bohemia through Hrubý's translation. By far the most important factor in this context, however, is the similarity between Velenský's translation of and his commentary on Erasmus' *Enchiridion* and Hrubý's edition of Erasmus' *Moriae Encomium*.

Hrubý's edition of Erasmus' work[11] begins with a number of passages from the *Adagia*, continues with his fairly free translation of the *Moriae Encomium* (made according to Všehrdý's method) and concludes with a commentary. It is in this last section that Erasmus' book is made intelligible to the ordinary people. Hrubý explains mythological and historical allusions, saying apologetically that scholars are in the habit of using such expressions and examples. He also says that Greek and Roman philosophers such as Plato and Cicero were very close in their ideas to the Christian truth, with the result that their classical writings can be put to very good use in the Christian religion. He then elaborates a number of Erasmus' ideas about the renewal of the Church and the purification of the Christian way of life. He sharply criticises those priests who are intent on acquiring money and power, but adds that the Hussite priests are also guilty of this fault. He condemns the great secular power of the popes and prelates and pleads for poverty to be practised by priests, as the "faithful Bohemians" want this to be

---

[10] A. Molnár: *Le mouvement préhussite et la fin des temps (ComViat,* 1958, 1).

[11] R. Říčan: *Die tschechische Reformation und Erasmus (ComViat,* 1973, 3), in which a detailed version of this work is provided. The original can be found in the University library at Prague (XVIII, D 38, fo 22b–29a).

practised. He also rejects the trade in indulgences, belief in purgatory and the worship of images. He recommends the reading of Scripture, because the simple evangelical truth is to be found in the Bible.

In addition to demonstrating his agreement with Erasmus in this way, Hrubý also includes a number of statements which seem to have been taken over from the Brethren. He warns his readers, for example, against riches and asks whether a sincere believer can engage in trade. He says that it is difficult to keep one's soul undefiled in the life of the city. He shows clearly that he is opposed to violence, declaring that to wage war is to go against the commandment to love one's neighbour as oneself. He even argues in favour of the communal sharing of property. Pražak[12] has seen in this an early form of class struggle, but —once again—completely overlooks the themes in the gospel which led to these criticisms of society, both in the case of the Brethren and in that of Hrubý.

The same tolerance which is recommended by Erasmus is also to be found in Hrubý when he takes his stand on the side of those who are wrongly called heretics by the Church. We should not, he insists, condemn others if we cannot see into their hearts, not even "the brethren whom we call Picards". Hrubý then speaks of intolerance in the context of the scholasticism practised at the University of Prague. The *studia humanitatis* is of the greatest utility for our knowledge of the Christian truth, he argues, but the theologians of Prague reject this study because they are not acquainted with it. Erasmus, on the other hand, calls on men to make use of it.

Finally, Hrubý makes a statement which Velenský was also to use later in an attempt to express the originality of the Bohemian Reformation and which also occurred in Archleb's letter to Erasmus:[13] Erasmus spread the Christian truth in the world, but it is the same truth that had already been known for a long time in Hussite Bohemia, the truth which "our enlightened Bohemians" had long confessed with all their strength and to which they still clung.

If we examine this commentary written by Hrubý and published in 1511, we find at once that it is strikingly similar to Velenský's foreword and appendix to Erasmus' *Enchiridion* published in 1519. Two conclusions result inevitably from a comparison of the two texts. The first is that Velenský was obviously inspired by Hrubý's edition of the *Moriae Encomium* to make a similar translation of and commentary on

---

[12] *op. cit.*, p. 448.
[13] The version is Říčan's, *op. cit.*, p. 187.

the same author's *Enchiridion,* since both works were expressions of a
"pedagogical humanism".[14] The second clear conclusion is that, as far
as the content of his work is concerned, Velenský was imitating his
older compatriot, the humanist Hrubý. This is evident because he,
like Hrubý, also explains the mythological stories for the benefit of his
simple readers. He also defends the classical, pagan philosophers.
Above all, he too stresses that, many years before Erasmus had begun
to write, the Bohemian Reformers had been confessing the Christian
truth. If we ask, then, whether Velenský was writing within the tradition of Bohemian popular humanism, we are bound, if we consider
this material aspect of his work, to answer in the affirmative. He was
undoubtedly influenced above all by Řehoř Hrubý.

The question as to whether the group of scholars who had joined the
Unitas Fratrum from the circles in the University of Prague can be
regarded as (popular) humanists is of secondary importance. If we
think of the renewal of the language of the people as the most characteristic ideal of these humanists, then these scholars certainly did not
form part of the movement of popular humanism. As far as we know,
a man such as Lukáš of Prague, who wrote a great deal in Czech
because of the lack of education generally among the members of the
Brethren, never concerned himself with this literary problem. If, on
the other hand, we regard the dissemination of (new) world literature
as an expression of "humanism", then Lukáš and others ought to be included among the humanists, since he translated parts of Erasmus'
Enchiridion in 1517, Valla's scientific contestation of the forged decretal
on the "Donation of Constantine" was very popular in circles composed of the Brethren and Claudianus followed the general tendency
among humanists of the period to publish classical works, printing
selections from Lactantius and Seneca and a new edition of the *Pastor
of Hermas.* Claudianus also prepared an edition of the New Testament
and published a map of Bohemia and several medical manuals were
moreover published in the language of the people by Lukáš' brother,
Jan Černý. All these works fit into the same framework of humanist
activity.

It is, however, not customary for those who specialise in the history

---

[14] This term is used by P. C. Boeren: *Nieuw contact tussen grieks-romeinse wereld en
christendom* in *Cultuurgeschiedenis van het Christendom* (Amsterdam, 1957). Boeren says
(p. 946): "... a method of formation, also useful outside the context of formal
education ... The name 'pedagogical humanism' would not be misplaced if applied
to this aspect of humanism".

of the literature of this period to include members of the Brethren among the Bohemian humanists, partly because their motives were not humanistic—they were above all concerned with the reformation of the Church. The popular humanists aimed at a change in man within a changed society. The Bohemian Brethren aimed, on the other hand, at a re-formation of the Church so that it would be possible to establish an environment in which man, changed by his faith, would be able to live in obedience to the law of Christ.

If, then, the Brethren were interested in the *literae humanitatis*, this was only within the context of their religious intentions, to which it was subservient. What is particularly striking in this connection is Lukáš of Prague's firm rejection of the study of the languages of the Bible, which would, in his opinion, simply hold up the work of the theologians! The Vulgate and translations from the Vulgate into the language of the people were, he believed, sufficient for the Church.

This is perhaps a suitable place to make a slight digression in order to justify our use of the word "Reformation" (in such phrases as the Bohemian Reformation, the Hussite Reformation and so on). It would be wrong if the reader had the impression that the Hussites, let alone the pre-Hussites, and the Brethren had any theological convictions tending in the direction of the essential Lutheran theme of "justification through faith". On the contrary, the Bohemian tradition was above all characterised by moralism and —sometimes—by legalism, with an occasional tendency towards donatism.

In his book *Forerunners of the Reformation*, H. A. Oberman[15] has drawn attention to a statement made by Luther distinguishing between the truth and the quality of life: *Doctrina et vita sunt distinguenda. Vita est mala apud nos sicut apud papistas; non igitur de vita dimicamus et damnamus eos. Hoc nesciverunt Wikleff et Hus, qui vitam impugnarunt. Ich schilte mich nit fromm; sed de verbo, an vere doceant, ibi pugno.*[16] It is true that neither Wyclif nor Hus made such a distinction between *veritas* and *qualitas*. In their case, ethics predominated, in Luther's, doctrine.

If we take as our point of departure the fact that ethical norms can be made radical without any violation of doctrine and that it is only when there is a renewal of doctrine that we can really speak of a "Reformation", then the (pre-)Hussites and the Bohemian Brethren can only be called precursors of the Reformation. To this can be added, in the positive sense, that a theologian such as Luther was powerfully influenced by the Bohemians (one of the works that influenced him was, for example, Lukáš of Prague's *Apologia*), so that it was partly thanks to these forerunners of the Reformation that he was able to become a reformer himself. The question as to whether a man is a precursor of the reform of the Church or not can only be answered in

---

[15] *Forerunners of the Reformation* (London, 1967), p. 10.
[16] WA *(Tischreden)*, I, No. 624, p. 294.

the light of the type of reform of the Church that is regarded as a decisive change—justification by faith alone.

If, however, the emphasis is placed on the fact that the Bohemians were aiming to achieve a radical transformation of the Church which was also decisive and had fundamental consequences (not simply a purification, in other words, but an elimination of the primacy as the mediating authority for the obtaining of salvation, on the basis of the gospel), then the struggle in the Church may well be called a "Reformation" in that sense of the word. Anyone who deprives the *Ecclesia Romana* of its hierarchy—initially, it is true, for ethical reasons, but this elimination could be realised, because the doctrine concerning the necessity of salvation had in the long run disappeared—and tends towards a Church without offices, a Church in which everyone is equal and each believer is a priest is clearly aiming at a fundamentally different Church.

We concluded from our reconstruction of Velenský's life in the previous chapter that he was influenced, during the period of his scientific training, by Renaissance thought in Paris, even though he may never have been in the city itself. Because of this, it is important to give a certain amount of attention to the French Renaissance and in particular to two leading thinkers who were, according to his own admission, so much admired by Velenský—Faber Stapulensis and Erasmus.

Faber was the scholar who had introduced a new way of interpreting texts into biblical studies, using the concordance system, by which one biblical text is able to throw light on another. He also compared the interpretations provided by the Fathers of the Church so as to be able, on the basis of their work, to correct what proved to be incorrect. His aim was to discover the *sensus spiritualis* of Scripture, which was bound to coincide with the *sensus litteralis*, since this had been inspired by God.[17] Faber regarded all typological and allegorical exegesis as a mutilation of the original intention of the Bible. A search had to be made for what the Bible itself intended to say.

A similar intention can be found later in Velenský's writings. In his foreword to the *Petrum Romam non venisse*, he wrote: "I quote Scripture according to its *germanum intellectum*." It is important, however, to stress here that Faber nonetheless continued to be a spiritual believer for

---

[17] This is entirely in the spirit of Thomas Aquinas: ... *primus sensus, qui est historicus vel litteralis. Illa vero significatio qua res significatae per voces, iterum res alias significant, dicitur sensus spiritualis; ... quia vero sensus litteralis est quem auctor intendit: auctor autem sacrae Scripturae Deus est* .... *Summa Theologiae*, q. 1, art. 10 *Sancti Thomae Aquinatis Opera Omnia, iussu impensaque Leonis XIII*, Romae, 1888, Vol. IV, p. 25. For Faber's exegetical method, see Henri de Lubac: *Exégèse médiévale. Les quatre sens de l'Écriture*, II/2 (1964), pp. 411–426.

whom the influence of the Holy Spirit was of far greater help than
grammatical exegesis in his attempt to discover the "true meaning" of
the scriptual texts which he approached and examined in the light of
this new method. It is above all necessary to emphasise this because
there is considerably less evidence of this attitude in Velenský's case.

Faber's *méthode du retour à la bible par la philologie et l'histoire*[18] emerges
clearly, for example, from his *Quincupla Psalterium*, published in 1509.
This contains five versions of the text together with a commentary by
Faber himself and includes a concordance (with reference to the prophets and the New Testament) and notes which throw light on grammatical and linguistic difficulties.

This new approach made a profound impression. In a letter to
Amerbach, Wolfgang Pratensis[19] wrote: *Videbis novum paraphraseos
genus*. In the same way, Beatus Rhenanus expressed his admiration of
Faber's method in a letter to Michael Hummelberger:[20] *Hic enim non
eas modo disciplinas quas liberales vocant, sed etiam ipsam theologiam supremam
suo candori restituere aggressus est*. Renaudet[21] does an injustice to Faber
by describing his approach as a *méthode érasmienne*. Faber had, after all,
arrived at this method quite independently—his early works, dating
back to the end of the fifteenth century, show that he was even then
already using the same method and, at that time (from 1495 onwards),
Erasmus was scarcely beginning his work in Paris and was entirely
unknown as a (biblical) scholar. His first study of the Bible based on
textual criticism dates back to 1505, when he had printed at Jodocus
Badius' press a work entitled *Laurentii Vallensis ... in latinam Novi
Testamenti interpretationes ex collatione Graecorum exemplarium Adnotationes*. This work was, moreover, not his own, but a manuscript which
he had found in the Norbertine abbey at Louvain and had (very
sparingly) edited and which consisted of notes on the New Testament
made by Lorenzo Valla. It was, however, precisely this work which
stimulated Erasmus to devote himself to a scientific study of the Bible.
As M. A. Nauwelaerts has said:[22] "Just as Valla had previously been
Erasmus' guide on the way towards the literature of humanism and
classical Latin, so too was Valla's book containing his notes on the

---

[18] A. Renaudet: *Humanisme et renaissance* (Geneva, 1958), p. 201.

[19] ibid.: *Préréforme et humanisme* (Paris, II, 1953), p. 516.

[20] *ibid.*, p. 516.

[21] *ibid.: Humanisme et renaissance*, p. 201.

[22] *Erasmus* (Bussum, 1969), p. 30. It is moreover legitimate to ask whether
Nauwelaerts has not, in this statement, underestimated the influence exerted on
Erasmus by his English friends.

New Testament the signpost to the study of the Bible and biblical theology".

We are therefore bound to agree with Faber's contemporaries in their recognition of him as an independent scholar who opened new paths of his own in biblical studies and in their conviction that he was not simply imitating Erasmus.[23] It is moreover quite clear from various parts of the *Petrum Romam non venisse* that Faber was for Velenský an inspiring example of the way in which scientific research could be done into the Bible. Not only does Velenský quote Faber's exegesis several times—in his own exposition of Paul's letters to the Romans and to Timothy—in which context he calls him "no mean exegete of the apostles" and one who "provides a very fine explanation"—he also applies Faber's comparative method to the work of the authors of the early Church and in this case too corrects their interpretation on the basis of this method.

It is also possible, however, that Faber may have been Velenský's model in another respect, namely in his attempt to prove that the evangelist Mark was not the same as Peter's travelling companion. Apart from the fact that he believed that he had found a point of contact for this theory in Faber's exegesis of the letter to Timothy (Mark must have brought the books and parchments with him from Troas, because he was chosen by the Holy Spirit to become the author of the gospel), he may also have thought of Faber's perspicacious argument[24] that Mary Magdalen was not the same woman as the woman who was a sinner in the gospel of Luke. Velenský uses an identical argument with regard to Mark, namely that the authors of the early Church concluded all too readily and merely on the basis of the identical names that the two persons were also identical.

In general, we are bound to conclude that this critical approach to the biblical text which enabled Velenský to use an *argumentum e silentio* about Peter's stay in Rome, is also the method employed by Faber in his commentary on Paul's epistles and the psalms—that is, the need to look above all for what the Bible itself intended to say. It is moreover evident from various quotations (especially in the third *persuasio*) that Velenský had Faber's commentary at hand when he wrote his treatise.

---

[23] In *Les origines de la Réforme*, Vol. II: *L'Église catholique; la crise et la renaissance* (Melun, 2nd edn., 1944), p. 396, P. Imbart de la Tour said: *C'est ainsi que son oeuvre précède et prépare celle d'Érasme.*

[24] In two treatises, both published in 1517, on Saint Ann and Mary Magdalen (see Imbart de la Tour, *op. cit.*, p. 560).

We must now attempt to explain why Velenský admired Erasmus more and credited him, as various statements made in his *Petrum Romam non venisse* show, with greater authority than Faber (some of whose biblical interpretations he corrects with an appeal to Erasmus' edition of the New Testament).

Despite his scientific approach, Faber was insufficiently critical. We have, for example, already seen that he did not doubt that the correspondence between Seneca and Paul, the Pseudo-Clementines and Dionysius the Areopagite were authentic. On the authority of Erasmus, on the other hand, Velenský insisted that (apart from the correspondence between Seneca and Paul) they were not authentic. The fact that Faber was not radical enough and that he did not go back completely, in other words, to the sources[25] was not the only reason why Velenský did not value him as highly as he did Erasmus. The difference in attitude and experience between the two authors[26] must undoubtedly have played a part. Faber was in the last resort a mystic, who was searching for the metaphysics of mysticism in his sources, both in the Bible and in the philosophers whom he so much admired. P. Imbart de la Tour[27] has said that *un souffle de mysticisme circule dans son oeuvre*, which accounts for his *intimité spirituelle* with the neo-Platonist Ficino. Renaudet[28] has said of him that *le saint Paul de Lefèvre est d'un spirituel et non d'un réformateur and that le Christ de Lefèvre demeure le Dieu métaphysique de Marsile Ficin, de Pic de la Mirandole et de Nicolas de Cues*. Although he also published one of Marsilio Ficino's works himself later (with a different intention, however), Velenský, who had a more analytical and historically critical sense, must in the long run have felt rather ill at ease in this mystical environment. It is, of course, true that Faber dissociated himself more and more from his earlier philosophical studies as time went by[29] in order to concentrate completely on biblical studies, but Velenský could not have realised this, since it only came clearly to light in the last period of Faber's life, when the *Petrum Romam non venisse* had already been written.

It is, of course, true that Erasmus was also a great admirer of Ficino,

---

[25] Imbart de la Tour, *op. cit.*, p. 395, assumed that Faber had only one manuscript at his disposal when he made his new translation of Paul's letters.

[26] Imbart de la Tour, *op. cit.*, p. 396: *Érasme est un plus grand cerveau, Lefèvre une âme plus haute.*

[27] *op. cit.*, p. 385.

[28] *Humanisme et renaissance*, p. 201.

[29] W. F. Dankbaar: *Op de grens der reformatie: de rechtvaardigingsleer van Jacques Lefèvre d'Étaples* (NThT, 1953/1954, pp. 327–345).

but Velenský found in him more what he was looking for—a critical approach to the material which would lead to a revelation of the various falsifications of the historical data and finally to a discovery of the true and reliable data concerning the primitive Church. Ultimately, then, what we find in Velenský's treatise is Erasmus' method —not simply an acceptance of the data provided by the Fathers of the Church, but a critical search to discover whether what they say can be true; an objective analysis of the facts mentioned in the epistles of Paul and in the Acts of the Apostles in order to make a reconstruction of how the reality must have been at the time, even though that reconstruction might be in conflict with the tradition of the Church. Erasmus too did not practise scientific research in an "objective" way, but incorporated into it on the one hand faith and on the other a need for renewal in man's life. This integration of the two factors is found to a much lesser extent in Velenský's work, but he makes it clear that he regarded the Dutch humanist as the highest authority in writing (in his third *persuasio*) that he followed the interpretation of "Origen, Chrysostom, Ambrose and many other learned exegetes" because "Erasmus does not change their interpretations in any way".

We must now turn to the question as to whether Velenský was influenced by Luther and, if he was, whether this is discernible in his writing. There can be no doubt at all that he admired Luther—this is clear from the fact that he published two of Luther's works, actively engaged in the task of uniting the Bohemian Reformation with the cause of Lutheranism and offered his own treatise to Luther for his opinion. In the preface to his *Petrum Romam non venisse*, moreover, he calls Luther a *pietatis christianae ardentissimum defensorem*.

It is, however, quite clear from the context in which Velenský mentions Luther why he admired the German reformer and in what respect he felt an affinity for him—in his treatise *De potestate papae*, Luther had attacked the very foundations of the papacy. Although there is no evidence for this assumption anywhere in Velenský's treatise, it is possible that he recognised that Luther had come to this opinion because of a deeper theological conviction—that salvation was not mediated through the primacy and therefore that the primacy was not necessary to salvation—but he did not recognise it as the most essential element. In other words, although he regarded the *sola Scriptura* as a *conditio sine qua non* for salvation, he found, as a humanist who approached all problems rationally, that the emphasis which Luther placed on the *sola fide* was essentially alien to his mentality.

Velenský was clearly more of an analytical historian than a theologian. He was therefore more interested in the historical evidence for the denial of the Petrine tradition than in questions concerned with guilt and its forgiveness. Just as it was not possible for Luther to be convinced by Velenský's argument, then, so too would it be wrong to look for any sign in Velenský's treatment of his subject that he was influenced by Luther.

The second sphere in which we must look for sources and backgrounds in Oldřich Velenský's method and view is the Reformation in Bohemia. If we take as our point of departure his main theme—that the papacy had to be opposed because it was an expression of the Antichrist who had made the Church corrupt since apostolic times—then a clear relationship is discernible with the Brethren. The members of the Unitas Fratrum based their attacks against the papacy in principle on a longing to return to the primitive Church and the consequence of this was a desire to renew society. There are many elements in the work of Lukáš of Prague which can also be found in Velenský's treatise. For example, in his commentary on the Book of Revelation, published in 1501, Lukáš criticised the Petrine tradition and, in his treatise "On the renewal of the Church" of 1510,[30] he analysed critically the emergence of the papacy and argued that the apostolic Church was normative. It is also possible to cite in this context other treatises written by members of the Unitas—a "Letter from the Brethren to Rokycana" (1471) and a treatise by the first leader of the Brethren, Řehoř (Gregory), published about 1470, which contains a passionate plea for a return to the Ecclesia primitiva.[31]

In the account of a journey to Italy in 1498 made by Lukáš of Prague and his secretary Tůma Přeloučský,[32] the latter provides a description of the martyr's death suffered by Savonarola. What is remarkable about this description from our point of view is that Velenský includes it almost word for word in the foreword to the Petrum Romam non venisse.

One document produced by a member of the Bohemian Brethren is of especial interest because it is clearly Velenský's most important source. This is Vavřinec Krasonický's "A refutation that Saint Peter

---

[30] For these works, see J. Goll: Quellen und Untersuchungen zur Geschichte der Böhmischen Brüder (Prague, 1878) and J. T. Müller, op. cit., in his appendix on the writings of Lukáš of Prague.

[31] Translations of these works will also be found in J. Goll, op. cit.

[32] Dated 1502; mentioned in A. Molnár: Voyage d'Italie.

ever occupied the papal see in Rome. A letter to Master Ždarský and, through him, to Master Hasištejnský".[33] Unfortunately, however, the text never appeared in print and the original is lost. There are two copies, which clearly have to be dated at the end of the sixteenth or the beginning of the seventeenth centuries. The conclusion that can be drawn from certain indirect indications in the text is that it must have been written shortly after the year 1500, but before 1505. Only one of the noblemen addressed in the letter is known—the Catholic humanist Hasištejnský. The other nobleman Ždarský is unknown.

The treatise opens with a detailed account of the conflicts among the Church's authors concerning Peter's life and this is followed by a defence of the view, based on the New Testament data, that Peter was never in Rome—and that he therefore could not have been the Bishop of Rome for twenty-five years—but that he was active as a preacher among the Jews in Judaea and the neighbouring regions.

Krasonický's method can be described as a process of elimination. Closely examining the text of the New Testament, he eliminates every possibility, in chronological order, of Peter's ever having been in Rome and in this way comes to the conclusion that the Petrine tradition in the Catholic Church is a fabrication.

Later on, we shall be discussing Krasonický's letter in greater detail, but for the present we must content ourselves by saying that it was Velenský's principal source when he wrote his *Petrum Romam non venisse*. The popular humanists of Bohemia may have stimulated him and the French humanists may have to some extent taught him the method that he used and have provided him with various exegeses, but, as far as the content of the *Petrum Romam non venisse* is concerned, Velenský's model was this treatise by Krasonický which was written in the tradition of the Unitas Fratrum. That is why, in any more profound investigation into Velenský's sources and backgrounds, we shall have to be concerned with the particular tradition of the Bohemian Reformation. Within this context, then, we shall discuss, in the following order, the Bohemian opposition to the Petrine tradition, which ended in Krasonický's treatise (Section 2 of this chapter), the

---

[33] *Odporové, že svaty Petr nedržel stolice papežské v Rime. Psaní panu Ždarskému a on panu Hasištejnskému.* Copies will be found in Prague (V.F. 41, fo 173–182) and Görliz (No. 8. 19, fo 97–113). The second copy contains the full text. According to Jaroslav Goll, *Časopis českeho musea*, 1878, p. 283, the copies provide a reliable version of the lost original. I have made use of the Prague manuscript. This does not contain the name of the author and bears the (short) title: *Psaní učiněné panu Ždarskému a on panu Hasištejnskému.*

views about the Antichrist and the primitive Church (Section 3), about the apostolic succession (4) and about the Bible as the sole authority (5). All these elements will be considered in the light of the part that they played among the Brethren and their predecessors in causing them to deny the Petrine tradition and also in the way in which they occur in Velenský's treatise as principal factors in the struggle against the primacy of the pope.

2. *The Opposition to the Petrine Tradition*

Any attempt made, in the light of the argument against the Petrine tradition found in this letter written by Vavřinec Krasonický, to go back in history in search of the very first denials of Peter's stay in Rome presumably lead to the Waldensians.

We read, for instance, in a treatise published in Rome in 1743 (*Adversus Catharos et Valdenses*) and originally written by the thirteenth century Dominican Moneta of Cremona,[34] that the Waldensians *dicunt Petrum nunquam fuisse Romae, unde arguunt nos de inquisitione ossium eius Romae cum in Novo Testamento nullum testimonium habeatur, quod Petrus fuerit Romae.* Another statement can be found in Robert Bellarmine's great work *Disputationes de controversiis christianae fidei adversus huius temporis haereticos*, published in 1590. In this, Bellarmine says that *primus qui docuit B. Petrum neque Episcopum fuisse Romae, neque Romam ipsam unquam vidisse, fuit Gulielmus* ... (Lib. II, cap. I, col. 712). This is a reference to William of Ockham, although the latter never explicitly questioned Peter's stay in Rome. He directed his polemics principally against the jurisdictional questions raised by the papacy.

The first author whose own work can be quoted as containing objections to the Petrine tradition is Marsilio of Padua, who was born in that town roundabout 1275 and became a *magister artium* in Paris in 1312. It was in Paris that he completed, twelve years later, on 24 June 1324, the book that was to occupy men's minds for centuries—*Defensor pacis*. The publication of this treatise made it necessary for him to flee from the French capital in 1326. He found refuge in Nuremberg, where his protector was Ludwig of Bavaria. He died in Nuremberg in 1343.

Marsilio's point of departure is a view of the state, based on an Aristotelian doctrine, according to which the powers belong to the

---

[34] Quoted by R. Bäumer, *op. cit.*, p. 21. The quotation is from Lib. V, cap. 2, fo 410.

authorities chosen by the citizens, these authorities being in turn accountable to the citizens who chose them. Marsilio saw the Church as part of the state and therefore as subject to the jurisdictional power of the state. In view of this, he believed that a priest could not exercise *potestas coactiva* or secular authority and that the pope could certainly not possess *plenitudo potestatis* or plenary powers. The only task open to the Church and the hierarchy was a spiritual one, but even in that purely spiritual sphere there were, in Marsilio's opinion, severe limitations to the power of the hierarchy, since ultimately only God had the last word. What is more, within the hierarchy the same elementary rules apply as in the state—the primacy of the pope was therefore, Marsilio taught, based on the choice of the bishops and not on any divine institution. For this reason, Marsilio believed that the authority of a council of the Church was always greater than that of any pope and any attempt on the part of a pope to exercise a *plenitudo potestatis* would inevitably result in the balance of society being disturbed.

Marsilio divided his work into three *dictiones* (I on the state; II on the Church; III—conclusions). All three parts of the *Defensor pacis* are, however, concerned with the same basic theme—the causes underlying the malfunctioning of society and the consequent absence of peace.

The most important part of Marsilio's treatise from our point of view is the *dictio secunda*.[35] The author's point of departure in this *dictio* is that Christ did not claim any *potestas coactiva* for himself, but on the contrary made himself subject to that secular authority. The apostles followed him in this. What is more, even within the circle of the apostles and their successors there was no order of priority with regard to power—they were all equal. In chapter 15, for example, Marsilio writes that, in *essentiali dignitate a Christo data*, the *presbyter* and the *episcopus* were equal in the *ecclesia primitiva*. It is never said even of Peter in the New Testament that he had more powers than the other apostles—on the contrary, Marsilio insists, all decisions were taken by the apostles in consultation with each other (Acts 15. 6, 25; 8. 14; Matt. 23. 8; Acts 4. 34). If, then, Peter had no power over the other apostles, his successors could not have had this.

What is more, no one could have been named as Peter's special successor because no apostle was designated to a particular territory (Matt. 28. 19: *docete omnes gentes*), because Peter had been in Antioch

---

[35] I have followed here the edition of the text prepared by W. Kunzmann and Horst Kusch: *Der Verteidiger des Friedens* (Berlin, 1958).

rather than in Rome and finally *quoniam si Roma fieret inhabitabilis, non propterea periret Petri successio.* Furthermore, Marsilio argues, if it is true that there were successors in Rome, then the bishops of Rome ought to be called the successors of Paul rather than of Peter (Acts 9. 15; Gal. 2. 7; Acts 22. 17). It can be said of Paul that he exercised the *officium episcopi sive pastoris* in Rome, *auctoritatem huius habens a Christo, et revelatione mandatum, et aliorum apostolorum electione consensum.* The same cannot be said of Peter: *dico per scripturam sacram immediate convinci non posse ipsum fuisse Romanum episcopum specialiter, et quod amplius est ipsum unquam Romae fuisse,* Marsilio states, since Luke, who wrote the Acts of the Apostles, and Paul, who was also in Rome, *de beato Petro nullam prorsus mentionem fecerunt.*

In chapter 16 of his treatise, Marsilio points out that it is clear from Acts 28 that Peter could not have been in Rome before Paul and that it can be concluded from Paul's letters that he never met Peter during his stay in Rome. It is possible, Marsilio says, that Peter was in Rome —*Romae vero non contradico*—but he certainly was not there before Paul.

Marsilio stresses that, in accordance with Christ's mission, the apostles and their disciples preserved their equality, but that the position of the bishop of Rome became more and more emphasised in the long run. It is clear from history that the bishops in other countries sought the advice of the bishop of Rome *in quibus dubitabant, tam de scriptura, quam de ritu ecclesiastico,* because the people were better instructed in *studia scientiarum.* This priority was, however, given voluntarily. When Constantine had been baptised by Sylvester, the latter Bishop of Rome was granted *iurisdictio coactiva* and thus acquired power over *agros, predia et possessiones plurimas.* In this way, the Bishop of Rome was invested with *dominio seculari,* thus becoming the main cause of the absence of peace in the Church and in the state (Cp. 18).

Marsilio's *Defensor pacis* continued to exercise an influence throughout the centuries on succeeding generations of writers (including, among others, Krasonický). We should not, however, conclude, from the consensus of opinions, that Velenský was directly dependent on Marsilio's work. All the same, there is a passage in his book that does not go back to Krasonický's treatise, but reveals such a close affinity with Marsilio's work in its choice of words and textual usage that this cannot be attributed to pure chance. We are therefore justified in concluding that Velenský must have had Marsilio's *Defensor pacis* in his possession when he wrote this particular passage. The text in question is the seventh *persuasio,* in which Velenský uses an argument very similar to that found in chapters 15, 16 and 17 in the *dictio secunda* of Marsilio's treatise.

Marsilio	Velenský
(15) quotes Gal. 2, according to which Paul was to go to the gentiles and Peter to the circumcised.	(7) quotes the same text.
(16) Paul therefore had to go to Rome; this cannot be said of Peter.	Why should Peter have forgotten this arrangement so quickly and have claimed other districts for himself?
(17) quotes Acts 28. 19–23, according to which the Christian sect was not known in Rome, which would be strange if Peter had been in Rome.	mentions the same text. What would Peter have done in Rome if Paul's words had been new to the Jews?
Anyone seeking the truth is bound to ask whether it is probable that Peter came to Rome before Paul.	Anyone who wants, can see now how credible it is that Peter was in Rome at that time.

We may therefore safely regard Marsilio as Velenský's spiritual father in this case. What is more, it is also possible to retrace the path along which his treatise, the *Defensor pacis*, was able to become so influential in Bohemia.

Georges de Lagarde[36] has pointed to Marsilio's influence on Wyclif and, through him on Hus: *le théocratisme de Wycliff aboutit aux mêmes conclusions que le positivisme marsilien: concentration de tous les pouvoirs coactifs au temporel comme au spirituel sur le chef d'une société unique civilement organisée.* The influence of Marsilio's treatise on Hus can be found, de Lagarde claims, in *la négation de la jurisdiction coactive du sacerdoce, la pauvreté apostolique, l'égalité fondamentale de tous les prêtres, la critique ardente de la donation de Constantin.*[37] What is more, several of the statements made by Hus in his *De ecclesia* are so closely related to certain texts in the *Defensor pacis* that we may certainly conclude that Hus both read and used this treatise.[38]

An even clearer clue can be found in 1466, when the German humanist, Gregory Heimburg, who was excommunicated in 1461 by Pope Pius II (after a conflict about the validity of the excommunication by the pope of Sigismund, the Duke of Austria, because the Duke had taken Nicholas of Cusa prisoner), came to the court of the Utraquist

---

[36] *La naissance de l'esprit laïque*, III (Louvain and Paris, 1970), p. 361.
[37] *ibid.*, p. 363.
[38] *ibid.*, p. 363.

king Jirik of Poděbrady in Prague as his advisor in foreign affairs. Heimburg greatly admired Marsilio of Padua and introduced his treatise to leading members of the court who were closely connected with the Utraquist Church. It is, however, not true to say, as some scholars have claimed, that Heimburg was the author of the *Confutatio primatus papae*, in which the *Defensor pacis, Dictio secunda* is very closely followed—this treatise was published in an edition on which his name appeared wrongly as author in 1550 by Flacius Illyricus and later, on the latter's authority, included in Goldast's *Monarchiae* in 1612.[39]

De Lagarde[40] has claimed that the author of this treatise was Matthias Döring, a Franciscan of Heidelberg, who must have written the book after 1443. He points out, however, that this mistake in attributing the treatise to Heimburg is really only *une demi-erreur*, because Heimburg was *un des derniers témoins de la survivance de l'esprit marsilien au XVème siècle*. This is very clear from the *Invectiva in Nicolaum de Cusa*,[41] a treatise which was written in 1461, defending Duke Sigismund against the charges brought against him by Pius II, and which became very popular in Bohemia.

This introduction of Marsilio's treatise into Bohemia was made much easier by the presence there of Martin Lupač. Lupač, who had originally been a priest in Chotěboř and had later become an auxiliary bishop in Prague, had been a disciple of Jakoubek and had for some time been criticising the Petrine tradition in very much the same way. He recognised the similarity between his ideas and those of Heimburg (and through Heimburg the views of Marsilio).[42] Although he died a few years later (in 1468), he was nonetheless able to use his influence to enable Heimburg's theories to be favourably received in Bohemia. He translated the German author's *Apologia contra Laelium*,[43] for example, into Czech.

A manuscript written by Lupač in 1467 has been preserved. In this "Letter from Martin Lupač to a friend"[44] the following statement

---

[39] Vol. I, pp. 557–563.

[40] *op. cit.*, p. 370. See also P. Polman: *L'Élément historique* (Gembloux, 1932), p. 193.

[41] Text in Goldast: *Monarchiae*, II: *Invectiva Gregorii Heimburg utriusque iuris doctoris in reverendissimum patrem, dominum Nicolaum de Cusa.*

[42] A. Molnár: "*Probacio preceptorum minorum*" *de Martin Lupač* (*ComViat*, 1966, 1/2); F. M. Bartoš: *Cusanus and the Hussite Bishop M. Lupač* (*ComViat*, 1962, 1).

[43] Text in Goldast: *Monarchiae* II: *Apologia Gregorii Heimburg contra detractiones et blasphemias Theodosii Laelii Felirensis Episcopi.*

[44] F. M. Bartoš provides a version of the content in his *Zapadlé dílko bratrské vědy* and Müller, *op. cit.*, provides various quotations (p. 150).

occurs: *Nulla est scriptura canonica de Petro, quod aliquando fuisset Roma et eam vidisset si vultis impugnare Antichristum, ad hoc oportet venire principum, quod sine ipsis nemo salvabitur et omnis auctoritas in plenitudo potestatis et graciarum... ex quo: ibi sedes Petri, ibi passus. Et tamen desuper nulla scriptura.*

What is more, Lupač also took over Marsilio's ideas regarding the silence preserved in the Acts of the Apostles and the epistles of Paul concerning Peter's possible sojourn in Rome. He denied the action that Peter was, according to the legends, reputed to have taken against Simon Magus, in this particular context opposing above all the account contained in the book of legends known as the *Passionale*. Lupač even went so far as to ask whether there had perhaps not been some false additions in the Bible to lead members of the Church to believe in a firm basis for the papacy. He was, however, convinced that no historical data could be found for this in the Bible and he concludes: "But you, with your learned and courageous preaching, tell me, whereas there is not a single word in the Bible that bears testimony to it, where and when Peter was in Rome".

Lupač can be regarded as an author who transmuted Marsilio's doubts about the Petrine tradition into a challenge to base this tradition on proofs, who changed the ideas held by Marsilio about the cause of the absence of peace in society (the unlawful exercise of the *plenitudo potestatis*) into the specifically Bohemian idea of the *fundamentorum fundamentum* of the Antichrist (the unlawful claim to the *sedes Petri*) and finally who in this way became instrumental in stimulating fresh historical research.

The challenge which Lupač issued to provide proofs of the Petrine tradition was not accepted by the Bohemian Catholics. With the emergence of the first generation of intellectuals in the Bohemian Brethren, however, this challenge was taken up enthusiastically and, what is more, in the spirit in which it was intended by the auxiliary bishop of Prague, namely that historical research would show that there were no proofs to be found, with the result that the basis for the authority of the pope would cease to exist. With this aim in mind, such leading members of the Bohemian Brethren as Lukaš of Prague and Tůma Přeloučský began to investigate the question. Lukáš even went precisely for this purpose to Italy in order to study the sources on the spot and to investigate the origins of various legends.

The first successful attempt, however, was not made until the beginning of the sixteenth century, when Lukáš' friend Vavřinec Krasonický wrote his treatise entitled "A Refutation that Saint Peter ever occupied the papal see in Rome. A letter to Master Ždarský and, through him, to Master Hasištejnský".[45] In this treatise, Krasonický conducts a discussion with two representatives of the Catholic party —the group of men who had been challenged by Lupač—appealing above all in this to Marsilio. He does this without ever mentioning Marsilio's name, but his use of the ancient legal title *důvodu* (the "jurist") as an indication of his source in precisely those places where he uses Marsilio's arguments (in the second *dictio* of his *Defensor pacis*) concerning the dubious nature of Peter's stay in Rome makes it quite clear that he was in this respect dependent on Marsilio.

Since what we have here is Velenský's most important source for his *Petrum Romam non venisse*, it is obviously worth while to provide a brief summary of the contents of Krasonický's treatise.

(fo. 173) After having pointed, in a very concise form, to the generally accepted tradition among Christians "that Peter was in Rome and held the office of bishop there, in the same way as the pope now carries out this function", Krasonický says: "I contest this view and I will follow Saint Peter on his journeys, at the same time showing that he could not have been in all these places if he was then in Rome".

(fo. 174) To begin with, he points to the conflicts that have taken place among authors in the Church with regard to the date of Peter's coming to Rome. He compares what Jerome had to say in this context with, among other things, the data found in the *Fasciculus Temporum* and the *Passionale* and Bede's calculation. He then concludes: "because these reports are in conflict with each other, they are false".

(fo. 175) The correct argument, Krasonický claims, has to be based on the period of Paul's conversion and his consequent visits to Jerusalem— firstly after three years and then after fourteen years, as he says in his letter to the Galatians. It is there that proof is to be found for the fact that Peter was still in Jerusalem at that time—eighteen years after Christ's death. Another proof is to be found in the Acts of the Apostles, where we read that, in the second year of the reign of the Emperor Nero—that is, thirty years after Christ's death—Paul came to Rome. At that time, Peter was still not there.

After this, Paul spent another two years in Rome and during this time wrote a letter to the Philippians, from which it is also clear that Peter was not present. The same conclusion can also be drawn from the (second) epistle to Timothy, which was written in Rome. In that letter, Paul wrote that Onesiphorus "often refreshed me; he was not ashamed of my chains, but when he arrived in Rome he searched for me eagerly and found me". Krasonický's comment is: "Is it not remarkable that Peter was not acquainted

---

[45] See Note 33.

with this, although he had been bishop of Rome for a long time then? But he knows nothing about Paul and Paul knows nothing about Peter".

(fo. 176) It is clear from the epistles to Timothy (2 Tim. 4. 5–6) and Philemon (verse 9) that Paul was quite advanced in years and at the same time that Peter was, however, not in Rome. "Surely," Krasonický observes, "he could not have kept his presence secret for such a long time?" In addition to this, the work was divided between Paul and Peter—Peter being sent to proclaim the gospel to the Jews, Paul being sent to the gentiles.

(fo. 177) According to the *Passionale*, however, all the Jews were driven out of Rome by the Emperor Claudius. What, then, Krasonický asks, would Peter have had to do in Rome? In this connection, Paul's letter to the Romans is important. Nothing—and this is understandable after what has been said in the preceding section—is said in that letter about Peter. "This," Krasonický affirms, "is a certain proof that Saint Peter was never there, let alone that he held the office of bishop there for twenty-five years". It is obvious, for example, from the story of Simon the tanner that Peter was in entirely different parts of the world—Joppa, going from there to Caesarea. It can also be seen that he worked in different districts from the letter that he wrote himself from Babylon, which does not mean the city of Rome,

(fo. 178) but an Egyptian settlement, which is now called "Chreyrum Babylon" and is also known as "Alktyrum". It is there, Krasonický claims, that Peter settled, after having visited Pontus, Galatia, Cappadocia, Asia and Bythinia. It is there too, he goes on, that John and the other apostles lived. Peter's second letter also gives the impression of having been written in a place a long way away from where Paul was.

(fo. 179) Nicholas of Lyra, who wrote a commentary on Holy Scripture, attempted to supplement many of the biblical stories with texts which would attribute more authority to Peter, but Nicholas' interpretation is unreliable. The same can also be said of the story in the Passionale about a meeting between Jesus and Peter when the latter fled from Rome (*Quo vadis, domine?*).

(fo. 180) And what, Krasonický asks, can be said about the tradition according to which a threefold fountain sprang up in the place where Paul's head was after it had been cut off? "I have asked various Bohemians who have recently been on pilgrimage to Rome whether they saw this fountain, but they knew only of a single or a twofold fountain". This tradition, Krasonický concludes, is no more than an invention of the imagination. If this legend about Paul's death is invented, however, Paul may have been released from prison and may not have died in Rome. Jerome, who in so many cases only declared that a matter was certain when the truth was established beyond dispute, ascertained dates concerning the apostles Peter and Paul, although this these are quite dubious.

(fo. 181) Finally, Krasonický discusses the donation of Constantine and Lorenzo Valla's demonstration that the decretals mentioning it were forgeries. In that context, it is said that there is no need for a pope of Rome to consecrate bishops. In Russia, Armenia, Romania and India there are bishops who are quite independent of the Church of Rome, just as Timothy and Titus—as is clear from the epistles of Paul—were also bishops without any confirmation by a bishop of Rome.

If this letter written by Vavřinec Krasonický is compared with Velenský's treatise *Petrum Romam non venisse*, then the extent to which Velenský was inspired by this short text of no more than nineteen handwriting-pages becomes abundantly clear. He follows the same order of arguments—firstly the conflicts among the writers, then the argument based on the data in the New Testament, followed by a hypothesis suggesting where Peter may in fact have lived and finally a refutation of a number of Roman objections based on legends. Velenský's choice of texts, quoted to illustrate his arguments, is also clearly influenced by Krasonický's treatise. Some of the rhetorical questions in the *Petrum Romam non venisse* are also closely related to statements in Krasonický's letter. (To give two examples: "Is it not remarkable that Peter was not acquainted with this, although he had been bishop of Rome for a long time?" and "Surely he could not have kept his presence secret for such a long time?".) Finally, Velenský also follows Krasonický in the emphasis that the latter places on the independence of the Eastern Church, in his clear appreciation of the work of Lorenzo Valla, in his criticism of Nicholas of Lyra and in his interpretation of the place name "Babylon". In a word, we may conclude that without this letter written by Krasonický to the noblemen Ždarský and Hasištejnský Velenský could never have written his treatise in the way in which he in fact wrote it. Lastly, we may also say that if he had not arranged his material in a more methodical way and supplemented it with a number of arguments which he found for himself and if he had not also dealt with the whole subject in a more scientific way—leaving out entirely, for instance, Krasonický's rather naive investigation into the legends!—then Velenský could certainly be described as a follower of Krasonický.

3. *The Antichrist and the Primitive Church*

Velenský states quite clearly at the very beginning of his foreword to the *Petrum Romam non venisse* that he believes that the papacy is a manifestation of the Antichrist: "Who would dare to deny that what was prophesied by Christ regarding the Antichrist is not found in the *Romana Ecclesia*? The *homo peccati* has been revealed and we can see him sitting *in loco sancto*". This idea of the Antichrist was characteristic of the Bohemian Brethren of Velenský's period. It originated, however, a century and a half before this time and was developed by the Bohemian reformers within the framework of their ideas about the *ecclesia primitiva*, which were in turn influenced by the ecclesiology that had been formulated in Bohemia since the time of Hus (following, but not always agreeing with the teaching of John Wyclif).

The origin of the concept of the *ecclesia primitiva* goes back to the fourth century and John Cassian (ca. 365–435) was probably responsible for it in the first place. In a study of the origin and functioning of the idea of the primitive church,[46] Glenn Olsen has pointed out that "the writings of John Cassian seem to contain the earliest references to the idea of the primitive church. Seizing upon a passage of the Scripture, Acts 4. 32 f, Cassian used the idea of the primitive church as a model by which to form and reform the monastic life of his own days".[47]

By the term *ecclesia primitiva*, Cassian meant the Church at the time of the apostles and he regarded *the vita apostolica* as normative for believers living during later periods, especially with regard to the practice of communal life and man's striving for perfection.

In the Carlovingian period, this idea of the primitive Church continued to be the norm. Olsen has provided us with a quotation from the *Vita Gregorii abbatis Trajectensis auctore liudgero* (a text dating back to the end of the eight century): *secundum formam primitivae ecclesiae*.[48] From the middle of the ninth century until the beginning of the eleventh, the concept of the *ecclesia primitiva* is no longer to be found in literature. After this time, it reappears, but only as a "neutral term to describe the earliest period of the church ...The canonist used the term *ecclesia primitiva* essentially to contrast ancient with contemporary usage".[49] The idea of the primitive Church as a normative model had therefore clearly disappeared by this time.

This normative character returned to some extent, however, when the *ecclesia primitiva* was equated with the pre-Constantinian Church (this was done, for example, by Bernard of Clairvaux) and the post-Constantinian period was characterised as the time when the Church became worldly. It is then that the view may have originated that there was a connection between the disappearance of the *ecclesia primitiva* and the activity of the Antichrist. This relationship played an important part in pre-Hussite teaching, in which two consequences which reacted upon each other resulted from the reformers' protest against the worldliness of the Church. The first of these

---

[46] *The Idea of the Ecclesia Primitiva in the Writings of the Twelfth Century Canonist,* in *Traditio,* Vol. XXV, 1969, p. 66.

[47] In *De institutis coenobiorum et de octo principalium vitiorum remediis,* II, 5. It is in this treatise that the term *ecclesia primitiva* was used for the first time. See also O. Chadwick: *John Cassian. A Study in Primitive Monasticism* (1950) and K. S. Frank: *Vita apostolica. Ansätze zur apostolischen Lebensform in der alten Kirche,* ZKG 82 (1971),

[48] *op. cit.,* p. 69.

[49] *ibid.,* p. 70.

is that the Antichrist was above all made manifest in the hierarchy of the Church, which was very remote from the *vita apostolica* in the *ecclesia primitiva*. The second is that the idea of the *ecclesia primitiva* was a powerful stimulus in the struggle against the Antichrist.

The explanation of the great influence that Wyclif had in Bohemia can be found in the contacts that had come about from the end of the fourteenth century onwards between England and Bohemia.[50] In 1382, Anna, the sister of Wenceslas IV, the king of Bohemia, married Richard II of England and one of the consequences of the close political ties that came about through this marriage was that Bohemian students came to study in Oxford. While they were there, they became acquainted with Wyclif's works and took them back with them to their own country. In 1390, Hus was already copying the English author's writings.[51]

Wyclif had strenuously opposed the ecclesiology of the Roman Church, which took as its point of departure the assumption that Christ had instituted the Church as an earthly organisation and had entrusted Peter with the task of governing it. Since Peter had exercised this right to govern the Church in his function as bishop of Rome, those who succeeded him in that episcopate also had power to govern the Church. They were *ex officio vicarii Christi*. Thanks to Peter's authority, they continued to enjoy this *ex officio* power, whatever their moral conduct might be.[52] In this way, the Church had become a clerical organisation—the community of believers had become institutionalised and the pope had *de jure* the power of Christ himself.[53]

The schism of Avignon, however, had opened many Christian's eyes to the impossibility of this ecclesiology—a distinction had to be made, in the opinion of many believers, between the Church as the Body of Christ and the Church as a human—and often all too human—institution. Wyclif made this distinction by presupposing that there was a *universitas praedestinatorum*, which was distinct from the Church as a clerical organisation. In this true Church, no part was played by jurisdiction and it was formed by those who had been predestined to be saved in the past and in the present and the future. There were no rulers in this true Church, only men serving one another as Christ

---

[50] R. R. Betts: *English and Czech Influences on the Hussite Movement*, in *Transactions of the Royal Historical Society*, 4th series, XXXI, 1939, p. 71–102.

[51] H. Kaminsky: *A History of the Hussite Revolution* (1967), p. 24.

[52] Brian Tierney: *Foundations of the Conciliar Theory* (1955), pp. 25–36.

[53] *ibid.*, p. 88.

had served others and the distinction between clergy and laity had no more significance. The only Christians who were *de facto* priests were those who lived according to the norms of the gospel. Whenever the hierarchy showed that it was determined to play a dominant part in the Church, however, it revealed that it was opposed to God and that its leader, the pope, was an Antichrist. Wyclif illustrated this tendency in chapter VI of his *Tractatus de potestate pape* and in his last treatise, *De Christo et suo adversario Antichristo*,[54] by comparing Christ's sayings with the words and deeds of the popes.

John Hus accepted Wyclif's view to a very great extent and included it in his main work, *De ecclesia*.[55] Like Wyclif, he too regarded the Church as the *universitas praedestinatorum*. Those unjust men who sought to rule over others ostensibly belonged to the Church, but were not predestined for salvation. The representative of power, the pope, could therefore not be the head of the true Church, since that head was Christ himself. The pope could only be called the *vicarius Christi* if he was predestined and as a consequence served his Lord. In not serving the Lord, he showed himself to be an Antichrist. In a letter written in 1413,[56] he wrote: *Si papa est predestinatus et exercet officium pastorale, sequens Christum in moribus, tunc est caput tante militantis ecclesie, quantum regit ... Si vero vivit Christi contrarie, tunc est fur, latro, ascendentes aliunde et est lupus rapax, ypocrita, et nunc inter omnes vivantes precipuus Antichristus.* It is clear, then, from this statement that, like Wyclif, Hus regarded the vicariate of Christ not as an office in the Church, but as a moral quality. In principle, every believer was a *vicarius Christi*. By making all believers equal, Hus took away the very foundation for the papacy: *Nullus papa est persona signissima illius ecclesie katholice preter Christum, igitur nullus papa est caput illius ecclesie katholice preter Christum.*[57] Like Wyclif, he also regarded the Donation of Constantine as the main cause of the Church's decline, since a secular leader was forced on the Church by that gift and that head gained juridical power.

Hus did not, however, follow Wyclif in every respect. He believed that it was still possible to recognise a bishop of Rome so long as that bishop behaved—because he was predestined for salvation—in a morally worthy way in accordance with the law of Christ. He therefore recognised the spiritual jurisdiction of the bishop of Rome. In this, he

---

[54] Both: J. Loserth, ed. (London, 1896, reprinted 1966).
[55] ed. S. Harrison Thomson (Cambridge Mass., 1956).
[56] Quoted by Werner, *op. cit.*, p. 11.
[57] *De ecclesia*, XIII, 107.

was different from Wyclif, who did not recognise anyone as holding
office of this kind in the Church, because he was an office-bearer and
therefore denied the equality of all those chosen and predestined to be
saved—an equality taught by Christ himself—and was consequently
an Antichrist. The conclusion that De Vooght has drawn from this[58]
is that Hus in fact recognised the primacy of the pope: *Huss affirmait
tout simplement que le pape était obligé à plus de vertu chrétienne que les autres
évêques* ·De Vooght's conclusion, however, does reduce to a rather
trivial level the fact that Hus seriously undermined the foundation of
the primacy of the pope—if the jurisdictional office of the papacy is
replaced by the moral quality of the pope, the ecclesiology of the
Roman Catholic Church is seriously impaired.

Different answers have been provided at different times to the question as to the extent to which Hus was dependent on Wyclif in his
teaching about the Church. At the end of the nineteenth century,
Johann Loserth suggested that "Hussitism is essentially Wycliffia-
nism"[59] and he supported this argument by comparing Hus' *De ecclesia*
with Wyclif's *De potestate pape*, in which many passages occur that Hus
had, Loserth claimed, "taken word for word from Wyclif".[60] According
to Loserth too, Hus "became a reformer from the time when he perused
the Englishman's works".[61] Loserth's argument has, however, been
radically contested by Paul de Vooght since Czech scholars have
pointed out[62] that Hus certainly included detailed quotations from
other authors in his work —this being clearly a feature of his style and
method—and that, for this reason, it is not possible to speak of any
exclusive dependence on Hus' part on Wyclif. De Vooght has argued
that attention has also to be given to those elements in Hus' work that
are not derived from Wyclif, since this reveals clearly that Hus made
a choice on the basis of his own vision. De Vooght says: *On ne choisit
pas uniquement par ce qu'on prend, mais aussi par ce qu'on laisse. J'ai tâché dès
lors de montrer l'indépendance de Huss par rapport à Wiclif dans ses positions
sur l'épiscopat, le sacerdoce, l'eucharistie, les indulgences, la communion des
saints, la pénitence et jusqu'à un certain point sur la notion de l'Église.*[63]

We have already seen that De Vooght has concluded from this that
Hus was wrongly condemned as a heretic *(Huss a préféré l'opinion catho-*

---

[58] *Hussiana*, p. 61.
[59] In his introduction to *Tractatus de potestate pape*, p. XLII.
[60] *ibid.*, p. XLIV/XLVII.
[61] *ibid.*, p. XLIII.
[62] Among others, Jan Sedlák: *Mistr Jan Hus* (Prague, 1915).
[63] *Hussiana*, p. 5.

lique traditionelle aux innovations hétérodoxes de Wiclif). But, as we shall also see later on, both de Vooght and Loserth have overlooked the important fact that Hus was also (and indeed primarily) influenced by a specifically Bohemian spiritual movement. We shall see that, in the process of ecclesiological development, Hus was at a point where many different lines of thought converged. Since he was not able to harmonise and unify all these various lines of thought, however, his work undeniably contains a number of contradictory elements. This aspect of Hus' work has provided various points of contact enabling different scholars to claim it as a vehicle for their own views. For Loserth, for example, Hus was simply a follower of the English movement to renew the Church. For the Marxist historians, he was a national hero who provided the necessary stimulus for a revolution against feudalism. For de Vooght, he was a good Catholic who had to be rehabilitated. The Protestant scholars Bartoš and Molnár are the closest of all to a correct interpretation in their more subtle assessment of Hus' position and their recognition of different spiritual backgrounds to his views. Both of these scholars regard him as a reformer who, as a child of his own times, was not able to throw light on all the different movements of the period, but did ascertain the direction which a reform of the Church had to follow.

The question concerning the relationship between the different influences on Hus' thinking and writing can also be answered as H. A. Oberman has done in saying[64] that "Hus stands in a succession, or school, of Czech reformers: he had therefore already available a blueprint for reform in which Wyclifite ideas could conveniently be sketched in", but that he did not assimilate the whole complex of Wyclif's ideas into his own thinking. It is, for example, clear that he rejected the donatistic tendencies in the writings of the English reformer. In any case, Hus' main problem was that he was unable to develop from his ecclesiology, in which he to a great extent agreed with Wyclif, a structure of the Church which would be effective in practice. The *universitas praedestinatorum* was, after all, the invisible Church and this could not provide an adequate alternative to the secularised hierarchical Church, especially since there was no visible dividing line between the pure Church and the "hierarchical Church of the pope, the cardinals and the prelates". Christians could live in a state of sin for a long time and still belong to the elect and vice versa:

---

[64] *Forerunners of the Reformation* (1967), p. 209.

Sic idem homo est iustus ex gratia predestinacionis et iniustus ex vicio deperdibili, qualis fuit Petrus in negando Christum et Paulus persequendo ipsum.[65]

For this reason, Hus' followers were obliged to modify his teaching about the Church. Jakoubek of Střiba, following Augustine's teaching, spoke about an *ecclesia mixta* as the reality with which Christians had to work. Within this visible Church, there were two distinct groups —the *congregatio sanctorum* and the community of hypocrites, the head of which was the Antichrist, of whom the pope was the incarnation. The activity of this Antichrist spread, Jakoubek taught, like a poison through the visible Church, but the *congregatio sanctorum* remained the true Church.[66]

Rokycana also tried to find some possible means of identifying these two groups within the Church and for this reason stressed the moral nature of this distinction in the *ecclesia mixta*, affirming that there was a Church of evil men, who were not predestined for salvation, and a Church of good men, who were. The Church was the community of those who were called to be saved, but, since all men were called to salvation, the true Church was formed by those who in fact responded to that call.

Finally, Brother Lukáš also regarded the Church as the community of those who were called to salvation and who responded to the call, adding, however, to Rokycana's teaching that the difference between the good and the bad men would not appear until the last day. He did, on the other hand, emphasise that it was to some extent possible to recognise this difference here and now, in that the true Church was above all a serving Church and the hierarchy, with the pope at its head, was not able, as a juridical power structure, to belong to this serving Church.

It is therefore clear from this search by the Bohemian reformers for an acceptable ecclesiology based on Wyclif's concept of predestination that it was very difficult to find a suitable alternative to the hierarchical Church with its jurisdictional structure which would function in practice. The only experiment that was successfully followed for a number of years was the community without any offices, composed of equal believers striving to lead highly moral lives according to the precepts of the gospel—Chelčický and Řehoř were leaders of such communities. It soon became apparent, however, that there was a

---

[65] *De ecclesia*, cp. IV (ed. Harrison Thomson), p. 27.
[66] Paul de Vooght: *La notion d'Église—assemblées des prédestinés dans la théologie hussite primitive (ComViat*, 1970, 3/4).

need, in practice, for some organisation and then the offices were restored and a *corpus mixtum* once again emerged. This happened because the priests and elders of the Jednota Bratrská, despite the fact that they were subject to such high moral demands, were sometimes compelled by the situation in which they found themselves to make decisions which were in the nature of a compromise and which could therefore be called into question and thus regarded by the extreme members of the Brethren as in conflict with the pure *lex Christi*. This is why Brother Lukáš' only course was to teach that the difference between predestined and rejected members of the Church would not be recognised until the last day at the time of God's judgement. De Vooght has concluded:[67] *L'Assemblée des prédestinés n'est pas une notion sur laquelle on puisse construire une Église entendu dans le sens d'une société d'hommes vivants. L'Église dans ce sens ne peut être qu'un corpus mixtum.*

It is clear that an ecclesiology which refuses to accord any place to a hierarchy and which regards every form of power exerted over others as a transgression of the law of Christ and therefore insists on moral behaviour as a sign of having been chosen is a pre-eminently suitable and fertile soil for the growth of a view according to which the leader of the hierarchy, the pope, is seen to be the Antichrist. A view of this kind had already been expressed by Wyclif in his *De potestate pape* and *De Christo et suo adversario Antichristo*. It was, however, in Bohemia at the time of Hus that these ideas about the Antichrist were developed very fully, above all by Nicholas of Dresden.

This German, who worked in Prague as the leader of a German school, but who was an ardent supporter of Hus and Jerome of Prague, wrote two books in 1412 and 1413 respectively, in which, following Wyclif, he drew certain conclusions from the thesis that the true Church of humble Christians, who were all equal, had been degraded by the hierarchy's quest for power to the level of a community of the Antichrist. The title of Nicholas' first treatise was *Tabule veteris et novi coloris seu cortina de antichristo*.[68] It contained nine *tabulae* or collections of texts from the Bible and statements by Christian authors brought together as documentation material for a description of Christ and the Antichrist, Peter and the pope and therefore of the *ecclesia primitiva* (the "old colour") and the *ecclesia moderna* (or "new colour"). This treatise was also illustrated, so that the reader could also have a visual

---

[67] *ibid.*, p. 132.

[68] Full text in H. Kaminsky: *Master Nicholas of Dresden. The Old Color and the New* (Philadelphia, 1965).

impression of the contrast between the two different churches.

The first *tabula* can be taken as characteristic of the whole book. Opposite Christ carrying his cross and saying: "If any man would come after me, let him ... take up his cross and follow me", there is an illustration of the pope riding on a horse, with the caption: *Sumus pontifex utens insigniis apostolice dignitatis.*[69] This contrast between Christ and the pope is heightened by a statement about the former: *Verus deus et verus homo* and another about the latter: *id est admirabillis, nec deus nec homo*, with, as a repetition of the same contrast: *Lege vitam Christi ab utero matris usque ad patibulum crucis et non invenies nisi stigmata paupertatis* and, directed at the pope: *in hiis Constantino successisti et non Petro.*[70]

Like Wyclif, Nicholas of Dresden also reveals that the pope's jurisdictional power was derived not from Peter but from the donation of Constantine. He does this by means of another contrast, beginning with a quotation from the decretal itself:[71] *Beato Silvestro et successoribus eius tradimus pallacium imperii nostri. Decernimus ut mappulis et lintheaminibus, id est candidissimo colore decoratos equos equitent, conferentes eciam diversa ornamenta imperialia et omnem gloriam potestatis nostre, et possessionum predia contulimus et rebus diversis ditamus.* This quotation is immediately followed by Jesus' saying: "Foxes have holes, and birds of the air have nests; but the Son of man has nowhere to lay his head" (Matt. 8. 20).

In the second *tabula*, a similar contrast is made between Peter and the pope by juxtaposing Peter's statement in Acts 3. 6: "I have no silver and gold" and the sentence from the decretals:[72] *Non habens titulum beneficii vel patrimonii unde possit congrue sustentari non debet ad ordines promoveri.*

These contrasts reach a climax in the eighth *tabula*, which contains an illustration of Jesus washing his disciples' feet contrasted with one of the pope whose feet are being kissed by believers. This is accompanied by the sarcastic comment: *Servus servorum dei ad oscula pedum beatorum.* The author also includes four lines of verse referring to the curia, which is compared with the disciples:

> *Curia vult marcas, bursas exhaurit et archas,*
> *si burse parcas, fuge papas et patriarchas,*

---

[69] *Decretals*, V, xxxiii[23].
[70] Bernard of Clairvaux: *De consideracione*, IV, iii.
[71] XCVI, dist. 14.
[72] III, v[4].

si dederis marcas, et eis impleveris archas,
culpa solveris quacumque ligatus eris.[73]

The ninth *tabula* forms a kind of conclusions and provides an image of the Antichrist accompanied by quotations from Nicholas of Lyra—the postil on 1 Pet. 5. 13: *Antichristus nascetur in Babilone. Babilon est Roma*, and the postil on 2 Thess. 2. 4: "The son of perdition, the opponent, who exalts himself against God, takes his seat in God's temple, to show that he is a god".

The following year, in 1413, Nicholas wrote another treatise with a similar aim, entitled *Consuetudo et ritus primitive ecclesie et moderne, seu derivative*.[74] This work is divided into three *partes*, the first of which begins with texts describing the *ecclesia primitiva* as a community of the Holy Spirit, without offices with jurisdictional powers: *Tempore apostolorum in primitiva ecclesia spiritus sanctus visibiliter operabatur; ... et sic sufficiebat quod ordinator diceret ordinando: sis presbiter, vel dyaconus, vel similia verba ...*,[75] and this was a matter of course, as *iure nature omnia sunt communia omnibus* and *in primitiva ecclesia omnes credentes, seu laici seu clerici, nihil possidebant, sed omnia erant eis communia*. In the apostolic Church, all believers were brothers, but the pope allowed no one to call him brother.

In the second *pars*, the Roman practice of excommunication is compared with the appearance of the *ecclesia primitiva* and in the third *pars* the author criticises the monastic orders and their rules, which he regards as a symbol of the decline of the Church.

What we find therefore in these two treatises of Nicholas of Dresden are many anti-papal themes of the kind that recur in Velenský's treatise *Petrum Romam non venisse*. We read, for example, that the Antichrist is in *loco sancto* ("Babylon is Rome") and that he does so because of the donation of Constantine, which made the original Church of believers who were all of equal status into an institution of power structures, the *ecclesia romana* thus coming to be in flagrant opposition to the *ecclesia primitiva*. Finally, there is the theme that anyone who wishes to return to the simplicity of the apostolic Church is threatened with excommunication.

---

[73] Reproduced by Kaminsky, *op. cit.*, as: "Money is what the Curia likes best / It empties many a purse and chest / If you are stingy with your marks / stay away from popes and patriarchs / But give them marks, and once their chests are filled / You will be absolved from the bondage of your guilt."

[74] Full text in Kaminsky, *op. cit.*

[75] *Sentencia Innocencii de ritu ordinacionis laudata est ab Iohanne Andree*, I, xvi[3].

A friend and supporter of Nicholas of Dresden was Jakoubek of Stříba. He recognised his own ideas in Nicholas' Wycliffian elaboration of ecclesiology, although he derived his views from a different and specifically Bohemian tradition.

This tradition goes back to the mid fourteenth century and its beginning can be traced to Jan Milíč of Kroměříž, the "Father of the Bohemian Reformation".[76] Milíč was a priest, who gave up his office in 1363 under the influence of the Waldensians and founded a centre in Prague where priests and those who had been rejected by society could lead a communal life ("Jerusalem") as a symbol of the pure way of life lived in expectation of the end of the world and the second coming of Christ. Milíč' preaching attracted the attention of the Inquisition and he was imprisoned in Rome in 1367, but released after a time. He died in 1374 in Avignon, where he was summoned for a cross-examination. It was during his captivity in Rome that he wrote the book that was to become so influential—the *Libellus de Antichristo*.[77]

In this treatise, Milíč' point of departure is that there is a direct relationship between the preaching of the gospel, the coming of the Antichrist and the second coming of Christ.[78] Preaching reveals the works of the Antichrist and at the same time prepares the way for the second coming of Christ, whereas, on the other hand, the Antichrist manifests himself more clearly and more openly as the preaching of the gospel is more purely directed towards Christ's second coming. This preaching must, Milíč taught, be based on the simple gospel itself. For this reason, theologians had to abandon scholasticism, which was based above all on logic and philosophy: *Qui ex virtutibus moralibus philosophie naturalis putant se posse salvari, nescientes caritatem expressam in evangelica lege.*

Milíč does not go so far as to identify the Antichrist with any historical figure, but he does admit that, at a certain moment in time, this Antichrist may be found in the person of the emperor,[79] in the monastic state or in the clergy. The only firm conclusion that Milíč

---

[76] R. Říčan: *Die böhmischen Brüder* (1958), p. 8.

[77] Published in the series *Věstnik kralovské české společ nosti nauk*, 1890. His *Sermo de die novissimo* is included in the collection *Reformačni sbornik*, VIII (1946).

[78] For Milíč' theology, see A. Molnár: *Le mouvement préhussite et la fin des temps* (*ComViat*, 1958, 1); E. Peschke: *Die Bedeutung Wiclefs für die Theologie der Böhmen* (ZKG, 1935, 54) and M. Spinka: *John Hus' Concept of the Church* (1966), from which the quotations are taken.

[79] He was once tempted to say that Charles IV (of Bohemia) was the Antichrist and was imprisoned for making this statement.

himself draws is that, in his own eschatological time—the schism of Avignon gave rise to eschatological expectations—it was necessary actively to look out for Christ's second coming.

Although it is certainly possible to regard Jan Milíč ot Kroměřiž as the founder of pre-Hussitism in Bohemia, it was his disciple Matěj of Janov who had a much greater influence on later developments in the country. Janov was born in or about the year 1350 in the district of Tabor, studied for a few years in Prague (not, however, at the university) and then went to Paris to complete his education. In 1381 he returned to Prague as a *magister parisiensis* and became a canon in the city. After a few years, he came into conflict with the episcopate because of his preaching, which was in the spirit of Milíč, and he was forbidden to preach for three years. It was during this period of enforced silence (1388 or 1389) that he wrote his major work, *Regulae veteris et novi Testamenti*,[80] a collection of treatises (not all of them his own work—he also included Milíč' *Libellus de Antichristo* in the book).

The work begins with the same theme as that of Janov's master, namely that there must be a form of preaching based on the simple gospel alone, so that faith will bring men to pure love *(fides caritate formata)*. Janov, however, introduced his own ideas about a radical reformation into Milíč' eschatological views, influenced in this by Joachim of Fiore. He believed that it was necessary for Christians to return to the *ecclesia primitiva* and to the simple life of faith that characterised the apostolic era. He was moreover very critical of the hierarchy, affirming that every good Christian was a priest, even though he may not have been ordained. On the other hand, an ordained priest living in sin was not even a Christian, let alone a priest.

For Janov too, the visible Church was divided into those members who were predestined for salvation and those who were rejected. Only those who had *fides caritate formata* and in whom the Spirit of Christ was active—*Ecclesia congregata ex multitudine solum electorum, quos vivificat et agitat spiritus Jesus Christi*—formed the *communio sanctorum*.[81] In contrast to the Church of the elect was the Church of the Antichrist, which was what Janov saw in the corrupt Church of his own times. The corruption was, in Janov's opinion, above all to be

---

[80] R. R. Betts: *The Regulae Veteris et Novi Testamenti of Matěj z Janova*, in *The Journal of Theological Studies*, XXXII, 1931, p. 344–351. The work was first published in 1908 (and the later volumes appeared between 1909 and 1926). The editors were Vlastimil Kybal and O. Odližilík (Prague).

[81] Liber III, treatise V (quoted in Spinka, *op. cit.*)

found in the priests, prelates and monks of the Church. The Antichrist was certainly manifest in every bad Christian (whose faith did not result in love), but the highest authority in the Church was the greatest Antichrist.

In principle, then, Janov's Antichrist was a collective reality, but because the antichristian influence on the Church was greatest in the case of those who had most power in the Church the *Summus Antichristus* must be, in Janov's view, the one who was at the head of the hierarchy. This individualisation within the collective reality made it possible for Janov to equate the pope and the Antichrist (in the same way that Wyclif had done: *Antichrist bedeutet ihm einfach ein Widersacher Christi in höherer Potenz*.[82] Essentially, however, the whole of the secularised Church was, in Janov's opinion, the Antichrist. It had fallen into egoism and this *amor sui ipsius* was the sign of the beast in the Book of Revelation. Egoism led inevitably to schism (here Janov is alluding to the schism of Avignon). The Antichrist disrupted the harmony of the Church by introducing many wilful laws and precepts.

Janov elaborated this theory by making a distinction in the *ecclesia* between the *varietas essentialis*, which was intended by God himself and was a consequence of many different effects of the Holy Spirit, and the *multiplicitas accidentalis*, which was was the result of an entire complex of (all too) human ideas and had to be eliminated from the Church. It was, Janov taught, through these accidentalia that the Antichrist acted in the Church as what Peschke[83] called *das Prinzip der Trennung*. This disturbance of harmony in the Church was caused by three main factors—the hierarchical structure had been allowed to develop too far, public worship had become too complicated and dogmatic pronouncements had become too remote from the original apostolic teaching. Sinful man was therefore able to find without difficulty points of contact in the life and teaching of the Church to express his *amor sui ipsius*—power and wealth and the inevitable consequences of these, divisions in the community of believers. Janov suggested, as a remedy against these tactics practised by the Antichrist, that Christians should aim actively to simplify and purify the Church, the model being the Church of the apostolic era, with an uncomplicated confession and an unhierarchical structure, a Church in which there was no opportunity for men successfully to achieve worldly power.

---

[82] Hans Preuss: *Die Vorstellungen vom Antichrist im späteren Mittelalter, bei Luther und in der konfessionellen Polemik* (Leipzig, 1906), p. 50.

[83] *op. cit.,*

Jakoubek of Stříba continued to propagate Janov's ideas. Jakoubek (ca. 1370–1429) was a magister at the University of Prague and, after Hus' death, an advocate of Utraquism (taking the initiative in the celebration of the Lord's Supper under both forms and by laymen). He made the Bohemian teaching about the *ecclesia primitiva* and the Antichrist more radical by linking it with Wyclif's ideas as presented by Nicholas of Dresden. Hans Preuss[84] has quoted from Jakoubek's treatise, *De antichristo*: *Antichristus est falsus Christus sive christianus, veritati vite et doctrine Christi fraudulenter contrarius, summo gradu malicie super habundans, sed vel ex toto vel ex maiori parte in malicie coopertus; summum gradum in ecclesia possidens summanque auctoritatem super omnem personam clericalem et laycam de plena potestate sibi vendicans* ... In this, Jakoubek is clearly completing Janov's idea—the Antichrist as a collective reality is seen as an individual in his teaching. What is more, this individual Antichrist was present for him in the concrete figure of Pope John XXIII (1410–1415) and he called on Christians to revolt against him and thus to restore the pure Church.[85] Jakoubek's teacher, Janov, had warned him against a violent rebellion and the shedding of blood when the Antichrist was revealed, but Jakoubek nonetheless wanted a drastic reformation. Under his influence therefore the Bohemian people actively resisted the Church of Rome, because, as the *ecclesia moderna*, it was the sphere in which the Antichrist worked.

This more radical version of the ideas about the *ecclesia primitiva* and the Antichrist was propagated above all by Jakoubek's friend Jan Želivský († 1422), who applied the various examples of the *ecclesia primitiva* directly to the contemporary situation in Bohemia: *In primitiva ecclesia numquam sancti volebant census accipere perpetuos.*[86] In this way, he intensified the conflict between the Roman Church and the Hussites —Christians ought not to obey the pope, he taught, because the pope himself did not obey the true vicar of Christ, Peter. Monks too were not really the successors of the apostles, because they did not live from the work of their hands. He also insisted that all priests who did not live as Christ had lived were in fact Christ's enemies: *ergo omnes sacerdotes symoniaci, dotati, avari, superbi, luxuriosi sunt dyaboli incarnati*,[87] in a word: *tales non sunt pastori ... sunt lupi* and their power was derived, not from Christ, but from the Antichrist.

---

[84] *op. cit.*, p. 56.
[85] E. Werner, *op. cit.*, p. 32.
[86] *ibid.*, p. 35.
[87] *ibid.*, p. 36.

Želivský also gives a prominent place in his teaching to eschatology, a subject which played an important part in Milíč' writing, but which Janov kept in the background. Once again, however, he applied this to the contemporary situation of conflict in the Bohemian Church. He compared the Emperor Sigismund, for example, to the red dragon in Apoc. 12 and looked forward to the new Jerusalem in the year 1412.[88] He therefore urged the people to make processions to the mountains as prophetic signs of the approaching end. By giving a political and a radically eschatological emphasis to the ecclesiological teaching current in Bohemia, Želivský stimulated the emergence of extreme resistance groups. Often using violent means, these Christians broke away not only from the Church of Rome, but also from the more moderate groups of Utraquists, who wished to secure stable relationships. His call also found a response, however, among several Christians who remained within the organisation of the Utraquist Church. Martin Lupač, a disciple of Jakoubek and Rokycana's auxiliary bishop, looking back to the martyrdom of Hus, wrote:[89] "What preacher today dares to call the Roman Church the synagogue of Satan, the whore of the Antichrist or the beast with ten horns (Apoc. 12)? We must find the spirit of bravery and resist". This call to the preachers of the Church was, however, not accepted by the Utraquists. The result of this was that Lupač was mistrusted in his own circle, but on the other hand became the confidant of the various communities of Brethren which began to emerge shortly afterwards.

After the bloody defeat of the Taborites, this militant form of reformation in Bohemia disappeared. The desire for a return to the *ecclesia primitiva* and the recognition of the Antichrist in the pope continued, but became rather a motivation for inner renewal and an attempt to renew society without using violent means, the eschatological expectations of these Christians gradually disappearing. For Peter Chelčicky, the pope was the Antichrist and obedience to the law of Christ meant leaving the established Church and leading a simple life without a hierarchical structure, all Christians being equal. This conviction continued to flourish after him in the community of the Brethren, especially in their initial complete rejection of all offices in the Church, but also later, when they continued to advocate the *ecclesia primitiva*. In a "Letter from the Brethren to Rokycana",[90] written in 1471,

---

[88] *ibid.*, p. 39.

[89] Müller, *op. cit.*, p. 150.

[90] *V Psani bratri Rokycanovi*, in Goll, *op. cit.*

for example, we read: *So gab es auch höchste Bischöfe der Christenheit nach dem H. Petrus, die in Armut beharrten und in Niedrigkeit auf Erden lebten, seinen Schimpf tragend, ihm folgend, von der Macht der Welt leidend, durch drei hundert Jahre, bis zum Kaiser Constantinus, den Sylvester in den christlichen Glauben aufnahm. Und dabei erlangte er weltliche Macht und Reichtum, Erhöhung und kaiserliche Würde und Lustbarkeiten des Fleisches.* Jaroslav Goll has also quoted from a treatise[91] which has been ascribed to one of the earliest leaders of the Brethren, Řehoř, and which must have been written roundabout 1471/1473: *Uns hat nicht als Muster gedient der Ursprung der Priesterschaft von den hohen Ämter der römischen Kirche, sondern das Beispiel der ersten apostolischen Kirche. Denn es gibt untrügliche Stellen in der Schrift, daß damals Bischof und Priester dasselbe gewesen sei, wie der H. Paulus an Timotheus und an Titus schreibt ...).*

When offices were restored in the Brethren, there was—entirely in the spirit of the quotations give above—no departure from the simple teaching that those bearing office had to practise a manual skill as their source of income. The idea of the Antichrist also persisted among the Brethren—in his commentary on the Apocalypse (1501), Brother Lukáš still regarded the pope as the incarnation of the Antichrist.

If we look at the whole of this process, then what emerge clearly are two basic underlying ecclesiological notions. Even though the different lines of thought came together at a later stage, these two notions were certainly the cause of a changed emphasis.

The first of these underlying notions was the expectation of the end of time that flourished during the fourteenth century. This was partly evoked by the schism of Avignon, which undoubtedly undermined the foundations of the Church. Milíč of Kroměříž interpreted this crisis in the light of the New Testament—the coming of the Antichrist meant that Christ's second coming would also take place very soon (Apoc. 14. 6–20; 19. 17–21). This inspired Milíč to activities with an eschatological and symbolic character. (His foundation "Jerusalem" in Prague is an example of this.) Molnár has therefore said of Milíč:[92] *Ce qui est essentiel chez Milíč, c'est le cadre eschatologique de son action symboliquement prophétique.* This "symbolically prophetic activity" was a form of preaching against the Antichrist and of preparation for the second coming of Christ. It was reminiscent of the *ecclesia primitiva*, but this idea was not used explicitly as the norm for combatting the

---

[91] *Jak se vidé mají míti k Rimské cirkví*, in Goll, *op. cit.*
[92] *Le mouvement préhussite et la fin des temps*, p. 29.

contemporary Church. The *ecclesia primitiva* does not in fact occur in Milíč' teaching as a model.

Milíč' disciple Janov, on the other hand, certainly used it in this way. Because he saw the presence of the Antichrist in man's desire for power, introducing division into the Church, he believed that the Antichrist could only be combatted and preparation could only be made for Christ's coming if Christians returned to the life and faith of the apostolic Church. What is particularly striking in this teaching is that, although there is not a complete disappearance of the expectations of the end of time, the *ecclesia primitiva* could become an aim in itself. It should, however, be pointed out that Janov used the idea of the primitive Church in a very specific way —not as a norm to find a solution to the problem of the hierarchy (which was at the same time indicative of uncertainty regarding dogma) that had arisen because of the schism of Avignon, but rather as an example of life in an eschatological era (which had been given a fairly permanent character). This was in striking contrast to the debates in conciliar circles, in which the concept was used as a rule with a different intention: "The dogmatic boundaries which had to be accepted by everyone were defined by the *ecclesia primitiva*... Dogma was ... what corresponded to the norms defined by the *ecclesia primitiva*".[93] These norms were required if a solution was to be found to the problem of the relationship between the *ecclesia universalis* (or the *congregatio fidelium*) and the *potestas papae*. The concept therefore functioned within the framework of an ecclesiology which aimed to preserve the hierarchy, but in a purified form. Janov's teaching, on the other hand, stressed the need to eliminate the hierarchy altogether, because it was an expression of power. His view resulted in a reformation of the Church in which there would be no further need for offices as an institution for the mediation of salvation. Conciliarism, on the other hand, preserved the clergy's function of mediating salvation and resulted in a restoration of the Church.

It is important, in conclusion, to point to the way in which Janov came to this idea of the *ecclesia primitiva* as a model. He began by analysing the errors in the Church of his own period and traced the cause of this decline to the fact that the hierarchy and public worship had been taken too far and that man's *amor sui ipsius* had made use of this. His remedy was to restore the apostolic Church, with its simplicity and its uncomplicated structure. In other words, Janov reached

---

[93] G. H. M. Posthumus Meyjes: *Jean Gerson* (1963), pp. 301/302.

the idea of the primitive Church by analysing his own period—he did not take as his point of departure the Bible as the authority which gave form to the life of the *ecclesia primitiva*. This is why Erhard Peschke has commented[94] that Janov was more concerned with the Church than with the Bible in his approach to the problem. At the deepest level, Janov's view of the Church was historical and analytical.

The second of these fundamental underlying notions in the ecclesiology of the Bohemian reformers can be traced back to Wyclif. Unlike Janov, the English reformer took the Bible as the only valid norm and based his criticism of the Church on it. It was, for Wyclif, the gospel which determined that no struggle for power should be allowed to take place within the community of believers. It was the "law of Christ" which imposed simplicity and equality on all Christians. As the norm for Christian life, the Bible said, according to Wyclif, that the Church had to be a community gathered around the commandment to love.

Wyclif's elaboration of this biblical basis of ecclesiology was quite rational. (This is why Peschke has called it the "biblical and rational" notion of the reformation in Bohemia.) Those who lived according to the law of Christ formed, he taught, the true Church of the elect, whereas those who did not live according to that law were the rejected, even though they were apparently within the Church. It was on the basis of this distinction that Wyclif developed his idea about the Antichrist and the restoration of the *ecclesia primitiva*—those who were predestined for salvation were, by living according to the gospel, *de facto* a priesthood within a pure Church. Because it was in conflict with the law of Christ, on the other hand, the jurisdictional hierarchy was an enemy of Christ and the Church of the Antichrist.

The difference between these two underlying notions, then, is to be found in the different points of departure chosen. In the case of Janov, the aim to restore the primitive Church was a reaction to a historical phenomenon (although this was, of course, analysed with biblical norms). In the case of Wyclif, on the other hand, the biblical norms themselves led directly to a simple Church of pious believers and, on the basis of this, the historically developed Church was shown to be a secular institution of power. The distinction is therefore one of subtle nuances. Janov was unable to complete his historical analysis without the aid of biblical norms. Wyclif, on the other hand, was unable to

---

[94] *Die Bedeutung Wiclefs für die Theologie der Böhmen* (ZKG, 1935, 54).

apply the biblical norms without at the same time having recourse to history. This resulted in Wyclif's and Janov's followers recognising each others' aims. Even Wyclif's idea of the *ecclesia praedestinatorum* occurred in the teaching of Janov, although it did not play a prominent part. Because of this, it was possible for both Wyclif's and Janov's trains of thought to go together in Bohemia and ultimately to result in a single common conviction, namely that the Church and society had to be renewed on the basis of the gospel.

We are bound to add, however, that it was especially at the time of the Hussite war that these two trains of thought influenced each other. The Hussites were combatted with great severity by the Church and this has two direct consequences. On the one hand, the Wycliffian community of the elect and Janov's *ecclesia primitiva* were able to acquire concrete form in the groups of the earlier Jednota Bratrská, which were often revolutionary in their renewal of society. On the other hand, it was easier for these Christians to identify their enemy, the Church, with the Antichrist.

Kaminsky[95] has said that "the similarities between the two types of reformism were to be sure more extensive than the differences, a fact that undoubtedly explains much of Wyclif's initial popularity among the Czechs", but he was also of the opinion that, after the two streams of thought had come together, Wyclifism predominated: "Matthew of Janov's doctrine was the dominant ideology of the first period, Wyclifism that of the second". This is certainly true if one thinks of Wyclif's biblical arguments about the poor Church and the rejection of papal primacy as well as of the pope as the Antichrist. Other aspects of Wyclif's work, however, were not definitively accepted, despite the fact that they were initially well received.

Wyclif, for example, believed that the law of Christ was, at the deepest level, identical with the natural law. The law of love and the natural law were able, in his opinion, to complement each other. This harmony had, however, been disturbed by sin, so that men had sometimes to be compelled to fulfil the commandment of love. When they reached this point, their human laws were able to conform to the commandment of Christ to love. Nicholas of Dresden clearly accepted this relationship between the natural law and the *lex Christi* when he wrote[96] that, in the primitive Church, *iure nature omnia sunt communia omnibus*. This idea, however, was completely rejected by Peter Chel-

---

[95] *A History of Hussite Revolution*, p. 25.
[96] See p. 107.

čický, who was nonetheless said "to hold Wyclif in high esteem because of his struggle against the Antichrist".[97] He took not creation, but man's sin, as his point of departure. Man, he taught, was in a radical sense turned away from God and there was no possible transition from evil to good. No human commandment could therefore ever be equal to the law of God.[98] This idea of Chelčický's was taken over into the theology of the Unitas Fratrum.

There was clearly a fundamental difference between the theological point of departure taken by Wyclif and that accepted by Chelčický and it was moreover only in their consequences, at the level of the simple Church of equals and the common struggle against the pope, that these two lines of thought came together. In view of this, as Peschke has observed, ... *ist festzustellen, daß die Ideen des Engländers dem Denken der Böhmen neue Richtung, Kraft und Gestalt gegeben haben, jedoch ... in umgedeuteter Gestalt wirksam geworden sind.*[99]

As we have already seen, Hus and his successors were unable to develop an effective structure for the renewed Church that they had in mind on the basis of their concept of the *universitas praedestinatorum*. They were stimulated by the conclusions that they had drawn from Wyclif's ideas, but the ideas themselves remained "foreign bodies" in the Bohemian tradition concerning the primitive Church and the Antichrist. This is why, in our opinion, Kaminsky's affirmation that Wyclifism predominated over Janov's teaching in the theology of the Bohemian reformers was really the result of his having paid too much attention to these conclusions drawn by the Bohemians regarding Church politics. The ecclesiology of Milíč and Janov continued to be influential in the Bohemia of later Hussitism and the Brethren. This is a fact that becomes quite evident in any attempt to trace, on the basis of statements made in the *Petrum Romam non venisse*, the tradition that had the greatest influence on Velenský.

In the first place, Janov's influence is clear from the the methodical order followed by Velenský in his treatment of the subject. Velenský concludes from an analysis of his own period that there is a need to restore the apostolic Church. The Bible does not form the basic point of departure for his reasoning, but "only" provides material for a description of the *ecclesia primitiva*. He observes that the Antichrist is reigning and this observation is not based—at least in the argument

---

[97] Quoted by Peschke, *op. cit.*
[98] See Peschke, *op. cit.*
[99] *ibid.*

found in the foreword—on an application of New Testament norms, but rather on a historical analysis. The pope, he says, takes action against good scholars and sincere reformers of the Church because of the existence of a power structure in which "one man rules over everyone". And this power is defended "with gnashing of teeth".

Velenský then goes on to investigate how this situation could have come about. Here too, his argument is not that the biblical norms have been neglected, but rather that history has been falsified by "mendacious bulls"; Velenský claims that "the Antichrist, under the name of Sylvester, regarded the secular kingdom as a gift from Emperor Constantine to himself". A very important part is played in Velenský's argument by the exposing of the Donation of Constantine by Lorenzo Valla. This is because it is only by means of such an analysis of the historical situation that any conclusion can be reached with regard to the action that should be taken against the Antichrist. What has to be done, Velenský concludes, is that Christians must return to the pure Church that existed before Sylvester secularised it with power and wealth and, what is more, this return is all the more important since the Antichrist continues, by means of his mendacious bulls, to defend this secularisation of the Church as intended by God.

As soon as Velenský begins to speak about this pure Church of the early period of Christian history as an ideal and therefore as the norm for the Christianity of his own times, the New Testament, of course, at once begins to play a part in his argument—like Janov, he too uses it in order to provide material for a description of the primitive Church. The Bible becomes the norm for judging the past and the present, but it is only used as a norm after is has already been made clear via a different way that there is a need for a norm of this kind. Velenský writes in this context: "Do you believe that the Church, which was founded by a poor Christ, and which was extended by poor apostles, ought to have so much wealth and power? And that in it one man should rule over everyone? The Church would then be nothing but a tyranny. Unfortunately, the Church has become just such a tyranny: the whore, Babylon, arrayed in purple". Because of this, Velenský insists, "she has therefore come into conflict with the words of Christ and with the rite and the example of the primitivae ecclesiae". Therefore, he concludes, it has to be said: "Come out of her, my people, lest you take part in her sins" and it is the task of the reformers "to expose the faults and sins of the Western Babylon".

Velenský's way of opposing the Petrine tradition, which he does in

imitation of Krasonický, provides a very good example of his preference for historical analysis rather than for the Bible as a point of
departure. He does not attempt to undermine the primacy of Peter by
showing that it is in conflict with the intention of the gospel, but rather
by pointing out that it is by historical research that it can be proved
that Peter was never in Rome. The very many quotations from the
New Testament that are used in this context function not as a basis for
a fundamentally theological protest against the primacy, but rather as
material for a scientific historical proof. It was moreover this way of
approaching the subject which was later to make Luther, reasoning
on the basis of biblical theology, say: *sed non evincit*.

It is clear, then, that Velenský was writing completely within the
tradition of Janov and was very remote from the biblicism of Wyclif.
The complete absence in Velenský's treatise of the theme of Christian
eschatological expectation, which provided both Milíč and Janov
with their most powerful motivation, may not be a reason for denying
a spiritual affinity between him and Janov. As we have already seen,
the theme of eschatological expectation became overshadowed by that
of the renewal of society in the case of Janov and, after the final defeat
of the Taborites, those expectations more or less completely disappeared in the later Utraquist Church and among the Brethren. There
can be no doubt, however, that Velenský's humanism was also a
reason why he did not connect the activity of the Antichrist with the
return of Christ. At the beginning of his foreword, he speaks about
"Elijah and Enoch, who came a long time ago", but he draws no
conclusions from this regarding Christ's coming. We may therefore
say that Velenský the humanist was hoping for a purification of the
Church on earth and not for a speedy end.

It is, however, not possible to discover any clear relationship,
especially with Janov, in the way in which Velenský speaks about the
Antichrist and the *ecclesia primitiva*. This, however, is understandable,
since the same statements had been made concerning these concepts
both by the Wyclifites and by those who followed the early Bohemian
tradition. In comparing the pope to the beast from the underworld,
for example, Velenský is calling to mind not only the *Tabulae* of Nicholas of Dresden, but also the teaching of Lupač and Brother Lukáš. In
this, he is completely within the whole Bohemian tradition of speaking
very strongly about the pope.

The same can also be said of Velenský's description of the *ecclesia
primitiva*. He fulminates especially against *pontifices, cardinales, patriar-*

chae, archiepiscopi, none of whom were present in the early Church, and sees them as characteristic of a hierarchy that has been carried too far. He recognises the need for simple offices in the Church, but emphasises that all those holding office should be equal, as in the early Church, when *presbyteri, episcopi vel seniores* were synonyms for the same office. He also insists that Peter had no knowledge at all of the "proud name *summorum pontificum*". It is not difficult to find quite specific sources underlying these statements. One of them was undoubtedly Janov, with his view that an exaggerated hierarchical structure is evidence of the tactics employed by the Antichrist. Another is Nicholas of Dresden, with his description of the simplicity of office in the apostolic Church and his proof that the different titles given to offices are in fact synonymous. Finally, there are the Bohemian Brethren with their rejection of the high offices. We are, however, bound to conclude that here too Velenský is interpreting the general climate of thought in the Bohemian reformation.

We may conclude by saying that Oldřich Velenský developed not only the material provided by Krasonický, but also the Bohemian tradition in general. In the first place, he continued in the same direction in using language and concepts which had become common property since Wyclif's and Janov's ideas had become merged together in the Bohemian reformation to describe the Antichrist and the primitive Church. In the second place, his treatment of these two subjects was above all derived from Janov's historical and analytical approach and this in turn also goes back to the pre-Hussite Bohemian tradition.

4. *The Apostolic Succession*

Any author who denied that Peter was the bishop of Rome and was therefore unable to regard the pope as the successor of Peter and who at the same time described the hierarchy, within the context of his views concerning the primitive Church, as a sign of the presence of the Antichrist was bound to make one of two choices. The first is entirely to reject the apostolic succession as such, as yet another aspect of the tactics employed by the Antichrist. The alternative choice open to such a writer is to provide an entirely different explanation for the concept of apostolic succession or to apply that concept in a different way. For which of these two alternatives, then, did Velenský opt? It is possible to answer this question at once by saying that his choice was certainly made within the framework of the ideas current among the Unitas Fratrum.

After a period during which they refused to recognise any offices at all, the Brethren found themselves compelled by practical needs which called for an authoritative government in the Church to appoint their own office-bearers once again in 1467. They then looked for a line of succession which had not been tainted by the period during which the Antichrist had been present in the Church, but which could really be connected with the purity of the primitive Church. It may perhaps seem strange that the Brethren did not in fact appoint functionaries, who could have been chosen as specialists from among the universal priesthood of all the believers without any form of ordination, since Wyclif had after all said that every Christian who followed the law of Christ was *de facto* a priest. This was, however, too modern a view for the times. Only a society which has become thoroughly familiar with the process of secularisation can begin to accept the idea that the visible Church can be administrated and governed by functionaries who have not been ordained and who are outside any succession. It was certainly not possible for the Bohemian Brethren to accept any idea of this kind. They could only choose between two possibilities—either a community of believers without any offices at all or officebearers who derived their official authority from a succession. And where succession via a worldly Church was unacceptable, because that succession had become in itself a manifestation of the Antichrist, then a link had to be sought with the pure Church of an earlier period. This connection could be made, in the opinion of the Brethren, along two possible ways. The first was via the Eastern Church, which had not suffered from secularisation since the time of the Donation of Constantine. The second was via the Waldensians, since, according to a legend which was generally accepted at the time, there was a line of succession through them which had originated in the Church before the time of Sylvester.

The Brethren had tried several times to establish contact with the Eastern Church. In 1491, Lukáš of Prague and several other members of the Brethren travelled through Greece and Turkey. In the long run, however, partly because these contacts were made difficult by the Mohammedan government, the links were broken. It is clear from this pre-history that Velenský had good reason to call the Eastern Church the part of the universal Church that had not been corrupted: "It is not without pain that the East looks to the West and sees how Christ has been banished from it". He also says: "The universal Church does not sing about this profane deceit, because the

Eastern Church has a different opinion" and adds: *quod satis scio*, that is, through Lukáš' accounts of his travels.

Much closer contacts were made with the Waldensians. Waldensian refugees, especially from Germany, had for many years found safety in the villages belonging to the Brethren and they became in the long run completely absorbed into the community. The Brethren themselves, however, also sought these contacts, because, according to a legend which probably arose in the fourteenth century, the origin of the Waldensians was to be found in the pure Church of the period before Pope Sylvester. This is also the reason why the Bohemians had their first bishop consecrated—not directly, certainly, but through his mediation—via a Waldensian bishop, who, they believed, was in the pure succession.

This is yet another reason too why Lorenzo Valla's exposure of the legend of Pope Sylvester was, in Velenský's argument, so important. On the one hand, the Donation of Constantine delineated the period at which the pure Church disappeared. On the other hand, it was clear from the fact that the story of Sylvester was a forgery that the process of secularisation in the Church which had begun at that time could not be explained away as God's will (or as a vision granted to Peter, as the legend had it[100]), with the result that, in both cases, a pure succession had to be traced back to the *ecclesia primitiva* before Sylvester.

In Velenský's treatise, however, the theme of the apostolic succession apparently played only a very subordinate part. He makes only a few scornful remarks about it: "They say that they have taken the place of the leading apostle and that they have therefore to transfer his inherited power to each other". It is, however, possible to defend the argument that it was precisely because of his critical attitude towards the apostolic succession that enabled him to reject the papacy, the latter, in his opinion, lacking a pure succession. On the other hand, however, it has to be pointed out that Velenský's attitude was to some extent ambivalent. He tries to prove that the Petrine tradition was not lawful and that this therefore deprives the apostolic succession of its basis. The apostolic era in a much wider sense, however, forms an entirely different basis and this can be obtained via the Eastern Church or the Waldensians. Velenský appears to accept this second line of succession, if we consider the emphasis that he places on the corruption in the Western Church and the need for any possible succession

---

[100] Ignaz von Döllinger: *Die Papstfabeln des Mittelalters* (1890[11]), reprinted Darmstadt (1970), pp. 61–125.

to proceed outside the official *romana ecclesia*. He does not, however, make any clear statement about the meaning of this succession or the need for it in the Church, with the result that his attitude towards this subject is like that of the Brethren generally, indecisive. There is also another undoubted reason for this ambivalence on Velenský's part and that is his humanism. A historical investigation into the origins of the various views about the apostolic succession attracted him more than making statements about the need for such a succession within the Church.

Roundabout 1525, that is, five years later, the author who inspired Velenský, Krasonický, stated, in his Treatise against Cahera,[101] "that no value should be attached to the external succession, indeed that it is even necessary to ask whether this can be found at all in the Church. And certainly not in the Catholic Church, since Peter was probably never in Rome". It is not really possible to say whether Krasonický thought in this case of Wyclif's distinction between *de iure* and *de facto* priesthood, but what can certainly be said is that the term "external succession" is used by Krasonický in a very obscure way. If it is not possible to express clearly how a spiritual succession is able to continue, the result will be that the term cannot be applied, in very much the same way as it proved impossible to find any marks which would serve to distinguish the concept of the *universitas praedestinatorum*. The use of the term "external succession" (as well as its ultimate rejection) is certainly not satisfactory, if we bear in mind that the Brethren eventually accepted the practice of consecrating bishops and followed a line of succession via the Waldensians, rather than choosing to have a *de facto* office (as a function) based on the universal priesthood of all believers. Finally, it should be noted that the term is nowhere to be found in Velenský's writings.

5. *The Bible as the Sole Authority*

The fact that Velenský was more inclined to investigate the subject from the historical and analytical point of view than from the standpoint of the Bible should not lead us to believe that the latter was not the ultimate authority for him. The very opposite is true—although his historical analysis led him inevitably to the *ecclesia primitiva*, the

---

[101] Text in Goll, *op. cit.* and a summary in Müller, *op. cit.* Why Krasonický expressed himself in this treatise more cautiously ("probably") than he did in his letter to Ždarský and Hasištejnský is not possible to explain.

New Testament data about the apostolic Church functioned in his case as the supreme authority. It has to be admitted, of course, that he usually quotes biblical texts as proofs in his historical analysis and uses them far less as authoritative statements to support his Christian convictions, thus showing that he was a follower of Janov rather than of Wyclif. On the other hand, however, Scripture is the only material that he uses as proof. It provides as it were the foundation for the conclusions that he reaches by means of historical analysis.

Which, then, has the higher status in Velenský's thinking and reasoning—the historical method or the authority of the Bible? In any attempt to answer this question, a distinction has to be made between the order of sequence and the order of precedence of the arguments used. In Velenský's order of sequence, historical research certainly precedes any appeal to the authority of the Bible. In his order of precedence, however, the biblical data have the last and indeed the only word as far as Velenský is concerned. There can be no doubt about this in view of the number of times that he quotes the *verba Christi* or the *lex Christi* as the supreme authority. Even in the very first line of the foreword to his treatise, almost as though his aim were to express his order of precedence in the sequence that he proposed to follow, Velenský makes a basic statement of principle: "There is no more atrocious form of superstition than that which has crept into Christianity through the activity of the Antichrist—the denial of Holy Scripture".

This raises the question as to the relationship between the Scripture and the Church. The Bohemian reformers recognised the truth of Augustine's statement: *Ego evangelio non crederem nisi me auctoritas ecclesiae commoveret*. But the *ecclesia* which has *auctoritas* must have been the *congregatio praedestinatorum*, the members of which understood the true spiritual meaning of Scripture, and not the *ecclesia romana*, in which the real significance of the Bible had been hidden beneath anti-Christian traditions. The Bohemian reformers therefore concluded that the Church of the Antichrist had once again to be made subject to the norms of the gospel.

The threefold doctrine of the coming of the Antichrist, the pure proclamation of the gospel and the second coming of Christ, in which the second, the proclamation of the gospel, had a twofold intention —both liberation from the Antichrist and (partly through this) preparation for the coming of Christ—was, of course, also taught by Milíč. As the Church became "poisoned" (to use Nicholas of Dresden's term) at all levels by the presence of the Antichrist, it became less and less possible to attribute any *auctoritas* to this visible Church, with the result that this authority was eventually assumed by the invisible Church of true believers.

Insofar as Velenský was completely within this tradition of the Bohemian reformation, he was able to make use of the biblical proof, in opposition to the exegesis of numerous authors in the Church since the time of Pope Sylvester, but in accordance with that of the Hussites and the Brethren. This biblical proof was moreover necessary to him as the basis from which he developed his ideas.

The way in which he used the Bible was also of course to a very great extent determined by the nature of the subject itself and the sources drawn upon. In his foreword to the *Petrum Romam non venisse*, Velenský was able to demonstrate his own particular scientific method, namely from an analysis of the contemporary situation in Bohemia, he concluded that the Antichrist was reigning in the Church. He further concluded that the rule of the Antichrist had been repelled by two combattants, in the first place, Luther, who had opposed the authority and the value of the papacy from a fundamentally theological point of view, and in the second place Valla, who had proved that the attribution of secular power to the pope was the result of a falsification of history.

It was, however, also necessary to carry on the battle in one more field if the primacy of the pope was to be completely eliminated. It had therefore to be demonstrated on the basis of data drawn from the apostolic era that the papacy was not lawful because Peter, whose episcopacy in Rome was regarded as fundamental, had never been in that city. Biblical evidence was required for this subject and this method and Velenský therefore states at the end of his foreword what his "manner of fighting" was: "I take my *militia* from Holy Scripture". It is clear from this, as it had already been made clear in his commentary on Erasmus' *Enchiridion*, that Velenský had been sufficiently influenced by the Bohemian reformation after the injection made by Wyclif and by the biblical humanism of Erasmus and Faber Stapulensis to be able to go back critically to the New Testament text stripped of all the traditions of the Church and at the same time to take the Bible as his point of departure and final authority.

In this perspective, it is possible to understand Velenský's two central arguments—his *argumentum e silentio* and his thesis that what cannot be found to have a biblical basis cannot be accepted as an *articulus fidei*.

The *argumentum e silentio* ("We may therefore conclude that Peter was never in Rome, since Holy Scripture is silent about this") can only be accepted if the Bible is used as the absolutely exclusive norm of truth. Tradition, after all, provides many arguments that can be employed to defend Peter's sojourn in Rome and not all of these are criticised by Velenský as being contradictory and therefore unreliable. This is why those who opposed Velenský later on and who recognised not only Scripture, but also tradition as the norm of truth were not convinced by this *argumentum e silentio*. They did not accept that there was a silence here. In other words, in opposition to Velenský's argument that it was only what was explicitly prescribed by the Bible that was legitimate and normative, his adversaries took their stand on the basis of the traditional canonical adage that everything that was not emphatically rejected by the Bible and that had been accepted by the Church, through the activity of the Holy Spirit, could be legitimate and normative.

In this context, it is important to note that Velenský was no longer able to use his *argumentum e silentio* in those cases (as in his seventeenth *persuasio*) where he was himself suggesting where Peter and Paul might have died. The silence of the Bible as a norm by which certain data could be eliminated acts in such cases against Velenský's own argument, with the result that such passages are among the weakest in the whole of his treatise.[102]

The Catholic authors of the sixteenth century responded to the challenge of the reformation and once again raised the question of the authority of Scripture and the related question of the part played by tradition. They stressed that history itself showed that the Bible could be interpreted in different ways. Imitating Erasmus, who asked in his *De libero arbitrio* (col. 1219): *quid opus est interprete ubi dilucida est scriptura? Si tam dilucida est, cur tot seculis viri tam excellentes hic caecutierunt, idque in re tanti momenti, ut isti videri?*, Eck stated[103] that, if the Bible was so clear in its intention, it was very unlikely that the true meaning had not been recognised for so many centuries and had only been understood at the time of the reformation. Pighius also made the celebrated statement that Protestants used the Bible *velut nasus cereus, qui se horsum illorsum et in quam volueris partem trahi, retrahi, fingique facile permittit.*[104] In his book *L'Élément historique dans la controverse*

---

[102] Luther's rejection (*sed non evincit*; see p. 139) may therefore also be partly based on this contradiction. He wrote, after all—in his treatise against Emser (see p. 141)—that Peter may have come to Rome after spending time in Jerusalem and Antioch.

[103] *Enchiridion locorum communium adversus Lutherum et alios hostes Ecclesiae* (1525), fo 35rv.

[104] *Hierarchiae ecclesiasticae assertio* (Cologne, 1538), fo 80r.

*religieuse du XVI*ᵉ *siècle*,¹⁰⁵ Pontien Polman provided a survey of the many authors who expressed themselves in this way and concluded that all of them in one sense or another believed that the one single cause of confusion in the Church of their own times was the practice of appealing exclusively to the authority of the Bible. The various subjective interpretations have to be subjected to a supreme authority and this can only be the Church, in which the Holy Spirit is active. In any attempt to define more precisely the way in which the Church operates as an authority in the matter of interpretation, great authority has to be ascribed not only to the pope and the councils of the Church, but also to the Fathers. The contradictions that are present in the patristic writings have, of course, been borne in mind, but, as Polman says, *ils font la distinction entre les Pères séparément et les Pères pris collectivement*. The unanimity of the Fathers, then, is of decisive importance in the interpretation of the Bible. Because they took this point of view, Velenský's opponents remained unconvinced by his list of contradictions in the writings of authors in the Church (given in his first persuasio) and were unable to accept his *argumentum e silentio*.

The fact that this *argumentum e silentio* prevailed in the case of Velenský himself can be traced back to a combination of considerations. Because of his humanism, he felt impelled to go back to the sources that were scientifically the most reliable, since they had been written by (Peter's) contemporaries. Because of his background of Bohemian Hussitism, he was unable to recognise the falsified tradition of the Church as a source of truth. (He regarded what the *ecclesia romana* called the activity of the Holy Spirit as the influence of the Antichrist.) Finally, because of the biblicism with which he had become acquainted in the Bohemian reformation and with which he was connected, he could let only the Bible have the last word.

In addition to these three reasons, Velenský also believed that the Roman Church had traditionally and wrongly tried to base *articuli fidei* on data taken from the post-apostolic period. There was, he argued, no need for Christians to believe in these data, because only what God himself had said in Holy Scripture called for faith: "It is not obligatory either for theologians or for the Church to believe in those things that are not derived from Scripture" (*persuasio* I). The "Roman tyrants", however, had made *fidei articulos* of these things, "so that what cannot be proved must nonetheless be believed".

What is remarkable in this context is that, in criticising the emergence and functioning of tradition in the Church in this rather crude way, Velenský was clearly taking no notice at all of the debates that had

---

¹⁰⁵ pp. 284–298.

taken place in conciliarism.[106] The conciliarists had also judged the *humanae traditiones* which had originated among the canonists very critically and had recognised that "not everything handed down by the Church belonged to the necessary truths of faith". They had also placed this criticism positively at the service of a renewal of the Church as a hierarchy of clergy. There is no indication anywhere in Velenský's writings that he was familiar with the concerns of the conciliarists. Even if he was aware of them, he was presumably not attracted by them. His reasoning is based on the simple combination of the three themes outlined above. Above all, he was convinced that authority could only be attributed to an article of faith if the dogma expressed in it did not go back to the time when the Church was in decline, but was traceable to the New Testament. If it went back to this source, it could be "proved". It should, however, be noted that even here Velenský does not reject his scientific approach through historical analysis—he stresses that the authority of the article of faith is based on the fact that it can be historically proved.

The value and significance of the article of faith, then, were quite different for Velenský than they were for the Lutherans. A few years later, Luther wrote that the article of faith was concerned with a necessity for salvation and that it was not really relevant whether or not a historical datum which could be proved was at the basis of it: *Wie wol ichs halt, S. Peter sey zu Rom gewesen, wolt ich dennoch nit drauff sterben als auff eyn artickel des glaubens.*[107] Velenský, on the other hand, was concerned not with the certainty of salvation, but rather with whether or not a statement about faith was historically reliable. This contrast between Velenský's position and Luther's can be expressed even more precisely—the ultimately decisive factor in the case of the former was rational proof; in the case of the latter it was faith seeking the certainty of salvation. In the case of both the Bible was the only ultimate authority, but whereas Scripture had above all a rational authority for the Bohemian humanist, it was for the German reformer a source for certainty in faith. Here too, then, it is clear that Velenský had a greater spiritual affinity with the early Bohemian tradition and with humanism than with the religious tradition of reformation which was handed on from Wyclif and the Bohemian Brethren to Luther.

This is, of course, the most important reason of all why Luther

---

[106] G. H. M. Posthumus Meyjes, *op. cit.*, especially pp. 264–267. The quotation will be found on p. 267.

[107] In his *Antwort auf das ... Buch Bocks Emsers* (see p. 141).

remained unconvinced by the *Petrum Romam non venisse*. It is undoubtedly possible to make an attack on the papacy which is much
more radical than that made by Velenský in his historical investigation.
This attack, which Luther himself made, is based on the fact that the
papacy is not necessary for salvation, a fact which clearly marked the
end of the primacy of the pope according to the Romam view. Luther,
in attacking the papacy from this vantage point, combined the *argumentum e silentio* with the necessity for salvation of the article of
faith, claiming that Peter may perhaps have been in Rome, but, since
the Bible is silent about this, the man who does not believe it cannot be
called a heretic, because he is not violating the word of God in this
instance. The Catholic defender of the papacy, John Cochlaeus, said
of this conclusion drawn by Luther: *Certe nisi hanc eis clavam eripiamus,
labefactabant protinus omne fundamentum nostrum.*[108] Our inevitable conclusion too is that, despite his own conviction that he would deal the
final blow to the primacy of the pope as an expression of the Antichrist, after the attacks made by Lorenzo Valla and Luther, with his
historical proof that Peter had never been in Rome, Velenský did not
in fact succeed in shaking the foundations of the Roman Church.

6. *Scientific Research*

Throughout this book, we have seen again and again how "scientifically" Oldřich Velenský investigated his sources and how clearly his
education as a humanist is revealed in this scientific research. In this
section, we shall attempt to support this claim with further evidence.

If we look at fifteenth century humanism as a whole, we are bound
to affirm that the aesthetic form of humanism which had emerged in
Italy as a Renaissance movement changed roundabout the middle of
the century into a philological and critical movement, with which the
name of Lorenzo Valla was closely associated. The aim of philological
research was above all to obtain certainty regarding the texts of
writings that had been handed down, because that certainty *(certitudo
principiorum)* could give access to the truth.

In Italy, this new tendency was certainly well received, but those
who followed it became too preoccupied with the search for a synthe-
sis between Plato and Stoicism on the one hand and Christian thought
on the other. In Europe north of the Alps, however, intensive research

---

[108] See p. 144.

was conducted into the biblical sources and the Fathers of the Church. This was not simply an objective scientific investigation, but was something that formed an integral part of the life of faith. Among the most important representatives of this biblical humanism were Faber Stapulensis, John Colet, Thomas More and Erasmus. Stapulensis and Erasmus wrote treatises in which they used the method of textual criticism developed by Lorenzo Valla with the purpose of making the Bible and the Church Fathers once again the source of a renewal of life and faith. Velenský followed the footsteps of these two great scholars. He clearly states that his sources in the *Petrum Romam non venisse* were Stapulensis' edition of Paul, Erasmus' edition of Lorenzo Valla's notes on the New Testament and the same author's own edition of the New Testament itself. He also made use of Jerome's commentary on the letters of Paul, which Erasmus had republished in a critical edition in 1516, and Erasmus' edition of Suetonius which appeared in 1517.

It was from these sources that Velenský took a number of facts and views about the dates of the New Testament epistles and the places from which they had been sent—data that he needed for his method of elimination—exegeses of passages which fitted into his own framework and several new ideas about documents belonging to the post-apostolic period which had been wrongly regarded in the Church's tradition as authentic. Not only was Velenský indebted to the work of Stapulensis and Erasmus for much of his own material, however —he was also sufficiently inspired by it to apply the same method of research to other texts.

A good example of this is his use of Jerome's treatise *De viris illustribus*, which is one of the most frequently quoted sources in the *Petrum Romam non venisse*. On the one hand, he cites Jerome as an authority; on the other, however, his attitude towards the Latin Father is critical and he often corrects him. For instance, he says that it is enough "to put one Jerome ... into the field against so many Lyras" as it is not necessary to send "a trained army against a great number of inexperienced troops" and he appeals to the authority of Jerome in order to refute a number of legends concerning Paul.[109] His comments on Philo[110] are entirely based on the *De viris illustribus*. In several passages, on the other hand, he rejects Jerome's data as unreliable, both in their details (an example of this is Jerome's wrong description of

---

[109] *Resp.* II and IV.
[110] *Resp.* VI and VII.

Paul's dwelling place in Rome as a *parva mansio*[111]) and as far as the main theme is concerned (Jerome stated that Peter came to Rome in the second year of Claudius' reign[112]).

This would seem to be a prejudiced selection, but on several occasions Velenský provides evidence of having examined Jerome's data critically, with the result that he was able, on the basis of his own investigation, either to agree or to disagree with Jerome. He added, for example, to Jerome's statement that the apostles held their meeting in Jerusalem eighteen years after the ascension of Christ[113] that "this is plausible, if the accounts in the book of the Acts are carefully examined". When, however, Jerome asserts that Mark wrote his gospel at the request of the brethren", Velenský comments[114] that Jerome said this "on the authority of Clement" and that this is wrong information, because "the books circulating under the name of Clement are, on the one hand, forgeries and, on the other, wrongly attributed to him". It is clear, then, that despite his great respect for this historian of the early Church—especially since Erasmus' edition of his work—Velenský was convinced that his own research should have the last word.

His attitude towards a celebrated historian of a much later period, Bartholomew Platina (1421–1481), a representative of Italian humanism, whose major work, *Opus de vitis pontificum* (1479), had been translated into Czech by Řehoř Hrubý with the aim of spreading the teaching of "popular humanism", was very similar. Velenský quotes and clearly agrees emphatically with Platina's statement:[115] "the confusion of the times, causing possible contradictions in the writing of history, must be taken into account, since nothing can for this reason be stated with certainty". Platina also wrote that Christians were safe up to the reign of Nero and Velenský notes that this is "sufficiently demonstrated".[116] All the same, he regards Platina's authority as having no more than a relative value and subjects it to careful examination. This is clear from a comment[117]—made in passing—about the historian's *Opus de vitis pontificum*, namely that it "makes use of the data pro-

---

111 *Persuasio* VIII.
112 *Persuasio* I.
113 *Persuasio* II.
114 *Persuasio* VI.
115 *Persuasio* I.
116 *Resp.* III.
117 *Persuasio* I.

vided by Orosius", who ought to have read the Acts of the Apostles and the letters of Paul more carefully![118]

The clearest example of all of Velenský's critical attitude, which enabled him either to agree with or radically to reject authorities in the Church, is the way in which he makes use of Nicholas of Lyra's postil, the *Postilla super bibliam*.[119] Lyra's notes on Rom. 16 are his authority for the statement that Paul was in Spain for ten years after his first period of imprisonment and that he returned to captivity in Rome afterwards.[120] In this, he declares his agreement with Lyra, since the same view is expressed by Stapulensis in his exegesis of Paul's letter. Velenský also used this place in Nicholas' postil as his source for Ambrose's statement about Narcissus[121] and Origen's dating of the letter to the Romans.[122] He also took John Chrysostom's exegesis of Jesus' lament over Jerusalem from Lyra's notes on Matt. 23. 34[123] and the postil on Philemon provided him with another of Chrysostom's exegeses.[124]

Velenský was able to agree entirely with Lyra's commentaries in these cases, but as soon as the Petrine tradition is discussed and Lyra says that: "the three years after which Paul came to Rome must be counted in the fourteen years after which he came there for the second time", Velenský strenuously opposes him. In this case, he declares that Lyra is "contradicted by so many good authorities" and Jerome's description obviously demonstrates "how clearly Lyra has gone astray".[125] He was also extremely sarcastic in his reaction to Lyra's notes on 1 Peter 5, that Rome is *figuraliter* described as Babylon. Here he says: [126]"Let Lyra play with his *figuris*". He then goes on to transpose the meaning of Lyra's postil, pointing out that, in the Apocalypse, Babylon is the seat of the Antichrist. He comments: "You see, then, what is produced by this *figurata interpretatio*—that it is permitted to fall away from this Babylon without being punished. Of what are we Bohemians therefore accused?". Once again, then, it is obvious that Velenský takes from his sources only what he believes

---

[118] *Persuasio* III.
[119] *Biblia cum glossa ordinalia. Nicolas de Lyra postilla* (ed. 1506, 1590, etc.).
[120] *Persuasio* X.
[121] *Persuasio* VI.
[122] *Persuasio* V.
[123] *Persuasio* XVII.
[124] *Persuasio* XI.
[125] *Persuasio* I.
[126] *Persuasio* II.

he can defend either as the result of his own research or by someone else's. He makes no appeal to authorities in the Church, but uses these as illustrative material for his own arguments.

He also approaches the source material in precisely the same way when he is discussing the data of the New Testament. On the authority of Stapulensis and Erasmus, he declares, for instance, that Rome was the place from which Paul sent his letters to the Philippians, the Galatians and the Ephesians.[127] In his fifth *persuasio*, however, where he has to give, within the framework of his thesis, evidence for the date of Paul's letters and the places from which they were sent, he provides an extensive argument of his own. He says in this context: "The second letter to the Corinthians was not written immediately after the first. For in the first letter, he (Paul) punishes the elder of the community and suggests that he should be removed from the unity of believers. According to the second letter, however, this man is received back into the community as a member after having confessed his guilt. If Paul wrote to the Thessalonians after all this, he must have come to Corinth a third time and composed his letter to the Romans there ..."

Velenský also provides similar arguments[128] with regard to the date and the place at which Paul wrote his second letter to Timothy. He argues that the author was at that time in prison and that he recalls in this letter his sufferings when he was previously in prison. It is therefore clear that he was writing from Rome, many years after his first sojourn in the city.

We have, moreover, already seen that Velenský does not accept everything uncritically from the books of his "teachers" with all the errors that this material may contain. A good example of this is found in his third *persuasio*, where he corrects Stapulensis' exegesis.

Velenský, we may conclude, put the principle of the humanists —a return to the sources—strictly into practice. It is understandable that he should have made mistakes when he did this, in view of the limited state of scientific knowledge at the time when he was living. There is, however, no doubt that Molnár was right when he described the *Petrum Romam non venisse* as *ein schönes Beispiel eines gelungenen Anlaufes zur historischen Kritik.*

---

[127] *Persuasio* VIII.
[128] *Persuasio* XII.

7. *Conclusions*

No one is ever completely original. Everyone's ideas are the result of influences that have come from the preceding generation or the environment and he may have imitated these unconsciously and uncritically or he may have reflected seriously about them. The greater the knowledge that a writer has of various traditions and views, the more clearly and frequently will traces of that knowledge be found in his work as expressions of those influences. These traces may be in the form of approval, rejection or correction. The author is independent insofar as he is able to select and correct on the basis of a view resulting from a critical examination of his sources.

In this sense of the word, Oldřich Velenský can certainly be called an independent writer, even though we would still insist on what we said at the beginning of this chapter, namely that Velenský did so much historical and exegetical research into other authors' works and made such extensive use of it in his own writing that he was not able to produce many new ideas of his own. It is, however, important at this stage to amend this statement in the following way. As a good humanist, he did not accept the scientific research carried out by others as authoritative, but he first checked it to be sure that it was reliable and only then assimilated it into his own argument as illustrative material. The most correct description of Velenský's practice in this instance is therefore that others provided him with a number of ideas. His work is characterised, both in form and in content, by his ability to select the sources available to him and, when necessary, to correct and supplement this material so that his own point of view emerges particularly clearly.

This is especially evident in the form of his treatise. He uses polemical material provided by Krasonický, but, unlike the latter, his composition is so clear and so conveniently arranged that the whole argument is much more convincing. Krasonický also employed the method of elimination, but the system that Velenský follows in his research is made quite clear by his division of his argument into *persuasiones*, each of which may begin with the statement that the passage to be discussed has later to be situated in time and may end with the conclusion that at that moment Peter was not in Rome. The author's addition of a second part containing *cavilli* or fallacious arguments to his treatise is, moreover, an excellent device, since this method makes it unnecessary for him to interrupt the logical sequence of the first part of the treatise containing the *persuasiones* by refutations of counter-arguments. In this way, these can be discussed separately (and at the same time presented in a clear arrangement).

In form and method, then, Velenský deals freely with his source. The same can be said about his attitude towards the material itself, in his treatment of which he is similarly independent. To a very great extent, for instance, he omits Krasonický's detailed discussion of legends, apparently in order to avoid distracting his readers from the main theme by all kinds of marginal questions. On the other hand, however, whenever it is essential to his subject to go into a legend, he discusses it, although he does so in a *cavillus* (because the legend—for example, the *quo vadis* story—is used as a counter-argument in the tradition of the Church). In an attempt to make the method of elimination even more effective, Velenský also adds his own exegesis to the material collected by Krasonický. If every possibility of a presumed sojourn by Peter in Rome is to be eliminated, it has to be possible to show by historical research that the apostle was also not in Rome in the last years of the reign of the Emperor Nero. And this can only be demonstrated by using data derived from the second epistle to Timothy, which is of a late date. A very striking factor too is that Velenský is more accurate than his teacher in mentioning his sources and that he takes trouble to verify the truth of Krasonický's argument by reference to recent scientific works.

Finally, it should be pointed out that Velenský also looked for the source on which Krasonický drew—Marsilio of Padua's *Defensor pacis*. This system, by which Velenský verified his sources, led him at least once—when it was most essential—to allow Marsilio's argument to prevail over Krasonický's. As far as the form alone of his treatise is concerned, then, we are bound to say that Velenský's attitude towards the material that he used was both independent and critical and that, as a humanist, he investigated his sources scientifically.

The same independent and critical attitude is also apparent from the content of the *Petrum Romam non venisse*. Velenský reveals himself here as a declared representative of the tradition of Matěj of Janov, with his purely historical approach to the subject. At the same time, however, he also assimilates the Wyclifian contribution to the reformation in Bohemia harmoniously into his argument. Kaminsky's thesis that Wyclifism predominated over Janov's doctrine in Hussitism cannot be applied in the case of Velenský. In his work, biblicism is completely absorbed into and interwoven with analytical historical research. He never gives the impression of trying to bring together two distinct trains of thought in his treatise. All the sources that he uses, whether he names them or not, and which are traceable to very different spheres —the literature of the Bohemian Brethren (Krasonický), Christian humanism (Erasmus and Stapulensis), pre-Hussitism (Janov) and Wyclifism (Nicholas of Dresden)—are so selected and arranged that together they form one single and well ordered argument. Velenský was never a mere compiler, but a man who contributed his own distinct view to the subject.

This original view can be described as follows. Krasonický had discovered a new way of refuting the belief that Peter had been a bishop of Rome with proofs derived from a process of historical investigation. This possibility was further developed by Velenský by means of a humanistic and scientific method, in which the specifically Bohemian protest against office as the foundation of the Church was furnished with new arguments. At the same time, however, this new possibility was placed by Velenský within the framework of earlier ideas about the Antichrist and the *ecclesia primitiva*, with the result that he was able to bring together in unity a great number of ideas and expectations that were current among the Bohemian reformers. Seen in this light, then, it is easy to understand why, according to Molnár, Krasonický a few years later called Velenský's treatise the model *par excellence* of how the primacy of the pope should be combatted[129] and why he did not in this context refer to his own work, but rather took over Velenský's corrections and additions to it!

The almost complete absence of any influence of the popular humanism of Bohemia in the *Petrum Romam non venisse* can be explained by the fact that the work, written in Latin, was not intended for the ordinary people of Bohemia, but was rather aimed at the intelligentsia of Europe. (It was perhaps partly for this reason that it was also published in Augsburg and Basle.) Comparisons with Hruby's commentary on Erasmus' *Moriae Encomium*, in which such an important part is played by the editor's exposition of the new science for the benefit of simple believers, are therefore not relevant, since this edition was published with quite a different intention. The Bohemian humanists, with their emphasis on the cultivation of the Czech language and the critical consciousness of the people, could not make any really

---

[129] A. Molnár: *Voyage d'Italie* (*ComViat*, 1962¹, p. 28) has pointed to a manuscript in the National Museum in Prague: VF 41, fo 59ᵇ,177.

substantial contribution to Velenský's special task, the denial of the Petrine tradition.

There can, of course, be no doubt that certain aspects of their writings inspired Velenský. Hrubý's claim, for instance, that the Bohemian people rediscovered the Christian truth before Erasmus certainly stimulated Velenský. It is important to note in this context, however, that Velenský substantiates this argument by using his sources, whereas Hrubý provides no argument to support his claim. The importance of Všehrdý and Hrubý here is that they brought the attention of their younger contemporary to Erasmus. For the same reason, it is not so relevant to compare Velenský's commentary on and foreword to Erasmus' *Enchiridion* with his *Petrum Romam non venisse*. It goes without saying that both documents contain several expressions, formulae and examples in which the same words are used. Both works were, after all, written at the same period and the sphere of interest and political activity in the Church within which Velenský was moving at the time must have had an influence on his choice of words and examples. We are, however, also bound to say of Velenský's edition of Erasmus' *Enchiridion* that the intention was quite different—that of educating the ordinary believers in popular humanism.

It is certainly beyond dispute that Velensky's other works must be taken into consideration as a background to the *Petrum Romam non venisse*. They point to the way along which Velenský travelled to reach his major work. At the same time, however, they also show that the *Petrum Romam non venisse* is not simply the end of a process of growth in Velenský's thinking—all the themes that occur in the preparatory phase recur in a radical form here—but also that Velenský had clearly not found the really effective method of fighting until he came to write this main work, namely the historical proof that Peter had never been in Rome.

Although Velenský's attention was brought to this method by Vavřinec Krasonický, his scientific assimilation of the material, his critical way of correcting and supplementing it and his skill in fitting the results of this research work harmoniously into the framework of the Bohemian traditions resulted in a treatise that heralded a new phase in the struggle against the papacy. The fact that, at this new stage of the struggle, hardly any part was played by Velenský's suggestions regarding the place where Peter and Paul were martyred is a clear illustration of the fact to which attention has already been drawn, namely that he did not apply his critical method to that part of his argument. The way in which the treatise was to continue to have an effect on the debate within the Church was precisely because of this to reveal the weak spot in his argument.

CHAPTER FOUR

THE REACTIONS OF VELENSKÝ'S CONTEMPORARIES

1. Luther

In a letter[1] to Spalatinus, dated 3 February 1521, Luther wrote that a *iuvenis eruditus e Bohemia* had given him a book in which the author had tried to prove, with eighteen *coniectures* that *S. Petrum nunquam venisse aut fuisse*[2] *Romam*, but that he was not convinced by these arguments *(sed non evincit)*. Despite the fact that the author's reasoning left him unconvinced, Luther very soon took over one part of the argument, namely that Peter could not have been a bishop in Rome for twenty-five years, as was generally asserted in the tradition of the Church. Only a few weeks after writing this letter, on 29 March 1521, he published a treatise against Jerome Emser entitled *Antwort auf das überchristlich, übergeistlich und überkünstlich Buch Bocks Emsers*.[3] In one chapter, *Von der Papisten Unfleiß*, Luther develops the thesis that the tradition concerning Peter's twenty-five years in Rome as bishop must be a lie because it is in conflict with the biblical data. It is clear that Luther did not originate this theme or the arguments supporting it, but that he had taken it from Velenský's *Petrum Romam non venisse*, since he had never before contested the Petrine tradition with arguments of this kind in any of his previous writings. Indeed, no questions had even been raised about the length of Peter's stay in Rome in the disputation at Leipzig in 1519. An even more convincing proof of Luther's dependence on Velenský in this case is that the arguments used in his treatise against Emser occur in the same order as those in the *Petrum Romam non venisse*. Writing at the end of the last century, Martin Spahn[4] was therefore quite right when he said *daß Luther ... seinen Angriffsstoff gegen Emser hat geschöpft* out of Velenský's treatise.

Luther opens his chapter with the assertion that the false tradition concerning Peter had already been in existence for more than a thousand years: *Auch S. Hieronymus ist yn dissen yrthumb gefuret. Szo gar zeyttlich haben die Papisten angehaben zu liegen, und so fort an die lügen von*

---

[1] WA *(Briefwechsel)* II, p. 375.

[2] G. Veesenmeyer, *op. cit.*, has suggested that Luther "made an error here; what he wanted to write was: *venisse Romam aut ibi passum fuisse*".

[3] WA, 7, p. 672 ff.

[4] M. Spahn: *Johannes Cochlaeus* (Berlin, 1898).

eynem auff den andern geerbet und gemehret. Like Velenský, then, Luther
also takes as his point of departure the unreliability of the early
Fathers of the Church as authorities in this historical question and the
consequent employment by later historians in the Church of doubtful
sources in their appeal to patristic authorities. Like Velenský too,
Luther therefore goes back to the New Testament data, which lead
him to a conclusion which is different from that reached via the tradition of the Church.

Luther then repeats the argument found in the *Petrum Romam non
venisse*, that John the Baptist appeared in the fifteenth year of the reign
of the Emperor Tiberius (Luke 3) and, *wie wol nit eygentlich yemant weiß,
wie lange sie geweret hatt, lassen wirß doch bey gemeyner rede bleyben, daß
Christus vierdhalb jar gepredigt hatt,* in other words, until the nineteenth
or twentieth year of Tiberius' reign. After this, Tiberius reigned for
another four years. After him Gajus four years, Claudius fourteen and
Nero fourteen years. This means that, between the twentieth year of
Tiberius' reign and the last year of Nero's, thirty-six years elapsed (and
at the end of this time Peter was presumably put to death by Nero).
If, then, Peter's stay of twenty-five years in Rome had commenced in
the fourth year of Claudius' reign, there would be another eleven
years (calculated from the time of Christ's ascension) in which he
might have been in Jerusalem and Antioch. Paul, however, writes in
Gal. 1 that he saw Peter for the first time in Jerusalem three years
after his conversion (which could only have taken place at the earliest
four years after the ascension) and then again fourteen years later. *Das
seyn zusammen achtzehen jar, die alleyn S. Paulus Petro zu Hierusalem gibt.
Wer weiß, wie lange er darnach blieben ist? Zu den achtzehen odder vielleicht
zwentzig jaren thu die sieben jar zu Antiochen und die XXV jar zu Rom,
so wirt S. Peter ym sechs odder sieben und vierzigsten jar nach Christus hymel-
fart gecreutzigt seyn von dem keyszer Nero, wilcher zehen jar zuvor, als ym
sechs und dreussigsten, todt gewesen ist.* Luther's conclusion is that those
who rely on human doctrines and neglect the teaching of the Bible
are bound to come to such nonsense.

Making use of Velenský's polemical method, Luther goes on to
affirm that, whereas some Christians maintain that Peter went to Rome
in the fourth year of Claudius' reign, others say that he went there in
the second year. Both are wrong, however, Luther insists, because,
according to Acts 18, Claudius drove all the Jews out of Rome. *Wie
kund denn S. Peter unter Claudio gen Rom komen haben? ... Kurtz umb,
unbestendiger und ungewisser historien hab ich nit gelesen denn von S. Peters we-*

sen zu Rom, das auch viel seyn, die da offentlich frey sagen, S. Peter sey nie gen Rom kummen.

This last, radical conclusion is not Luther's own. He preferred to assume that Peter was in Rome, but he could not regard it as an article of faith in view of its uncertainty: *Wie wol ichs halt, S. Peter sey zu Rom gewesen, wolt ich dennoch nit drauff sterben als auff ein artickel des glaubens.* We only have to believe, Luther insists, *on was uns Got yn der Schrift zu glauben hat gepotten.* This means, however, that the teaching about the papacy *yn dreck und sand ist gesetzt,* since, if it is not necessary to believe that Peter was in Rome, *so ist auch nit nott zu glauben, das der Babst seyn stuel erb und Babst sey.*

It is clear from this why the conclusion reached by Luther the theologian was different from that to which Velenský came via his historical analysis. For Luther, the important question was whether it was necessary for salvation to recognise the papacy. If this was not made explicit in Scripture, the answer had to be that it was not necessary to salvation, even though it might appear from other data that Peter was in fact in Rome. The historical basis was not of decisive importance. The only ultimate criterion for Luther was whether the Bible had anything to say about God's intention in this matter.

Luther's point of view emerges very clearly at the conclusion of his argument, where it also becomes apparent why he said that he was not convinced by Velenský's reasoning *(sed non evincit).* He supplies several possible reasons for defending Peter's sojourn in Rome: *Ich denck aber, das yemand vielleicht gesagt oder geschrieben hab, Sanct Peter sey nur nach dem XXV jar gen Rom kummen, und das haben denn etlich vorstanden, er sey XXV jar zu Rom gewesen.* He may (as Paul claims) have been, after eighteen years in Jerusalem and seven years in Antioch, in Rome for another eleven years, after which he may indeed have been crucified in the thirty-sixth year after the ascension during the reign of Nero.

It is evident from the very fact that he suggests this that Luther did not follow Velenský to the end in his method of elimination. He did not, for example, make use, as Velenský did, of the exegesis of the second epistle to Timothy and the end of the Acts of the Apostles as proof that Peter was not in Rome at the time of Nero. Luther's ultimate conclusion, however, was that it *eyn yrthumb ist, das er ym dritten odder vierten jar Claudii gen Rom kommen sey.*

Luther remained reticent all his life with regard to the question as to whether Peter ever went to Rome. In a *Tischrede*[5] of 1 August 1537,

---

[5] WA *(Tischreden)* III, No. 3620 (pp. 461–462).

he said, for example: *Ego nescio, an Petrus Romam venerit, quia historiae varietas me absterret.* In 1545, he said:[6] *Wie wol hie sind etlich gelerten, die wollen, das S. Peter nie gen Rom sey kommen. Und solt den Babst sawr werden, sich zu wehren wider solche Schrifft. Ich will hierin nicht Richter seyn, S. Peter sey da gewest oder nicht.* Finally, in January 1546, he said once again:[7] *Paulus ist gen Rom komen, ob aber S. Peter hinkomen und zu Rom gewesen sey, das weis ich nicht.*

This uncommitted attitude on Luther's part can be explained by the fact that he was essentially not interested in the problem. His view that the papacy was not necessary for salvation was in no way influenced by whether or not it was possible to prove that Peter had been Bishop of Rome. He was swayed more by theological than by historical arguments and this is the essential difference between him and the *iuvenis eruditus e Bohemia*, who regarded the papacy as overthrown as soon as its historical basis had been undermined.

Luther's refusal to make any radical statements as to whether the tradition concerning Peter's sojourn in Rome was reliable can also be found in the circle of his collaborators and disciples. In the *Chronica durch Magistrum Johannem Carion* (fo. 82b), which was edited by Melanchthon and published in 1532 in Wittenberg, we read, for example: *Zu zeiten Neronis ist Sanct Petrus der Apostel zu Rom gecreutziget.* Two years later, *Ein kurtzer auszog aus der Cronica Naucleri* was published in Magdeburg, in which the author, Nicholas Amsdorf, said that Peter may have come to Rome in the fourth year of Claudius' reign, but that that was uncertain (fo. 2v). Robert Barnes, the author of the first Lutheran history of the popes, the *Vitae Romanorum pontificum quos papas vocamus*, which appeared in 1536 in Wittenberg with a foreword written by Luther himself, insisted that Peter had been Bishop of Rome for twenty-five years (fo. B). He was, however, acquainted with the fact that *quidam negant Petrum venisse Romam*, a denial based, among other things, on controversy between authors in the Church: *Quidam dicunt Petrus (ut Orosius) primo anno, quidam secundo anno Claudii, ut Platina, alii 4 anno Claudii eum Romam venisse dicunt.*

This partial or complete acceptance of the Petrine tradition in Lutheran circles has led R. Bäumer[8] to conclude in regard to Velenský's reasoning *daß es ... nicht um eine protestantische, sondern um eine böhmische Kritik handelte.*

2. *Cochlaeus*

Luther's viewpoint, as expressed in his treatise against Emser, was at once contested. The first man to oppose him was John Cochlaeus.[9]

---

[6] WA, 54, 254 (*Wider das Bapstum zu Rom von Teuffel gestifft*).
[7] WA, 51, 136 (*Zwo schöne und tröstliche predigt*).
[8] *op. cit.*, p. 23.
[9] Also known as John Dobneck (1479–1552).

This humanist and theologian, who had, among other things, been friendly with Ulrich von Hutten—whose attention he had drawn to the treatise on the *Donatio Constantini* published in 1440 by Lorenzo Valla—had been a deacon at the Liebfrauenkirche at Frankfurt am Main since 1518 and assisted the papal nuncio in various cases at the court of Charles V. In this last capacity, he took part in the Diet of Worms on 17 and 18 April 1521 and a week later, on 24 April, had a long and profound conversation with Luther. From that moment onwards, he was convinced that there was no way of reconciling the different points of view and he began to oppose Luther in numerous writings. As soon as Luther's *Antwort auf das überchristlich, übergeistlich und überkünstlich Buch Bocks Emsers* came into his hands, he brought it to the attention of the nuncio, Jerome Aleander.[10] He did this in two letters[11] written on 11 and 22 May 1521, in which he declared:[12] *Lutherum scripsisse in novissimo contra Emsero libro teuthonico S. Petrum non fuisse Romae XXV annis, imo dubium esse an unquam Romae fuerit.*

Aleander reacted quickly, summoned Cochlaeus to Mainz on 1 June and commissioned him to translate the text in question into Latin, *quo legere posset quidnam hoc esset monstri.*[13] The translation was soon finished and was sent ten days later by Cochlaeus to the inquisitor van Hoochstraten in Cologne, with the request that it should be sent on to the nuncio, who had in the meantime departed. In an accompanying letter,[14] he stressed that the treatise was dangerous *(molitur enim nebulo totum diruere papatum)* and asked whether the nuncio would persuade a scholar in France or the Netherlands to reply to Luther.

This was not, however, the end of the affair for the pugnacious Cochlaeus. Between 2 and 9 June (on the same days, in other words, that he had been translating Luther's text for Aleander), he had written a treatise of his own as a defence, in which he had assembled all kinds of proofs of Peter's sojourn in Rome. He sent this treatise on 19 June to Pope Leo X, asking for his consent to publish it.[15] If any alteration had to be made to the text, he declared, he would accept it, since what was at stake was not his own cause, but a defence of the papacy. He

---

[10] † 1542; Aleander was librarian at the Vatican and from 1520 onwards nuncio at the court of Charles V.

[11] W. Friedensburg: *Beiträge zum Briefwechsel der katholischen Gelehrten Deutschlands im Reformationsalter*, ZKG XVIII, 1897 (p. 106 ff).

[12] *ibid.*, p. 116.

[13] *ibid.*, p. 116.

[14] *ibid.*, p. 115.

[15] *ibid.*, p. 116.

also emphasised how important the subject was in his opinion: *Certe nisi hanc eis clavam eripiamus, labefactabant protinus omne fundamentum nostrum.*[16] There was, however, no answer from Rome.

The absence of a reply from Rome is possibly the reason why Cochlaeus' treatise was not printed until 1545, when it came from Weissenhorn's press in Ingolstadt, with the title *Assertio pro Hieronymo Emsero, contra Lutherum. De XXV annis S. Petri in Ecclesia Romana.* A German version of the treatise prepared by John Dietenberger,[17] however, appeared as early as 1524: *Ob Sant Peter zu Rom sey gewesen.*[18] Although both Cochlaeus and Dietenberger had been familiar with Velenský's treatise for some time when this German edition of Cochlaeus' text appeared, there is no hint in the latter (or even in the 1545 edition of Cochlaeus' treatise) of any reaction to Velenský's publication, despite the fact that there are sufficient points of departure here and there in the text for polemics against Velenský. For example, at Eii[19]—where the author provides a survey of the heresies of the Waldensians, the Picards, Wyclif and Hus—the author says: *aber diesen unsinnigen Zweifel* (that Peter may not have been in Rome) *hat keiner nie für bracht.* This is, of course, a clear reference to Luther's remark: *das auch viel seyn, die da offentlich frey sagen, S. Peter sey nie gen Rom kummen.* We are therefore bound to assume that the whole text of Cochlaeus' treatise was finished in June 1521, when Luther's treatise against Emser was still being disputed.

Veesenmeyer[20] was not of this opinion. He believed that Cochlaeus did not independently think up all the arguments used in his treatise against Luther, but that he employed the theses which John Fisher had used against Velenský in the treatise that had been published in the meantime, in October 1522 (*Convulsio calumniarum Ulrichi Veleni Minhoniensis*). Cochlaeus would, however, have been prevented by his own pride from admitting that he was dependent on Fisher and this is also why he ignored Velenský's treatise and made it appear as if he had himself thought up all the counter-arguments against Luther.

---

[16] *ibid.*, p. 116.

[17] 1475–1535. His biography was written by Herman Wedever: *Johannes Dietenberger. Sein Leben und Werke* (Freiburg, 1888).

[18] *Ob Sant Peter zu Rom sey gewesen. Antwort Doctor Jo. Cochlei. Auff Martin Luth. disputation, ob Sant Peter zu Rom sey gewesen. Durch Doct. Johann. Dieten. vertütscht* (Strasbourg, 1524).

[19] This and the following quotation have been taken from Wedever's version of the text, *op. cit.*

[20] *op. cit.*, p. 147.

Veesenmeyer's theory is, however, not tenable. Cochlaeus follows the order of Luther's argument in his attack against it, whereas Fisher discusses Velenský's *persuasiones*. What is more, as we shall demonstrate when we come to discuss another polemical work by Cochlaeus,[21] the latter was certainly inspired by Fisher's treatise, but his argument is elaborated entirely in his own way.

Since the original Latin edition of Cochlaeus' book was not published until after the first battle had been fought, it is obviously preferable to regard the German version as the contribution to the polemics. This is not only chronologically more correct—it also does no serious harm to Cochlaeus' contribution to the debate, as far as the content of his treatise is concerned. For, although the German version is in certain places more detailed than the Latin original—for example, especially in the presentation of the events in which Cochlaeus himself took part (his stay in Worms and Trier, for instance, where he met Luther), where Dietenberger is clearly including information that came to him by word of mouth—as soon as the arguments in the debate with Luther are mentioned, Dietenberger follows Cochlaeus' original text quite faithfully. This is why we may safely affirm that this is the Cochlaeus who spontaneously wrote his defence in June 1521 speaking.

The counter-argument can be divided into six different aspects. In the first place, Cochlaeus discusses Luther's thesis that the New Testament has nothing to say about Peter's having stayed in Rome. His reply to this is that there is a great deal in which Luther believes which is not to be found in Scripture—for example, the doctrine of the Trinity. He accuses Luther of contradicting himself: *Wir glauben —sagstu—der gemeinen Rede, dasz Christus gepredigt habe fierdhalb Jahr*; why, then, Cochlaeus goes on, do you not believe in the "common saying" that Peter was in Rome for twenty-five years? That is, after all, *viel allgemeiner bestätigt* than the length of Christ's ministry of preaching. About Peter's sojourn in Rome have written *einmüthlich und einmündig zugleichen die Schreiber der Historien ... auch die heiligen Doctores der Kirche Hireneus, Damasus, Eus., Hier., und viele andere treffliche hochgeachtete Lehrer.*

This proof of the reliability of Peter's stay in Rome on the basis of the unanimity of the witnesses was denied by Velenský, who provided detailed examples of the contradictions existing between the different

---

[21] See p. 149, 167.

witnesses. The fact that Cochlaeus overlooked this is a further indication that his text must have been finished when Velenský's treatise came into his hands.

In the second place, Cochlaeus disputes Luther's use of the New Testament data. His reply to Luther's statement that, if the tradition concerning Peter's sojourn in Rome is true, he could not have been so long in Antioch and Jerusalem, despite Paul's reference to the latter, is: *Deine Rechnung ist falsch, denn du sollst nicht wähnen, daß Sant Peter hat alle die Zeit zu Rom müßig gesessen, und nimmer keinen Fuß aus Rom bewegt, sondern ist dar und her gegangen, wo solchen Fürsten der Anfang des Glaubens und ander Noth erfordert hat.*

In the third place, Cochlaeus calls Luther's chronology into question. According to the "papists", Luther had cynically observed, Peter was eighteen years in Jerusalem, seven years in Antioch and then twenty-five years in Rome, after which he was crucified during the reign of Nero—but at that time Nero had already been dead for ten years! Cochlaeus' answer to this is that Luther *die verschiedenen Zeitpunkte, in welchen Petrus in der heil. Schrift gelegentlich einmal in Hierusalem und Antioch erwähnt wird, als dauernden Aufenthalt rechne.* When Luther does this, however, *zählt er närrisch.* Cochlaeus suggests therefore: *Siehe die Chronica Eusebii ein wenig baß an, so wirst du finden, daß St. Peter im fünften Jahr nach der Auffahrt des Herrn die Kirche in Antioch. gegründet habe.* What is more, Cochlaeus also affirms that Paul did not say, as Luther claims, that Peter was in Jerusalem for eighteen years. What he said was that he saw him there twice in eighteen years, *aber nicht daß er sei achtzehn Jahre allein blieben zu Hierus., als du fälschlich ihm zugibst.* Jerome, Cochlaeus declares—overlooking in this case Luther's statement that *S. Hieronymus auch ym dissen yrthumb ist gefuret*—is precise in the time that he gives for Peter's stay in Rome, saying that he was there from the second year of Claudius' reign until the last year of Nero's. During this time, Cochlaeus believes, Peter undoubtedly went quite often to Jerusalem—if the Jews went there every year at the Passove, why should Peter not have made the journey three or four times in twenty-five years?

This is a clear example of the fact that, contrary to what Veesenmeyer suggests,[22] Cochlaeus did not *mit Fishers Kalb gepflügt habe,* since Fisher agreed that Jerome had made an error in his dates. What is more, if, as Veesenmeyer also suggested, Fisher was really such a

---

[22] *op. cit.*, p. 147.

model for Cochlaeus, he would not have gone on appealing to Jerome in this pertinent way.

In the fourth place, Cochlaeus also questions Luther's sources and asks what witnesses he can bring forward against the Petrine tradition. He has not a single proof at his disposal, Cochlaeus states, that Peter was never in Rome. All that he says is that "there are many who say openly that he never came to Rome". Cochlaeus, who can bring forward names in support of his defence, challenges Luther to do the same: *Sag doch, wer sein die, welche es sagen? Warum nennst du sie nicht mit ihren Namen?*

Cochlaeus was, of course, wrong in thinking that Luther believed that Peter was never in Rome. This can probably best be explained by the shock effect produced by Luther's remark, apparently made in passing, but certainly made quite consciously, that there were "many" who defended the radical standpoint. Should we perhaps conclude from this that Cochlaeus suspected that Luther was himself one of those radical thinkers who believed that Peter was never in Rome? It is also clear from this that Cochlaeus was not at the time acquainted with Velenský's treatise. Why, if he had been familiar with it, would he call so insistently on Luther to name his sources of information?

In the fifth place, Cochlaeus adduces various interpretations of passages in Scripture not discussed by Luther. Quoting 1 Pet. 5. 13, he says—in complete contrast to Velenský's exegesis—that the "Babylon" mentioned in the text is the city of Rome. He also quotes the "prophecy of Christ" in the last chapter of the gospel of John, according to which Peter "will stretch out his hands" (John 21. 18), *das heißt gecreuzigt würde* and he asks when that prophecy was fulfilled.

In the sixth place, Cochlaeus uses historical arguments. He points out that Rome has been regarded throughout the centuries and by the whole Christian world as *Grab der Apostel* and as the Church taught by Peter. Luther alone, Cochlaeus claims, questions what has never been denied by any heretic, *weder Marcion, noch Montan oder Manichäer, auch kein Feind wie Cels., Porphir. und niemant.* According to Tacitus too, many Christians were martyred during the reign of Nero and who would believe *daß sie ohne einen Bischof gewesen seien?* If Peter was not that bishop, Cochlaeus insists, let Luther say who he was.

Another proof is provided by the existence of the Church in the Via Appia mentioned by Hegesippus and where pilgrimages have been made for centuries. Cochlaeus claims that he can also produce other evidence and asks what Luther can say against it. All that he can produce, apparently, is Paul's statement that he saw Peter in Jerusalem in the eighteenth year after the Lord's ascension. But how is he able to conclude from this that Peter had never previously been to Rome? *Ich habe dich zu Worms geschweigt im 21. Jahr, folgt daraus, daß du im 20. Jahr nicht zu Wittenberg gewesen sei? Es haben mich viele zu Rom gesehen im 18. Jahr, folgt darum, daß ich vor nicht zu Köll oder Nürnberg gewesen sei?.* It cannot be regarded as proof, Cochlaeus insists, that Luke does not report this fact, since there is a great deal that he does not report (for example, that Peter was in "Ponto or Bithinia", which is something that Peter himself tells us in his first epistle). The result is that nothing can be proved by the silence of the New Testament.

A survey of the contents of Cochlaeus' treatise brings us inevitably to the conclusion that, although the author's point of departure for his opposition to Luther was the latter's denial that Peter was in Rome for twenty-five years, the polemics are in fact concentrated on the statement *daß auch viel seyn, die da offentlich frey sagen, S. Peter sey nie gen Rom kummen.* Although Luther himself refused to make any decision as to whether Peter was in Rome or not, he nonetheless supported this statement with the argument that the Bible is silent about the Petrine tradition.

In his treatise, then, Cochlaeus was attacking through the person of Luther, the much more radical spokesman behind him. Shortly afterwards, he was to become acquainted with the work of this unknown author.

The fact that Cochlaeus first became familiar with Luther's view of Peter's episcopate in Rome and then became acquainted with Velenský's treatise —and therefore engaged in polemics in this order—is presumably the reason for the misunderstanding in Pontien Polman's exhaustively documented work, *L'Élément historique dans la controverse religieuse du XV*e *siècle.* Polman regarded Luther as the spiritual father of the contestation concerning Peter's twenty-five years' episcopacy and Velenský as the author who took this argument to a more radical level by denying in his *Petrum Romam non venisse,* which was published *un peu plus tard* (p. 153) than Luther's treatise against Emser, that Peter was ever in Rome.

It is also worth noting that Emser himself wrote a reply to Luther's treatise against him: *Quadruplica auf Luthers jüngst gethane Antwort, sein Reformation belangend* (1521). [23] Like Cochlaeus, he also provides detailed quotations from the Church Fathers in defence of Peter's twenty-five

---

[23] Text in E. L. Enders: *Luther und Emser. Ihre Streitschriften aus dem Jahre 1521* (Halle, 1891), pp. 129–183.

years' episcopacy. Emser mentions the *Quo vadis* legend, the accounts of the controversy between Peter and Simon Magus, the relics in Rome and, as scriptural evidence, 1 Pet. 5. 13, saying that "Babylon" must be a reference to Rome.

In the meantime, Aleander, who had left for the Netherlands, had still not reacted to Cochlaeus' letter. The latter therefore wrote once more, on 27 September,[24] to the nuncio, asking him whether he had received his translation of Luther's treatise. At the same time he also sent Aleander his treatise *Assertio pro Hieronymo Emsero*, which he had sent to the pope, and Velenský's treatise *Petrum Romam non venisse*, which had shortly before this come into his possession and which had revealed to him that it was precisely here that it was necessary to look for the source of the affirmation that Peter had never been in Rome (and certainly had not been there for twenty-five years). It was this Velenus who was meant by the statement "that there are many who say openly that Saint Peter never came to Rome".

Aleander confirmed in a letter written in October[25] that he had in fact received the translation and asked Cochlaeus to be patient. The latter, however, could not remain patient and began to write a defence against Velenský's treatise. A great deal of this work, *De Petro et Roma adversus Velenum Lutheranum*,[26] was written in January 1522. It was not published, however, until February 1525, when it was printed by Quentell in Cologne, and, since it only began to play a part in the debate from the time when it was published, it is better not to discuss the arguments that it contains here. Keeping to the chronological order of the polemics, we must consider the work of other authors first. It can, however, be said at this point that Cochlaeus himself published a part[27] of his treatise in German in 1537, with the title: *Von der Donation des Keysers Constantini, und von Bepstlichen Gewalt*.[28]

3. *Aleander*

Cochlaeus alarmed Aleander sufficiently to make him set to work without delay in his own sphere, that of Church politics. The papal

---

[24] W. Friedensburg, *op. cit.*, p. 123.

[25] *ibid.*, p. 126.

[26] *De Petro et Roma adversus Velenum Lutheranum, libri quatuor, Johannis Cochlaei, artium et sacrae Theologiae professoris egregii atque ecclesiae divae virginis Frankfordiēn Decani* (Cologne, 1525).

[27] Bii^r to Ci^v.

[28] *Von der Donation des Keysers Constantini, und von Bepstlichem Gewalt. Grundtlicher bericht aus alten bewerten Lerern und Historien. Auch etwas vom Laurentio Valla, vom Cypriano, vom Ireneo, Hieronym, etc.* (Cologne, 1537).

nuncio at once informed the Bishop of Strasbourg, William, Count of Hohenstein, and asked him to send a copy of Velenský's treatise in Latin and in German to Eberhard von der Mark, the Cardinal of Liège, so that the latter would be fully documented and able to present the matter to the emperor, Charles V, and discuss it with him.

The nuncio not only tried in this way to persuade the secular authorities to take action—he also brought the whole question to the attention of the Vatican. On 13 October 1521, he wrote a letter to the vice-chancellor, Medici,[29] in which he stated that the deacon at Frankfurt, Cochlaeus, had sent him a treatise in which it was asserted *quod Petrus nunquam fuerit Rome, imo etiam intus habetur Paulum non fuisse passum*. He also promised to send this treatise, which was, he said, greatly esteemed by the Lutherans, with his letter so that it would be possible to see in Rome that they were dealing with a "real Achilles". He would, he went on, have liked to spend the following winter in the *bibliotecha Pallatina*, a library that he knew so well, in order to compose a treatise *contra questo ribaldo libro*, but he had to remain at his post in order to combat the danger. A Catholic scholar should, he suggested, undertake to write a defence. He also wrote in his letter, with regard to the author of the treatise in question: *Esso libro ancorchè l'habbi titulo di un quidam* ... (and here a name must have been omitted; we have therefore to supply "Ulricho Veleno") ... *et intus quell lui se nomina Boemo*.

Aleander, however, thought himself that it was more probable that the author's identity would be found among the humanists of Germany or the Netherlands. In any case, he said, the style of the treatise made it clear that it had been written by someone educated in humanism. He was also able to be more concrete in his conjecture about the identity of the author: *quello amico*, whom he suspected was the author, "when he was taking breakfast with me last Sunday, praised the treatise very highly. When I observed that the contents were shameless, he flared up violently and insisted that I should point out one single error in the book. When, with the aid of quotations from St Paul, I at once named two very clear examples, he fell into great confusion and did not for long continue with the subject".

What is remarkable is that Aleander does not mention the name of the man whom he suspected was the author of the treatise anywhere

---

[29] T. Brieger: *Quellen und Forschungen zur Geschichte der Reformation. I. Aleander und Luther* (Gotha, 1884), No. 48 (pp. 268–271). P. Balana, *Monumenta reformationis Lutheranae*, 1884, also mentions this letter, but makes a number of corrections in it (p. 294).

in this letter. The reason may, of course, be that he was really a "friend" whom he did not want to attack directly and implicate with the Vatican. In that case, it might have been Erasmus, who studied with Aleander and shared his room in Venice in 1508 and who was living in the same district as Aleander in 1521, at the time of the controversy. (From the end of May, Erasmus was in Anderlecht; on 28 October he left the southern Netherlands, present-day Belgium, for Basle.) Another comment made by Aleander also points to Erasmus as the author: "that it is barbarous—*come dire in linguaggio Greco*—that such a famous man should conceal himself in silence". If indeed Erasmus was the author, in Aleander's opinion, this would explain why the latter did not fall in with Cochlaeus suggestion to ask a scholar from France or the Netherlands to reply to Luther's treatise against Emser, but rather passed the request on to Rome. If Erasmus was Luther's informant, it would have been a very delicate matter to find the right person to compose a reply to the treatise in question.

The nuncio was, however, not successful in persuading the Church authorities to act quickly in this matter. It was not until 1559 that Velenský's treatise appeared in the index of forbidden books compiled in the pontificate of Paul IV, his name being mentioned among the *auctores, quorum libri et scripta omnia prohiberentur*. Later, it appeared in the index of the Council of Trent (1564) among the books *primae classis*.[30] Bartoš[31] has quoted Jan Blahoslav, the Bohemian philologist and historian, who wrote in his *Grammatica česka*, which was published in 1571, that *huius nomen papistae in catalogo damnatorum scriptorum inter ficta nomina recensent*. The reason why the name Ulrichus Velenus Minhoniensis was included in the Venetian Inquisition which, in 1554, formed the basis for both these indices, under the heading of "pseudonyms", is probably because Velenský's first opponent, Cochlaeus, had already declared, with regard to the treatise, *nescio cuius filii terrae, qui se Velenum nominat*.[32]

It is clear from the fact that Velenský's treatise was not officially forbidden until the fifteen-fifties that the Church authorities were not really alarmed by Aleander's warnings. It is also possible that it was no longer necessary to forbid the book for some time because interest in it had receded after the initial violent polemics. The new German edition brought out in 1551 by Flacius Illyricus and the renewed inte-

---

[30] F. H. Reusch: *Der Index der verbotenen Bücher*, I (Bonn, 1883), p. 234.
[31] *Zapadlé dílko*, p. 4.
[32] *De Petro et Roma adversus Velenum Lutheranum* (Aiv).

rest in the treatise that resulted from this is the most probable reason why it was placed on the index. If this is the case, then the date of publication of the Italian edition of the *Petrum Romam non venisse*—1556— is even more remarkable, since it may perhaps indicate that its inclusion in the *index librorum prohibitorum* had quite the wrong effect!

4. John Fisher

Although Cochlaeus and Aleander were the first to take action against Velenský, the first theological work written against him was by John Fisher, the Bishop of Rochester. This English humanist, who was a friend of Erasmus, had been planning to publish this work as early as the spring of 1522, but publication was to some extent delayed by the state of war that prevailed—England's support of Charles V in the latter's struggle against the French king, Francis I. The work was, however, published in the autumn of 1522—the first edition of the *Convulsio calumniarum Ulrichi Veleni Minhoniensis* was printed by Willem Vorstermann of Antwerp on 30 October.[33] Despite the fact that communications had been made difficult by the war, a second edition was printed by Conrad Resch in Paris in 1525.

In his introduction, Fisher says that Velenský's book came into his possession thanks to *egregium virum dominum Tunstallem*. Since this churchman, Cuthbert Tunstall,[34] was particularly zealous in his search for forbidden books, this may mean that the *Petrum Romam non venisse* was already circulating as illegal reading in England in 1521.

Fisher's book is thoroughly scientific in its plan and intention. Following an introduction, it includes an *autorum catalogus, quorum testimoniis in hoc libello utitur, praeter sacras literas et rationes quas adducit*, in which thirty-nine Church authors are named. The literal text of Velenský's treatise is included in the sense that, after each *persuasio* and *cavillus*, there follows (for the sake of the readers) a *summa calumniae* prepared by Fisher and then the author's *responsio*. In each *responsio*, the course of the argument in the relevant persuasio by Velenský is closely followed, with the result that what emerges is a counter-argument which takes every aspect into consideration. Only Velenský's

---

[33] *Convulsio calumniarum Ulrichi Veleni Minhoniensis, quibus Petrum nunquam Romae fuisse cavillatur per Joannem Rossensem Episcopum, academiae cantabrigiensis cancellarium. Petrus fuit Romae.* A photomechanical reproduction of *Joannis Fisheris Opera* was made in 1967 in Farnborough (from the 1597 edition).

[34] Tunstall was born in 1474, became Bishop of London in 1522, was dismissed in 1531 by Queen Elizabeth and kept a prisoner in the Tower; he died in 1539.

foreword, which provides the best insight of all into his attitude, is not included by Fisher and therefore not disputed by him. We can only guess why Fisher did not consider this foreword.

As a result of Fisher's method, the sequence of subjects discussed is determined by Velenský's argument and above all by the latter's method of elimination. For this reason, the *Convulsio* opens with an examination of the question as to whether there is any contradiction among the historians about when Peter arrived in Rome. Fisher believes that, with regard to many events in the ancient world, there can be no agreement about dates and years: "This can be seen everywhere in Holy Scripture, to say nothing of profane historians". One example that he gives is the list of generations provided in Gen. 11 in the Hebrew text and the Septuagint and the version given in Luke 3. But, Fisher says, *quamquam tanta legatur in annorum numeris discrepantia, nemo orthodoxus de historiae veritate secum animo vacillat.* Another example is the existence of different interpretations of the vision of the "seventy weeks" in Dan. 9. Fisher here mentions Jerome's summary of the many divergent opinions in this case and says: *Et quamquam isti sic inter se disgladientur, Danielem tamen omnes vera scripsisse nihil haesitamus.* There is a similar difference of opinion regarding the date of Christ's death. The day given by Tertullian is different from that suggested by Ignatius or John Chrysostom. "But just as no one ever doubted for this reason that Christ died for us," Fisher insists, "so too does no one need to doubt, because different dates are given, that Peter was in Rome. What is more, these differences prove ultimately to be less important than one would expect. Jerome provides an exact calculation, showing that the apostles met together in council eighteen years after the Lord's ascension, that is, in the ninth year of Claudius' reign. This is not in conflict with the tradition that Peter was Bishop of Rome for twenty-five years, since Peter had already been in Rome for several years at the time of the council and travelled to Jerusalem for that occasion. Velenus' argument that we are bound to conclude from Claudius' edict against the Jews that Peter could not have been in Rome at that time is not valid. Peter was obedient to his mission and did not fear death. What is more, he was probably protected by friends in Rome. With regard to Jerome's calculation, which leads us to conclude that Peter was the Bishop of Rome for twenty-five years, there is no contradiction among the authors: *In hoc omnes consentiant, non Latini solum, verum etiam Graeci.*"

No conclusions can be drawn also from the omission of Peter's name from Paul's letters, although Velenus does draw such conclusions, Fisher points out. In his greetings, after all, Paul usually misses out those who are best known. In the first epistle to the Corinthians, for example, Paul mentions none of his friends, although he worked there for eighteen months. In the second letter, Stephen, Achaicus and Fortunatus are not named. There is no greeting for the bishop of the community in the letter to the Galatians, although there must have been a leader there. Only Euodia and Syntyche are mentioned in the letter to the Philippians and no mention is made of Bishop Archippus in the letter to the Colossians. The only conclusion that can be drawn from this, Fisher claims, is that Paul was not in the habit of greeting the *praefectos ecclesiarum* by name in his epistles.

The same can be said of the absence of any data concerning Peter in the concluding chapters of the Acts of the Apostles. All that Luke has to say about this period in Rome is that Paul proclaimed the gospel to all those who came to him in prison. He has nothing to say, Fisher points out, about "those who were in the Emperor's house" (although these are mentioned in the letter to the Philippians), about the letters written by Paul, about Paul's transference to the praetorium or about his defence. This is why it is impossible to draw any conclusion at all with regard to Peter from Luke's silence, Fisher states. What is more, he goes on, if we were to argue in the manner of Velenus, we would be able to claim that Peter was never in Antioch, simply because Luke does not mention this datum.

Fisher next deals exhaustively with Velenský's exegesis of Paul's letters to Timothy. The author's statement that everyone left him in the lurch at the time of his defence cannot be used as an argument for denying that Peter was ever in Rome, since Paul is referring here, Fisher points out, to his own servants. Peter was not one of their number and had his own work: *curam egit gregis sui*. Add to this that Paul was supported by the Holy Spirit and it is at once clear that Peter realised that he could not desert his flock for the sake of Paul. Furthermore, Velenus' argument that Onesiphorus would not have had to look for Paul for such a long time if Peter had been in the city of Rome in order to inform him is, Fisher insists, unacceptable, since Onesiphorus came from Ephesus and was therefore not known to Peter. In this context too, Fisher refutes Velenský's argument based on the correspondence between Paul and Seneca with the words: "Scholars dispute the authenticity of this correspondence. Erasmus regards it as false and that is enough for me".

Fisher gives a great deal of attention to Velenský's argument that the contradictory data concerning the date and place of Peter's death as a martyr lead inevitable to the conclusion that he did not die in Rome and that a more plausible assumption is that he was martyred in Jerusalem. In his reply, Fisher provides many examples showing the diversity of opinions regarding the date of Christ's death, at the same time pointing out that this has never resulted in a complete denial of the Saviour's death as such. He also says that, if there is any contradiction of this kind concerning the date and place of Peter's martyrdom, this should not be a reason for doubting the truth of his death as a martyr.

In reply to Velenus' supposition that he was martyred in Jerusalem, Fisher declares that no one—*Graecus aut Latinus, doctus aut indoctus*—ever thought of such a *mendacium*. As he has already said several times, he points out, no one has ever claimed that Peter suffered martyrdom during the reign of Vespasian, so that this possibility is excluded. The same also applies to Peter's death in Jerusalem—no one has ever made this claim either. After all, if Peter really died in Jerusalem, surely his grave would have been there?

Fisher also believes that Velenus was misinterpreting Scripture when he supported his argument with a quotation from Christ's words over Jerusalem "killing the prophets" and his inclusion of Peter among the prophets. In the first place, Fisher says that Christ mentions no name in this context. In the second place, however, it is not in any sense necessary to conclude from the statement that Peter and Paul were handed over to the Jews to be killed that they were martyred in Jerusalem, just as it does not follow from the statement *Christus a Romanis crucifixus erat* that *igitur Romae crucifixus*.

Fisher also attempts to show that Velenský is mistaken in his exegesis in other cases spread over the whole of his treatise. Peter was not going against his mission to work among the circumcised when he went to Rome. Did not Paul, the apostle to the gentiles, go first to the synagogue wherever he went? The figure known as Mark in the letter to the Colossians was certainly Peter's helper and the author of the gospel and not the same as the Mark Aristarchus of the epistle to Philemon. "Babylon" is also not an Egyptian city, but Rome, since it would be remarkable if, assuming that the *princeps apostolorum* went to Egypt, no author knew anything at all about it. A final example of the way in which Fisher corrects Velenský's exegesis is this—it cannot be concluded from Scripture that Christ will remain in heaven until he comes again at the last judgement. (Velenský used this argument to deny Christ's appearance to Peter in Rome.) Surely, Fisher asks, Paul says in 1 Cor. 9 and 15 that he has seen Christ? And above all, Christ is still *vere praesentem in altaris sacramento*.

Finally, it should be noted that Fisher's argument is weaker when, at the end of his treatise, he attempts to build up counter-arguments in reply to Velenský's *cavilli*.

Fisher does not, for example, succeed in refuting Velenský's argument based on the contradiction to which the latter pointed between Nicholas of Lyra and Jerome with regard to the time of Peter's coming to Rome. Despite detailed calculations and numerous quotations, he is bound to admit that Jerome made a mistake when he said that Peter went to Rome in the second year of Claudius' reign; a mistake, Fisher adds, "that was also pointed out by Bede".

The only objection that he is able to raise against Velenský's comment that the books of Dionysius the Areopagite were forgeries and could therefore not be used as proofs is that Erasmus rejected the authorship, but not the contents. The only argument that he can put forward against Velenský's assertion that Hegesippus could not have been a reliable witness because he could not have experienced what he described, since he came to Rome much later is, moreover, the rather naive defence that Hegesippus may nonetheless have written his book a long time before he came to Rome and that the very fact that Ambrose later translated his work into Latin must be regarded as proof that it was reliable.

A final example of the weakness of Fisher's arguments against Velenský's *cavilli* is his opinion about the truth of the Donation of Constantine. It is of no importance to him whether the declarations about this matter are authentic or false. What he regards as important is whether the matter itself is true or not. And, in his opinion, there can be no doubt—the territory over which the Church had authority was extended by the emperor's gift.

Fisher's treatise ends with a *totius operis conclusio*, in which the traditional view of the Church is interpreted. The three fundamental data, Fisher says, are firstly that Peter is *primus inter apostolos a Christo constitutus*, secondly that Christ called him the rock *super quam ecclesiae suae structura consurgeret* and thirdly that Christ said to him: *Ego oravi pro te Petre, ut non deficiat fides tua*. The conclusion that has to be drawn from this is that Peter must occupy first place in the Church.

Fisher finally stresses that Antioch, where Peter was initially, was dominated by non-believers and that the same applied to Jerusalem, where James was bishop and to Achaia, where Andrew worked. The territories in which the other apostles proclaimed the gospel also fell into the hands of non-believers. Only the city to which Peter brought the gospel became the source of faith: *fides per Petrum praedicata Romae, non deficit hactenus*. The only conclusion that can be drawn from this, Fisher declares, is *Petrum vere fuisse Romae*.

If we consider Fisher's treatise as a whole, we are struck by the fact that this humanist, unlike such contemporaries as Cochlaeus, bases his argument to a relatively small extent on the tradition of the Church as an indisputable point of departure. On the contrary, he attempts above all to show on the basis of an exposition of certain passages from the New Testament that Velenský' point of view is untenable. This is undoubtedly partly a result of the plan of his treatise—he allows the sequence and the nature of the subjects that he discusses to be prescribed by Velenský. When, however, Fisher discusses questions concerned with the value and reliability of the data provided by the Fathers and historians of the Church—and he also does this because Velenský raises precisely these questions—then it is noticeable that he stands at a certain distance from his material. Following his friend Erasmus, he recognises that certain sources which are accepted by the tradition of the Church are not authentic and he is prepared to admit that the traditional data may indeed be contradictory.

If we bear in mind that his method is to allow Velenský first to express his opinion fully by including his text integrally in his treatise, then we are bound to describe Fisher as an extremely worthy opponent of the Bohemian author and as a good representative of the humanism of his period in his attempt to approach his subject as objectively and as scientifically as possible. We shall see that this first treatise written by a representative of Roman Catholicism marked a culminating point in the polemics which was not attained again in the later history of the controversy.[35]

After making his contribution to the debate, Fisher had nothing more to say in connection with Velenský and his treatise. In his later works, there is only one reference to Velenský—and that is indirect. This is found on his treatise *Sacri sacerdotii defensio contra Lutherum*, published in 1525 by Quentell at Cologne.[36]

---

[35] With the exception of Bellarmine, who, two generations later and working with Fisher's text of the *Petrum Romam non venisse*, wrote a worthy reply.

[36] CCath. IX. In Bviii^v: *Ostendimus in libello quodam adversus Velenum scripsimus,*

5. *Simon Hessus*

This first theological opposition to Velenský provoked a defence, when Simon Hessus—as Otto Clemen has shown,[37] a pseudonym for Urbanus Rhegius, who had been a preacher in Augsburg since 1520—wrote his *Apologia Simonis Hessi adversus D. Rossensem Episcopum Anglicanum super concertatione eius cum Ulrico Veleno*.[38] It is dated July 1523 and was printed by Adam Petri of Basle together with the treatise *De auctoritate officio et potestate pastorum ecclesiasticorum*, which is wrongly attributed to John of Wesel.[39]

In his introduction, the author says that Velenus' book came into his hands recently and that he would have give it no attention if John Fisher had not found it worth while to reply to it. Having read both treatises, he did not want to pass judgement and say who was victorious in the debate. He simply wanted to place on record that polemics of this kind were very advantageous for true Christianity. His treatise begins with the affirmation that what is being discussed is not a question of faith: *Quod absurdius aut fingi aut excogitari potest, quam, quod humanis conciliis est receptum, in fidei articulum nobis vertere?* It would be just as wrong to say that Velenus was a heretic because he could not believe that Peter was condemned to death in Rome as it would be to say that a man who could not believe that John Fisher was the Bishop of Rochester was a heretic or a schismatic.

It is at once clear from the very beginning of Hessus' treatise that the high level of debate at which Fisher's treatise is written is not present in this case. Luther's affirmation that whether the Petrine tradition is accepted or not is of no importance in the question as to whether the primacy is necessary for salvation is obviously reduced here to a popular level by an epigon in an argument against Fisher. The situation becomes even more doubtful when Hessus attempts to establish that it is not necessary to salvation to accept that Peter was the Bishop of Rome by asking "what we ought to think of the salvation of James, who was put to death by Herod Agrippa before it was possible for Peter's primacy in Rome to be known to him". What is more, Hessus soon departs from his original aim of refuting Fisher's

---

non ante finiendam eam successionem, que cepit a Christo quam omnia, que per Christum praedicta sunt, evenerint.

[37] *Zentralblatt für Bibliothekswesen*, XVII, p. 589.

[38] *Apologia Simonis Hessi adversus D. Rossensem Episcopum Anglicanum super concertatione eius cum Ulrico Veleno, an Petrus fuerit Romae et quid de primatu Romanis pontificis sit censendum.*

[39] O. Clemen, *op. cit.*, p. 589.

disputation of Velenský's thesis, going off in his own direction and expressing his own view as to how the papacy functions. He believes that an idol has been made of Peter and that Peter's successors have claimed for themselves the right to define new articles of faith, which is something that is reserved for God alone. If the popes had never abused their office, no one would ever have been opposed to them and there would never have been a Velenus to doubt that Peter was in Rome.

According to Paul, Hessus argues, "if a revelation is made to another sitting by, let the first be silent" (1 Cor. 14. 30). Yet the pope insists that the whole council should obey him. Christ moreover does nothing that he has not seen the Father doing, but the pope only does what turns out to be best for him and the cardinals.

Hessus goes on to show, by means of three examples, how the popes have, since time immemorial, sown discord by defining new dogmas and proclaiming new commandments. In the first place, although many of the Fathers of the Church celebrated Easter on 14 Nisan, a Roman Bishop[40] condemned all those who did not celebrate Easter on a Sunday. This gave rise to the first schism, that between the Eastern and the Western Churches. Ought this sort of action to take place for the sake of a mere trifle? A similar confusion—in the second place—caused the Greek Christians to fall away and this too was something of minimal importance—whether leavened or unleavened bread should be used in the Lord's Supper.[41] As soon as the pope becomes tyrannical, Hessus observes, the Holy Spirit leaves him. In the third place, the most cruel wars were caused in Bohemia because the laity were refused the chalice. It is to be feared, Hessus comments, that even more radical schisms will come about if more articles of faith of that kind are proclaimed.

After elaborating in this way his thesis—which owes little to principle and is in the main purely pragmatic—that the cause of all schisms is the faulty conduct of the pope, Hessus returns to consider Fisher's treatise as such. His argument, however, never reaches a high level. He accuses Fisher of "senseless reasoning" when the latter asserts with Velenus' arguments (and by this he means the uncertainty of the

---

[40] Victor (189–198).

[41] In 1053, the Patriarch of Constantinople, Caerularius, sent a letter to Bishop John of Trani, accusing the Latin Christians of various heresies, including that of using unleavened bread at the Lord's Supper. This letter came into the hands of Pope Leo IX, who initiated a sharp correspondence. This debate resulted in a complete and final breach between the Eastern and the Western Churches (1054).

fact if the data are contradictory) that Christ did not die on the cross, since Velenus drew his conclusions from contradictory human opinions, whereas Christ's death on the cross is a fact of salvation based on scriptural evidence. But it is, after all, absurd to think that Fisher ever made such a crude statement! His argument was clearly that no one would deny Christ's death despite the fact that the data differ and that, for this reason, not so much importance ought to be attached to the differences between the data in the case of Peter's sojourn in Rome.

Hessus' final tirade against Fisher is concerned with the latter's appeal to Jerome. He ought, Hessus suggests, to stop quoting Jerome's words as though the latter were the oracle at Delphi. After all, he did not regard his own opinion or that of others as infallible. Moreover, he often contradicted himself, not only in his exegesis, but also in the statements that he made concerning faith. Yet Hessus says this, despite the fact that Fisher himself stood at some distance from the Fathers of the Church and even admitted that Jerome had made a mistake in what he said about the date of Peter's arrival in Rome.

At the end of his treatise, Hessus declares that he is reluctant to discuss Fisher's arguments any further, since "in this sphere no good piety can come about". All that the person who reads Hessus' treatise objectively can conclude, however, is that the author has really not discussed Fisher's arguments at all. It is a polemical pamphlet which does not in any way contribute meaningfully to the debate. There is neither any exegetical elaboration of the New Testament passages discussed by Fisher nor any reply to Fisher's thesis that it is not possible to deny the Petrine tradition simply because of the diversity of the data.

Finally, Hesus does not even support Velenský's judgement of the papacy on the basis of the behaviour of individual popes. Velenský was of the opinion that the papacy would fall if the historical foundation was undermined. The fact that he regarded individual popes as representatives of the Antichrist was simply the consequence of his point of departure —because Peter was not the first Bishop of Rome, his successors had to be regarded as "tyrants" who exercised authority in an unlawful manner and who claimed powers in matters of faith without any legitimate basis for this. Whereas the moral aspect predominated in Hessus' case, in Velenský's it was no more than an epiphenomenon of a fundamentally wrong point of departure in the early Church.

6. *Other Supporters and Opponents*

Velenský's views had in the meantime become well known, not only because they had been disseminated through the medium of his own treatise, but also because of the publication of the book written by his authoritative opponent, John Fisher. For this reason, then, it is not surprising that the effects produced by his ideas can be detected in many different works published in the years that followed, in the form either of support or of opposition.

These continued effects of Velenský's ideas can be divided into three groups. In the first place, there are certain references in the writings of the *Schwärmer* who were glad to make use of them as points of contact for their own ideas against the Church. In this group can also be included those references found in works published by lay preachers who were influenced by the Reformation. In the second place, the leaders of the Reformation also made use of Velenský's arguments, though they were in general rather more careful. In the third place, Velenský's influence can also be detected in a number of counter-arguments used by Roman Catholic theologians, though these are noticeably few.

(ad 1)

As early as 1522, the author of the so-called *Türckenbüchlein*[42] which was printed by Johann Prüß in Strasbourg stated that a Bohemian scholar had recently demonstrated that Peter never went to Rome and that this scholar proved his point *mit vil beweglicher Ursachen*.

A year later, Balthasar Stanberger of Weimar[43] published his *Dialogus zwischen Petro und einem Bauern*. The treatise was printed by Michael Buchführer in Erfurt.[44] In it, Peter is introduced, complaining to a peasant that the Roman Church has made him a *mörder, dieb und blutsauger der armen leut*, although he never desired silver or gold, but has always clung to God's word. The peasant also asks Peter: *Du lieber Petre, was haben denn unsere pfaffenn furgebenn, damit wir arme leut also jemerlich vorfurt und noch teglich forfurt werdenn? Sagt doch der Babst, du lygst zu Roem begrabenn, hat dir auch einn kirchenn in deinem namen lassen bawenn,*

---

[42] *Turcken puechlein. Ein nutzlich gesprech, odder underrede etlicher personen, zu besserung Christlicher ordenung und lebens, gedichtet.*

[43] In another text *(Dialogus oder gesprech zwischen einem Prior, Leyenbrüder und Bettler)*, the author calls himself *Baltasar Stanberger zü Weimar in dem Fürstlichen schloß.*

[44] Text in O. Clemen: *Flugschriften aus den ersten Jahren der Reformation* (Leipzig, 1909), pp. 187–199.

und gewint grosz gelt mit deinem leychnam. Peter's answer to this question is: *Hastu doch vor wol vornommen, das ich gehn Rom nie kommen noch gewest bin. Sy werdens auch also nit erweisen kunnen.*

It is, however, unlikely that Stanberger read Velenský's treatise himself—he probably learnt of his ideas through other works. He makes Peter say, for example: *Martinus Luther, mein brüder und mitapostel Jesu Christi, der dem Babst und seinem anhang die wahrheit sagt, sagt das ich zü Rom nie kein babst gewest und auch dahin nie kommen noch das regiment da innen gehabt.*

One author who clearly read Velenský's treatise, however, was Sebastian Franck. The title of the third part of his *Geschichtsbibel*, published in 1531,[45] is, *daß Petrus nach dem Leiden Christi nie gen Rom sei kommen, achtzehn anzeigung aus der Schrift und Chroniken.* This part contains an almost literal reproduction of Velenský's eighteen *persuasiones.* Indeed, they are copied so literally that they include even the mistake that Velenský made in calculating the number of years in Claudius' reign—an error that occurs in both Latin editions of the treatise. Franck only abbreviates the *cavilli*, including them in one chapter. Since the author does not add any commentary of his own to the text, but does on the other hand—by never mentioning Velenský's name at any point— give rise to the impression that he is providing his own arguments, we may undoubtedly speak in this case of a classical example of plagiarism. This would also explain why Franck does not include Velenský's foreword in his book—it would, after all, be clear from that foreword that he was not the original author. There were many later editions and translations of Franck's *Geschichtsbibel*; the result of this is that the argument contained in the *Petrum Romam non venisse* became known to very many readers, who did not, however, learn who the spiritual father of the work was.

Roundabout the time of the opening of the Council of Trent, but probably going back to an even earlier work written at the beginning of the fifteen-thirties in Strasbourg, a treatise entitled *Der new Deutsch Bileams Esel*[46] was published (also in Strasbourg) by the printer Jacob Cammerlander. The author is unknown, but suggestions have been made[47] that it was Pamphilus Gengenbach or Nicholas Manuel. A

---

[45] *Chronica, Zeitbuch und Geschichtsbibell von anbegyn biß in diss gegenwertig MDXXXVI iar verlengt, Anno MDXXXI* (2nd edn.).

[46] Full text in K. Gödeke: *Pamphilus Gengenbach* (1856). A photomechanical reprint of this text was published in Amsterdam in 1966 .(See pp. 310–342).

[47] *ibid.*

dialogue between Christ and Peter occurs in this treatise with the following text (strophes 665–676):

Christus: *Vnd Petre waißt nit wer der ist* (The pope)
er rhümbt sich doch zu aller frißt
Wie er hab sein gewalt von dir
den du empfangen hast von mir
Habst ihn auch gesetzt gen Rom
Vnd ihm die gantz Welt vunderthon
drumb hat vns diß schmack gethon
die gantze Christenheyt verfürt
das mann kein frummen nirgens spürt.
Petrus: *Gen Rom binn ich doch kummen nie*
wie kenn ich dann inn diese mühe ...

Finally, there is the treatise written by Balthasar Fontana, a Carmelite from Locarno, in March 1531, entitled *Epistola ad universam Christi in Germania Ecclesiam*,[48] in which Velenský's name is mentioned, although his arguments are not discussed. The passage in question has a pathetic note: *Lachrymosis suspiriis degentes in tenebris obsecramus humiliter, ut praecipue omnia opera divinissimi Zwinglii, famosissimi Lutheri, resolutissimi Melanchthonis, accuratissimi Oecolampadii, solertissimi Pomerani, illuminati Lamberti, ingeniosissimi Veleni, elegantissimi Brentii, acutissimi Buceri, studiosissimi Leonis, vigilantissimi Vteni ad nos pecuniis nostris mediantibus transmittere dignemini.* If any importance at all can be attached to the adjectives that the author has so liberally distributed throughout this passage, then the one which describes Velenský and distinguishes him from the others is certainly striking.

(ad 2)

Like Luther, the other leaders of the Reformation were rather more reserved in their attitude towards Velenský's radical denial of the Petrine tradition. In 1534, for example, Bullinger wrote to Oswald Mycenius:[49] "With regard to the question as to whether Peter did or did not see Rome, I have no opinion at all. On the one hand, I am prepared to believe the evidence of the early Fathers, but, on the other, I am also inclined to accept what Velenus affirms". *Ego vero me in hac caussa levicula quisquam coget in verba Veleni.*

---

[48] In *Historiae Ecclesiasticae Novi Testamenti seculi XVI. Authore Joh. Henrico Hottingero (Pars II: Continens Historiam Reformationis)*, ed. Joh. Henr. Hambergeri (1665). The text is on p. 271 and 618 ff.

[49] *Epp. Eccl. Helvet .Reformatorum*, ed. Füslin, p. 131.

Calvin is also not very pertinent in what he says. His view of the Petrine tradition can be found in Book IV, caput 6 of his *Institutio religionis christianae*.[50] There he writes: "although everyone says that Peter was a bishop in Rome, this is, it seems to me, not at all certain. What Eusebius says about the twenty-five years' episcopate in Rome can be contradicted without difficulty. Paul, after all, writes in his letter to the Galatians that Peter was still in Jerusalem about twenty years after Jesus' death and afterwards spent some time in Antioch (according to Gregory, seven years). The period between the death of Jesus and the end of the reign of Nero, who put Peter to death, covered more than thirty-seven years. This therefore leaves at the most ten years during which Peter can have been in Rome. Another reasoning is, however, also possible. There is no mention at all of Peter in Paul's letter to the Romans—which was probably written four years before he went to Rome—and this would not have happened if Peter had been bishop there. What is more, there is also no mention of Peter in Luke's description of the way in which Paul was received by the brethren in Rome." The same can also be said of the letters that Paul wrote from Rome, Calvin writes, since *il ne dit pas un seul mot, par lequel on puisse coniecturer que sainct Pierre fust là*. And when Paul says in 2 Tim. 4 that everyone has deserted him, *Où estoit alors sainct Pierre? Car s'il estoit à Rome, sainct Paul le charge d'un grand blasme, d'avoir abandonné l'Évangile*. "Another argument is that the early authors do not agree about Peter's successor, one naming Linus, another Clement", Calvin writes, *finalement, les choses de ces temps-là sont tant embrouillées de diversité d'opinions, qu'il ne faut pas legièrement croire tout ce qui est escrit*.

It is clear that, although he does not mention the author's name, Calvin makes use of Velenský's arguments and, what is more, that he follows the order of the *Petrum Romam non venisse* (and sometimes even uses the same words). On the other hand, he overlooks those *persuasiones* which deal with the death of Peter and Paul in Jerusalem, although he recognised the "Babylon" mentioned in the first epistle of Peter as a town in Egypt. This is clear from his commentary on Genesis[51],

---

[50] Latin edition, 1536; afterwards published in French (CR XXXI–XXXII), pp. 680–681.

[51] CR XXIII, p. 159. Cf. the commentary on Peter, CR LXXXIII, p. 292, Cp. V, 13: *Quae in Babylone: Multi ex veteribus Romam aenigmatice putarunt notari. Hoc commentum Papistae libenter arripiunt, ut videatur Petrus romanae ecclesiae prae fuisse ... Si alexandrinam ecclesiam Marcus constituit, diuque illic episcopatu functus est, nunquam potuit Romae esse cum Petro ... Quam itaque Marcum tunc secum Petrus comitem habuerit, quum scripsit hanc epistolam: Babylone fuisse probabilius est.*

in which he has this to say about Gen. 10. 10: *Terra Sinhar addita est ad notem discriminis*: *quia altera quoque Babylon Aegypti fuit, quam hodie Cairum vocant.* All the same, in his conclusion he confines himself to the cautious statement that, in his opinion, Peter's episcopate in Rome *n'est gueres certain, comme il me semble.* In this, then, he is close to Luther.

(ad 3)

The reactions experienced in Roman Catholic theological circles at the time on are few in number and moreover give the impression that these theologians learnt about Velenský's views through the writings of other authors and that they did not, in several cases, even know the name of the author of the treatise.

This is most apparent in the case of Johannes Eck, the great defender of the papacy for a period of several decades. On 7 February 1520, he completed his *De primatu Petri libros III*, a treatise which Johannes Metzler S.J.[52] believes was Velenský's point of departure for writing his *Petrum Romam non venisse.* Although Metzler's suggestion is untenable because of Velenský's themes and sources on the one hand and the total absence in his work of any allusion at all to Eck, it does point to the remarkable fact that, although Eck's interpreters have made a connection between him and Velenský, it is not apparent in any of Eck's writings that he knew Velenský and was opposed to his ideas. This is all the more striking since a scholar such as Eck must have been familiar with the work of Fisher (which was published in 1522) and must therefore have become acquainted with Velenský's name and ideas. All the same, he does not mention Ulrichus Velenus at all in his *Enchiridion locorum communium adversus Lutherum et alios hostes ecclesiae*, published in 1525. One explanation for this may be that, like Cochlaeus, he perhaps regarded Velenus as a pseudonym and, what is more, as a pseudonym for Urbanus Rhegius. He certainly speaks in his Enchiridion of a *novum mandacium Urbani Riegeri aut alterius Lutherani* and in this context points to the statement that Peter was never in Rome. If this theory is accepted, it is possible to draw the conclusion that Eck was combatting Velenský in his *Enchiridion*, but was doing so in the person of Urbanus Rhegius.

This theory is in no sense weakened by the fact that Rhegius mentioned Ulrichus Velenus Minhoniensis in the *Apologia* which he wrote under the pseudonym of Simon Hessus and which may also have been

---

[52] See his introduction to the Eck edition: *Epistola de ratione studiorum suorum* (*CCath*, 2), p. 58.

read by Eck (it was published in 1523). After all, even if Eck had known that Hessus was a pseudonym used by Rhegius, he may well have assumed that Rhegius was defending a work of his own against Fisher written under a different pseudonym.

A Roman Catholic author who undoubtedly read Velenský's book and discussed it in detail in a reply is Gregorio Cortese, a monk of Monte Cassino who later became a cardinal and the visitator general of the Benedictines. This reply, the *Tractatus adversus negantem Petrum Apostolum Romae fuisse*,[53] was written in 1523 and dedicated to Pope Adrian VI.

Cortese mentions neither the name of the author nor the title of the book that he is attacking. He declares in his foreword that he is writing "against the man who was the first to venture to deny not only that Peter was the bishop of Rome, but also that he had ever been in that city". He also describes the treatise as "a book which assures its readers not only that Peter did not die in Rome, but also that he had never been there". Cortese avoids mentioning Velenský's name because he regards "Ulrichus Velenus Minhoniensis" as a pseudonym: "He aroused my suspicion because he did not want to make his name and his fame known among later readers with this shameful action".

The first part of Cortese's book is devoted to a general consideration of the subject and contains many quotations from the Fathers of the Church on which the author bases his defence of the Petrine tradition. In this way, his argument follows very much the same course as Cochlaeus' and Fisher's. Whereas Fisher, however, builds up his argument with New Testament data, Cortese only makes use of Scripture in his argument insofar as the Fathers quote from it. What Cortese does, however, point out—and this is something that his contemporaries did not do—is that Velenský's view is an elaboration of what had been suggested centuries before by Marsilio of Padua: "The first man to defend this position seems to have been Marsilio of Padua, who published, under the protection of Ludwig of Bavaria, a work against the popes of Rome which he called the *Defensor pacis*".

In the second part of his treatise, the author follows Velenský's reasoning very closely: "Since we have already said that we are not at all convinced by his arguments, it is necessary to quote these". The method, then, that Cortese follows is to contrast each *persuasio* with a *dissuasio*. He does not, however, produce any new ideas. He denies

---

[53] In *Gregorii Cortesii Mutinensis s.r. ecclesiae presb. Cardinalis. Epistolarum familiarium liber* (edn. *Venetiis. Apud Franciscum Franciscium senensem.* 1573), pp. 300–362.

that there is any contradiction among the authors writing within the Church concerning the Petrine tradition—certain data may, in the course of time, not have been in agreement with each other, but *de rebus ipsis nulla sit ambiguitas*.[54] Cortese is also unable to accept that the tradition concerning Peter's sojourn in Rome might be contradicted by scriptural evidence—Peter returned to Jerusalem from Rome for the apostolic council, but his seat remained in Rome because his care extended to all the churches (and not simply to the circumcised). He also wrote his letters from Rome. Cortese does not go into Velenský's foreword, although it is clear that he was familiar with it because he makes use of the quotation from Juvenal to point to the divine punishment that will befall his opponent.

As we are discussing these polemical treatises in chronological order, we must now consider in greater detail a work by Cochlaeus which we mentioned at the end of the section on that author—the *De Petro et Roma adversus Velenum Lutheranum, libri quatuor*. This was published in February 1525 by Quentell of Cologne, but Cochlaeus says, in his foreword dedicated to Christopher, the Bishop of Augsburg, that he had already written this work three years before against a man "who called himself Velenus". He had, however, refrained from publishing it at the time, on the one hand because John Fisher had, in the meantime, published his book and, on the other "because he was reluctant to discuss a matter which was known to the whole world". Now that the Lutheran sect was spreading so quickly over the whole of Germany, it had become obvious to him that he had to make public what he had written then.

Veesenmeyer[55] also assumed in this case—just as he did in the case of Cochlaeus' treatise against Luther (the *Assertio pro Hieronymo Emsero*)—that Cochlaeus was here boasting that he was himself the spiritual father of the counterarguments. He assumed that Cochlaeus has "passed Fisher's work off as his own" (*mit Fishers Kalb gepflügt habe*) and that the date when the work was conceived—1522—was fabricated so as to make it seem as though his text was completed at an earlier date than Fisher's.

Veesenmeyer was, however, wrong in this assertion. In the first place, he was mistaken because certain details in the text point clearly

---

[54] Cortese regarded the book named by Velenský, *Fasciculus temporum*, as providing faulty evidence: "It does not agree with Jerome, Eusebius and Orosius and is therefore not reliable".

[55] *op. cit.*

to January 1522 as the time when the treatise was written. Leo X, for example, is named as the pope who had recently died and his successor was not yet known to Cochlaeus.[56] What is more, he states in another book, written on 27 February 1524 in the form of a letter *(Responsio in epistolam cuiusdam Lutherani)*:[57] "A few years ago, I replied both to Luther and to Velenus", *Luthero quidem XXV annos neganti, uno libello, Veleno autem, neganti totam substantiam facti, quatuor libris.*[58]

The most important reason, however, for regarding Cochlaeus as an independent opponent of Velenský is the fact that he provided a complete counter-argument against Velenský's foreword, whereas Fisher did not deal at all with this foreword in his treatise. In addition to this, Cochlaeus also provided eighteen *demonstrationes*, as a counter-part to Velenský's *persuasiones* and there is no evidence here of any dependence on Fisher. When, however, Cochlaeus attempts to refute each of Velenský's *persuasiones* and *cavilli* separately and in great detail —in the same way as Fisher had done—we find arguments that had already occurred in Fisher's treatise. These, however, function as points of departure for Cochlaeus' own elaboration and can be regarded more as sources of inspiration than as examples to be imitated.

We may therefore conclude that large parts of this work, in particu-lar the polemics against Velenský's foreword and the eighteen *demon-strationes* in fact originated in January 1522, but that the systematic disputation of Velenský's *persuasiones* and *cavilli* may have been written at a later date, when Cochlaeus had already been inspired by Fisher's treatise, *Convulsio calumniarum Ulrichi Veleni Minhoniensis.*

In Book I of his treatise, Cochlaeus refutes Velenský's foreword by following the latter's argument very closely and therefore beginning by criticising the exegesis of the passages concerning the Antichrist. He quotes evidence from the Old Testament prophets and the gospels to show that the Antichrist was not expected until the apocalyptic end of time and that he cannot therefore be regarded as a figure in history.

Cochlaeus also defends the pope against Velenský's charge that he took action against Hus, Wyclif and Jerome of Prague as well as the

---

[56] Leo X died in December 1521; Adrian was elected pope on 9 January 1522.
[57] Published on 13 June 1524 in Stuttgart.
[58] Veesenmeyer regarded even this statement as wrong, believing that, thanks to Fisher, Cochlaeus would have gathered together sufficient evidence to be able to refute Velenský, yet he announced here that his book would be published (in 1525), pretending, however, that it had been written as early as 1522. Veesenmeyer writes: *Er (Cochlaeus) wollte wahrscheinlich schon voraus die gelehrte Welt auf dieses herrliche Product begierig machen.*

Hussites generally. Hus and Jerome were not, Cochlaeus insists, condemned by the pope, but by the council; in the same way, the pope did not cause the misery of the Hussite war. Bohemia itself was guilty of this, he argues, because it had been influenced by Hus (just as there now influences in Prague emanate from Wittenberg). Finally, Wyclif died before he could be executed, with the result that his bones were later scattered over the sea.

Cochlaeus discusses in detail Velenský's image comparing the pope with a three-headed Cerberus which had already lost two heads in attacks by Valla and Luther. He admits that Valla was right in describing the declaration concerning the Donation of Constantine as a forgery, but he upholds the transference of authority by the Emperor Constantine to Pope Sylvester as a historical fact. Against Luther too, he argues that, since the Antichrist cannot, according to the evidence contained in the Bible, reign in the Church, the Spirit of Christ is active in it and statements made by the Church about the powers of the pope cannot simply be set aside.

Book II contains the eighteen *demonstrationes* in which Cochlaeus attempts to argue in favour of Peter's sojourn in Rome. The emphases laid by the author in his argument are clearly revealed by the fact that it is only in the first *demonstratio* that he provides evidence from the gospels, whereas, in all the other *demonstrationes*, this evidence is taken from the Fathers of the Church. It is also remarkable that the scriptural texts which he discusses are not used to reconstruct the historical situation (as was the case in Velenský's treatise), but are rather employed in a traditional manner. Cochlaeus accords central importance to Luke 22. 32, because it was to this text that the Council of Nicaea appealed and the Church of Rome followed the council in this. He then quotes Matt. 16. 17, 18 and 19; 17. 27; 18. 22; 26. 52 and John 21 as evidence "that Peter's chair is based on the gospel", but he does not provide any exegesis in support of this statement.

Books III and IV are devoted to a systematic refutation of Velenský's *persuasiones* and *cavilli*, in which several main ideas recur again and again. Cochlaeus uses three leading counter-arguments against Velenský's argument that the data provided by the Church Fathers and the later historians of the Church contradict each other. In the first place, he argues that it is not justifiable to conclude from the contradictory nature of these data that the event in question did not in fact take place. The example that Cochlaeus quotes here is the same as Fisher's, namely that the evangelists differed in their statements concerning the time of Jesus' death. In the second place, Cochlaeus insists that there is no real contradiction concerning the time of Peter's arrival in Rome provided that an "inclusive" calculation is made. In other words, the same time may be meant by the second year of Claudius' reign as by the fourth year. In the third place, the author argues that Velenus is inconsistent in regarding the data provided by pagan authors as reliable and those provided by writers in the Church as unreliable.

Cochlaeus does not accept Velenský's *argumentum e silentio* because, apart from Peter, many other leaders in the early Christian community are not named in the epistles. Like Fisher too, he mentions the absence of any reference to John in the letter to the Ephesians and to James in the letter to the Hebrews. He also points out that neither Luke nor Paul have anything to say about the crucifixion of Andrew, the beheading of Bartholomew or the assumption of Mary into heaven.

Cochlaeus also argues against Velenský's claim that the assembly of the apostles at Jerusalem is evidence that Peter did not come to Rome at that time and, what is more, he does so in the same way as Fisher in his treatise, insisting that Peter travelled from Rome to Jerusalem for the occasion.

We may therefore make this general statement about Cochlaeus' counter-arguments. In opposition to Velenský's contention that an *argumentum e silentio* is provided by the canonical books, Cochlaeus quotes excessively from the patristic writings and in this way appeals to the tradition of the Church in order to supplement Scripture. In this sense, then, Spahn[59] was quite correct in his assertion that Cochlaeus gathered *ein massigeres Material* together in order *sich mit ungeschickter Breite auf den Beweis einzulassen.*

In the same year that Cochlaeus' *De Petro et Roma adversus Velenum Lutheranum* was published—1525—the Dutch theologian Albertus Pighius wrote his *Adversus Graecorum Errores*,[60] which was devoted above all to the papal negociations with the Eastern Church, in Rome, where he held the position of *cubicularius secretus* to Pope Clement VII. In the last part of this treatise, the author is concerned with a defence of the primacy of the pope. He refers to the arguments used by the opponents of the Petrine tradition—the silence preserved in the Acts

---

[59] *op. cit.*, p. 98.

[60] See H. Jedin: *Studien über die Schriftstellertätigkeit Albertus Pigges* (Münster, 1931), pp. 14 ff, 85 ff. The quotations are taken from Jedin, Polman, *op. cit.*, and Bäumer, *op. cit.* The work itself: *Cod. Vat. lat.* 7804.

of the Apostles concerning Peter's episcopate and the contradictory statements made by different authors in the Church with regard to when Peter came to Rome. Pighius does not regard these arguments as decisive and goes on to mention many Fathers of the Church who spoke of Peter's episcopate in Rome and to quote from their writings. He freely admits that there is no agreement between them concerning the date of Peter's arrival, but *ut tamen demus non omnes convenisse de anno adventus Petru in urbem, illi tamen in hoc consentiunt: quod idem Romae fuerit coronatus martyrio post gestum in ea per annos aliquot episcopatum*. He also asks why cities such as Jerusalem or the Egyptian Babylon did not make any claims to be the seat of the primacy if Peter was martyred there. As far as the silence about Peter in Paul's letters is concerned, Pighius says that Peter interrupted his twenty-five years' sojourn in Rome several times, for instance, when the Emperor Claudius banished the Jews from the city.

In 1538, when he was provost at Utrecht, Pighius wrote a work that was entirely devoted to the papacy: *Hierarchiae ecclesiasticae assertio*. This treatise was published in Cologne. After having outlined his points of departure in Book I, the author goes on, in Book II, to discuss the thesis that the unity of the Church is guaranteed not only by love and grace, but also by the existence of a hierarchy with one man at its head. In Book III, he provides an exegesis of the biblical texts on which the papacy is based and, in Book IV, he deals with the primacy itself.

In the third book, Pighius provides a summary of the arguments of his opponents, as he had done in his *Adversus Graecorum Errores* of 1525, and—again as in his earlier treatise—contrasts these with the testimony borne by the Fathers, quoting especially and at length from Eusebius' *Historia ecclesiastica*. He also discusses the *argumentum e silentio*. In the case of Paul and Luke, this *silentium* has an obvious explanation, Pighius claims. There are, he says, certain other facts in the lives of Peter and Paul which are not mentioned in the Acts of the Apostles (for example, Peter's sojourn in Antioch, Paul's journey to Arabia and the meeting between Peter and Paul in Antioch) and Paul perhaps did not meet Peter in Rome because the latter was not continuously in the city. (During the persecution of the Jews in Claudius' reign, Pighius claims, Peter handed over the leadership of the community to Linus and Cletus.) He was, after all, responsible for the whole of the Church: *Quem alioquin existimandum non est, ita perpetuos XXV annis desidisse Romae, ut urbis portas egressus nunquam fuerit ad alios quoque instruendos et confirmandos in fide* (fo. 110[r]).

It is clear from these two treatises, that Pighius was completely familiar with the arguments used in the *Petrum Romam non venisse*, but that he was not concerned at any point with polemics directed against Velenský as the author of the text. He was rather intent on refuting the opponents of the papacy who used these arguments.

For the sake of completeness, we must briefly consider three authors who published treatises defending the papacy, but did not directly or explicitly oppose Velenský's argument, although they were writing during the same period.

In 1520, the Franciscan Thomas Murner wrote his *Von der babstenthum*,[61] in which he declares *das alle historien ußweisen, wie Petrus VII iar ʒu Antiochia residiert hab, darnach in Italiam gon Rom kummen sey, und da alß in einer hauptstat der gantʒen wel ungehindret XXV jar und siben monat seinen stul regieret.* Polman was mistaken[62] when he quoted this sentence to illustrate Murner's opposition to Velenský, since Murner's treatise was published at the same time as Velenský's and this statement could not therefore have been a reaction to the *Petrum Romam non venisse* or to Luther's treatise against Emser. If any polemics were intended at all in this case, then they must have been directed against the Waldensians, who were, after all, the first to question the Petrine tradition.

The second author whom we have to consider here is Johannes Faber, who wrote his *Malleus in haeresim Lutheranam* in 1524.[63] The first sentence in this treatise makes it quite clear that the author is confining himself to an attempt to refute Luther's ideas concerning the papacy, as set out in the book that he wrote in 1519, *De potestate papae: Editus est a Martino Luthero libellus potestate papae inscriptus.* The entire plan of Faber's work is based on this—again and again the author quotes from Luther and then gives his reply.

He does not, however, entirely ignore the fact that a change took place in Luther's view of the papacy after 1519, by his having taken over Velenský's arguments with regard to Peter's twenty-five years' episcopate in Rome. He challenges the assertion that certain conclusions can be drawn—as Luther does—from the silence preserved in the Acts of the Apostles about Peter's episcopate in Rome. Surely, he says, nothing is said also about John's exile to the island of Patmos in

---

[61] Text in *Deutsche Schriften*, Vol. VII, ed. Franz Schultz (Berlin, 1918–1931), quotation on p. 23.

[62] *op. cit.*, p. 471.

[63] *CCath.* 23/24.

the Acts of the Apostles? What is more, it is clear from Acts 28. 3 and Romans 16. 3–17 that there were Christians in Rome before Paul came there. This, Faber concludes, must have been the result of Peter's work in the city. He also quotes writers active during the apostolic era as witnesses—Pseudo-Hegesippus, Dionysius of Corinth and the statement made by the Presbyter Gaius and quoted by Eusebius: *Ego habeo trophaea apostolorum* (p. 387).

The third author whom we must discuss in this context is Kaspar Schatzgeyer, who published in 1525 a treatise entitled *Traductio Sathanae, hoc est diabolicae fraudis detectio qua sub scripturEs praetextu disseminat errores*.[64] This Franciscan, who was provincial of his order in Munich from 1514 onwards, was deeply concerned with questions about the relationship between the pope and the council. In this matter, he on the one hand interpreted conciliarist—and even Marsilian— ideas and, on the other, corrected these ideas again and again, giving them a curialist interpretation. The point of departure for his treatise was Luther's appeal to a council against the pope.

To begin with, Schatzgeyer admits that the authority left by Christ to his apostles was the same for all of them. At the initial stage of the Church's existence, this jurisdictional power was a requisite for all the apostles. Immediately afterwards, however, the authority of Peter emerged as the *potestas ordinaria*. The authority of the other apostles ceased when they died, whereas the powers of Peter are lasting in the Church: *Soli Petro Christus plenariam dedit potestatem institutione ordinaria perpetuo in ecclesia durata.*

With regard to the *locus classicus*, Matt. 16. 18 *(Tu es Petrus, super hanc petram aedificabo ecclesiam meam)*, Schatzgeyer says that the foundation is not Peter himself, but the statement of faith pronounced by Peter. This pronouncement of faith, however, is tied to the person —and to his successors. Because Christ wanted to make Peter the head of the Church, God granted this revelation to him. Nonetheless, Schatzgeyer points out, the *magisterium fidei* is not exclusively confined to the papacy. It may be necessary for difficult questions of faith which concern the salvation of souls *per se et directe* to be brought before an ultimately normative body, namely the council with *potestas plenaria* which can count on the help of the Holy Spirit, because the

---

[64] In *Opera Omnia* (Ingolstadt, 1543), fo 260ᵛ. For an assessment of Schatzgeyer's work, see C. H. Klomps: *Kirche, Freiheit und Gesetz bei dem Franziskanertheologen Kaspar Schatzgeyer* (1959).

latter has been promised to the Church as a whole. The council cannot, however, act without the pope as *caput subalternum*.

As far as the papal office itself is concerned, Schatzgeyer goes on, it is clear from Scripture that all striving for human glory must be rejected. A primacy of honour therefore cannot exist. The primacy of the pope is always a question of giving service. The greatest servant has the highest office. The primacy is therefore at the summit of the Church's service for the sake of the salvation of all believers.

In view of the author's aim and the structure of his argument which is closely connected with that aim, it is easy to understand that there are only very indirect points of contact between Schatzgeyer's and Velenský's views—the former's historical point of departure, that of the situation of the early Church, is not really historical at all, since it contains a theological decision. Moreover, his assessment of the papal office in the course of history does not result, because of its theological content, in a posing of the question as to whether the claims on the part of the pope to authority are legal or not. On the contrary, Schatzgeyer concludes by pointing directly to the scriptural basis for the pope's task of serving the Church.

7. *Conclusions*

The polemics were in fact concerned with the relationship between Scripture and tradition, but, because of the way in which this problem was approached and the importance attached to scriptural and traditional data, it is necessary to describe the clash of opinions rather more subtly than might appear at first sight. What appears to be simply a struggle between Rome and the reformers emerges, on closer inspection of the arguments employed, to be a situation in which great and even fundamental antitheses exist within the parties themselves.

Velenský's point of departure was determined by the influence exerted by the Bohemian Brethren, namely that historical investigation was bound to reveal that the papacy was based on a falsification of history by the tradition of the Church. A revelation of this falsification would, the Brethren believed, deprive the papacy of its foundation and enable the continuation of that papacy to be seen simply as an activity of the Antichrist. Lupač had already outlined this programme and Krasonický had begun to elaborate it.

This, then, was the point of departure which determined Velenský's method. The earliest sources for historical research into the Petrine tradition as the foundation of the papacy were, in his opinion, the data of the New Testament, which were for this reason of greater value than the tradition of the Church. Velenský's consistent research into the Bible with the aim of refuting the Church's tradition was therefore based not on a fundamentally theological choice of Scripture as the only source of truth, but rather on practical scientific considerations.

Velenský also believed that he had achieved his aim when he had been able to deny the Petrine tradition on the basis of the *argumentum e silentio* provided by the New Testament and of a refutation of tradition by verifying it against the current philosophical adage that the truth is firmly established only when all the reports about it are in agreement with each other. In this way, the illegality of the primacy of Rome as the *successio* of the episcopate of Peter was demonstrated and that was sufficient proof for Velenský.

The three great opponents in the continuation of the struggle —Luther, Fisher and Cochlaeus—clearly recognised this point of departure and this aim, together with the method that resulted from it and their reactions were all perfectly adequate, although of course each reacted in accordance with his own view.

Luther also regarded tradition as unreliable and only accepted the biblical data. He rejected, however, Velenský's practical scientific reason for accepting the scriptural data only as material used for proof. For Luther, the *sola scriptura* was not a scientific and experimental statement, but rather a necessity of faith. He regarded the question concerning the mediation of salvation through the papacy as of primary importance and an analysis of the historical data as no more than a support for his main purpose. He was essentially not interested in historical research of this kind. Velenský's proof was therefore not sufficient for him. He extended the lines fundamentally: *Wie wol ichs halt, S. Peter sey zu Rom gewesen, wolt ich dennoch nit drauff sterben als auff ein artickel des glaubens.* If, on the other hand, it was not necessary for salvation to believe that Peter was in Rome, Luther believed, *so ist auch nit nott zu glauben, das der Babst seyn stuel erb und Babst sey.*

This essential attack against the papacy was, moreover, not completely absent from Velenský's writing. He too used the argument that the Petrine tradition was not an "article of faith" because it lacked any basis in Scripture. He also alluded to the necessity for salvation, when he said in his first *persuasio*: "neither theologians nor the Church herself are obliged to believe those things which cannot be traced back to Scripture and which are dubious because they are contradictory". Because of his historical purpose, however, he was unable to draw the extreme and fundamental conclusion, namely that, if acceptance of the primacy was not an article of faith and therefore not necessary for salvation, the foundation of the papacy was essentially infringed, even if it was admitted that Peter was in Rome. Velenský, however, was not able to admit this, because for him the historical proof that Peter was not in Rome was quite conclusive. Luther, on the other hand, admitted this freely, because it gave all the more emphasis to the fact that the fundamental decision was taken for a different and deeper reason. In the tension between Scripture and tradition, then, Velenský opted, as a humanist historian, for *sola scriptura* on the basis of rational considerations, whereas Luther used the principle of *sola scriptura*, as a theologian, with his eye on the certainty of salvation.

In this respect, the Roman Catholic theologian Fisher was closer to Velenský. He too gave preference to evidence from Scripture because —like Velenský—he believed that the papacy would fall if its historical foundation was undermined. His polemics were therefore directed towards showing—if need be together with a repudiation of the Church's tradition—by exegesis that no *argumentum e silentio* was provided by the New Testament. Since he naturally believed that the function performed by the papacy in mediating salvation was an essential one, he too, like Luther, extended the lines further to include the necessity for salvation. In view of the fact, however, that this necessity for salvation was rooted historically in the Petrine tradition, he was bound to engage in polemics with Velenský in the sphere of historical investigation. This was a sphere in which Luther was not interested, but which was of the very greatest interest to Fisher. For this reason, it is probable that Velenský would have had a deeper understanding of the point of view of his opponent Fisher in this case than of that of his "supporter" Luther.

Cochlaeus, whose work was perhaps at a lower scientific level than Fisher's, saw even more clearly that the real danger to the papacy came, not from Velenský, but from Luther. This is why he reacted to Luther's affirmation that the tradition concerning Peter's sojourn of twenty-five years in Rome could not be correct, but that the apostle may perhaps have stayed there for a shorter time with the comment that this attacked *omne fundamentum nostrum*. Moreover, it was not historical analysis that had, in Cochlaeus' opinion, undermined this foundation of the Church, but that fact that Luther had been able to set aside the historical evidence as unimportant to the certainty of salvation. This points clearly to the incorrectness of Veesenmeyer's statement that Cochlaeus was simply guilty of plagiarism, "passing Fisher's work off as his own". Cochlaeus in fact penetrated at once to the heart of the problem and warned the Church authorities. Fisher, on the other hand, overlooking the deepest problem, defended history with arguments drawn from history. In that sphere, he was undoubtedly more skilled than Cochlaeus, which is, of course, one reason why, when the latter came to oppose Velenský later, in 1525, he relied to a great extent for his inspiration on the data gathered by Fisher. In this way, he came to follow the same line of thought as Fisher—in other words, he discussed especially the reliability of the historical data.

The front line opponents in the combat can therefore be described in the following way. Cochlaeus reacted spontaneously, aware of the fundamental theological threat to the primacy and reacting to Luther when he separated the necessity for salvation from the question as to whether the Petrine tradition was or was not reliable. Fisher's reaction to Velenský (and Cochlaeus' in his later publication), on the other hand, was based on Velenský's denial of the reliability and his subsequent declaration that the papacy was illegitimate because of this. It is quite possible that, in his perspicacity, Eck saw these front lines and their consequences very clearly, with the result that he confined his polemics to Luther.

Having mapped out the struggle in this way, it is not difficult to place the other participants in the debate. On the Protestant side, Simon Hessus is close to Luther—he did not want to pronounce any verdict on the conflict between Velenský and Fisher about the reliability of the traditional data—a clear statement that he regarded this debate as of secondary importance—but he did, on the other hand, want to make it clear that no question of faith was involved. In this way, Hessus succeeded in reproducing Luther's point of view very well, although he did not always do this in an equally dignified way.

Bullinger and Calvin took up the same position as Luther. An analysis of the historical data, leading to a refutation of the Petrine tradition, is interesting and it gave support, of course, to their fundamental rejection of the papacy—in this Calvin almost literally included a great deal of Velenský's evidence —but, in the whole of the structure of the theology of the Reformation, it only played a modest part which was in no way essential. It is only in Book III of the *Institutio religionis christianae* that Calvin discusses this question.

The situation was, of course, quite different in the case of the

Schwärmer and their writings. According to the extent in which they were orientated towards humanism or social revolution fitted Velenský's attack against the primacy into the framework of their own thinking. Sebastian Franck was impressed by the detailed evidence that Velenský had assembled, but, for Balthasar Stanberger, it served as support in his claim that the Petrine tradition had made the pope into a *mörder, dieb und blutsauger der armen leut*. Finally, the author of the *New Deutsch Bileams Esel* was able to make use of Velenský's arguments in his protest against the power structure of the papacy. In all these cases, however, the discernment that characterises Luther's approach is lacking.

On the Roman Catholic side, very few were aware of the real problem. Aleander hardly reacted at all when Cochlaeus pointed out to him that the foundation of the Church was undermined by Luther's far-reaching statements, but he wrote to Rome in order to set the Church machinery in motion when Velenský's historical analysis threatened to attack the Church's tradition. The treatise written by Gregorio Cortese, the cardinal who moved in Vatican circles, cannot, however, be regarded as a reaction to Aleander's alert,[65] although it only deals with the opposition to the Church's tradition and with arguments in defence of that tradition and draws exclusively on that very same, challenged tradition.

There is no doubt that the debate about the value of the Church's tradition which was set in motion by Velenský led the Catholic polemicists to stress once again the authority of the Fathers of the Church. In contrast to the mutual contradictions with regard to marginal subjects, they stressed unanimity with regard to what was essential. In this unanimity, they saw the possibility of using tradition as an authority in the exposition of Scripture. That is why we find, in Velenský's opponents, constantly recurring series of quotations from the Fathers and other authors in the Church.

By wanting to do battle on this particular field, however, they were in a weaker position than their opponent, because Velenský, inspired by the ardent advocates of the renewal of the Church in Bohemia and formed by critical humanists, was well motivated and able to expose the weaknesses of the Church's tradition. It is possible that what is revealed here is a tragic aspect of the Reformation period: because the secondary element, tradition, had been raised in the Church to the level

---

[65] Cortese wrote (p. 315) that he had received the treatise from Ottobonus Fliscus.

of the fundamental and essential, the Roman Catholic defence against an essential attack—by Luther—had to be conducted with secondary means. What is perhaps even more important, when an attack took place—by Velenský—on this secondary field and the weakness of this foundation was revealed, the Roman Catholic defenders reacted as though the struggle was concerned with essential things. It was only a few individuals who understood where and by whom the foundation of the Church had really been attacked.

CHAPTER FIVE

THE CONTINUED EFFECT ON LATER WRITERS

1. *Flacius Illyricus*

In 1551, Matthias Flacius Illyricus, a Church historian of Magdeburg, published a work entitled: *Verlegung zweier schrifften eines Augsburgischen Münchs, mit Namen Joannes Fabri, von des Babsts Primat und von Beicht. Durch M. Flacius Illyricus. Item achtzehn beweisungen, das S. Petrus zu Rom nicht gewesen sey.*[1]

The John Fabri mentioned in the title of this treatise was a Dominican (from Heilbronn, not Augsburg) who had, in October 1550, published a book entitled *Von Ankunfft und herkommen der Römischen Bischöff von Petro bis auf Julium den Dritten.*[2] In this book, he had defended the papacy against attacks by Lutherans: *Laß dich durch die Mißbräuche etlicher römischer Bischöfe nicht also ärgern, daß du darum den von Christo hinterlassenen Stuhl wolltest verachten, schänden oder schmähen ... Wiewohl das bös Leben der bösen römischen Bischöfe soll gehaßt werden, soll doch in ihnen der Stuhl Petri, den sie besitzen, auch die Schlüssel und Gewalt von Christo ihnen gegeben und befohlen, geehrt werden.*[3]

Flacius reacted at once to this[4] (his foreword is dated 20 August 1550, but this is an error, since Fabri's foreword is dated 7 October 1550; Flacius' reply has therefore to be situated at the beginning of 1551). He accuses Fabri that *er lügt, daß es stinken möchte.* He regards above all what Fabri says of Peter's sojourn in Rome as poisonous lies suggested to the Church by the devil. In order to reveal these lies, he supplies *achtzehn beweisungen, das S. Petrus zu Rom nicht gewesen sey.* This part of Flacius' treatise is clearly an almost literal translation of Velenský's *Petrum Romam non venisse,* although the latter's foreword is omitted.

Fabri, however, replied to Flacius in his treatise *Quod Petrus Romae*

---

[1] Magdeburg, n.d. (Foreword 20 August 1550).

[2] A survey of the contents and bibliographical details will be found in Nikolaus Paulus: *Die deutschen Dominikaner im Kampfe gegen Luther* (Freiburg, 1903), pp. 243–244.

[3] Quotation in Paulus, *op. cit.,* p. 244.

[4] And also to an earlier treatise which Fabri wrote in 1550: *Von dem Eyd Schwören. Auch von der Widertauffer Marter* (Ingolstadt). See also N. Paulus, *op. cit.,* p. 242.

fuerit, et ibidem Primus Episcopatum gesserit, atque sub Nerone martyrium passus fuerit: *Et an fundamentum Ecclesiae dici possit*,[5] in which all the arguments used by Cochlaeus and Fisher are once again reviewed. This work remained unpublished for some time, however, until it was discovered by Nicholas Mameranus, a poet and historian from Luxemburg, who had it printed on 20 September in Dillingen, with Fabri's consent. Mameranus wrote a foreword for this edition, quoting a number of passages from Scripture and the Fathers which might serve as a defence of Peter's episcopate in Rome.

It is clear from these polemics not only that Flacius was familiar with Velenský's treatise, but also that he had it in front of him (probably in the Latin version)—he made a new German translation of it. We may conclude from this and from his vehement opposition to Fabri that he was convinced by Velenský's arguments (although he does not mention the latter's name anywhere in his writing). This conclusion is, however, only partly true. Flacius' position is the same as that taken earlier by Luther, who, in his treatise against Emser,[6] rejected, with arguments provided by Velenský, Peter's twenty-five years as bishop of Rome, but left it open as a possibility that the apostle may, after having stayed for eighteen years in Jerusalem and seven in Antioch, have gone to Rome and been put to death there during the reign of Nero. It is notable that, when Flacius was concerned with this subject once again three years later—in his *Historia certaminum inter Romanos Episcopos et sextam Carthaginiensem synodum Africanasque Ecclesias, de primatu seu potestate Papae, bona fide ex authenticis monumentis collecta*[7]—he wrote: *non constat plane, Petrum fuisse Romae*.[8]

Anyone taking this statement out of its context, as Cullmann has done[9], and translating it as: *es sei nicht absolut sicher, daß Petrus in Rom gewesen sei*, is not accurately reproducing Flacius' hesitation, because he is not reporting the reason for this statement. Flacius himself took over—in the same way as Luther had done—Velenský's argument. It is *propalam falsum*, Flacius argues, when the papists write that Peter was in Rome for twenty-five years, since he stayed in Jerusalem for eighteen years, was then in Pontus and also another seven years in

---

[5] N. Paulus, *op. cit.*, p. 245, where another title of this treatise is given: *Testimonium scripturae et patrum, B. Petrum Apostolum Romae fuisse* (Antwerp, 1553).
[6] See p. 139, 141.
[7] Basle, 1554 (Henrichus Petri).
[8] In the supplement: *Contra commentium primatum papae*, p. 167.
[9] O. Cullmann: *Petrus, Jünger—Apostel—Märtyrer* (Munich and Hamburg, [1]1952), p. 77.

Antioch. If this had been followed by twenty-five years as bishop in Rome, then he would have died long after the reign of Nero, "by whom it is said *(dicitur)* that he was put to death". It is, however, certain that Peter was not in Rome when Paul came to the city, Flacius says, and that Paul had nothing to say about Peter in the letters that he wrote from Rome.

If we examine the whole of Flacius' treatise, it becomes quite clear that his hesitation as to whether Peter was ever in Rome was based not only on the fact that the apostle could not in any case have been bishop there for twenty-five years, but also—as in the case of Velenský—on the division of tasks between Paul and Peter. In connection with Gal. 2, he wrote[10] that Peter *ipse velit praedicare Judaeis, Paulus debeat concionari gentibus*, from which may it be concluded *ei et a Christo potissimum super et inter Judaeos apostolatum, episcopatum, seu papatum concreditum mandatumque esse: et eum tum ante Hierosolymitanam synodum, tum postea potissimum Judaeos docuisse, eoque potissimum ibi sedisse aut stetisse, ubi plurimi Judaei fuerunt, id est in Syria et aliis orientalibus partibus. Nam Romae non ita multi fuerunt: quandoquidem et nondum fuerant sic dissipati sicut postea in eversione Hierosolyma, et Claudius eos Roma penitus expulerat.*

The statement: *non constat plane, Petrum fuisse Romae* must therefore be understood as a cautious indication that no absolute certainty can be obtained regarding this matter, although the available data argue in favour of a denial of Peter's sojourn in Rome.

The subject is also approached in the same cautious way in the *Ecclesiastica historia*.[11] Oscar Cullmann said[12] that Flacius *in diesen Magdeburger Zenturien vom Martyrium des Petrus und des Paulus in Rom spricht* and F. C. Baur said[13] that this work *keinen bestimmten Zweifel gegen die angebliche Thatsache ausspricht*. Once again, however, we are bound to question whether Cullmann—and in this case Baur—have correctly reproduced Flacius' train of thought. It would certainly seem as though no problem is raised here in what Flacius says about the death of Paul and Peter in Rome: *Sub finem suum Nero praestantissimos duos apostolos, Petrum ac Paulum, Romae scribitur (!) interfecisse:*

---

[10] *op. cit.*, pp. 124–125.

[11] *Ecclesiastica historia, integram ecclesiae Christi ideam, quantum ad locum …* (The "Magdeburg Centuries"), Basle, 1559–1574. Centuries 1/3 were written by all the contributors in 1559; Centuries 4/13 were written (in 1560–1569) without Flacius, because of his involvement in the controversy over original sin.

[12] *op. cit.*, p. 77.

[13] *Paulus, der Apostel Jesu Christi* (2nd edn., Leipzig, 1866), p. 317.

quorum prior crucis, alter gladii supplicio est affectus. Eusebius libro secundo, cap. vigesimoquinto. Nonnulli affirmant, eodem die factum; alii variant, diversos quidem annos, sed eundem mensis diem constituentes.[14] But here too it is possible to recognise the cautious manner in which Flacius always speaks about this subject. Not only does he give several different opinions—he also and above all is on his guard against making any pronouncement of his own, saying that "it is written" *(scribitur)*, in other words, "it is written by Eusebius".

A similar method of approach is also found in the passage in the *Ecclesiastica historia* on *Argumenta contra primatum Petri*.[15] Among the arguments that Flacius brings forward against the primacy of Peter is not Velenský's, but the statement that Peter and Paul were put to death by Nero. This is, however, expressed in a rather detached manner and Flacius also mentions his sources: *Paulus et Petrus Romae a Nerone interfecti et sepulti dicuntur (!), teste Tertulliano et Egesippo apud Eusebium.* Here too Flacius is very reluctant to make a statement of his own and later on in the same work we find the reason for this reluctance. In the chapter *De vitis doctorum*,[16] he provides a summary of Velenský's argument—the calculation that Peter could not have been in Rome for twenty-five years, the fact that Peter is not named as the bishop of Rome in Luke's Acts of the Apostles and the silence preserved by Paul about Peter in his epistles. Flacius' conclusion, however, is not like Velenský's, but rather in the spirit of Luther—it is at least clear, he says, that *Petrum vel non fuisse Romae, vel alio tempore fuisse, ac brevius.*

We may therefore conclude that Flacius used Velenský's treatise repeatedly in order to derive from it arguments that he could employ to deny Peter's twenty-five years' episcopate in Rome, but also that, in imitation of Luther, he left it open as a possibility that the apostle may still have come to Rome during the period that was not covered by the New Testament sources. This second conclusion implies that Flacius rejected Velenský's theory that Peter probably died as a martyr in Jerusalem, even though this theory is not mentioned anywhere in his writings.

It is, moreover, clear that Flacius found Velenský's treatise extremely valuable as a refutation of the papacy—so valuable in fact that he published an Italian translation of it in 1566: *Trattato nel quale con certis-*

---

[14] *Cent.* I, lib. II, cap. III (col. 28).
[15] *Cent.* I, lib. II, cap. VII (col. 527).
[16] *Cent.* I, lib. II, cap. X (col. 561–562).

simi ragioni nella sacra scrittura, si manifesta, come Pietro Apostolo non mai fu à Roma, ne ancò pati in quella il Martirio: la onde si uede quanto debolmente il Romano pontifice si vanta di esser successore di Pietro. This time—in contrast to his German translation of 1551—he included the complete foreword and mentioned the name of the author: Ulrico Veleno Minoriense.[17]

Finally, Flacius' contemporary, John Funck, should be mentioned, since his position was almost identical. Funck published his *Chronologia, hoc est omnium temporum et annorum ab initio mundi usque ad 1552 computatio* in Basle in 1554. On the one hand, he includes in this treatise Velenský's argument with regard to the silence preserved in the New Testament about Peter's sojourn in Rome and the hypothesis that the "Babylon" of Peter's first letter may have been a Jewish settlement in Egypt and concludes from this that Peter could not in any case have been in Rome for a long time. On the other hand, Funck says—entirely in the spirit of Luther, that he does not venture to make any pertinent statements about the matter. He does, however, make one important statement: *Non est articulus fidei, nec haereticus consensus, si quis non omnia credet, quae Pontificii ad suam tyrannidem stabilendam excogitarunt* (fo. 78)

2. *Bellarmine*

Flacius' writings did not immediately give rise to a renewed debate about the views of Oldřich Velenský. We may, however, regard as direct reactions to his work the placing on the index of forbidden books in 1559 and 1564 of the *Petrum Romam non venisse*[18]—as an anonymous work, however—and the writings of Lindanus and Sanders.

William Lindanus, the Inquisitor of Friesland and, from 1569 onwards the Bishop of Roermond, wrote his *Panoplia evangelica, sive de verbo dei evangelico libri quinque* in 1560. It was published in Cologne. In Book I of this work, the author points to the contradictory interpretations that can be made when the Bible is regarded as the only authority. In Book II, he demonstrates the value of the Church's tradition and in this case especially the writings of the Fathers as authoritative in matters of interpretation. In Books III and IV, he attempts to show that the teaching and the institutions of the Church were already in existence in the apostolic Church. Finally, in Book V, he challenges the views of the Protestants in these questions.

Book IV of Lindanus' treatise contains the author's polemics against Flacius—and even more against Calvin and Funck (and, in passing, Velenský). Lindanus, however, does not provide any new arguments.

---

[17] See Appendix, No. 6.
[18] See p. 151.

He regards it as sufficient to appeal to the unanimity existing among the Fathers of the Church: *Petrum igitur Romae fuisse, licet capitis sui periculo docuerit ipse, omnesque veterum scriptorum chorus constanter simul et concorditer sonet* (p. 441). A little later, he makes a similar statement: *Petrum Romae fuisse, affirmant, ut qui de eo amplius dubiter rectior, utrum unus Sol, an duo sint, quaerat. Quis hoc vanum esse cum Calvino, aut Veleno, afferere audeat* (p. 442). In Lindanus' opinion, the arguments used by Calvin to throw doubt on Peter's episcopate *tam sunt ridicula* (p. 444) and he believes that Funck ultimately *Petrum Romae fuisse negare non audebat* (p. 444).

Two years later, Lindanus returned to the same subject in the work that he published at that time in Antwerp, *Tabulae grassantium passim haeresium*. The *tabula secunda* of this work is devoted to a discussion of the contradictions existing among the views of Luther's followers. In it, Lindanus writes:

$$
\left. \begin{array}{c} Petrum\ Romae \\ fuisse \end{array} \right\} \quad ait \quad \left\{ \begin{array}{c} Lutherus\ in \\ Homilia \end{array} \right\} \quad negat \quad \left\{ \begin{array}{c} Sebast.\ Franck \\ Velenus \end{array} \right.
$$

The Englishman, Nicholas Sanders, who fled from his own country in the reign of Queen Elizabeth and published his treatise *De visibilii Monarchia Ecclesiae, libri octo* in 1571, made hardly any contribution to the discussion. He reacted to Flacius' arguments against Peter's episcopate, but, in his counter-argument (in Book VI, cap. X), he mentions only the exegesis of 1 Pet. 5. 13 and the customary quotations from the Church Fathers. After this, he draws the remarkable conclusion that *est igitur in Verbo Dei satis aperte significatum, quod Petrus Romae fuerit* (p. 217). On the basis of the same evidence provided by the Fathers, he concludes in Book VIII: *Non papam, sed protestantes Antichristi membra esse*.

For the sake of completeness, it should also be noted that the well-known French jurist, Francis Balduinus, played an indirect part in the debate. He wrote a foreword for the edition of the *Optati Afri, Milevitani episcopi, libri sex de schismate Donatistarum adversus Parmenianum* that he prepared for publication in 1563 in Paris. In this foreword, he pointed to an inconsistency in Calvin's teaching. In the *Institutio christianae religionis*, Calvin accepted Peter's sojourn in Rome as a possibility, but in his commentary on the epistles of Peter he denied it (p. 120). This intellectual comment can, however, not be regarded as a real contribution to the controversy. The humanist Balduinus, who had initially been in sympathy with the aims of the Reformation, but had later returned to the Catholic Church, never really felt committed to questions concerned with the primacy.

It was not until 1586 that a radical theological contribution was made to the controversy by a leading Roman Catholic. It was in that year that the Jesuit scholar who was a professor in Rome (and from 1599 onwards a cardinal in that city), Robert Bellarmine, published the first volume of his major work—containing his lectures to his students—*Disputationes de controversiis christianae fidei adversus huius temporis haereticos*.[19] It is the *controversia tertia (De summo pontifice)* of this comprehensive work that deals with the papacy[20] and it contains among other things a detailed refutation of Velenský's treatise.

Bellarmine begins[21] by reviewing the work of those authors who have questioned whether Peter was even in Rome: *Primus quod sciam, qui docuit B. Petrum neque Episcopum fuisse Romae, neque Romam ipsam unquam vidisse, fuit Gulielmus quidam, Ioannis Wiclefi praeceptor, ut Thomas Waldensis refert lib. 2, doctr. fidei, art. 1, cap. 7. Hunc sequutus est Uldalricus Velenus Lutheranus, qui librum integrum de hac re edidit, in quo XVIII persuasionibus (sic ipse eas vocat) demonstrasse se putat, Petrum nunquam fuisse Romae, et tam Petrum, quam Paulum non Romae, sed Hierosolymis esse occisos. Pro quo opere, ad finem libri affirmat, se sine ullo dubio immarcescibilis coronae praemia a Deo percepturum. Et sane si mandacia coronantur a Deo splendidissimam coronam sine ulla dubitatione Velenus accipiet.*

He then goes on to name Flacius as representing the same point of view: *Illyricus quoque in libro contra primatum Papae: Demonstratio, inquit, certa est Petrum Romae non fuisse.* By not quoting Flacius completely,[22] Bellarmine is able to accuse the author of the *Historia certaminum inter Romanos Episcopos* of making a statement that he in fact never made. When, however, he comes to mention Calvin, he quotes him correctly: *Ioannes Calvinus, lib. 4. Institut. cap. 6, par. 15, postquam rem totam esse dubiam ostendit, ita concludit: Tamen, inquit, propter scriptorum consensum, non pugno quin illic mortuus fuerit, sed Episcopum fuisse, praesertim longo tempore, persuaderi nequeo.* To this he adds, quite correctly, giving Flacius in fact his proper place[23]: *Similia habent Magdeburgenses Centur. 1, lib. 2, cap. 10, col. 561.*

---

[19] Ingolstadt, 1590.

[20] Liber I: *De primatu S. Petri in Ecclesia militante*; Lib. II: *De successione Romani Pontificis in eo primatu*; Lib. III: *De Antichristo quod nihil commune habeat cum Romano Ponifice*.

[21] Lib. II, cap. I (col. 712).

[22] In Flacius (*Historia certaminum inter Romanos Episcopos...*, p. 267), the whole sentence reads: *Demonstratio item certa est, Petrum Romae non fuisse, quod Paulus Romam et Romae scribens ac tam multos mediocre Christianos salutans et nominans nunquam tam vel unico verbo Petri tanti viri mentionem faciat.* This was a commentary on his statement: *Non constat plane, Petrum fuisse Romae.*

[23] This gives the impression that Bellarmine did not regard Flacius as responsible for the work of the Centuriators of Magdeburg.

From this review, Bellarmine concludes that he has to reply to four questions: *Primo, an Petrus fuerit Romae? Secundo, an sit mortuus Romae? Tertio, an fuerit Episcopus Romae? Quarto, an Romanum Episcopatum semel susceptum nunquam mutaverit?* To this he adds that what must above all be discussed is the question of the validity of the office of *multi Romani Pontifices nunquam fuerint Romae* (the Avignon popes) and that there must also be an exposition of the problem as to why Peter, who was the bishop of Antioch, nonetheless obtained the primacy in Rome.

Bellarmine deals in great detail with the task that he set himself. The point of departure that he takes is the text at the end of the first letter of Peter: *Salutat vos Ecclesia in Babylone collecta, et Marcus filius meus*. He says, quoting Eusebius, Jerome and Tertullian, that Rome was regarded in the early Church as this "Babylon", but he also notes that Luther was inclined to the same opinion, because he wrote about *Babylonica captivitate*, and that the centuriators of Magdeburg called Rome by the same symbolic name in many passages in their well-known "Centuries".[24] Velenský is therefore, he concludes, alone in his view that the Babylon mentioned by Peter must be sought in Egypt, as the later "Chayrum". Furthermore, when Velenský changes the evidence found in the Apocalypse—the "Babylon" mentioned in that book, Bellarmine insists, is clearly Rome—into a cynical attack against the *romana ecclesia* ("then we must quickly leave this fiendish Babylon"), he ought to remember that *Babylonem vocari non Romanam Ecclesiam, sed Romanam urbem, qualis erat Ioannis tempore*.

After having defended Rome as the place from which Peter sent his epistle, Bellarmine employs the concluding passages from the Acts of the Apostles and the letter to the Romans to support his argument that Peter must have been in Rome for a long time. There were evidently, according to the end of Acts and Paul's letter, many Christians living in the capital, Bellarmine concludes, and asks: *Petro igitur quis hos Christianos fecerit, si Petrus non fuit Romae?*

He then mentions Velenský's view of this question, namely that the Christians began to go to Rome after Christ's death, during the reign of Tiberius. His reply to this is that Velenský's appeal to Tranquillus and Tertullian in this case was mistaken. The former was not referring to the Christians in his *Vita Tiberii* and the latter was stating the very opposite, that Pilate wrote to Tiberius about the many converts, whereupon the emperor brought the matter before the senate. Tiberius

---

[24] Bellarmine mentions *Cent.* I, Lib. II, cap. 4 (col. 56).

therefore only knew of Christ's fame from Pilate's letters. The Fathers of the Church must for this reason have been right, Bellarmine says, when they said that Peter was the first to work under the Romans and that this happened at the time of Claudius.

Bellarmine's third argument is in support of the thesis that Mark wrote his gospel in Rome, leading to the conclusion that Peter must have preached there. He has several reasons for refuting Velenský's counter-argument that John Mark, Peter's disciple, was different from Mark Aristarchus, the evangelist. Bellarmine insists that it was Mark and Aristarchus who were different. Two different persons, Mark and Aristarchus, feature in the letter to Philemon and the fact that they are different emerges even more clearly from the letter to the Colossians, where, in his final greetings, Paul writes: *Salutat vos Aristarchus concaptivus meus et Marcus consobrimus Barnabae.* The fact that Mark was the bishop of Alexandria cannot be regarded as proof that he could not have written the gospel in Rome. He was, Bellarmine suggests, later sent to Egypt by Peter.

Bellarmine next discusses the question as to whether Peter died in Rome.[25] His point of departure is that, until the fourteenth century, no one ever doubted that Peter and Paul were buried in Rome and he finds this firm conviction understandable, since so many writers in the early Church reported this fact. In this context, he quotes Eusebius, Hegesippus, Chrysostom, Tertullian, Ambrose, Jerome, Augustine and other Fathers of the Church and goes on to affirm that Velenský has nothing valid to say against this unanimous testimony, apart from his description of the *Quo vadis* story as a falsification, basing this conclusion on his exegesis of Acts 3, which teaches that Christ will not return to this earth before the day of judgement. Bellarmine rejects this exegesis and refers to Acts 9 (Christ's appearance to Paul on the road to Damascus) as an example of scriptural teaching that Christ certainly appeared to his apostles after his ascension.

In the following chapter,[26] Bellarmine defends the thesis that Peter was the Bishop of Rome until he died with the argument that, in the early history of the Church, no city is mentioned as having claimed to be the episcopal throne of the apostle with the exception of Antioch and Rome. In support of this thesis, he quotes many authors in the Church who have called Peter the first Bishop of Rome.

After having outlined his own point of view in this way (namely

---

[25] Lib. II, cap. 3.
[26] Lib. II, cap. 4.

that Peter was in Rome, that he was bishop there and that he died there) and having supported his standpoint by appealing to many authorities in the Church, Bellarmine goes on[27] to discuss and refute systematically Velenský's treatise *Petrum Romam non venisse*, observing correctly that it was the persuasiones elaborated in that work *quibus Calvini et Illyrici argumenta continentur*.

Bellarmine's arguments, however, are the same as those adduced by Cochlaeus, Fisher and Cortese. His reply to Velenský's statement concerning the contradictions existing among authors in the Church about the year that Peter is reputed to have come to Rome is that *discordiam de tempore—si qua esset—quo Petrus Romam venit, non infirmare sententiam nostram, quod Petrus Romam venerit*. He also gives as an example that this uncertainty regarding the date is of no importance for our evaluation of the fact the difference existing among the evangelists with regard to the day of Jesus' death: *Nam constat apud Christianos, Christum esse mortuum in cruce pro nobis: tamen maxima discordia est de tempore, quo mortuus est*. He then comes to the counter-argument: just as the contradictory statements about the date was an argument for Velenský not to believe in Peter's sojourn in Rome, so too is it possible for complete unanimity concerning the fact to be an argument for being certain about Peter's episcopate. Bellarmine moreover insists that there is no real contradiction among the *bonos auctores*—if Eusebius and Jerome wrote that Peter came to Rome in the second year of Claudius' reign, their statements do not contradict Orosius' comment that the apostle came to Rome *in exordio regni Claudii*. Bellarmine's observation is: *Nam si regnum Claudii tres in partes dividas, id est, in exordium, medium et finem, annum secundum ad exordium pertinere videbis*. He goes on to say that all the authors who have spoken of twenty-five years as the length of Peter's episcopate (Damasus, Isidore, Bede and others), have agreed about this dating, since *nec enim sunt anni XXV usque ad annum XIV Neronis, nisi a secundo Claudii numerare incipiamus*. Bellarmine also dismisses the *Fasciculus temporum* and the *Passionale* mentioned by Velenský as unreliable sources. The first, he claims, can be traced back to Marianus Scotus,[28] who frequently contradicted himself in his *Chronicum*.

Bellarmine's reply to Velenský's argument that historical uncertainty exists regarding Peter's successors is very similar. He first defends the thesis that a difference of opinion concerning the lists of

---

[27] Lib. II, cap. 5/11.
[28] † 1080.

bishops does not in any sense give rise to uncertainty regarding Peter's episcopate and then goes on to show that there was in fact a great measure of agreement with regard to the first bishops of Rome.

In opposition to Velenský's argument that contradictions in the presentation of secondary facts cause doubt about the primary fact, Bellarmine defends the thesis that this method is incorrect, because, among all the authors whose statements are mutually contradictory, there is unanimity about the primary fact and he insists that the contradictory character of these writings can to a great extent be disproved by careful research.

Bellarmine next discusses Velenský's *argumentum e silentio* based on the New Testament. Here too, we find a familiar reasoning, namely that Peter remained in Jerusalem for the first five years after Christ's ascension. During the fifth year, he went to Antioch, where he was bishop for seven years. During that period, he travelled around Pontus, Asia, Galatia, Cappadocia and Bythinia from Antioch. After spending these seven years at Antioch, he returned to Jerusalem, where he was imprisoned by Herod, but set free by an angel. That same year—the second year of Claudius' reign—he went to Rome, where he remained for twenty-five years as bishop. During his episcopate in Rome, he returned temporarily to Jerusalem, when Claudius banished all the Jews from Rome. When he was in Jerusalem, he was able to take part in the council of the apostles. When Claudius died, he went back to Rome and stayed there until his own death. If this is really the story of Peter's life, Bellarmine concludes, then Velenský's argument, which was based on the assembly of the apostles in Jerusalem, and claimed that Peter was at that time not yet in Rome, is untenable.

Bellarmine also denies that any evidence is provided by the lists of greetings in Paul's epistles. John is not named in the letter to the Ephesians, although he was the Bishop of Ephesus, and James' name is absent from the letter to the Hebrews. What is more, Paul wrote his letter to the Romans at a time when Peter was not in Rome.

The *argumentum e silentio*, Bellarmine argues, cannot be applied in the case of very many other subjects contained in the New Testament: *Alioque quia Mattheus non scribit in Evangelio Christum circumcisum; Marcus non meminit praesentationis; Lucas non meminit stellae novae; Ioannes non dicit Christum natum de Maria Virgine; ista omnia erunt falsa, quod absurdissimum est.* For this reason, he concludes, no importance can be attached to the silence preserved by Paul and Luke about Peter's sojourn in Rome.

Bellarmine also deals with the way in which Velenský uses Scripture in other cases. He regards the exegesis which Velenský provided of division of tasks between Peter and Paul that was made in Jerusalem as incorrect: *Petrus praedicaret omnibus, et ubicunque vellet, sed principaliter Iudaeis; Paulus omnibus, et ubicunque vellet, sed principaliter Gentilibus.* This is, in any case, Bellarmine stresses, clear from the apostolic practice. In his journeys, Paul went first to the synagogues of the Jews, whereas Peter also went to Antioch and Asia. Moreover, Velenský's conclusion from Matt. 23 that Christ was here predicting the death of Peter and Paul as martyrs is completely groundless. The *prophetas et sapientes et scribas* mentioned in that chapter of Matthew's gospel cannot, after all, be the apostles, Bellarmine argues, since it is well known that Andrew was put to death in Achaia, Philip and John were killed in Asia, Thomas died in India, Bartholomew in Armenia and Matthew in Ethiopia. What is more, Velenský ought not to appeal to Nicholas of Lyra and Jerome to support him in this absurd claim, for both these authors said quite clearly that Peter and Paul were put to death in Rome.

Finally, Bellarmine gives a certain amount of attention to a number of other sources, notably Linus' account of the Passion and Josephus' works. Linus, he asserts, is not an authority to whom any appeal can be made—Velenský admits this, yet quotes Ambrose via this source. Josephus also is unable to support Velenský's claims—if Peter was really put to death in Jerusalem, why does Josephus not say, in Book XX of his *Antiquitates*, in which he records the actions of the high priest Annas, that the latter also put Peter to death?

If we examine Bellarmine's argument as a whole, we are bound to observe that, after the exhaustive refutations written by Cochlaeus, Fisher and Cortese, no new elements are added to the polemics with Velenský. Bellarmine is also, on his own admission, to some extent dependent on Fisher. He himself writes[29] that his attention was brought to the heresy that he is attacking by a book published a long time previously by Johannes Rossensis, *beatae memoriae viro*, but goes on to say: *sed librum ipsum* (that is, Velenský's treatise) *videre nunquam potui.*

It was therefore thanks to the scientific honesty of Fisher—who included the whole of Velenský's treatise in his own—that Bellarmine was able to become acquainted with the literal text of the *Petrum Romam non venisse.* What is more, since Bellarmine constructed his

---

[29] Lib. II, cap. 11 (col. 740).

argument in imitation of Fisher, it is not surprising that he, like the English bishop himself, conducted the polemics entirely within the sphere defined by Velenský—in other words, he too combatted a historically analytical argument with historical arguments. Bellarmine did not, moreover, discuss in this context the fact that the historical reliability—or unreliability—of the Petrine tradition is not essentially important in a defence of the papacy, since the foundation of the primacy is only undermined when its necessity for salvation is disputed. He does not, moreover, even consider this question in the following *capita* of his *De summo pontifice*, in which Velenský is not mentioned at all, but Luther, Calvin and Flacius are attacked. Bellarmine there continues to discuss the Petrine tradition and defends the validity of the Petrine succession as continued by the bishops of Rome.

Hardly any advances were made in the controversy concerning Velenský's views in the reactions evoked in the Protestant camp by Bellarmine's great work. Following Flacius in the Magdeburg Centuries, it was generally accepted as a fact that Peter was in Rome and all that was rejected was his twenty-five years' episcopate in that city. What appears to be the closest approach to Velenský's view is to be found in the teaching of Amandus Polanus of Polansdorf (1561–1610), a theologian at Basle, who prepared three theses for the disputations that he was to conduct at the university in 1596—these provided the possibility for criticism of the Petrine tradition. Under the collective title of *De regimine ecclesiae*, there was a debate on a thesis entitled *Contra Petri Apostoli primatum in Ecclesia* on 16 September 1596, on a second thesis *Contra ementitam successionem Pontificum Romanorum in Episcopatu Romano* on 14 October and on a third thesis, *De primatu Papae et de Antichristo*, on 25 November.[30] The defenders follow, very summarily, the ideas contained in the *Petrum Romam non venisse* concerning Peter's absence from Rome, but Polanus himself does not take over Velenský's arguments.

Polanus' own opinions are expressed most clearly in what he wrote in his *Kurtzen Inhalt der gantzen Lehr, welche in der theologischen Schul der lobliche Universitet Basel geführt wirdt*:[31] (68) *Wir lehren, daß alle Bischoff*

---

[30] In 1597, 24 theses by Polanus, including the three mentioned here, were published together in *Sylloges thesium theologicarum, ad methodi leges conscriptarum et Disputationibus Roberti Bellarmini praecipue oppositarum atque in vetusta Academia Basiliensi ad disputandum propositarum ab Amando Polano a Polansdorf. Pars prima, Basileae 1597*. A very short version of Velenský's persuasiones appears on p. 43.

[31] Published in 1600. The text is published in Ernst Staehelin: *Amandus Polanus von Polansdorf* (Basle, 1955), pp. 111–130.

unter einander gleich seyen, und keiner unter ihnen ein allgemeiner Bischoff sein oder genennt solle werden, derhalben auch kein Römischer Papst nicht, welcher in der That auch kein Bischoff ist, dieweil er das Amt eines Bischoffs nicht thut; daß alle die Bischoff oder Seelenhirten, so die Lehr, welche Petrus verkündiget hat, führen, Petri Nachfolger seyen im Amt, die Gemeind Christi zu weyden; der Römisch Papst aber seye keines wegs Petri Nachfolger, dieweil er weder die Lehr, welche Petrus verkündigt hat, führet noch auch seinem Leben und Wandel nachfolget. Later in the same treatise, Polanus also says: (73) *Wir lehren, daß der Widerchrist mit seinem Anhang mit nichten die Kirch Gottes seyen, sondern derselbigen abgesagte Feind, daß der Römische Papst der Widerchrist und die Päpstler, das ist: alle die, welche sich mit der Gemeinschafft deß Papsts verunreinigen, das Reich deß Widerchrists seyen, derhalben die nach dem Wort Gottes reformierte Kirchen recht, wol und gottseliglich gethan, daß sie sich von der Päpstischen Kirchen abgesöndert haben.*

The most that can be concluded from these quotations is that Polanus was influenced by Velenský's ideas about the Antichrist, but a more plausible assumption is that the author is here reproducing a criticism of the papacy that was universally accepted in Protestant circles. This also emerges from a work which Polanus published previously, his *Partitiones theologicae juxta naturalis methodi leges conformatae duobus libris, quorum primus est de fide, alter de bonis operibus* (Basle, 1590). In this treatise (p. 154), Polanus writes that the *Antichristus est Papa Romanus* and that *Ecclesia Antichristi est Ecclesia Romana, falso dicta Apostolica et Catholica.* He does not, however, have anything at all to say about the Petrine tradition in this earlier work.

Another Protestant theologian who, like Polanus, questioned the reliability of the Petrine tradition, but did not directly combat it, was Daniel Chamierus. In 1626, he published, in Geneva, his *Panstratiae catholicae.* The title of Liber XIII, Cp. IV of this work is *Utrum Petrus fuerit Episcopus Romanus* and Chamierus' reply to this question is:[32] *Ac sane non tantum de eo nihil scriptura testatur: sed nonnulla sufficit in contrarium argumenta. Imo in ipsa Ecclesiastica historia multa sunt quae scrupulum moveant... Sed fuisse Petrum Romanum Episcopum, quomodo Linum, Cletum, Clementem, hoc vero pernego, et Papistarum afferentium argumenta solide confuto.*

One of the few men to take over almost entirely the argument contained in the *Petrum Romam non venisse*—with the exception of the suggestion that Peter and Paul were put to death in Jerusalem—

---

[32] *Tomus secundus,* p. 483.

was Velenský's well-known compatriot John Amos Komenský. In 1626, he wrote, at the age of twenty-five, a "Warning against the Antichrist and his Temptation",[33] which was clearly intended to be defence of the Reformers' position against Bellarmine,[34] and in which one chapter was devoted to the question as to whether Peter was ever in Rome. In Caput XV, the author states "that the Roman Church was not founded by or on Peter, because he had no episcopate in Rome and was never even there".[35]

Although Komenský elaborated this statement with the help of the arguments contained in the *Petrum Romam non venisse*,[36] this does not necessarily mean that he ever read the treatise himself. He may, after all, have taken over from Bellarmine the latter's version, in his work, of Velenský's argument. Komenský nowhere mentions Velenský's name in his own treatise and this may point to the fact that Velenský's treatise never came into his hands, since he is very particular in recording his sources. He even mentions, for example, John Bale's *Acta Romanorum Pontificum*,[37] which provided very few arguments.

3. *The Polemics in the Netherlands*

It can be stated that the Protestant theologians of the sixteenth and seventeenth centuries generally speaking accepted the classical tradition of the primacy of Peter, sometimes with amendments, and certainly not emphatically opposed it. In Protestant circles, Velenský's treatise was forgotten. It was only in the Netherlands that the ideas contained in the *Petrum Romam non venisse* were kept alive by a number of theologians, either by defending them or by attacking them.

Even before Flacius Illyricus had once again drawn attention to Velenský's ideas, John Anastasius Veluanus showed clearly, in his

---

[33] *Retuňk proti Antikristu a svodum jeho.* Text in *Dílo Jana Amose Komenského*, II (Prague, 1971).

[34] Directed especially against *De verbo Dei non scripto, De romanis pontificis ecclesiastica monarchia* and *De summo pontifice*.

[35] *Že římská církev ad Petra a na Petru založena neni: totž že Petr Biskupstvi římského nezačal, ani v Římě jak živ nebyl* (p. 96, *op. cit.*).

[36] In six points: 1) the silence preserved in Acts; 2) the mission given to Peter to work among the Jews; 3/5) the silence maintained in the letters of Paul and 6) the calculation, made according to the method of elimination, of the number of years when Peter could not have come to Rome (*op. cit.*, pp. 97–99).

[37] See p. 196. (Komenský mentions this work in Cp. XIV.)

treatise *Der Leeken Wechwyser*,[38] published in 1554, that he was a follower of the Bohemian humanist. The examples and arguments that he uses in his chapter *Van den Antichrist*[39] give the impression that they are taken from the *Petrum Romam non venisse*. He has, for instance, this to say about the pope: "He has placed three crowns on his head, thereby making it arrogantly known that the three supreme princes, that is, emperors, kings and dukes, must continue to be his sworn servants" *(Hy set drie kronen op synen kop, vnde gifft dar mit houerdich to kennen, dat die drie hoichste fursten, nemelick keysers, kunningen, vnd hertogen, noch syne geswoirne knechten zyn moeten).*

Another statement reminiscent of Velenský is what Veluanus says about Peter's sojourn in Rome: "Several early Christian teachers have written that Peter was in Rome. Others, however, have produced evidence against this from the writings of the apostles, Paul's letter to the Romans and the epistles that he wrote when he was in prison in Rome, making it much more credible that Peter was not in Rome ... This can be seen from the following examples. In Rom. 16, Paul greets all the leading preachers who were in Rome at the time. In Phil. 1, he speaks about his work there and about the help that he gave to so many Romans with his preaching. Writing to Philemon, he names his most important fellow-helpers in Rome. Writing to Timothy, in the last chapter of the other letter he says, just before his death: 'They have all deserted me. Luke alone has remained with me in Rome.' But nowhere does Paul say that Peter was in Rome or that he did anything either at his time there or before his time. We may therefore conclude from this that it would be far more reasonable to call the Roman bishops Paul's successors than those of Peter" *(Etlicke alde doctoren schryven, dat Petrus to Romen zy gewest. Etlicke bewysen nu hier tegen vyt den wercken der apostelen, vyt Paulus breef an den romeren vnd mit syn epistelen vyt de romsche gefencknis gescreuen, viel geloifflicker to zyn, dat Petrus nyt to romen zy gewest ... Dit merckt aldus. Rom. 16. begruet Paulus alle principale predicanten die der tyt to Romen waren. philipp. 1 vertelt hy syn arbeyt vnde wie viel die Romer mit syn predicken geholpen zynt. An Philemon benoemt hy syne principale mithelpers to Romen. An Timotheus int leste capitel des anderden breefs sprickt hy kortelick vur syn doot aldus. Sie hebben myn al verlaten, Lucas is to romen allene by my gebleuen. Mer hy melt nergent, dat Petrus to Romen zy gewest, of dar ytwes gedain heft,*

---

[38] Text in *Bibliotheca Reformatoria Neerlandica* IV, ed. S. Cramer and F. Pijper (The Hague, 1906), pp. 125–376.

[39] *op. cit.*, pp. 365–368.

by syner tyt, of vor syner tyt. Hyr vyt follicht, dat die romsche bischopen viel billicker Paulus dan Petrus nafolgers genant zyn sollen).

Whereas the above passages are very reminiscent of Velenský's *persuasiones*, other arguments used by Veluanus clearly come from the tradition initiated by Marsilio of Padua: "Christ sent out his apostles with equal power to bind and to loose; he made no one subject to the commandments of another, to preach the gospel on another's instructions or to keep another's decrees" *(Christus heft syn apostelen vytgesandt mit ene gelycke macht in bynden vnd ontbynden, nymant gestalt onder des anders gebyden, dat euangely to prediken na des anders beueel, of des anders insettingen to halden).*

After this refutation of the Petrine tradition by Veluanus, there was, not only in the Netherlands, but also in the whole of Europe, a period during which the subject was hardly discussed at all. It was only roundabout the turn of the century that the theme was taken up again, the first interpreter of Velenský's views after this interval being John Bale (1495–1563), an Anglican bishop who, after his conversion to Calvinism, fled to the Netherlands. As early as 1538, when it was published in Basle, he wrote a treatise entitled *Acta Romanorum pontificum, a dispersione discipulorum Christi, usque ad Paulum quartum.* It was, however, not until many years after Bale's death, in 1615, that this work was published in Leiden and provided with a commentary written by John Martin Lydius.[40]

In the chapter *De Petro Apostolo*,[41] Bale states that, although the papists claim *(ut somniant Papistae)* that Peter was the Bishop of Rome for twenty-five years, the historical truth is that he worked mainly, on the basis of the division of tasks between himself and Paul, in Judaea: *In Iudaea ergo, ac finitimis regionibus, Christo mandato obstrictus permansit, praedicans in maritimis urbibus Evangelium regni Dei.* This, Bale believes, is borne out by the miracles that God performed through him—the cure of the paralytic Aeneas in Lydda, the raising of the dead Tabitha at Joppa and the baptism of the centurion Cornelius. All these signs prove that *illum nec sedisse, nec mortem obiisse Romae.*

Bale does not elaborate this theme any further, nor does he provide any arguments based either on the New Testament or on the contrarieties found in patristic writings. The consequence of this is that his

---

[40] *Scriptores duo anglici, coaetanei ac conterranei; de Vitis Pontificum Romanorum. Videlicet: Robert Barns et Johannes Baleus.*

[41] Liber I, p. 19.

treatise can be regarded as no more than a modest beginning to the later debate in the Netherlands.

All the same, Bale's work did inspire a Dutchman to write a history of the popes in which the Petrine tradition is disputed in a spirit much more akin to that of Velenský. In 1632, James Revius, who, from 1614 onwards was a preacher in Deventer (and from 1642 onwards governor of the Staten-College at Leiden), published his *Historia Pontificum Romanorum*.[42] In his foreword to this book, he wrote that he had made use of the chronicle of the popes written by Platina[43] and Bale's *Acta Romanorum Pontificum* and that it was his intention in his book to call to mind again and again the actions performed by the Antichrist so that *doctrinam de Antichristo in ecclesia puram conservari*.

Revius begins his chronicle with a consideration of Peter, *unicus, creditus papa I* and refutes the affirmation that the apostle spent twenty-five years in Rome as its bishop. In this, he uses the same arguments—in a very concise form—that Velenský had employed in his *Petrum Romam non venisse*—the chronology which can be reconstructed from the data supplied by the New Testament is not in accordance with the interpretation provided by the Fathers of the Church, in other words, if Peter, after having gone to the assembly of the apostles in Jerusalem, had then gone to Rome and had stayed there for twenty-five years, he would have lived about five years longer than Nero. What is more, Revius claims, *an vero unquam Romam viderit, variant patres*. Irenaeus speaks of Peter's sojourn in the capital lasting many years and Origen, on the other hand, says that he came to Rome only towards the end of his life, *quod facit statu minandae nostrae sententiae, de falsimonia 25 annorum regiminis*, Revius concludes. Other Church Fathers, he goes on, teach that Peter was put to death by the Jews. He provides three remarkable pieces of evidence in this context—Chrysostom's *Homilia* 76 on Matthew, Jerome's commentary on Matt. 23 and Nicholas of Lyra's gloss on the same passage. Where these are the same—not very convincing—examples that Velenský provides in his persuasio XVI and where they are also not to be found in Revius' source, John Bale's *Acta Romanorum pontificum*,

---

[42] *Historia Pontificum Romanorum, Contracta, Et compendio perducta usque ad annum aerae Christianae MDCXXXII, a Jacobo Revio* (Amsterdam, 1632). See also E. J. W Posthumus Meyjes: *Jacobus Revius, zijn leven en werken* (Utrecht, 1895), pp. 226–240.

[43] *Historia B. Platinae de vitis pontificum romanorum*, written in 1479 (but published for the first time in the Netherlands in 1643, 1645 and 1664).

this may well show that Revius was in fact familiar with the text of
the *Petrum Romam non venisse*. It would, after all, have been purely by
chance that he might have found these same misinterpreted quotations himself as evidence.

Finally, Revius states that it is not true to say that Peter was the
head of all the bishops, because both at that time and much later the
Christian communities were governed *communi presbyterorum consilio*
and there was, as Jerome affirmed, no difference in rank or authority
between the presbyters and the bishops. It should also be pointed out
here that this argument is also not to be found in Bale's work and
would seem to have been taken over from Velenský.

Shortly after the publication of Revius' history of the popes, in
which the author opposed the Petrine tradition, one of his most famous
contemporaries and compatriots, Hugo Grotius, joined in the conflict and, although he expressed his views in this matter only in the
form of marginal notes in other works, he nonetheless defined his
position very clearly.

In 1640, when he was in Paris as the envoy for Sweden, Grotius
wrote a *Commentatio ad loca quaedam Novi Testamenti, quae de antichristo agunt, aut agere putantur*,[44] with the aim of showing that it was
fundamentally incorrect to identify the pope with the Antichrist and
in the hope of removing one of the obstacles which stood in the way
of the reunion of the churches that he so much desired.[45]

In this work, he discusses five chapters of the New Testament,
2 Thess. 2, 1 John 2 and 4 and Apoc. 13 and 17. This is followed by
an *Appendix ad interpretationem locorum Novi Testamenti, quae de antichristo agunt, aut agere putantur*,[46] in which Grotius defends the whole
Petrine tradition, including the traditional teaching that Peter was
Bishop of Rome for twenty-five years.

His point of departure is an acceptance of the authority of the
magnus auctor Hieronymus and the *viri diligentes Eusebius, Orosius et alii*.
When these authors state that Peter was the Bishop of Rome for
twenty-five years this must be the truth, Grotius says, and any calculation of the year when the council of the apostles was held in Jerusalem is no longer important. Peter, *primus in Ecclesiarum cura*, may have
gone to Rome before that time and may have returned to Jerusalem for

---

[44] In *Hugonis Grotii Opera omnia theologica*, three volumes (Amsterdam, 1679), III,
p. 457.
[45] W. S. M. Knight: *Life and Works of Hugo Grotius* (London, 1925) pp. 278–280
[46] *op. cit.*, p. 475.

the sake of the council. *Non sequitur*, he claims, *hoc vel in illo anno Romae non fuit Petrus, ergo toto illo temporis spatio ibi non fuit.* Peter's episcopate in Rome was also not in conflict with his task of preaching the gospel to the Jews, since there were—a fact that is clear from Paul's epistle to the Romans—many Jews in Rome who had been converted to Christianity and were therefore *ad curam Petri*.

Grotius also saw no reason for not regarding the name "Babylon" in Peter's letter as a symbolic name for Rome. Surely, he asks, the same name is used for Rome in the Apocalypse? Those who claim, moreover, that Peter was crucified by the Jews are *homines stulti*. Suffiently convincing proof is provided by the complete agreement regarding Peter's crucifixion in Rome among all Christians, even Greek Christians, Novatians, Donatists and those who had an interest in not believing it.

Grotius names none of these whom he opposes in this work. He may, of course, have been thinking of Bale when he speaks of *qui Petrum ab Iudaeis cruci affictum tradidere*. Later on, he mentions Calvin several times. It is therefore possible that, in his discussion of the refutation of Peter's twenty-five years' episcopate on the basis of calculation of the date of the council of Jerusalem, he was thinking of Calvin's *Institutio religionis christianae*.

Much more thorough and more fully documented than any of the writings mentioned above is the work of Claudius Salmasius (1588–1653). This French theologian had fled from his own country and, after spending a short time in Sweden, settled in the Netherlands, in Leiden, where he succeeded Josephus Justus Scaliger (1540–1609)[47] It was there that his *Librorum de primatu papae pars prima (cum apparatu)* was published in 1645. It is clear from the detailed apparatus which precedes the work proper that his plan was to include in the *secunda pars* of the treatise a critical examination of the Petrine tradi-

---

[47] For a long time, Scaliger has been regarded, on the authority of Fr. Spanheim (see note 57), as a representative of those theologians, who accepted the Roman Petrine tradition. H. J. de Jonge (*The Study in the New Testament* in *Leiden University in the seventeenth Century*, Leiden, 1975), however, has made clear, that Scaliger in his notations on the New Testament—published after his death—has shown himself a opponent to that Petrine tradition. For example, he makes the statement: *De eius Romam adventu, sede 25 annorum et supremo capitis supplicio ibidem, nemo qui paulo humanior fuerit credere posset.* As an illustration of the fact that Scaliger's view must be known to many people—and even was of such an importance, that it overshadowed all preceding publications—de Jonge mentions a remarkable sentence of Pier Francesco Foggini, librarian of the Vatican (1741): *ante eum* (that is Scaliger) *nemo dubitavit Romam Claudio imperante Petrum venisse.*

tion in the Church. This second part, however, was never published. Many Christians assume, he wrote in his book, that Peter was the first bishop of the city of Rome, *cum satis constat Petrum nunquam Romae fuisse. Certe hoc probabimus in altera parte de primatu.*[48] All the same, he still provides a number of arguments which support his own position in this first part of the work.

He takes as his point of departure the assembly of the apostles in Jerusalem, at which, according to Gal. 2, Peter was given the task of preaching the gospel to the Jews. Peter carried out this task by travelling around in Judaea and the surrounding country. His journeys took him to Antioch—where he also had successors, none of whom claimed the primacy for themselves—and Egypt, which was the country from which he wrote his first epistle. The "Babylon" which the writer mentions as the place from which the letter is sent is, Salmasius claims, the Egyptian town of that name. (Like Velenský, Salmasius also names his sources: Strabo, Caelius and Volateranus.) The only reason for regarding the name "Babylon" as allegorical is the mistaken assumption that Peter was the Bishop of Rome. If, however, it is assumed that Peter did not depart in any way from his task of proclaiming the gospel to the Jews in Judaea and the surrounding districts, there is no reason for regarding the name "Babylon" as allegorical.

Peter must, moreover, have had successors in Egypt, who made as little claim as the bishops of Antioch to the primacy: *Quo iure autem de primatu Petri contendet Roma cum illis urbibus, quas prius accessit Petrus quam Romam veniret et in quibus episcopus longe ante instituit atque Ecclesias fundavit, quam Romae ullos constitueret? Quae primae Petrum habuerunt civitates, meliori ac maiori iure primatum sibi vindicare possunt, quam Roma quae ultima omnium Petrum vidit.*[49]

It is clear from the declared intention of his treatise that the author was only concerned to refute the Petrine tradition within the framework of his own deliberations about the primacy and we cannot conclude from his marginal observations about the Petrine tradition that he was familiar with Velenský's treatise. It is evident from his announcement of a separate discussion in a second part of the work that he must have had many arguments in reserve. At the same time, however, it can also be seen from the provisional indications that he provides in the first volume that his conclusions are exactly the same as Velenský's.

---

[48] p. 14.
[49] p. 15.

His frequent use, in parenthesis, of the statement *Petrum nunquam Romae fuisse*, his exegesis of the conclusion of the first epistle of Peter and his employment of the word *fabula* to describe the Petrine tradition of Rome—all these leave us in no doubt about his view. The same can also be said of his summary, which once again points to a second part:[50] *De Petro fabulam esse docebimus, qui Romae nunquam fuerit, et cui Apostolatus non gentium, non Romanorum, sed Iudaeorum concreditus est, nisi mentitum esse Paulum velimus. Ergo Paulus primus Ecclesiae Romanae fundator est.*

Half a century later, Salmasius' arguments were refuted by a contemporary who, like himself, had also settled in the Netherlands, Jacques Basnage. After having been a preacher in Rouen, where he was born, he became the leader of the Walloon community in Rotterdam in 1691. From 1709 until his death in 1723, he served the Walloon community in the Hague.

In 1699, his comprehensive history of the Church, the *Histoire de l'Église depuis Jésus-Christ jusqu'à présent*, was published in Rotterdam. In the first volume,[51] he deals with the *établissement du Siège de Rome* and discusses Salmasius' exegesis of "Babylon" as the place from which the first letter of Peter was sent: *Saumaise soutient que Saint Pierre quitta de bonne heure l'Empire romain,[52] passa à Babylone où étaient un grand nombre de Juifs, à la conversion desquels il travailla pendant toute sa vie; que ce fut là qu'il écrivit sa lettre, et enfin qu'il y mourut.* Basnage then goes on to add that it is quite possible that Peter may well have made many different missionary journeys to places where many Jews were living, *mais cela n'empêche point que Saint Pierre qui était chargé du soin de la circoncision ne soit allé à Rome pour travailler à la conversion des Juifs, qui y résidaient au delà du Tibre en assez grand nombre.* Basnage here appeals to the traditional teaching of the Church: *En effet, tous les anciens qui ont parlé de Saint Pierre le font mourir à Rome, et comment résister à une si grande nuée de témoins? Il s'agit d'un fait, et on ne peut connaître la vérité de ce fait que par l'autorité et par le nombre de ceux qui en ont parlé.* Basnage certainly recognises the differences that exist between the various early writers in the Church regarding their versions of the secondary facts, but—in the manner of Bellarmine—he points to their complete agreement with regard to the primary fact: *S'il n'y avait qu'un petit*

---

[50] p. 21.

[51] Livre VII, chapitre III (p. 347).

[52] This is not what Salmasius had written (his words were *Petrum nunquam Romam fuisse*).

nombre d'anciens qui déposassent sur ce fait, leur autorité ne serait pas si grande; mais, malgré la variation de leurs récits, ils s'accordent tous sur le martyre de cet apôtre à Rome.

What is remarkable here is that Basnage only discussed Salmasius' book and not the dissertation of Friedrich Spanheim Junior, which had been published in the meantime, *De ficta profectione Petri Apostoli in urbem Romam, deque non una traditionis origine,* and in which the Petrine tradition was refuted in far greater detail and in a much more radical way.

This professor at the University of Leiden, who had been teaching at Heidelberg until 1670, wrote, in 1679, his *Dissertationum Historici Argumenti Quaterni,* in which was included a *Disquisitio Historica qua Petrum Apostolum Romae nunquam fuisse conjectatur.*[53] This work is divided into four parts, the first providing a very well documented survey firstly of the authors of the early Church who wrote about the Petrine tradition, then of the details of Peter's biography to be found in the writings of the Church Fathers and finally of the Protestant authors of the more recent period who were concerned with the problem of the reliability of this Petrine tradition. Spanheim's conclusion is that these Protestant scholars, almost without exception, recognised Peter's episcopate in Rome as a historical fact, but, despite this, he maintains that Peter's sojourn in Rome was not simply doubtful, but completely in conflict with the truth.

In *pars secunda* of his *dissertatio,* Spanheim points to the *vanitas* of the Petrine tradition and mentions—before proceeding to his arguments— as scholars who have previously given their attention to the same subject: *Claudius Salmasius, in Apparatus ad libros de Primatu, post Ulricum Velenum, Illyricum...* It should be noted that, in contrast to his reference to the title of the work as well as the author's name in the case of Salmasius, Spanheim does not mention the title of Velenský's book. We are, however, bound to assume that Spanheim read the *Petrum Romam non venisse,* since the argument that follows in the second part of his work is exactly the same as that found in Velenský's treatise. Spanheim in fact provides eight *rationes,* in each of which an argument against the Petrine tradition is developed, together with the refutation of the arguments of the opponents in each case.

In *ratio prima,* Spanheim discusses the silence in the Acts of the

---

[53] The same article can be found in his posthumously published *Opera* (Leiden, 1703), *tomus secundus,* on pp. 331–380, where it is entitled: *Dissertatio tertia de ficta profectione Petri Apostoli in urbem Roman, deque non una traditionis origine.*

Apostles with regard to Peter's episcopate in Rome and opposes Bellarmine's view that it is not possible to derive an *argumentum e silentio* from this.

Ratio altera draws the reader's attention to the similar silence about Peter in Paul's letter to the Romans. Spanheim replies to the objection that Peter was not in Rome at that time because he had been banished from Rome by Claudius on the one hand with an argument that the date of the letter is arbitrary in view of the fact that Peter's absence from Rome had to be defended and, on the other, with the thesis that any such flight from Rome on the part of Peter would be in conflict with the *officium boni pastoris*.

Ratio tertia alludes to other proofs in the epistle to the Romans which show that Peter had not previously been in Rome. Christ, for example, is praised for the work that he did among the Romans, so that Peter could not have been the *fundator ecclesiae Romae*.

In *ratio quarta*, the author provides an exegesis of Gal. 2: the *apostolatum circumcisionis* is, according to Spanheim, Peter's task. Since this letter was written after Peter's and Paul's tasks had been divided, we are bound to conclude that the writer of the letter regarded this division of tasks as having taken place.

Ratio quinta points to the fact that Peter is also not mentioned in the other letters that Paul wrote from Rome. Spanheim draws particular attention to 2 Tim. 4. 16 ("At my first defence no one took my part") and, in this context, there is an almost literal quotation from Velenský's treatise: "It is therefore better to believe that Peter was not in Rome than to cause him shame by saying that he left Paul in the lurch".

Ratio sexta contains a commentary on I Clement, in which Peter and Paul are both mentioned, but *cum discrimine*—there are hardly any data about Peter, but many about Paul. Peter's biography must, Spanheim concludes, have been unknown in Rome at that time and this would be inexplicable if he had been the Bishop of Rome.

In *ratio septima*, the author shows that the Roman writers who described the life and works of the emperors Claudius and Nero, Tacitus and Suetonius, had nothing to say about Peter and finally, in *ratio octava*, there is an *argumentum ab inductione, nec sub Tiberio Romae fuisse Petrum, nec sub Cajo, nec sub Claudio, nec sub Nerone* ...

It is clear, then, from this survey that Spanheim took over, apart from a few exceptions, the whole of Velenský's thesis and that he also employed, at least partly, Velenský's method of elimination. P. Martin has written:[54] that, in Spanheim's treatise, *les dix-huit persuasions et les sept réponses d'Ulrich Vélénus sont présentées sous une forme plus sérieuse et plus scientifique*. This evaluation, however, does not do justice to Velenský's work. Spanheim is more diffuse in his refutation of the tradition of the early Church, but he is certainly no more serious and scientific in the development of his ideas than the author from whom he derived those ideas.

Pars tertia of Spanheim's *dissertatio* contains a great number of quotations from the Church Fathers which have a bearing on the Petrine tradition. In his discussion of these, however, the author adduces no new counter-arguments.

In *pars quarta*, Spanheim discusses the text in the first letter of Peter (1 Pet. 5. 13) in which "Babylon" is named as the place from which the epistle is sent. To the question as to whether *Romam figurate Babylonem appellari*, Spanheim's reply is that—if this name was customary—something about it ought to be found in Clement, Ignatius, Irenaeus, Tertullian or Origen, but there is nothing. Spanheim therefore concludes, like Velenský and Salmasius before him, that the Egyptian Babylon—*hodie Cairo*—is the place where Peter must have written his letter.

Finally, at the end of the fourth part of his work, Spanheim questions the origin of the *fabula* of Peter's twenty-five years' episcopate in Rome, but concludes that he cannot find any answer to this question—*origo est obscura*.

A little later, Spanheim's dissertation was challenged by Samuel Basnage, a namesake and compatriot of the Jacques Basnage mentioned previously in this chapter. Although he originated in Bayeux, he was appointed in 1691 as preacher to the Walloon community of Zutfen, where he remained until his death in 1721.

His Church history in three volumes, *Annales politico-ecclesiastici, annorum 645 a Caesare Augusto ad Phocam usque*, was published in Rotterdam in 1706. In this work,[55] he provides a good summary of Spanheim's eight *rationes* and this is followed by his refutation of the earlier writer's arguments. In the first place, he points out, that the Epistle of Clement, which was written in Rome and addressed to the Corinthians, alludes to Peter's and Paul's sojourn in Rome. In I Clem. 6. 1, there is, he notes, a text which refers to "those who have, through

---

[54] *op. cit.*, p. 20.
[55] pp. 727–728.

many torments, become the finest examples in our midst (ἐν ἡμῖν)."
This text can only refer to the two great apostles.

In the second place, Samuel Basnage speaks of the important argument that the spot on which Peter died is well known. If this is an incorrect tradition, the author argues, how is it possible to explain that it has long been believed, not only in the Church of Rome, but also on Greece and France and Carthage, that Peter died in Rome? And how can it also be explained that it took such a short time for the truth about Peter's death—assuming that he was never in Rome—to be distorted?

In the third place, it should not be forgotten that it was an honour for the Church to have been founded by an apostle. In that case, it is remarkable that only one Church, the Church of Rome, claimed that honour for itself with regard to Peter. If Peter had really died in another place, then other churches would undoubtedly have claimed that they possessed the apostle's tomb!

In the fourth place, whenever the bishops of Rome have taken action against well-known opponents, like Cyprian, they have always appealed to the authority of Peter. And they would have had no reason for doing this if they had not been certain of Peter's sojourn in Rome.

In the fifth place, it should be remembered, the author points out, that the members of the early Church had the habit of gathering together at the tombs of the martyrs. It is from this time that Peter's tomb became well known. Since then, moreover, Christians have continuously recalled Peter's coming to Rome and his death in the city and this commemoration has never been called into question.

4. *Conclusions*

It has already been pointed out in the introduction how the controversy about the Petrine tradition was continued into the nineteenth and twentieth centuries. The arguments used, however, have been so different from those employed by Velenský that the debate during these later centuries cannot be regarded as a continuation of the effect or influence of the *Petrum Romam non venisse*. This treatise, published in 1520, stimulated thought and discussion among many scholars in the generations that followed and this resulted in research in the territory, originally explored by Velenský, continuing for several centuries. So many new data were, however, introduced into the debate by this continuing research that the territory itself was greatly enlarged and even changed. Until the beginning of the eighteenth century, the polemics—in which Spanheim and Basnage, for example, had participated—still took place within the limits defined by Velenský's arguments. In the centuries that followed, however, this was no longer the case. On the one hand, scientific research into early Christian literature has produced a great deal of new material which Velenský could never have had at his disposal and has, moreover, opened the way to many new hypotheses.[56] On the other hand, many new points of view have also emerged as a result of developments in the nineteenth and twentieth centuries in the spheres of liturgical studies and archaeology and these too could not have been available to Velenský. Any consideration of this discussion would in fact lead us into an entirely different subject matter. For this reason, we shall conclude our investigations with the above description of Spanheim's views, since this author is the last whose writings preserve a clear echo of Velenský's thought.

If we look at the whole period from Flacius Illyricus to Spanheim what strikes us most of all is that only one representative of the Romam Catholic Church made any contribution to the debate—Robert Bellarmine. This theologian wrote an extremely workmanlike treatise but, following his great predecessor and example, John Fisher, was not able to add any new elements to the controversy.

The very limited extent to which the Roman Catholic Church was involved in the continuing debate is undoubtedly connected with the

---

[56] A good example of this is the theory developed by C. Erbes in his article: *Petrus nicht in Rom, sondern in Jerusalem gestorben* (ZKG XXII, 1901, pp. 1–47, 161–231). Erbes based his hypothesis that Peter was put to death in Jerusalem on his interpretation of the Πράξεις Πέτρου (the so-called "Marcellus text", which was translated by Faber Stapulensis as *Lini episcopi de passione Petri*—see *Act. Ap. Apocr.* I, 11, 12). Agrippa and Albinus, the figures named in these *Acta* as the prefect of the city of Rome and the most prominent citizen respectively and as those who were responsible for Peter's death are, of course, known to us from other sources. The first is the King Agrippa before whom Paul was summoned to appear and to defend himself (Acts 25. 13–26.32). The second, Albinus, is the Roman governor who, according to Josephus, succeeded the Festus mentioned in the Acts of the Apostles in 62 A.D. This ancient Jerusalem tradition concerning Peter's death was, Erbes claimed, taken over by Rome and transposed into a Roman situation, becoming well known as such roundabout the year 170. It was, according to Erbes, self-evident that, after the destruction of Jerusalem and the decree forbidding the Jews to live there, no tradition developed concerning Peter's tomb in the city: *Nach der Zerstörung gab es kein Jerusalem mehr ... Es was dort ein neues Geschlecht hingezogen, das wußte nichts mehr von Petrus* (op. cit., p. 214).

fact that so few Protestants also participated and that these were moreover not really united among themselves. Leaving Grotius on one side, because his reasons for defending the Petrine tradition show his attitude towards this question at least to be more Catholic than Protestant, the theologians of the Reformation can be divided, broadly speaking, into three categories.

The first group consists of those who accepted Velenský's arguments without hesitation. Those who belong to this group have, over the whole period, always been exceptional and they have also only been active in a restricted area. The members of this group are Komenský in Bohemia and Veluanus, Revius, Salmasius and Spanheim among those who published works in the Netherlands. Bale cannot really be included among this very small number of authors because, apart from simply denying it, he wrote scarcely anything about the Petrine tradition as such. Even Salmasius does not really belong to this group—if we confine our assessment of his attitude simply to what he says in the first volume of his *De primatu papae*, the only one that was published—since he was above all concerned with questions about the legitimacy of succession in the primacy and it was only within that framework that he revealed himself as a defender of views of the kind expressed by Velenský.

The second group contains a much larger number of Protestant theologians who, following Luther, Calvin and Flacius, have questioned the tradition of Peter's episcopate in Rome, but have tended to regard the matter as of secondary importance because they have not thought of it as necessary to the life of faith and for salvation. It would be quite correct to include Salmasius and Polanus among these theologians. Their opposition to the legitimacy of the primate was, after all, not simply a juridical matter—they were also concerned to show that the papacy was not necessary for salvation.

The third group is also small and consists of those Church historians who, like both the Basnages, had historical aims in their opposition to Velenský's views and their defence of the Petrine tradition. If these men had been living a few centuries later and if they had consequently had at their disposal the knowledge acquired in the nineteenth and twentieth centuries, their position would have been understandable. As authors writing in the seventeenth and eighteenth centuries, however, all that they were able to do was to have recourse to the authority of the writers of the early Church.

This reference on the part of these Church historians to unconditional acceptance of the Church's tradition is at the same time accompanied by a phenomenon discernible in the work of many other Protestant theologians writing at the same period,[57] even though they make no explicit statements about it—they have a reserved attitude towards approaching the Church's tradition too critically. For all of them, Jerome is a *magnus auctor* and Eusebius and Orosius are among the *viri diligentes*. No one ventured to contradict their authority. It is not possible to say with certainty whether the hidden reason behind this attitude was a need to be regarded by scientific Catholic historians and theologians as equally objective and scientific. In any case, the triumphalism of, for example, Henri de Valois, who, in 1659 in his Latin edition of the Greek Church historians,[58] wrote[59] that nothing was better known, more certain and more soundly based in the whole history of the Church than the fact that Peter came to Rome, can be more clearly understood in the light of this attitude of reserve on the part of the Reformers. Even more striking, however, is Velenský's courage as an objective and scientific historian in going against the generally accepted view of his own times and venturing to challenge the historical reliability of the Petrine tradition.

Our final conclusion, however, must be—just as it was in our retrospective view of the preceding period—that Luther's theological approach to the papacy gained the upper hand in Protestant circles over Velenský's historical analysis. If, in the Reformers' view, the papacy was not essential to Christians in the matter of certainty of salvation, the controversy as to whether the Petrine tradition was or was not historically reliable was a question of secondary importance.

---

[57] Spanheim *(op. cit.)* mentions C. Molinaeus (1500–1566), F. Junius (1545–1602), J. Scaliger (1540–1609), J. Casaubon (1599–1614), D. Chamier (1570–1621), N. Vedel († 1642), J. Selden (1584–1654), D. Blondel (1591–1655), J. Usher (1580–1659), H. Hammond (1605–1660), J. Pearson (1615–1686), J. Fell (1615–1686), H. Dodwell (1641–1711) and G. Gave (1637–1713).

[58] Henricus Valesius *(pars prima): Eusebii Pamphili ecclesiastica historia. Libri de vita Constantini. Constantini oratio ad Sanctos, graece et latine cum annotationibus* (Paris, 1659). The entire work in three volumes was also published in Amsterdam in 1695: *Historiae Ecclesiasticae Scriptores Graeci. Ex Interpretatione Henrici Valesii.*

[59] *op. cit.,* Vol. I, *Annotationes in Librum* II, cp. XV: *Atque nihil in tota historia Ecclesiastica illustrius, nihil certius atque testatius, quam adventus Petri Apostoli in urbem Romam* (p. 30).

APPENDIX ONE

A SURVEY OF THE EDITIONS OF THE PETRUM ROMAM NON VENISSE

1.

IN HOC LIBELLO GRAUISSI || mis | certissimisq, & in sacra scriptura fundatis racionibus || uariis probatur: Apostolū Petrū Rhomam nō uenisse, || necq illic passum, proinde satis friuole & temere || Rhomanus Pontifex se Petri successorem || iactat & nominat &c̄.

On the title page, there is a woodcut showing the risen Christ opposite Peter (with a key) and Paul (with a sword and a book). The colophon on [H iv^r] reads: *Finit libellus bifariam diuisus, VIII kalendas || Decembris, Anno Virginei partus. || M.D. XX.*

The format is quarto and the signature is A–H iv (all the iv references are missing, whereas G ii is immediately followed by H).

The printer is not named, but at the end of the nineteenth century there was complete agreement about the press where this treatise must have been printed—the form of the letters was that of Sylvan Otmar of Augsburg.[1]

The author's name is given above the foreword as *Vlrichus Velenus Minhoniensis, benigno lectore salutem.*

2.

IN HOC LI || bello grauissimis, certissimisq, & || in sacra scriptura fundatis ratiōi || bus uariis probatur, Apostolū Petrum Romam nō uenisse, || necq illic passum, proinde || satis friuole, & temere || Romanus Pontifex se || Petri successorem ia= || ctat, & nomīat &c̄.

Around the title is a border, divided into four blocks and heavily decorated with *putti*, elephants and camels; below, on the right, in the bottom block is a date: *. 1519 .*

The format is quarto, the signature is a–f iv (from b onwards the iv references are missing) and there are *custodes.*

---

[1] Otto Clemen in *Zentralblatt für Bibliothekswesen* XVII (1900), p. 587; *ibid.*: *Flugschriften aus den ersten Jahren der Reformation*, Vol. III, 5 (1906–1911), p. 187.

The concluding lines read: *Distichon ad Lectorem.* || *Quicquid id est, uanum, uero seu uerius ipso,* || *Syncere trutines lector amice uelim.*

The printer and the date of printing are not given in the text. The name of the author—*Vlrichus Velenus Minhoniensis*—is given, in the same way as in No. 1, above the foreword.

For a long time, opinions differed with regard to the printer and the dating of this edition. The date that appears in the bottom block of the border around the title does not necessarily indicate that the book was printed in that year. The *Short Title Catalogue* of the British Museum (1962 edition) gives behind the title of the treatise: [*A. Cratander, Basle, 1520?*], but the *General Catalogue of Printed Books* (also of the British Museum), which was published in 1964, although the data in this edition go back to 1955, gives in the case of the same copy the year 1519, but does not give the place. According to the *Catalogue Général des Livres imprimés de la Bibliothèque National* (1959), *l'encadrement porte la date: 1519.* The *Nederlandsche Bibliographie van 1500 tot 1540* of W. Nijhoff and M. E. Kronenberg (1923) gives the date of publication: *(c. 1520?)* and the printer as Mich. Hillen van Hoochstraten, in Antwerp. M. E. Kronenberg herself, however, corrects this statement in an article in the journal *Het Boek* (year 13; September 1924).[2] She writes: "We have wrongly ascribed the work written by Velenus to van Hoochstraten of Antwerp. On closer inspection, it became clear to me that it was printed by Andreas Cratander at Basle. I found the same border round the title with the same heavy decoration of *putti*, elephants and camels in a completely identical form in another of Cratander's works. The two initials and the type-faces of the book also occur in the prints by Cratander which are to be found in the Koninklijke Bibliotheek. There can therefore be no doubt that the book was printed by Cratander."

Otto Clemen, who had originally given Lazarus Schürer of Schlettstadt as the printer, on the basis of the border round the title, corrected his opinion at almost exactly the same time as M. E. Kronenberg. In the *Zentralblatt für Bibliothekswesen* (1923, year 40), he wrote that the woodcut in question occurred both in Schürer's and in Cratander's work, with the difference, however, *daß in der Cratanderschen Ausführung die Jahreszahl 1519 von zwei Punkten eingeschlossen sei, während sie bei Schürer fehlen.*

---

[2] The second series of the Dutch journal specialising in books and libraries, published by M. Nijhoff, The Hague; the article (p. 254) is entitled *Een onjuiste toeschrijving in de Nederlandsche Bibliographie van 1500–1540.*

We may also conclude that Cratander must have been the printer from the fact that he published Erasmus' *Dulce bellum inexpertis* in a German translation in 1519, using the same woodcut.

A different light seems to have been thrown on this question by the authoress of an article in the commemorative book on Cratander that was published in 1966: *Andreas Cratander—ein Basler Drucker und Verleger der Reformationszeit.*[3] In her essay, entitled *Künstler und Formschneider der Offizin Cratander*, Margarete Pfister-Burkhalter writes:[4] *Vermutlich schärfte sich mit wachsender Erfahrung sein* (that is: Cratander) *Sinn für Qualität, daß er diese Bordüre an Lazarus Schürer in Schlettstadt weitergab, der sie 1520 als Titelrahm benützte zu Willibald Pirkheimers Eccius Dedolatus.* Two observations arise in this context. In the first place, we are bound to conclude that the *Petrum Romam non venisse* must have been printed before this sale by Cratander took place and this therefore points to the date 1519. In the second place, there is the question as to whether—and if he did—why Schürer removed the fullstops on each side of the year 1519 from the woodcut.

In a reply[5] to my request for further information, Dr Pfister-Burkhalter retracted what she had said in this article. She wrote: *Die vier Leisten der Schlettstadter Ausgabe Pirkheimers bei L. Schürer von 1520 scheinen nur identisch mit denen bei Cratander [1519], sind aber von anderen Holzstöcken abgezogen, was zahlreiche Abweichungen verraten. Nicht nur die fehlenden Punkte bei der Jahreszahl .1519., sondern die ganze Zahl ist anders. Alle vier Leisten unterscheiden sich in kleinen Einzelheiten... Da es sich bei den Schlettstadter Leisten offenbar um ziemlich getreue Nachschnitte handelt —vielleicht vom gleichen Formschneider—bleibt leider die Frage offen, wann Lazarus Schürer in den Besitz seiner verwendeten Holzstöcke kam.*

Despite the fact that it has been possible to reach agreement about the identity of the printer, it has not been possible to do this with regard to the date of publication. There are unfortunately in the Druckerei Cratander A.G., which still exists in Basle, no archives going back to the first few decades of the sixteenth century, from which data might be obtained concerning a date of the *Petrum Romam non venisse*. The content of the treatise, however, points to a date of publication which could not have been later than the autumn of 1520. In his foreword, Velenský writes that the pope "ensnared" Luther "with his rage" and, if this does in any way have a bearing on a con-

---

[3] Published by Helbing und Lichtenhahn, Basle.
[4] p. 68.
[5] dated 2 November 1973.

crete fact, the obvious one is the papal bull *Exsurge Domine*, which is dated 15 June 1520, but which, of course, only became generally known a few moths later. What is more, the author says that John Reuchlin and Ulrich von Hutten were "treated unjustly" by the pope and this may have been allusion to the pope's orders to have the latter arrested and the former's book *Augenspiegel* condemned. Both of these papal decisions were taken in June 1520. If this Cratander edition was published before Otmar's, then, on the basis of these indications provided by the text itself, they can only have been separated by a very short space of time.

The Czech Church historian F. M. Bartoš, who was intensively engaged in a study of the treatise in 1925,[6] has said that both Latin editions were published "extremely probably at the same time" and has based this statement on the great interest in the work at the beginning of the Reformation.

3.

IN DISEM BŮCHLIN WIRT MIT MANCHER || *lay tapffern/ bestendigen* | *vnd in der schrifft gegründten vr=* || *sachen* | *klårlich bewert* | *das der hailig Apostel Petrus* || *gen Rom nicht kōmen* | *noch alda den tod gelit=* || *ten* | *darauß volget* | *wie sich der Rômisch* || *Papst* | *vnbillicher weiß* | *ain nach=* || *kommer Petri růmet vnd auß* || *schreibt* 7c̄.

Under the title is the same woodcut as in the edition given here as No. 1. Above the foreword the author's name is missing (elsewhere in the text the name also is not to be found). There are also no references to the printer and year of publication. At the end are the words: *GOT SEY LOB VND EER.*

The format is quarto. The signature is A-Giv (the iv references are missing).

It is unanimously accepted that the printer of this edition must have been Sylvan Otmar of Augsburg, on the basis of the use of the woodcut and the type-faces employed. A very careful examination of the woodcut has revealed that this is less worn than the woodcut used in the Latin edition of 24 November 1520. In four different places, the line drawing is sound in the German edition, but damaged or interrupted in the Latin edition. The only conclusion that can be drawn

---

[6] *Zapadlé dílko bratrské vědy* (Věstnik KČSN, I, 1925, Prague).

from this evidence is that what we have here is an edition which was published before the one given above as No. 1 and that the date of this edition must be before 24 November 1520.

There are, however, also indications of a different kind which lead us to conclude that this edition was published after November 1520 and before the spring of 1521. The edition certainly gives the impression of having been a translation of the Latin edition. There is clear evidence of faults in the Latin edition having been corrected in this German version (for example, an error in the calculation of the number of years of Claudius' reign) and of the titles of books, which were given in too summary a form in the Latin edition, having been completed. On this basis of this evidence, the publication of this edition ought to be dated after the publication of editions Nos. 1 and 2. On the other hand, in a letter written by the papal nuncio Aleander on 13 October 1521 and addressed to Rome,[7] there is reference to a Latin and a German copy of Velenský's book. If we assume that at least a few months elapsed between the publication of this German edition and the time that Aleander became acquainted with it, then we come to a date that could not possibly be later than the summer of 1521.

This contradiction in the data can only be solved if we assume that the text of the Latin edition (of Augsburg) was ready at an earlier date and that the German translation contained corrections of this text but was in fact printed first.

The fact that Kuczynski,[8] like Weller,[9] reported, without further comment: "(Augsburg, S. Otmar, 1521)" has to be explained as a conclusion drawn from Aleander's letter to Rome, a conclusion which, however, overlooks the evidence provided by a comparison between the woodcuts in the two editions.

4.

Achtzehen tapffere || beständige und in der schifft gegründte Ursachen und Bewehrung || daß Sant Petrus der Apostel nach dem Tod des HErrn Christi nach Rom nicht kommen || noch alda den Todt gelitten. Sieben loß Ursach der ROMANISTEN || damit sie sich gegen obgesetzte Bewehrung zu hüten

---

[7] T. Brieger: *Quellen und Forschungen zur Geschichte der Reformation*, I, *Aleander und Luther* (Gotha, 1884), p. 268.

[8] A. Kuczynski: *Thesaurus libellorum historiam reformationis illustrantium* (1870–1874).

[9] Emil Weller: *Repertorium typographicum* (1864), No. 1959.

vermeinen: Und sieben beständig Antwort auf dieselben || welche sie ganzt ab=
räumen und hindan werffen. Daraus folget || wie sich der Römisch Babst un=
billiger weiß ein Nachkommer Petri rühmet || und ausschreiet.

This second German edition is mentioned by Weller[10] under
No. 1960. He gives, however, no indication either of the division of
the letters or the lines in his rendering of the title or as to where copies
can be found. His description is quite summary: *o.O.u.J. (1521). 4*

Von der Hardt, to whom Weller refers, gives, in his survey of the
books contained in the *Biblioteca domestica Brunsvigae*,[11] a division of the
lines, but a different date: 1524.

I am not familiar with any of the copies of this edition.

5.

In 1551, Flacius Illyricus prepared a German edition as the second
part of his treatise entitled: *Verlegung zweier schrifften eines Augsburgi-*
schen Münchs, mit Namen Joannes Fabri, von des Babsts Primat und von
Beicht. Durch M. Flacius Illyricus. Item achtzehn beweisungen, das S. Petrus
zu Rom nicht gewesen sey.

It was published in Magdeburg and the foreword is dated 20 August
1550. It has, however, been pointed out by Nikolaus Paulus[12] that the
writings of the Dominican John Fabri, against which Flacius' polemics are directed, contain a foreword dated 7 October 1550, with the
result that Flacius' reply could not have been published before 1551.

The text of Velenský's treatise—without the foreword, however—
is to be found on D–F iv. There is no mention of Velenus as the
author.

6.

TRATTA= || TO NEL QUA || le con certissimi || ragioni nella sa=
|| cra Scrittura, si manifesta, come || Pietro Apostolo non mai fu à || Roma,
ne ancò pati in quella il || Martirio: La onde si uede quan= || to debolmente
il Romano || pontefice si vanta di es= || ser successore di Pietro.

---

[10] *ibid.*

[11] Herm. von der Hardt: *Antiqua literarum Monumenta* (1691), Vol. II, p. 118.

[12] Nikolaus Paulus: *Die deutschen Dominikaner im Kampfe gegen Luther* (Freiburg,
1903), p. 244.

The data *ANNO 1566* is given below the title.

The format is octavo and the signature is A–[M viii] (the vi, vii and viii references are missing). As the second part of this book is included: *VERISSI= || MA ET VTI= || lissima legenda || aut Historia de S. || Petri Episcopatu uel Papatu. || M. Fla. Illyri.* The date is given below as *M.D.LXVII.* The signature is N–[N vi].

As the third part is included: *CONTRA || COMMENTI= || tium primatum || papae || authore Matth. Flac. Illyr.*[13] This title page contains the year: *ANNO M.D.LXVII.* The signature is [N vii] - [Q viii].

The colophon on [Q viii] reads: *Ratisponae excudebat || Ioannes Burger.* The authors name is given again above the foreword: *Al Benigno lettore salute, Vlrico Veleno Minoriense.*

The combination of this exact Italian translation of Velenský's treatise and two Latin treatises by Flacius in one continuous signature lead us to the obvious conclusion that Flacius Illyricus was also the translator of Velenský's text. In that case, he would probably have made the translation one year before writing the two other treatises.

In an article published in 1827, Veesenmeyer[14] wrote that he would find it more plausible to regard Vergerius[15] as the translator, but in that case the edition would have been posthumous, since Vergerius died in 1565. Veesenmeyer was hesitant to call Flacius the translator: *Wenn wir sonst etwas Italienisches von Flacius hätten, so wäre ich geneigt die Übersetzung ihm zuzuschreiben. Es mag also ungewiß bleiben, wer die Arbeit geliefert habe ...)*

F. M. Bartos[16] is in no way hesitant—he simply assumes that Flacius was the translator.

There are copies of this Regensburg edition in Ulm and Munich.

7.

E. L. Enders wrote in his book on Luther's correspondence

---

[13] This work also occurs as the continuation (also with consecutive signature) of the Basle edition (1554 Henrichus Petri): *Historia certaminum inter Romanos Episcopos et sextam Carthaginiensem synodum, Africanasque Ecclesias, de primatu seu potestate pape, bona fide ex authenticis monumentis collecta. Auctore Matthia Flacio Illyrico.*

[14] G. Veesenmeyer: *Sammlung von Aufsätzen zur Erläuterung der Kirchen-, Literatur-, Münz- und Sittengeschichte* (Ulm, 1827), p. 149.

[15] Pietro Paolo Vergerio (1497–1565), in 1536 bishop of Capodistria, 1548 because of his conversion to protestantism, dismissed.

[16] *op. cit.*

(*Luthers Briefwechsel*, Vol. III)[17] that a German edition of Velenský's treatise appeared in 1618, but he has not given the title of this edition. Presumably he took this datum from Weller's book,[18] in which a later edition is mentioned under No. 1960 as *Achtzehn wolgegrundte Argument u.s.w. 1618. o.O. 8.*

All other data are missing.

8.

In his *Monarchiae S. Romani Imperii sive Tractatum de iurisdictione imperiali seu regia sive pontificia seu sacerdotali ...*, published in Frankfurt in 1618, Melchior Goldast includes the text of Velenský's treatise, which appears in part III[19] and is entitled:

VLRICHI VELENI MIN= || HONIENSIS ||TRACTATUS|| quod Petrus Apostolus nun= || quam Romae fuerit.

Velenský's foreword is missing from this version. The treatise is dated: *Anno Domini 1523.*

9.

VLRICHI VELENI, || Minhoniensis || Libellus, ||Quo || Petrvm Romam Non || venisse || demonstratur. || Editio recognita.

Below this title the date is given as *Anno MDC LX.* The format is quarto and the signature is A–H iv (1–64). The name of the printer is not given.

The unnamed publisher has provided this edition with a foreword in which he includes the Latin title almost word for word. He also writes that this book "from the previous century" came into his hands "a short time ago" and that the author's arguments so convinced him that he wanted to make the treatise public again. In the text, names, titles and important or interesting statements are printed in italics.

In view of the fact that the whole of Velenský's foreword is included in this edition, the publisher must have possessed one of the Latin

---

[17] Stuttgart, 1889, pp. 82, 83.
[18] *op. cit.*
[19] pp. 1–16. (A–Bii^v).

editions of 1520 and, what is more, it is clear from the punctuation and the spelling that this Latin edition must have been Cratander's. The publisher[20] was Johann Konrad Dannhauer (1603–1666), a Lutheran theologian who was a deacon of the Thomas Church at Strasbourg.

[20] *WA (Briefwechsel)* II, pp. 259–261.

SYLVAN OTMAR'S EDITION (AUGSBURG, 1520)

Reproduction of the exemplar, possessed by the Universiteitsbibliotheek Amsterdam, Coll. Ev. Luth. Sem.

In hoc libello grauissi

mis/ certissimisq₃,& in sacra scriptura fundatis racionibus
uariis probatur: Apostolū Petrū Rhomam nō uenisse,
necq₃ illic passum, proinde satis friuole & temere
Rhomanus Pontifex se Petri successorem
iactat & nominat &c̄.

IVVENALIS.

Aude aliquid breuibus Gyaris,& carcere dignum
Si uis esse aliquid. probitas laudatur,& alget,

Vlrichus Velenus Minhoniensis,
benigno lectori salutem.

NOn possum persuaderi,benigne lector,ut ullam
uel Poeticâ fabellâ, uel supstitionem Iudaicam,
eque ficticiâ, eque ridiculâ ac nociuam credam: atqea
est,q̃ scripturarũ neglectus in Christianismum hodie de
Antichristo intrusit. Cuius aduentus ex tam euidentissi
mis cõiecturis, ex tam certissimis indiciis, a Christo &
Apostolis,ceu digito monstratis,nescio qui uideri non
potest?Nisi forte hoc iam nr̃a meruere cõmissa,ut occe
cati ac improuidi,repétina Dei ira,uelut inter oscitátes:
quod dicit̃,opprimamur,fœdũq̃ interitũ sera deplora-
mus penitentia, Dũ Antichristũ uenturũ interim expe-
ctamus,présenté cõniuemus.Heliã & Enoch uenturos
nobis pmittimus. Quę quidé.si carnaliter,atq̃ in corti
ce futura credimus, Iudaicis fabulis,ut doctissimus Ieronimus ad Marcellâ scribit,acquiescere necessum é,ut
uidelicet rursus edificet̃ Ierusalem, & hostię offerantur
in templo,& spiritali cultu imminuto, corpales reuiui-
scant cerimonię:Sed quia totus ille liber Apocalypseos
Ioannis,unde hęc de Antichristo, Helia & Enoch opinio,spiritualiter intelligendus est,quum quot uerba tot
mysteria habeat, Heliam Enoch & Antichristũ iamdiu
uenisse, & tot annis tyránidé suâ in Ecclesia exercuisse,
& etiã nũ exercere certũ est.Quis em̃ tam semel exuisset
pudorem,ut tergiuersari audeat , quicquid a Christo &

A ij

apoſtolis prꝫnunciat ū de Antichriſto nouimus,in Ro⸝
mana eccleſia non inueniriꝾ quꝓ tanta tꞛcꝫ imanis inua⸝
ſit abhomiatio,ut fideles interea uiuere tedeat, dū nihil
horū non ueniſſe, quꝫ d e Antichriſto prꝫdicta ſunt,ſu⸝
is oculis cōtemplant̄ , in alteriuſꝗ Chriſti obſequium,
ſeſe accerſiri , immo cogi ſentiunt ꝰ Porro ſi aduen⸝
tus Heliꝫ, ſecundarium quoꝗ Chriſti aduentum prꝫce
dere debet,nó carnaliter ꝑfecto id,ſed in ſpū intelligen
dum eſt.Quꝫadmodū Ioannes ille Baptiſta interrogan⸝
tibus Herodianis,an ipſe fuiſſet Helias,non ſe Heliam
eſſe ingenue reſpondit , Chriſtus uero eū fuiſſe Heliam
libere ꝑfeſſus eſt,cū alias,tū eo loci,ubi apoſtolis pcó⸝
tantibus. Quid ergo ſcribe dicunt , ꝗ Heliam oportet
primū uenireꝾrñdit.Dico uobis,quia Helias iam uenit,
& nó cognouerūt eū, ſed fœcerūt in eo quecūꝗ uolue⸝
runt, de quo Angelus apud Lucam ꝓdixerat, prꝫcedet
ante eū in ſpiritu & uirtute Heliꝫ.Perinde & nunc,dum
miſteriū hoc iniquitatis oꝑatur , & reuelatus eſt homo
peccati , & ſedere uidet̄ abhominatio ꝓphana in loco
ſancto , iamdudū Helias & Enoch in ſpiritu & uirtute
uenerunt,qui cū hic Antichriſto depugnēt,qui fideles,
ne ei uel ad horā cedant,dehortent̄ admoneantꝗ.Atꝗ
promouerēt certe plurimū , ꝗmnis cū uitꝫ ſuꝫ maximo
diſpendio , Nempe quos ille in camino ſuo truculentiſ
ſime ꝓpediē exurere nó uertur, Hiꝫronymū Sauonaro
rolam, uirū oīm ſuffragio facile doctiſſimū , & pietatis
Chriſtianꝫ haud ſegnē patronū, Florentiꝫ tercium met
uulcano tradidit,Britanniꝫ Ioānis Vigleph oſſa,homi⸝
nis nó facile cum quouis alio cōferendi, poſtliminio in
Oceanū ſpargenda decreuit, ne quid memoriꝫ ipſius

apud poſteros remaneat, neue cũ Chriſtianis cõmune
quidpiã habere uideret́ ne humũ qdē.Quidni cõmemo
rem, Ioannem Hus ac Hieronymũ prꝫſtantiſſimos aca
demi ꝫ Pragēſis Magiſtros: quos pſide ad Conciliũ ac
citos, nulla diſcretõe, ſed mera ſua tyrannide, flãmis cõ
cremauit: quod toti Chriſtianorũ orbi teſtatiſſimũ eſt́
Quid de noſtris temporib9 dicã ꞉ Ioannē Reuchlinum
IoannēPicũ Mirandulanũ, literarũ columina, q́m ille ini
que tractauerit́ Sed necdũ contra Doctorē Martinum
Lutheriũ. pietatis Chriſtianꝫ ardentiſſimũ inueſtigato
rem ac defenſorem , & Vlrichũ Huttennũ, ſtrēnuiſſimũ
Germaniꝫ equitē auratũ, ira ſua deferbuit, at indies ſuo
illo feruentiſſimo iracundiꝫ igne, cõtra eos ardet ac fla
mas intentat, Et ne hic oblitus uidear, quãtꝫ cladis Boe
miꝫ iampridē auctor fuerit, ut mactata tot Chriſtiano
run̩ corpa, flumina ſanguinis funderent.Gemit Anglia
ſua pertefa iniurias, Necꝫ ſine dolore ꝑſpectat Oriens,
Chriſtũ exulare in occidente uidens, At uero diuina bo
nitate, breui iam futurũ ſperamus, ꝙ dominus iniquum
hunc, ſpũ oris ſui iugulabit, ut tandem in maieſtate ſua
& decore aduentus , quaſpiam fidei reliquias adhuc in
mundo reperiat.Feruente em̃ diſceptationũ ac cauillo
rum in extricabilium in mundo, ſtudio, Theologia fri
gebat. pietas Chriſtiana extincta eſt.At regione, incale
ſcéte Theologia, iam rigent cõtentiones:depercũt Pon
tificiꝫ frauduēltiſſimꝫ traditionis Chriſti ptꝫcepta eua
cuans̃. Vbiꝗ pietas quꝫrit ꞉ ueſtigia quibus inauia de
uenerat Eccleſia deprꝫhendunt́ ꞉ Quomõ tñ hic Anti
chriſtus in priſtinã conditionē reduci nõ patit́ ꞉ ſed in
dignat́ ꞉ſed frendet dentibus꞉ & quod poſtremũ eſt꞉pe

A iii

rire uult potius q̃m corrigi . Qui tot iam retro ſęculis:
ipſiſſimus triceps ille infernalis Cerberus : in cuius ſig-
num triplicē defert coronā: ne cui capiti ſua deſit: toto
mundo iugiter oblatrabat: ſuo ueneno neminē non in-
toxicans:ſuā detrectantē cathenā neminē non mordēs.
Sed iā duobus amiſſis capitibus:mitior eſt aliquáto be
ſtia:Quoꝝ unius in eo duello iacturā paſſa eſt:quo Lau
rentius ille Valla : acerrimus literarū & pietatis cenſor,
ac uerus ille Hercules ei occurrit:unūꝗ uaſtū caput mu
crone amputauit : Cuius latratus:totus orbis moleſte,
nec ſine damno ferebat:dū ſub Silueſtri noīe:Lateranen
ſe palaciū:omnibus aliis facile pręcipuū:Romam:& to
tius Italię ac occidentaliū regionū ꝓuincias, loca:ciui-
tates:Conſtantini Impatoris munificentia ſibi donatas
adſtrueret: ut hac ſola uoce : nihil iā prope in mūdo ui-
deat:quod ſibi non arrogaſſet:Quā ucro ſtrennue:& q̃
fortiter id ſibi eripuerit Laurentius: cōmenticias etiam
Bullas ueriſſime reprobans:hoc cōſtat oīnib⁹.Nec mi
nus tamen animoſe hac tempeſtate noſtra D.Martinus
Lutherius: uelut alter quidā Theſeus beſtiā inuaſit:ca-
putꝗ detrūcauit alterum : dū eum primatū quo in totū
debachabat mundū illi abſtulit: ficticia Decretaliū deli
ramenta, ſolidiſſimis teſtimoniis expugnans . Sed hui:
nondū ſentit uulnera:uel ſaltem diſſimulat beſtia, dū ſu
pręmū illud:ac cęteris robuſtius caput illeſū adhuc cō-
ſyderat:quo ſe ſucceſſorē Petri: cuius principatus inter
Apoſtolos obtigiſſe uidet : oblatrat: e quo quidē capite alia, quáuis detruncata : iterato ſubnaſci uidentur.
Non aliud:ait:Cōſtantinū mouit, quo in Eccleſiā foret
munificus, niſi ꝗ Petrus ei ſtertenti in ſomnis apparue

rit:quędã ne demandauerit obeunda: Pro cuius reuerē
tia expergefactus ille tandē,impio se abdicauit, illudqʒ
in Siluestrũ reiecit:& alias Ecclesias omes parere eidem
iussit:& uoluit quo primatus Romani Pótificis erigať:
quem Christus Petro etiam obtulisse: quamuis uarie ei
uisus est . Vide nenias:& unde exurgunt? Restat illi ca
put, quo se Petri successorem iactat:In qď quia neminē
adhuc ensem distrinxisse uideo , cũ tñ omniũ quibus se
defendit bestia hec:puppis (ĩn adagio)sit & prora:diui
na ope subnixus, q̃uis uiribus impar:sed tñ diuinis scri
pturis cõfisus:cũ bestia cõgrediar: hocqʒ quod residuũ
est caput illi auferam.Et ne quē lateat pugnandi mod9:
sacrę literaturę militiã in suas acies primũ distinguam:
quę ut ęque sunt fortissimę , ita citra timorē eas in ho
stem producã : cominus uel eminus cũ eo pugnaturus.
Atqʒ eo prostrato: deinde & spoliũ auferã , deqʒ arma
tura ipsius prędã faciam: Septem quosdã cauillos qui
bus sese muniri solet ille,certioribus testimoniis deprę
daturus, Necqʒ hic alicuius facio eorũ calumnias:apud
quos pietas heresis est:q̃muis certo sciã:millies mē here
ticũ uocitaturos . Enimuero candidũ lectorem interim
moneo:ne ptinus ipso libri offendať argumento: inqʒ
ipso uestibulo eius horreat animus: Cõscientiã meã ob
testor , nullas huc fraudes,nulla mēdacia:nec dolos me
intrudere uoluisse : sed ut quęqʒ scriptura germanũ ha
buisse mihi uisa'intellectũ: ita'in meas hasce psuasiones
adduxi . Quod si q̃uid sinistre ac perperã dictũ quis in
ueniat:statim suggillet:oblitteret ac deleat,& me ad di
scendũ propensũ, obiter docere nõ negligat : Nõ enim
piget me:ut cũ Augustino dicã, sicubi hesito q̃rere, sed
nec pudebit,sicubi errauero:corrigere,Vale.

Liber hic duas habet particulas : quarū prior decem &
octo comprehendit persuasiones , ꝗ Petrus nunꝗ post
Christi passionē Romę fuerit : & ꝗ Hierosolomis & nō
Romę passus sit.

Altera particula septem habet cauillos : quibus Rom.
Curia illis persuasionibus occurrere cōsueuit: Quibus
tamen uicissim septem correspondēt responsiones: eos
non aliter atꝗ rudera quędam dissipantes.

⟨⟩Prima persuasio.

Vum diligētissime euoluerim, quotquot ad ma-
num fuerant hystoricorū ac Theologorū: eosꝗ
nō infimę conditionis libros , de aduentu Petri
Romā: de passione & authore mortis ipsius: nihil aliud
ꝗm meras controuersias illic reperire potui: cū nemini
fere cū alterō satis conueniat: sed quilibet suū proferat
iudiciū: uel hoc solo suspectū: ꝗ a cęteris dissentiat omī
bus. Et ut paucos cōmemorem e multis . Quidā in exordio Imperii Claudii Petrū Romam uenisse cōtendūt:
quorum e numero est Orosius historicus non triuialis:
Quidā anno Claudii secūdo: & illi sunt Hieronimus &
qui suę innituntur authoritati . Quidā anno eiusdē imperii quarto, atꝗ est liber ille: qui tempoꝝ historias: ceu
fasciculo quodā cōprehendit . Pręterea: ab his omnib9
dissentit liber ille qui sanctorū uitas enarrat: & cōmuni
ter passionale nominaꞇ, Is eñ anno post passionē Chri
sti: Petrū Romā applicuisse testaꞇ: qui quidē annus tre-
decimus fuisset impii Claudii. Similiter qui annos mun
di: & annos ab urbe condita recensent: usꝗ ad aduentū

Petri Romā uel eius paſſionem, q̄m mutuo pugnēt ne
mini obſcurū eſt, qui modo Eneades Anthonii Sabelli
ci, hiſtoriā Pontificū Platinę, ipſumq̃ Oroſium uiderit.
Quę quidē diuerſitas, & ſi nil aliud eſſet teſtimonio, ſu
ſpectū tñ Petri Romā aduentū redderet, & falſam hanc
ꝓbaret coniecturā, q̃ Petrus unq̄m Romę fuiſſet. Quę
tñ adeo inualuit, ut tot ſeculis qui ei reclamare auſus fu
iſſet, habuerit adhuc neminem, Et parū abfuit, ne Ro
manenſiū aulicorū tyrannis, in fidei articulos eam retu
lerit, ut quod nulla ratione probari poteſt, ſola neceſſi
tate credi uideaꞇ. Accedit ad hęc, licet neuter hiſtorico
rū cum altero ſentiat, tñ aduerſus legem Chriſti, q̄ſi ex
cōpoſito omẽs decertant, ut uel hoc unū uanas eorū fa
bulas ac deliramenta ꝓdat. q̃ cū Paulo, apoſtolorū om
niū in ſcribendo locupletiſſimo, cū Luca euangeliſta ſi
mul & Aꝑlicarū actionū hiſtoriographo, inexcuſabili
ter contendant, ut inferius liquido ꝓbabiꞇ. Si nulla eſt
ſacrę ſcripturę adſtipulatio qua id cōfirmari poſſit, &
tam remota hiſtoria adeo cōfuſa eſt & fallax, nō ſtulte
Petrū nunq̄m Chriſti poſt paſſinoem Romę fuiſſe cre
diꞇ, Alioqui ſi illic eū aliq̄ñ fuiſſe uerū eſſet, uero omĩa
(dicente philoſopho)cōſonarent, At diſſonante lege,
diſſidentibus mutuo hiſtoricis, quis niſi emotę mentis
uerū hoc aliq̄ñ putauerit. Quāta ſit em in tam uetuſtiſſi
mis rebus, tā remotę hiſtorię fides, argumento eſt Bar
tolomeus ille Platina, qui Ro: Pontificū res geſtas de
ſcribens, ac multo etiā poſteriora iſtis tpa tractans, ſępi
us cōquęriꞇ uariationē hiſtorię, maiorū neglectū, tem
porū perturbationē quibus diſtrictus, nihil interea af
firmare audet. Nempe, ſi Petrus Romanorū fuerat epi

B

ſcopus, dicant quē ſibi ſucceſſorē noiauerit? & quis iñ
locū ipſius fuiſſet ſuffectus? Si Linū dixerint, latinorū
turba obiter reclamabit, quoue id ꝓbent, diē dicet. im⸗
mo & Grecorū plurimi in hac cauſa latinos non deſti⸗
tuent, Chryſoſtomo in ſecundā ad Timotheū epiſtolā
dicente. Hunc Linū, aiunt quidā, ſęcundū poſt Petrum
Romanę eccleſię Epiſcopū fuiſſe. Donat9 uero Terēti
anus interpres inquit. Aiunt, uſurpat̃ de re incerta, quā
nos dicimus eſſe falſā. Sin aūt Clementi hic honor dabi
tur, qd̃ multis placet, plures adhuc erunt qui id impro⸗
bent, & hanc gloriā erga Linū reponant: Clementem nõ
primo nec ſc̃do, ſed tertio gradu primū, poſt Petrū ſta⸗
tuentes. Deinde, Pius ne Anicetū, uel Anicetus Piū prę
ceſſerit? Vrbanus ſub Diocletiano ne, uel ſub Aurelio
Anthonio degerit? Cornelius ſub Gallo, an ſub Volu⸗
ſiano uel forte Decio paſſus ſit? hiſtoria uariat, nec ali⸗
quid certi de his rebus definire poteſt. Nec mirum, ſi &
multo his poſteriora tempora, eorúꝗ geſta, adeo ſunt
hiſtoricorū figmētis deprauata, ut nemini poſt hac inte
grū ſit res grauiores eorū libris tueri: Siquidē id meret̃
(ut habet ꝓuerbiū) mendax, ne ſi uera tandem dixerit,
ei credat̃. Porro ſi ne Theologi eadē hic ſentiūt. falſitas
exinde illorū emergit. Diſcordia ẽm in ſcriptoribus, ut
dixit ille, teſtimoniū eſt falſitatis, Immo Auguſtinus ue
ritatē ex eo cognoſci docet, ſi ſcriptores cõcorditer in
ea cõuenerint, neꝗ unus diſſentiat ab altero, uel a pluri
bus plurimi: Et idē Auguſtinus, cū in multis aliis locis
ad Hieronimū & Fortunatū, tū & hic ad Vincentiū, de
quoꝗlibet etiā ſanctiſſimorū hoīm ſcriptis loqui. Hoc
genus (inquit) literarū, ab autoritate Canonū diſtin⸗

guendū est, Non enim sic legunt, tānꝗ ex eis ita testimo
nia ꝑferant, ut contra sentire nóliceat: Et nó Theolo⸗
gis dumtaxat:in eiusmodi rebus ex sacra scriptura non
deducibilibus,& ex eorū uarietate dubitabilibus crede
re nó adstringimur:sed nec ecclesię quidē, ut Thomas
in quodlibetis disputat. Eapropter, ad hunc modū ser⸗
moné claudere licet, ꝗ Petrus nunꝗm post passionem
Christi Romę fuerit, de cuius aduentu illuc: diuina scri⸗
ptura silet:historia secum diuariat. Doctores minus di⸗
gni sunt ꝗm quibus hic credatur:presertim dum ita mu⸗
tuo disceptent.

⁋ Persuasio sęcunda.

    Petrū Romam uenisse in exordio: uel secundo: uel ꝗ
to imperii Cęsaris Claudii: hoc est viii. ix. uel xi. post pas
sioné Christi anno dicentes: eorū imprimis refellit opi⸗
nio: qui Petrū in oriente quinꝗ : uel sedm alios: septem
annis sese cōtinuisse: tandé Antiochiā diuertenté, septé
annis in episcopali sede resedisse: & in Ponto: Galatia:
Bithinia ac circumiacentibus Asię puinciis aliquā mo⸗
ram cū fęcisse adstruunt: Non em: si id uerū esset: Ro⸗
mā uenire nisi post xiiii. aut xv. annos: hoc est septimo
uel octauo Claudii anno potuisset. Quibus patrocina⸗
tur gestoꝗ Apostolicorū scriptor Lucas ca. xv. Contro
uersia enim inter quosdā de hęresi phariseorū ex una &
Paulū ac Barnabā ex altera parte: de circūcisione obser
uationeꝗ legaliū habita: eas ob res discutiendas : in Ie⸗
rusalem illi descenderunt. Et factū est cōsiliū Aposto⸗
lorū & seniorū: Inter quos Petro primę loquendi porre
cte sunt partes: quāꝗ Iacobi Ierosolimitanorū pręspite
ri sententię: omes tandé subscripserint: eiusꝗ approba⸗

                                                B ii

uerint oratiunculá:Quę res manifeſtat Petrũ nõdũ Romam diuertere potuiſſe.ſed una cũ Iacobo:& quibuſdã
aliis Hieroſolymę manſiſſe:Vel forte in partibus Iudeę
Chriſtũ aliquãdiu docentē Hieroſolymã tunc tpis redi
iſſe:Et tñ multorũ eſt opinio : Hieronimo ſup epiſtolã
ad Galatas dicente:ꝗ circiter decimũ octauũ annũ poſt
Chriſti in cęlũ aſcentionem id factũ fuiſſet. Quod facil
limũ eſt creditu: ſi quis modo ſeriē rerũ ab apoſtolis ge
ſtarũ diligentius examinauerit. Cui ergo maior habēda
fides:Lucę ne Euangeliſtę:qui rebus ab apoſtolis factis
uel interfuerat ipſe:uel a Paulo apoſtolo (cuius indiuiduus fuerat comes: & quo pñte hanc ſcripſerat hiſtoriam)erat edoctus?An iſtis bellantibus mutuo hiſtorico
rum ac Theologorũ opinionibus? Qd̄ ſi id neceſſario
mihi dabit ː ut Claudii primũ nono aut undecimo ĩpii
anno Petrus Romã uenerit: & ibidē uigintiquinꝗ annis Epiſcopatũ tenuerit:iam nõ a Nerone:ſed Veſpaſia
no potius martyriũ paſſus fuiſſet: qd̄ neminem adhuc
unꝗm uel dixiſſe uel ſcripſiſſe cõperi.Et hinc manifeſta
riũ eſt: ad nonũ Claudii annum Petrum Romam uenire
non potuiſſe.

⸿Perſuaſio tertia.

Deniꝗ ꝗ ne nono quidē anno illuc uenire potuiſſet:
eiuſdē imperii ꝓ Petrus: Tranquillus in Claudio eſt au-
thor:qui Chriſtianos tunc tpis Roma fuiſſe pulſos ſcri
bit:Claudius:inquit: Iudęos impulſore Chriſto aſſidue
tumultuantes Roma expulit . Vbi Oroſius addubitat
Vtrũ contra Chriſtũ tumultuantes Iudęos coerceri &
cõprimi iuſſerit:an etiã Chriſtianos ſimul:uelut cogna-
tę religionis homines:uoluerit expelli ꜝQui profecto ſi

uel hiſtoriā rerū geſtaꝝ ab apoſtolis : uel ſaltē Paulinas
legiſſet epiſtolas : non ambigeret Chriſtianos Iudeorū
impietate & uerſucia:Cęſarē ac populum Ro:ad uindictā excitante una cū eiſdē Roma expulſos fuiſſe: Quip
pe uel apoſtolo ad Romanos in epiſtola id teſtāte:Inter
alios nanꝗ Chriſtianos quos ſaluere iuſſerat:Salutate:
inquit:Priſcillam & Aquilā : adiutores meos in Chriſto
Ieſu:qui ꝓ anima mea ſuas ceruices ſuppoſuerūt:Quos
ſane niſi Chriſtianos Apoſtolus nouiſſet : in cathalago
ſalutandorū Chriſti fideliū neutiꝗm repoſuiſſet : Attñ
quomō Iudeus genere Aquila ille fuerat:ꝗmuis in Chriſtum una cum coniuge crędiderit: nihilominus hunc tñ
Lucas in actibus Iudęū Ponticū nominat in hęc uerba.
Poſt hęc inquit:egreſſus ab Athenis Paulus: uenit Corinthū & inueniens quendā Iudęū noīe Aquilā : Ponticū genere:qui nuper uenerat ab Italia: & Priſcillā uxorē
eius . Eo ꝗ ꝑcepiſſet Claudius diſcedere oēs Iudęos a
Roma:acceſſit ad eos:& quia eiuſdē erat artis:manebat
apud eos & operabaꞇ . Et ne quis dubitet Chriſtianos
eos fuiſſe,addit Lucas in calce capi: duodeuigeſimi dicens: Iudeus quidā Apollo nomine Alexandrinus gñe
uir eloquens:deuenit Epheſum:potēs in ſcripturis : hic
erat doctus uiam dñi: & feruēs ſpiritu loquębaꞇ :& do-
cebat diligenter ea quę ſunt Iheſu : ſciens tñ baptiſma
Ioannis:Quē cū audiſſet Priſcilla & Aquila: aſſumpſe-
runt eū:& diligentius expoſuerunt ei uiā dñi:hęc Lncas
ad uerbū. Et totū hoc caput declarat Priſcillā & Aqui-
lam Chriſtianos ex Iudeis factos: Roma una cū aliis ex
pulſos fuiſſe:Quod iterū docent Paulinę literę:quas no
uiſſime iaṁ:ubi tempus reſolutionis ſuę propinquaue-

B iii

rat,ad unice dilectū difcipulū Timotheū fuum miferat:
Saluta inquit Prifcillam & Aquilā:Vnde non folū Chri
ftianos, fed finceriffimos quoqʒ Chriftianos eos fuiffe
cōftat,ut pote quos Apoftolus data modo occafione
nunꝗ nō falutabat.Nil hic moror, qd' Stapulenfis tam
in hac ad Timotheū,ꝗm ad Romanos in Epiftola inno
uat,uerba Apoftolica ad hunc modū exponens:falutat
uos Prifcilla & Acyla,uel Prifca & Acyla.Origenē,Chri
foftomū Ambrofiū, & tot doctiffimos alios interpʒtes,
imo & ueterem ipfam traductōem cui in hac parte Eraf
mus nihil derogat,hic fequi malo.Quid reftat igit' dice
re.ꝗm Petrū ad nonū ufqʒ Claudii annū Romā non ue
niffe?Qui enim illac uenire tunc potuerit,cū cęteri oēs,
cū Iudei tū Chriftiani inde pellerent,& in tantū ftoma-
charetur Roma ? Qui fi poft hac Romā aliquando ue-
nierit,ac uigintiquinqʒ illic delituerit annis,Vefpefiano
eius imputaretur martyrium, quod de tam benigniffimo erga oīnes principe credere nephas eft, & nemo eft
omnium qui hoc affirmare audeat.

¶Perfuafio quarta.

Pergamus iā eo ordine oftendere, ne ad uigefimū q-
dem annū poft Chrifti paffionē, uel in celū afcenfionē
Petrū Romam uenire potuiffe,Quod ex uerbis difcipu
li,a fufpectione apud Galathas fefe purgantis clariffi-
mum eft,Dicit em in ea quam ad Galathas dederat epiftola non a quopiam hoīm, fed folo Chrifti munere,
euangelicū mifteriū fibi contigiffe.Et quod dixerat,nec
cuiꝗm uideret falfum probat inquiꝗens poft miraculo-
fam fuā ad fidem Chrifti cōuerfionē, nō in Ierufalem ad
Apoftolos fe declinaffe:fed protinus Arabiā abiiffe:tā-

dem iterato Damaſcũ repetiiſſe, & tum tertio loco pri
mum tribus reuolutis annis Ieroſolymam uidendi Pe∢
tri gratia trãſmigraſſe. Deniꝗ poſt quĩdęcim dies poſt
ꝗm Petrum & Iacobũ fratrem domini uĩdeat͡, dicit ꝗ
iterum Ieroſolimã reliquit, ac in partes Sirię & Cilicię
deuenit. Deinde aſſumpto Barnaba & Tito. poſt inte∢
gros quatuordecim annos͜, rurſum Ieroſolymã rediit,
quo euangeliũ quod in gentibus prędicauerat cũ his ꝗ
Apoſtoloꝗ uidebant͡ columnę conferet & iterũ Petrũ
una cum Iacobo & Ioanne illic reperit:Et ſic certum eſt
totis illis ſeptemdecim annis Ieroſolimis & in collimi∢
taneis regionibus Petrũ ſeſe continuiſſe͜,nec unꝗm Ro
mam receſſiſſe.Additis eĩ quatuordecim annis quib⁹
Ieroſolymã reuenerat͜,ad annos tres quib⁹ ͵pxime poſt
cõuerſionẽ ſuã uiſitauerat Ieroſolymã:decem & ſeptem
anni ͵pueniunt. Demũ poſtꝗ Petrus aliꝗ̃diu citra Pau∢
lum moraret͜͡,Antiochiã ueniens in eum incidit quẽ ille
acerrime illic obiurgauerat.͜& idem in facię reſtitit:eo ꝗ
nõ recte ambulaſſet ad ueritatẽ euangelii : & ſimulatio∢
ni nõ modo ipſe fuit obnoxius: ſed ad hãc alios quoꝗ
iã tum ͵ptraxerit:Dixi inquit Cęphę corã omnibꝰs:ſi tu
cum Iudeus ſis:gentiliter uiuis & nõ Iudaice : quó gen∢
tes cogis iudaizare͜,Inter ꝗ repręhenſionẽ Petri & priſti
nam eoꝗ ab inuicẽ diſceſſionẽ aliquid tpis certe inter∢
uenerat.Ad hęc͜,poſt Chriſti aſcenſionẽ: nõ mox Paul⁹
Chriſtum agnouit͜, nimirum qui dum Stephanus ſaxis
obrueret͡ enecareturꝗ aſſiſtens:mortẽ ipſius in deliciis
habuerat.Dicit͡ eĩ Actoꝗ ſeptimo, Teſtes autẽ depo∢
ſuerunt ueſtimenta ſua:ſecus pedes adoleſcentis quoca
bat͡ Saulus : Et ſoluſmet inferius ca. xxii. ad Chriſtum

queribundus loquit̄.Cum funderetur sanguis Stepha-
ni testis tui: ego astabā & consentiebam: & custodiebā
uestimenta interficientiū illū.Vide q̄ hoc tempus ab a-
scensiōe Christi,ad usq̄ obiurgationē Petri Antiochię
a Paulo factā facile uiginti etiam annos superet, Quibus tn̄ Petrum certū est Romę nondū fieri potuisse,q̄-
uis nec postea unq̄m illic fuerit,Verū,demus hoc aduer
sariis,q̄ Petrus anno uigesimo Romā appulisset, Iā ad
tredecimū usq̄ annum imperii Claudii ille aduentus p̄-
rogaretur, Quod si huc trahantur uigintiquinq̄ anni,
quibus Romanā moderatus est Ecclesiam, interim Ve
spasiani temporis eius mors irrogaret̄. Quod ois omnium historicorū libri ut falsissimū auersatur,Produca-
mus huc Romanorū imperatorum tpa,quo res fiat eui
dentior.Lucas euangelii sui ca.tertio, anno impii Cęsa
ris Tiberii quindecimo Christū dedit uerbū dei p̄dicare
incępisse,qui tandē post tres annos & aliquot mēses p̄
dicationis suę mortē sustulit,anno eiusdem imperii de-
cimooctauo uel ultra,Tiberio post passionē ipsius annis tribus impante,post hunc Caius Gallicula annis tri
bus,mēsibus decem,& octo diebus imperans uita functus est,Claudius anno quatuordecimo imperii morit̄:
Nero totidem annos in impio explesse dicit̄. Otho Sil
uius infra lxxxxv.dies imperiū alteri cessit,Aulus Vitel
lius octo mensibus impauit.post hunc Vespasianus de
cennio Romanis sese impatorē pręstitit: Sub quo Chri
stiani pacifice Romę degebāt, nullis ab eo uexati perse
cutionibus. Quę igit̄ iniquitas in tam benignissimum
principem hanc reiicere iniuriā,tanquā ille Petri interfe
ctor aliquando fuerit.

ℂ Perſuaſio quinta.

Sub hęc,neq̨ tunc tpis qn̄ Paulus Romanis ſcripſerat Petrū Romę fuiſſe, hęc ipſa epiſtola ad Romanos
porrecta argumento eſt.Quā quidē, ſatis longo tpe ab
Apoſtolo non fuiſſe deſcriptam cōſtat.In q̃ ipſe,ut Ori
genes meminit, omnibus numeris abſolutior fuerat,q̃ʒ
dum Corinthiis ſcripſerit.Et iccirco poſt utrũq̨ ad Co
rinthios epiſtolā hác ſcriptā fuiſſe, cōtendit Origenes:
Athanaſius uero, & poſt primā quoq̨ ad Teſſalonicē-
ſes, Attamē alteram ad Corinthios, nō mox poſt eam
quę prior eſt exarauit Apoſtolus. Si quidē in ea quę pri
or eſt,inceſtū quendā Corintheorū eccleſię ſeniorē, qui
cū uxore patris rem habuerat,acriter taxat. & ex unita-
te fideliū,emancipandū pręcipit, huncq̨ ſpiritui mali-
gno in poteſtatē tribuit,mo do ſpūs in diem dn̄i Chriſti
Ieſu ſaluus fieret,In altera uero, poſtq̃m ille reſipuit, ac
admiſſum digna cōpunctiōe atq̨ pœnitudine defleuit:
rurſum unitati,membrorūq̨ Chriſti cōmunioni reſtitu-
tus eſt.Ac tandē poſt miſſas ad Teſſalonicenſes literas
ubi iā tercio Corinthū uenerat:per Pheben Cenchreen-
ſem fęminā, ad Romanos epiſtolā direxit,in cuius calce multos fratrū nominatim ſaluere iubet.Et qui pridē
illius opera in Chriſtū crediderunt, & qui quapiā in eū
dexteritate uſi ſunt, Tū qui eccleſię illius antiſtites ac ſe
niores fuerunt.ueluti Narciſſum:Andronicū:Iuliā:Pri-
ſcillam & Aquilā. Qui igit̃ fieri potuit:ſi Paulus Petrū
tunc Romę fuiſſe credidiſſet,ut digna hunc ſalutatione
non dignaret̃ꝰ cuius ille obſeruantiſſimus eſſe, & nihil
honoris ei nō deferre pro ſua canicie, & Apoſtolatꝰ ho
neſtate debuerat, Sed inelectabilis hęc eſt ratio, ℗etrū
C

Romę tunc tpis nõ fuiſſe, Faceſſat ergo uafricia Roma
na hanc ſibi gloriam ambire, nihil enim ęque falſum eſt
atcʒ hęc arbitraria ęſtimatio.

⟨Perſuaſio ſexta.

Accedit & iſtud ad corroborandũ, qʒ Petrus ad ea
tpa, quibus Paulus Romanis literas deſtinauerat, Romę nõ fuiſſct, quia diuus Ambroſius, ſup epiſtolam ad
Romanos, in quibuſdã uetuſtis codicibus dicit ſe legiſ-
ſe Narciſſum illo tempore Romę pſbiterũ fuiſſe: cuius
domũ Apoſtolus ſaluere iubet, hic tñ, inquit diuus Am
broſius , officio peregrini fungebat, exhortationibus
firmans crędentes. Quod ſane nuperus Romanus prę-
ſbiter neutiɋ̃ſ faceret: a quo nihil tã eſt alienũ q̃m uerbi
diuini prędicatio. Et id propter, uelut claudus (ut Plau
tino utar dicterio) ſutor, domi totos ſedet dies, cupedi
arum deliciis uoratrinã explens . Niſi forte oſtentandę
pompę cauſa, ad Lateranenſe palatiũ interdũ prorepat:
Porro ut ad rem ueniamus, hic ſcito eſt opus, apud pri-
mitiuã ęccleſiam nullos fuiſſe, qui dicerent ſummi pon
tifices, Cardinales, Patriarchę, Archiepiſcopi. Nempe
quę duos ſolũ eccleſiaſticos habuit ordines: Preſbiteros uidelicet & Dyaconos: ut ex ea claret quã Philippē
ſibus Apoſtolus e Roma dederat epła, Paulus inquit &
Timotheus ſerui Iheſu chriſti, Omibus ſanctis qui ſunt
in Chriſto Ieſu, qui ſunt Philippis cũ Epiſcopis & Dya
conibus, Nam iidē uocabant preſbiteri, epiſcopi uel ſe
niores, ut ex epiſtolis Paulinis eſt manifeſtiſſimũ, Quin
in Actis quoɋ̃ Apoſtoloʒ, ad Epheſinę eccleſię p̃ſbite
ros inquit, Quia uos ſpũſſanctus poſuit epiſcopos re-
gere ęccleſiam dei, Et Petrus, qui & ipſe preſbiter mul-

tarum ecclesiarũ fuerat: ad p̃sbiteros diſperſionis Pon-
ti:Galatiȩ:Capadotiȩ: Aſiȩ & Bythiniȩ ſcribens:ſenio-
rem ſe nominat dicẽs: Seniores ergo qui in uobis ſunt:
obſȩcro conſenior & teſtis Chriſti paſſionũ : Ignoraue
rat:credo:tũ adhuc ſupcilioſum ſummoꝗ pontificũ no
men:uel abhorruerat planc. Et ut regrediamur ad prio-
ra:Prȩſbiteri dicebant:qui eccleſiis ueluti quidã proceres prȩerãt:Vnde apoſtolus in priori ad Timotheũ epi
ſtola.Qui bene:inquit:prȩſunt p̃ſbiteri: duplici honore
digni ſunt.Et ad Titũ: Huius rei gratia reliqui te Cretȩ:
ut ea quȩ deſunt corrigas: & cõſtituas per ciuitates prȩ
ſbiteros:ſicut ego prȩſcripſi tibi : Igiť hic p Narciſſum
prȩſbiteꝗ:ſeniorẽ aut Epiſcopũ Romanȩ eccleſiȩ fuiſſe
intelligimus:qui nõ modo eius:ſed & aliarũ circũiacen-
tiũ eccleſiaꝗ & Chriſti fideliũ curã gerebat: cuius etiam
familiã: ob ingenuas eius uirtutes Paulus ſalutare p̃ce-
pit: Inſup Andronicus & Iulias:duo e ſeptuaginta duo
rum Apoſtolorũ numero : ut Origenis eſt opinio: Ro-
mȩ ea tempeſtate fuerant:Quos hac prȩrogatiua hono
ris:ad Romanos in epiſtola ſalutat apoſtolus: Salutate
inquit: Andronicum & Iuliam cognatos meos & con-
captiuos meos :qui ſunt nobiles in Apoſtolis:qui& an
te me fuerunt in Chriſto Ieſu: Adde: Priſcilla & Aquila : ut Ambroſii ſuffragatur authoritas: non ocioſe Ro
mam uenerunt : Qui quoniam ꝓpenſiores erant inde-
uotione: ideo ad cõfirmationẽ Romanorum miſſi fuiſſe intelligunť:de quibus ad hunc modũ Paulus loquiť:
Salutate Priſcillam & Aquilã: adiutores meos in Chriſto Iheſu:qui ꝑ anima mea ſuas ceruices ſuppoſuerunt:
Eapropter quid opus Roma tunc habuerit Petro uete-

C ii

rano & iam uiribus defecto,nō coniicio. Nempe cū ha
buerit legittimū p̄sbiterū Narciſſum,apoſtolos Chriſti
doctrina inſignes,Andronicū & Iuliam, & coopatores
in euangelio nō contemnendos Aquilā & Priſcillā?Sed
hoc citra omnem cōtrouerſiam uerū eſt., q̄ Romę tunc
tempis nō fuerit:Nam ſi neminē non ſalutat eorū Ap̄s:
uel qui ſeniores fuerant,uel qui cognati & cogniti,quō
unū Petrū non ſalutaſſet, quo cū firmiſſimā amicitiam
& ſocietatē iampridē iniuerat:& eius uidendi deſyderio
antea Ieruſalem petere nōdubita uerat.Et hinc apparet,
uſq̄ adNeroniani impii tp̄a Petrū Romę nō fuiſſe, Qd̄
ſi uiginti & quincq̄ annis illic reſederit,a quo tandē mor
tem paſſus eſt?Hic tuſſiunt Romani ſycophantę, non
ſecus ac indocti quicq̄ cantores, qui locū fęcerunt pro
uerbio,hęſitatio cantorū,ut cōmuniter dicit̄,tuſſis eſt.

      ⟨Perſuaſio ſeptima.

Huc producā,& quod Apoſtolus ad Galatas narrat
in epiſtola, Creditū eſt inquit mihi euangeliū prępucii,
ſic & Petro circunciſionis.Qui nācq̄ operatus eſt Petro
in Apoſtolatū circūciſionis. Qui nancq̄ operatus eſt &
mihi inter gentes.Tandem manifeſtat,quō pactus fuiſ
ſet cū Iacobo,Petro & Ioanne,in ſynodo quę Ieruſoly
mis ſup legaliū obſeruatione habita eſt, ut ipſi in circū
ciſionē,hinc uero inter gentes cū Barnaba,predicatū p̄
ficiſceret̄.Quō itacq̄ tam cito Petrus pacti imemor fie
ri potuit,& alienas partes ſibi uſurpare,cū Roma toci
us paganiſmi mater tunc fuerit?Qn̄ immo,ſi circūciſio
nis fuerat Apoſtolus,quō Romę tot annis,ad Pauli ui
demus illac aduentū, cū Iudęis nihil ei fuerat negotii?
Adueniente nancq̄ illac Paulo, ut Lucas in Actis Apo

ſtoloꝛū ait,dicunt Iudei ad eū,Deſecta hac notū eſt no⸗
bis,quia ubiꝗ� ei cōtradicitur . Rogamus eṁ te audire
quę ſentis.Nos eṁ neꝗ lꝝas accepimus de te , neꝗ ad⸗
ueniens aliquis fratrū, nūciauit aut loqutus eſt quid de
te malū. Quos tandē copioſa illa ac uberrima oratione
ſua alloqutus eſt Paulus,a mane uſꝗ ad ueſperā ſermo⸗
nem ‚ptrahens.E quibus aliqui dictis crediderūt,quidā
uero rennuerunt credere,Et nunꝗ̷ antea audita aurib9
haurientes,adinuicē tumultuabāt & multā inter ſe ha
bebant queſtionē.Quid ergo Romę tanto tpis interual
lo fęcerat Petrus, ſi Iudęis ea quę a Paulo audierant no
ua & inaudita uidebāt.Nec aliquem ſe prius audiuiſſe
dixerunt,qui eius ſectę inſtituta & ritus eis declaraſſet?
Et proinde Paulū,ut quę ſentiat diceret , uelut uno ore
poſtulabant oēs,Videat qui uult,ꝗm ſit tutū Romę Pe
trū aliquando fuiſſe credere.

ℂ Perſuaſio octaua.

Iam ad ea uſꝗ peruenimus tempa , quibus Ieruſoly⸗
mis ludeoꝶ coactus inſolentia Paulus,ad Cęſarem ap⸗
pellauit,ac Romā deductus, cathenis horrendus in car
cerē coniectus eſt:illicꝗ in conductu ſuo:quod ei carce
ris fuerat loco,toto biennio permanſit , Nec profecto
parua hęc erat manſio,ut Ieronymus in epiſtolā ad Phi
lemonē loquiꝷ ad quā Iudęorū turbę quottidie cōflue⸗
bant.Nā ſuſcipiebat oṁes, ut in Actis Lucas ſcribit,q
ingꝛędiebāt ad eū prędicans regnū dei, & docens quę
ſunt de dño Iheſu chriſto cū oṁi fiducia ſine ‚phibitio⸗
ne,allectans ad fidem Chriſti hoi̅es,ut uerbis ita & lite⸗
ris,Multos eṁ,eo cōcionante,non modo plebęos,ſed
& de regia Neronis,Chriſti fidē ſuſcępiſſe:ipſius epiſto
                                                    C iii

lę oſtendũt:Ad Philipenſes eĩ e cõductu ſuo ſcriptitás
Salutant uos, inquit,oés ſancti, ac quidẽ maxime, & q
de Cęſaris domo ſunt.Quin epiſtolas quoq; aliquot in
uinculis dictaucrat.pia admonitióe,& Chriſtiana pieta
te plenas,ne ecclcſię Chriſti pulchre ab eo inſtitutę,eius
abſentia in deterius laberent,Nã quos uiua uoce cõue
nire nõ poterat,ſcriptis tantiſp admonebat,ne ſuę ,pfeſ
ſionis obliti,a Chriſto aliqñ excideręt,pcipue Galathis
poſt pſeudo aptos,retro a Chriſti fide ac ſuis rudimẽtis
abeũtibus,epiſtolã e Roma ſcribere nõ dubitauit, uerbis etiã aſperioribus eos cõmonefaciens ne uafricia &
aſtu,a Chriſto abduci ſeſe paterent,Deũ obteſtans,q̃ q̃
cũq; illũ in mandatis dederat,ea nõ ab homibus,neq; p
hoíes nact? unq̃; fuiſſet:ſed ſola benignitate Iheſu Chri
ſti:Nimirũ quib? tã firmiter cręndi oporteat:ut ſi angel?
quoq;,uel ipſemet ſecũdario ad eos aliqñ uenerit, ac di
uerſum quiddã docere uoluerit,pbroſum ac execrabile
id fieret,in q̃ epiſtola,Petri aliquot locis meminit,cuius
teſtimoniũ in hoc negotio,ut Galatis qd̃ dixerat facilius pſuaderet,mirũ in modũ illi fuerat neceſſariũ, Nõ tñ
uſpiã eius mentionẽ facit,an Romę ipſum tũc habuerit
collegã,uel ſi eis quę ſcripſerat, & ille ſubſcribere uolue
rit,Qui certe,ſi tũ Romę fuiſſet, ſaltẽ eius noíe eos ſalu
taſſet, quo facilius tã eminentis Apoſtoli uocabulo p-
moti reſipiſcerent,& ab extranea doctrina ſegregati, ad
mentẽ rediręt quádoq;,Attñ nihil hoꝝ fęcerat apts, qd̃
maximo eſt teſtimonio , neq; ea tẽpeſtate Petrũ Romę
fuiſſe,Cũ tñ uigintiquinq; anni,uel ſcd̃m quoſdã uigin
tiſeptẽ,a Chriſti paſſione aut aſcenſióe pterierint, Cęte
rũ neq; in ea quã ad Epheſios Romę ſcripſerat epiſtola
ullã eius mentionẽ facit,Cuius tñ hęc ſemp alias fuerat

cõſuetudo,ut collegaꝝ ſuárum noīe, in Chriſtũ crẹden
tes ſalutaret.　　　🄲Perſuaſio nona.

Inditio ſunt,Petrũ tpe Pauli Romẹ nõ fuiſſe,& literẹ
quas p Epaphroditũ ad Philipéſes dederat apſus, in q⸗
bus multoꝝ eos admonet, & q̃ erga illũ tunc tpis gere⸗
bant manifeſtat,maxime aũt q̃ntũ illic in euangelio ꝓ⸗
fẹcerit dicens ſua occaſiõe paſſim Romẹ euangeliũ prẹ
dicari ab oībus,eodẽ quidẽ impetu,q̃muis diuerſo ſtu⸗
dio.Quidá em̃ uinculis & cõſtantia iꝑius animati,ſince
ro affectu,& uere Chriſtiana intẽtõe:fidẽ Chriſti Romẹ
oſ timore exuto,inuulgabát. Quidá uero ſola cupidita
te nocédi Paulo:ad euágelizandũ Chriſtũ trahebantur:
Putabát em̃ fore: ꝗ Neronis Tyranni:cui nomẽ Chri⸗
ſti fuerat poſũ:puocata iracũdia:Paulina gſia in euan⸗
gelio faceſſeret:ac Tyrañus in eũ:uti eius ꝑfeſſionis au
thorẽ:grauius aíaduerteret.Fit em̃: q̃ maxime nobis no
citura ſciuerint: hẹc ad noſtrã ꝓniciẽ inimici palã euul⸗
gant:Tũ ait Paulus ſibi nõ eſſe curẹ: dũ quouis mõ euã
geliũ annũciet:& Chriſtus orbi innoteſcat:ſũũ hoc ad
uitã:ſiue ad mortẽ illi ſit ceſſuꝝ. Maluit em̃ cũ euágelii
lucro mori: q̃ abſcꝗ ꝓfectu uiuere:res ꝓfecto miraculo
digna:ſi Petrus tũc Romẹ fuerat:q̃madmodũ multis iã
annis inibi agere debuerat:quõ Chriſti nomẽtã moleſte
a Paulo Roma audierit:ut ſubornati in hoc etiã pleriꝗ
hoīes doloſi ſub Chriſti ꝓdicatõis obtẽtu Pauli exitiũ q̃
rerẽt:Nũ uero ocioſus tot annis illic delituerat:& Chri⸗
ſti occultauerat fidẽ Petrus:timés ne in eũ ſeuiſſet tyrã⸗
nus:utcꝗ facili⁹ eoꝝ inſidias q aduerſabáṫ Chriſto ſub
terfugerit? Nã ſi annuatim euágeliũ:Romẹ ꝓdicauerat:
ea res nõ debuit eſſe Paulo timori:ſiquidem Roma tot
iam annis antea Chriſtũ patientiſſime a Petro audierit:

Immo quantumcumqʒ tumultuante Roma : tyrannus
ad uindictā irritaret , in Petrū primitus resultasset hęc
iniuria, ut pote qui caput eius negocii fuerit , Ecquid
igitur formidarat Paulus,ne faba hęc in suo qd dicitur,
cuderet capite nō uideo. Ad hęc,in fine eiusdem episto
lę subdit,Salutant uos omnes sancti, maxime uero qui
de Cęsaris aula sunt, Maxime prorsus dicere debuit Pe
trus,oím nostrū ueluti quidā antesignanus, En q̄m inse
curū est dicere,etiā tunc tpis Petrum Romę fuisse,dum
Paulus captiuus illic teneretur , hac persuasione clarissi
mum est.

C̣Persuasio decima,
Colosensibus per Tychicū ac onesimū scribens Pau
lus in recessu epistolę addit Salutat uos Aristarchus cō
captiuus meus,& Marcus cōsobrinus Barnabę & Ihe-
sus qui dicit iustus,qui sunt ex circūcisione. Ii soli sunt
adiutores mei in regno dei,qui mihi fuerunt solatio. Sa
lutat uos Epaphras qui uestras est,seruus Ihesu Christi.
Salutat uos Lucas medicus Charissimus,& Demas. Vi
de q̄m oés nominatim enumerat,qui tunc ei aderant &
coopatores eius erant in regno dei,hęc est ecclesia Chri
sti,Gregorius em̄ inquit. Sępe in sacro eloquio regnum
cęlorū pn̄tis tpis ecclesia dicitur. Et Christus Apud Lu
cam,regnū dei,inquit intra nos est, Quas ob res Paul9
dicit.Ii soli sunt adiutores mei in regno dei . Quid ergo
Petrus,nūquid tanq̄m ueteranus quidā ac emeritus miles in ociū tunc se recępat,ut non pro sua uirili euange-
licas adiuuaret partes , cooperatorqʒ in regno Christi
non fieret? quod de Perro sentire horret animus: proin
de nō te habuit tunc Roma Petre. Nā si fuisses Romę

& Paulũ eundẽ Chriſtum prędicantem nõ iuueris: eius
iam factionis fuiſſes Apoſtolus:quę non Chriſtũ ędifi-
caret,ſed deſtrueret ac demoliretur. Omne enim regnũ,
Chriſto dicente,in ſe diuiſum deſolabiť , ac domus ſupra domũ corruet.

ℂ Perſuaſio Vndecima.

Oneſimus , quẽ phrygẽ genere quidã fuiſſe putant,
philemonis Colloſſei ſeruus, cõpilatis rebus quibuſdã
ipſius Romã fugitiuus uenerat,illicꝗ Paulo de Chriſto
concionante audito , Chriſti nominis factus eſt candi-
datus ac baptiſmate in Chriſticolarũ conſortium aſci-
tus, Porro ne quid labis priſtinę ſceleſtę uitę in eo re-
manſerit,cõſcientiã Apoſtolo aperuit, & iniuriam quã
domino ſuo intulit,rebus quibuſdã illius ſurreptis con
feſſus eſt, Quẽ Paulus,quia nimirum adamarat,nõ ſibi
temperare potuit , quin protinus benigno ac ſcito epi-
ſtolio eũ Philemoni reconciliaſſet, hanc ſibi iniuriã in
Philemonẽ bene meritus donari poſtulans . Et ſi quid
damni re pecuniaria , aut alia quęuis, Oneſimi pfugio
acceperit, p eo ſe uadẽ ponens,oĩaꝗ ſe depenſurũ eius
loco pmittens . Et in Epiſtolii principio Philemonem
Appiam uxorẽ ipſius, & Archippũ Coloſenſis Eccleſię
epiſcopũ ſalutans , quo id facilius p quo interpellaue-
rat,ut ſenſit Chriſoſtomus, impetraſſet, Timothei nomẽ adiungit dicés, Paulus ſeruus Chriſti Ieſu & Timo
theus frater Philemoni &c . Cur hic Petri nomẽ in ſalutatione Paulus ſupprimit, ſi Timothei appoſuit,qui
facilius tã magni euangelici pconis authoritate motus:
offenſam forte Oneſimo cõdonaſſet ? Proh pudet me
tot ſęculorũ,quibus Paulinę litterę tineis corroſę , ſitu

D

ac pedore fedatę,intra angulos delituerāt, paſſimq; ab
omibus negligebant,Quarū lectio tot erroribus, ne in
ecclefia fubnafcerent,uel fola occurrere potuerit,Quid
em tā manifefte oftendere potuit Petrū Romę nó fuiſ
fe, q̃m hęc ad Philemoné epiſtola a Roma p Onefimū
trānfmiſſaꝰSed nunquid forte Philemoné, & p̄ſbiterū
Colloſſenſem Archippū , noíe Petri faluere iubet Apo
ſtolus,ad finé epiſtolę ꝓperemus,Salutat te Epaphras꞉
inquit,cócaptiuus meus,Marcus,Ariſtarchus, Demas
& Lucas adiutores mei,O infœlicem Petrū,ſi tū Romę
fuerat,& Paulū in hoc honeſtiſſimo deſtituit negotio.

❡Perfuafio duodecima.

Peracto iam dicto biennio , multifq; Romę ad fidé
Chriſti cóuerſis,ac epiſtolis hinc inde p eccleſias tranſ
miſſis,tandé Paulū in libertaté aſſeruit Nero,e cópedi
bufq; dimittere fœcit, Quod ipfemet ad Timotheū te
ſtat̃ Paulus dicens,liberatus ſum de ore leonis,Capti
uitas eterñ hęc intra hoc quinquennium fuerat, de quo
Trayanū impatorem ſex, Aurelius dicere ſolitū memo
rat,procul diſcant cuncti principes Neronis quinqué
nio , Adeo eñ comis, benignus, affabilis & modeſtus
quinq; primis ſui impii annis Nero fuerat,ut de eo Trā
quillus ſcribens꞉a pietate hūc impii exordia fęciſſe dixe
rit, Et tantū aberat ut infra hoc quinquéniū Nero mor
ti deuouerat q̃npiam , q̃ moleſte & indignanter eis qui
mortis ſententiá in aliqué pronunciauerint, pro cóſue
tudine fubſcribere etiam fuerat ſolitus.Nā ſemel admo
nitus, ut in ſupplitio cuiuſdā capite damnati ex more
fubſcriberet,Quā uellem꞉inquit neſcire literas,Hic igi
tur pro ſua erga oés beniuolentia Paulū tunc tpis di

miſit liberũ,Reliquis aũt nouē imperii ſui annis,,in oēm
luxum turpitudinē,truculentiã adeo ſe effudit,ut impie
tate oēs facile: ſceleſtiſſimos etiã homines ſuperaſſet:
QuáuisIoſephus libro antiquitatũ uigeſimo: ca:ſexto:
nimis incertã de Nerone eſſe hiſtoriã tradat: dicit náq̓:
Multi de Nerone hiſtoriã cõſcripſerunt : quorũ quidã
pro gratia beneficiorũ eius neglexcre ueritatē:Alii uero
ꝓpter odiũ & eius inimicitias: ſic impudenter mēdatiis
inuoluti ſunt:ut aperta reprẽhenſione ſint digni.Ideo ſ̨
uiēte iã Nerone:ac tyranno nõ impatore exiſtente:poſt
decēniũ iterum Paulus in uincula relapſus eſt: & pcius
q̃m unq̃ȝ antea ab eo habit9. Vñ epiſtolã illã:qų ad Ti
motheũ habeť altera:ſcribēs: prioris captiuitatis memi
nit his ferme uerbis: In priua mea defenſione nemo mi
aſtitit: ſed oēs me dereliquerunt:nõ illis imputeť: dñus
aũt mihi aſtitit:& cõfortauit me:ut p me pr̨dicatio im
pleať & audiant oēs gentes:& liberatus ſum ex ore lco⸗
nis:Vbi tunc Petrus fuiſſe cenſendus eſt?Rom̨ reuera
nõ fuit : alioqui Paulo cauſam ꝑ capite apud Neronis
tribunalia peroranti: & ſeſe defendēti eũ nõ adfuiſſe:ini
quũ prorſus fuiſſet.Quē ſi ex induſtria quoq̃ȝ derelique
rit:nulla excuſatõe deinceps dignus haberet̃:Ego tamē
millies tolerabilius iudico : Petrũ nunq̃ȝ Rom̨ fuiſſe
credere : q̃m hanc calumniã:q̓ Paulũ deſtituiſſet : in tã
ſublimē Apoſtolum reiicere.

    ¶ Perſuaſio tredecima.

    Notũ eſt Lucam euangeliſtã : & Apoſtolicarũ actio⸗
num hiſtoriographũ : indiuulſum totius pegrinationis
Pauling fuiſſe ſociũ:quē ille filii ſemper dilexit loco:ho
norificamq̃ȝ eius mentionē pleriſq̃ȝ facit in locis : dicēs

                           D ii

illius maximā laudē in euangelio fuisse: Nam cū oēs eti
am a Paulo defecerint: hic solus nunq̃m ei non adhere,
bat:Nō minis : non uinculis: nō sexcentis psecutioni,
bus perterritus : Cuius historia ad hęc usqʒ tpa:quibus
Paulus uinctus e Ierosolymis Romā perductus:ibiqʒ in
cōducto a milite custoditus est:peruenit.Veluti eius rei
capite ultimo copiose meminit: quō uidelicet Paulus
Romā perductus fuerit : quō fratres qui eo tpe Romę
fuerant ad Appii forū ei ebuiā uenerint: quō triū dierū
spacio euoluto:Iudeos ad se accitos habuerit:quō col,
loquutus cū eis fuerit:quō eos confutauerit: & singula
ordinatim ‚psequit́:Nullam tñ alicubi mentionē de Pe,
tro facit:an uel alloquio Paulū aliqñ dignat9 fuisset to
to hoc biennio:Vel quid rerū Petrus Romę fęcerit inte
rim, dū Paulus uerbū dei ardentissime illic tū depredi,
casset.Et tñ tunc tpis hanc historiā fuisse scriptam crę,
ditur,qñ Paulo Romę in cathenis degenti ille intrepide
ministrauerat Qui usqʒ adeo Pauli studiof9 fuerat:ut qc
qʒ hactenus de eo comperat, cuncta in suā historiā dili,
gentissime cōgesserit:etiā Ieronymo de uiris illustribus
attestante, Lucę inquir historia usqʒ ad bienniū Romę
cōmoranti Paulo peruenit,id est usqʒ ad quartū Nero,
nis annū.Ex quo intelligimus in eadē urbe librū esse cō
positū:Igitur uisio nem Pauli & Teclę, & totā baptisa,
ti Leonis fabulā, inter Apochriphas scripturas cōputa
mus.Quale eñ est,ut indiuiduus comes Apostoli inter
cęteras eius res hoc solū ignorauerit́hactenus Ierony,
mus.At quid hoć́nonne nō solū Apocryphū,sed plus
q̃m falsissimū erit , Petrū romā sęcundo Claudii anno
uenisse , ibiqʒ uigintiquinqʒ annis episcopatū tenuissé́

Cuius Lucas in tam p̄stantiſsima diligentiſsimaq̃ hiſto
ria nullam mentionē facit, Qui dubio procul, ſi tūc Ro
mę fuiſſet, nō hoc toto biennio ocioſus cōplicatis, ut
dicit́, manibus illic ſediſſet, uel ſaltem nō ſic delituiſſet,
quin a Paulo uel Luca cōſpici inueniriq̃ interdum potuerit.

℃ Perſuaſio Quatuordecima.

Circiter uigeſimū ſeptimū poſt aſcenſionē Chriſti ad
patrem ac Neroniani imperii quartū aut quintū annū,
Petrū Romę nondū fuiſſe, id iam tā manifeſtū, q̃m qđ
manifeſtiſſimū eſt. Sed quia neq̃ ultimo Neronis anno
hoc eſt poſt paſsionē Chriſti, & eius ad parentis dexte-
ram aſcenſionē triceſimoſeptimo illic uenire potuerit,
hoc deducit. Qm̄ Paulus e manibus Neronis elapſus
in Hiſpaniā: ut Lyra & alii quidā uolunt, & partes occi
dentis iter adornauerat. Eius cm̄ intentionis Apl̄m fuiſ
ſe, etiā cū Romanis literas ſcripſerat certū eſt, Peractis
aūt ibi decē annis, rurſum ad Neronis manus đeuenit,
& mortē accelerare uidens, ſcripto Timotheū cōmone
facit, ut aſſumpto ſecū Marco Romā ſeſe recipiat eo q̃
pręter Lucā: nullus iā ei reſiduus fuerit collega: Sed quō
tuis dictis, mi Paule. fidē habere potero, cum tota hęc
Romana colluuies, a ſecundo Claudii anno uſq̃ finem
imperii Neroniani Petrū perpetuo Romę duraſſe exer-
ta uoce, p̃clamet? Qui ergo fieri potuit, ut ſolus cū Luca Romę fueris? O doctor gētiū facile id tuę cedo ue-
racitati Petrū Romę nunq̃z te uidiſſe, & aliis recedenti-
bus, ſolū cū Luca remanſiſſe, Nihil me mouent uerba ſa
crę ſcripturę Tyrannorū, qui Chriſtū ac tua dicta adul-
terare fœdiſſimeq̃ p̃ſtituere in deliciis habēt. Cęterum

eadē epiſtola ſcribit. Det miſericordiā dominus Oneſi-
phori domui, quia ſepe me refrigerauit, & cathenā meam non erubuit, ſed cū Romam ueniſſet, ſollicite me q̄-
ſiuit & inuenit, det illic dominus inuenire miſericordi-
am a deo in illa die. Non obſcurū eſt ex his uerbis, quā-
tę gratitudinis erga eos fuerit Apoſtolus, qui officium
aliquot in eū cōtulerint, ut nō poſſit hic ſatis gratulari,
ac ſuū gaudium uerbis exprimere quod ei conciliaue-
rat Oneſiphorus ſuo aduentu, Qui peregre ueniens, nō
tamen conquieuit, donec hunc inueniſſet, Potuit certę
Oneſiphorus hic a Petro ſi tunc fuerat Romę, cercior
effici, quo locorū Paulus Rome ſeſe continuerit, & liberatus fuiſſet multū anxia, illa ſollicitudine, qua Paulū
hincinde per Romam diſcurrēdo inueſtigauerat. Mirū:
ſi Paulus neminē pręterit, a quo aliquod perſentiſcerit
beneficiū, q̄ Petrum Romanum, ut aiunt, incolā, ſuum
nunquā ſcribit aduiſitaſſe carcerem, Quē tamen aman-
tiſſimū ſui ſemper habuerat fratrem, Nempe a quo in
Catholica illa ſua Paulus Chariſſimus nominatur frater. Quāobrem ueriſſimū eſt ad ultimum uſq̄ Neronis
annū Petrum Romę non fuiſſe, Cū nec, ſaluere iubens
Timotheū, fratrum qui Romę tunc aderant nomine,
Petrū admemoret. Salutant te Eubolus & Pudens & Li
nus & Claudia, & fratres omnes, Non uideo. Cur ex in
duſtria ſupprimere Petri nomē uoluiſſet, cuius alioqui
ſemper fuerat obſeruantiſſimus, Quomodo iccirco uiginti & quinq̄ annis Romę egit? quomodo a Nerone
paſſus eſt, cum nec ſub eius imperio uenire quoq̄ illac
potuerit.

¶ Perſuaſio quindecima.

Præter epiſtolas iam dictas, Pauli e Roma miſſas,
ſunt quædam aliæ familiariores reſponſiuæ epiſtolæ ipſi∢
us ad Senecam, Neronis imperatoris præceptorem ſcri
ptæ, Quas ego nonnullis argumentis, tunc fuiſſe ſcri∢
ptas arbitror cũ Paulus ſecundo iam Neroni præſenta∢
retur. Primũ, quia iam Nero Cæſar furibundus, atrox,
petulcus, adulter, & omni prope uiciox contagio fue∢
rat pollutus, quod de priori eius quinquennio nullus
credere poteſt. Secundo, quia id temporis Paulinæ quæ
dam epiſtolæ, quas ubi in priori captiuitate Romæ tene
retur, ad quaſdã eccleſiarum direxerat, ad manus Sene∢
cæ iam tunc deuenerant, ex quibus ille nonnihil profæ∢
cit. Quod priori biennio, quo Romæ tenebat Paulus,
fieri non potuit, Tercio, ꝙ Seneca in una Epiſtolarũ ad
Paulũ deſcriptarũ, Romani incendii a Nerone facti me
minit, quod ad finem declinante Neronis imperio fa∢
ctum eſt, Cum Oroſius non ita multo poſt, Petrum &
Paulum communi mendacio deceptus, a Nerone mar∢
tyrium paſſos ſcribat, Et ſequenti mox autumno, peſti∢
lentiam Romæ obortam adeo magnam, ut uno autum
no ad trigintamilia hominum uita deceſſerint, Quam
peſtilentiam Neronis imperio decreſcente factam, Sue
tonius in uita ipſius deſignat. Illis itaꝗ ambobus Ro∢
mæ exeuntibus, Paulo in carcere Seneca in regia Ne∢
ronis cum alter de altero magna ſibi polliceretur, &
neuter neutrum alloqui potuiſſet, uel quod inde utri∢
ꝗ immineretur periculum, quandoquidem lege cau∢
tum fuerat, ne quiſpiam Chriſtianum aut Iudæum al∢
loquæretur, uel qued Senecæ non fuerat integrum

Paulinū carcerē aduifitare, ne quid exinde tyrannū of
fenderet, aut ipfe quoqʒ cōiiceret in carcerem: Quapro
pter epiftoliis hanc colloquendi farciebant penuriā, &
quidē mutuū amorē utrinqʒ pre fe ferentibus, neuter tū
Petri alicubi meminit, qui uigintiquinqʒ annis iam tum
Romę agere debuerat, nondū tn̄ fuerat Senecę doctiffi
mo, in Chriftianofqʒ benigniffimo homi cognitus, Cui
proculdubio nonnihil gratificatus fuiffet, fi quod Pau
lus ob carceris impedimentū non poterat, ipfe eius de
fiderio fatiffęciffet, & de Chrifto fecū cōfabulatus, in
numerū Chrifti fideliū afferuiffet. Quod Paulus etiā fa
cere debuit, ut ablata fibi Senecā alloquendi copia, cū
ad Petrū nulli Apoftolorū poftponendū relegaret, qui
nihilo deterius fidei Chriftianę primordia ei tradiderit,
Sed quis, ni forte exoculatus non uideat omnia hic re
pugnare peftiferę huic opinioni, qʒ Petrus Romā unqʒ
uenerit, a Nerone paffurus, cū tot rationibus cōuinca
tur, ad ultimū ufqʒ Neronis imperii annū, Petrū Romā
nunqʒ ueniffe, tantū abeft, ut martyriū ab eo paffus fue
rit, Nā legirur & in ea quę tertia eft Senecę ad Paulū epi
ftola, qʒ eius plurimū rei caufa Nero apoftolo fuerat in
dignatus, qʒ a ritu & fecta priftina Iudeorū qui pharife
us olim fuerat, non folū ipfe recefferit, fed & aliis hoc
fuaferit faciundū. Quod plane Petrus prior Paulo Ro
mę facere debuerat, fi tot annis ante aduentū in urbem
ipfius, illic refederit.

℄Perfuafio Sedecima.

Neminem adeo hebetē ac ftupidū puto, quin intelli
gat Petrū nō modo Romę paffum nō fuiffe, fed ne euim
fuiffe illic quidem. Et ne quis moueat inuerecunda illa

Romanę Curię uoce,tot teſtimonia pferentis,perpendat ſecū:qm item de paſſione Petri & Pauli alterutrum coueniant Authores,Ambroſius ſermone illo ſexageſimoſeptimo , de Petri & Pauli martyrio diſſerens dicit, Vna die, uno in loco,unius tyranni tolerauere ſententiam,& hęc cū multis aliis cōmunis eſt ei opinio,immo totius Romanę eccleſię, in eorū ſolennitate decantantis,Glorioſi principes terrę , quō in uita ſua dilexerunt ſe,ita & in morte non ſunt ſeparati,Falſa uero eſſe hęc, paſſiones utriuſcz,ſub nomine diſcipulorū Pauli cōfictę produnt,dū necz cū iſtis,necz ſecū conueniant, Qd em hic dicit una die eos paſſos fuiſſe,id Linus apertiſſime negat,& hoc uaria quidē ratiōe,quas ego ob proli xitatē huc nō adduco , uerū lectorem ad paſſiones illas per cōmenticiū Linū deſcriptas,& a Iacobo Stapulenſe latinitati donatas remitto . Dionyſius uero , non ille Pauli diſcipulus, ſed neſcio quis mendaciſſimus nebulo priori opinioni ſubſcribit. Sed nunqd & uno in loco paſſos cōcorditer omes ſcribunt? hic uide medacio rum portenta:Quidā em hoc fatentur ingenue,cantante etiā Romana eccleſia , ne in morte eos fuiſſe ſeparatos,ſed ſicuti una die ita in uno loco morti fuiſſe tradi tos.At Linus Petrū in loco,qui Naumachia appellaba tur,cruci prępoſtere affixū ſcribit, In quo autē Paulus ceruicē amiſerit,nō meminit.Sed hoc uno ſatis teſtatur noluiſſe ſe dicere,uno in loco paſſos,cū alios apparito res & carnifices:alios mortis ſpectatores eorū utricz aſ ſignet.Porro Dyoniſius ille,apertis uerbis ab eorū diuariat ſententia, Nā inquit,cū ad mortem ducerent: & ab inuicē ſepararent ,Petro dixiſſe Paulū,Pax tecū fun

E

damentū ecclefiaᵹ: & paſtor ouiū & agnorū Chriſti,De
inde ᵱ Neronis edicto ambo ad exiciū peruenerint, ne
hic quidē confentiunt: Nam cū oēs eius rei Neronē ᵱ-
nunciēt authorē:folus tñ Lynus:Agrippā Petrū interimere impaſſe teſtaᵗ . Scribit nanᵡ: ᵱ petro Romᵉ de
gente:multᵉ fexus fᵉminei monitu petri:illecebris luxu
riᵉ abrenunciauerunt: inter quas Agrippᵉ cōcubinᵉ ᵮ-
tuor fuere: quarū cōtinentia indignationis materiā A-
grippᵉ prᵉbuerat:ita ut petrū cruce interimere iuſſerit:
Hac de re:quāuis tota Roma tumultuareᵗ:imperatore
tñ nihil fciente . Et multa funt figmenta quibus illi mutuo diſſident:dū nihil certi fup ea re pronunciare noue-
runt:Quᵉ ibi ergo fides:ubi nulla eſt concordia? Nā uel
hoc folū diſſidiū mendaciū eorū prodit. Necdū unū ui
dimus arbitrū:qui hanc intolerabilē inter eos litem diri
mere aliᵱñ aufus fuiſſet:Hiſtoriᵉ eñ:quā de nerone qui
dam nobis reliquerunt:infecurū eſt credere:ut iam Iofe
phi adfcripfimus uerba.Immo res profecto miranda:ᵱ
Iofeph⁹ ipfe:qui a Vefpafiano expugnata Ierofolyma:
Romā perductus eſt ibidéᵡ agens Domiciani fere fupa
uit tempa . Et hiſtoriā Iudaici belli in urbe cōfcribens,
Vefpafiano eiufᵮ filio Tito nomiatim dicauit:in eaᵡ a
Nerone interemptorum:ut etiā alias in Antiquitatibus
meminit:nec ullā mentionem de petro ac paulo facit:
Qui tñ erga Chriſtianos fauentiſſimus fuerat:& arre-
pta occafione: nō fine honoris prohemio eorū folebat
meminiſſe: Velut Ioannis Baptiſtᵉ in Macheronta Ca-
ſtello obtruncati:libro Antiquitatū duodeuigefimo:Et
Iacobi apſi: fratris Chriſti Iheſu:ac Ierofolymitanorū ᵱ
ſbiteri:libro uigefimo : Id propter crediderim ego uitᵉ

exitũ.Ierofolymis ũnà cũ Iacobo & quibufdã aliis pe҂
trũ accepiffe:Siquidẽ Iofephus: & alios nonnullos tũc
tpis cũ Iacobo:ab Anano Iudeoꝝ pontifice interfectos
fcribit:Nam & ipfa reclamat ratio: petrũ una die interi
tũ cũ Paulo habuiffe : Qui a Chrifto uocatus : uxorẽ &
liberos:immo focrũ:quã Chriftus a febre uexatã:prifti҂
nę fanitati reddidit: habuiffe legit : & oĩm Apoftolorũ
habebatur annofiffimus : ut pote cuius caniciẽ Paulus
(ut Athanafio placet) reueritus: pòft tres cõuerfionis
fuę annos: eius uidendi gratia Ierufalem acceffit : cũ tñ
ipfe adolefcens adhuc fuerit : ut actorũ habet feptimo
Attñ in euangelica functione: tã diu uerfatus eft : ut ad
difcipulos unice fibi dilectos fcribens : ętate fe iam cõ҂
fectũ aliquoties fateret . Quis fe cõmittat Labyrintho
huic inextricabili:quẽ uobis tortuofiffimis fuis opinio
nibus : uelut mufcipulas quafdã adornant fcriptores?
nec quippiam tã certi alicubi occurrit quo ceu filo quo
dam ducti ad exitũ eaꝝ pueniamus.

❡ Perfuafio decima & feptima.

Oftenfo ꝗ petrus Romę mortẽ nõ receperit : reftat:
dicere: ubi locorũ ꝑ Chrifti nomine paffus fit . Et ante
ꝗm id probe:id teftor prius: nullũ teftimoniũ diuina ex
literatura huc trahi poffe quo quis paulũ indubie Ro҂
mę paffum fuiffe a Nerone oftendat: Nã dũ poftremo
iã neroni oblatus fuerat:& ad Timotheũ fcribens : hęc
interpofuit uerba.Ego iam delibor:& tempus refolutio
nis meę inftat:In eis Paulus decrepitam: & nõ martyriũ
fuum intellexerũt. Quẽ interea dũ hęc fcripferat : ualde
fenio detritũ : & decrepitũ plane fuiffe:fi non alio tefti҂
monio: certe uel hoc folo cõftat : Qñ ante decẽ annos

E ii

Philemoni fuo fcribens : fenem fe nominauit : Cū talis
fim inquiens:ut Paulus fenex. Quātū uero putas intra
hoc decenniū cōtinuis laboribus: oīm ecclefiarū follici
tudine:corpufculū Pauli exhauftū eft & maceratū:ut in
dicare Timotheo fuo chariffimo cogeret:quo Romam
acceleraret : fuoꝗ aduentu morte ipfius puerteret : qua
ipfe breui fuerat refoluendus:Nam ꝗ fpūfanɛto illuftra
tus:liberatione fui e carcere puiderit: uerba ipfius indi⸗
cant : Significans eɱ quó in priori ante Neronis tribu
nal ftatione:caufam fuā folitarius: & oɱi patrono defti
tutus porauerit : a Neroneꝗ ereptus fuerit: fub hꝗc ita
loquit : liberatus fum de ore leonis. Et liberabit me do
minus:ab omni opere malo: & faluū faciet in regnū fuū
cꝗlefte: hoc eft ad minifteriū corpis fui myftici : ecclefiꝗ
fanɛtꝗ:Queadmodū per regnū cœlefte: Gregorii autho
ritate: ecclefiam in facris fcripturis fꝗpiufcule nominari
diximus: Sicut eɱ fua fpes nō illū fefellit: ubi in priote
captiuitate cōftitutus: Philemoni fcripferat: para mihi
hofpitiū: Nā fpero per oratiões uɼas donari me uobis:
Ita neꝗ hic eū decepit : Sūt eɱ pleraꝗ alia teftimonio:
eū a Nerone liberatū etiā fecundario fuiffe : ueluti Epi⸗
ftola illa Senecꝗ: quꝗ Apoftolo in carcere degenti mife⸗
rat ipfe:Ex quibus pcliue eft creditu:Neronis uiolenti⸗
am Paulū euafiffe : Verū ne hic longius iufto immore⸗
mur:iam Petrū & Paulū Ierofolymis paffum:teftimoni
is irrefragabilib9 cōfirmabim9: primitus folius Chrifti
uerbis:ad fcribas & pharifeos:immo ipfam Ierofolymā
apud Matheum & Lucam loquentis: Ve uobis fcribꝗ
& pharifei hypocritꝗ: qui ꝗdificatis fepulchra prophe⸗
tarum & ornatis monumenta & dicitis: fi fuiffemus in

diebus patrū noſtrorū:nō eſſemus filii eorū in ſangui⸗
ne ͺppheta℣. Itaℷ teſtimonio eſtis uobismetipſis: quia
filii eſtis eorū qui prophetas occiderunt . Et uos imple
te menſuram patrū ueſtrorū.Ideo dico uobis.Ecce ego
mitto ad uos prophetas & ſapientes & ſcribas : & ex il
lis occidetis & crucifigetis : & ex eis flagellabitis in ſy⸗
nagogis ueſtris : & perſequimini de ciuitate in ciuitatē:
ut ueniat ſuper uos &c̄.Tandem dicit Irl̄m Irl̄m quę oc
cidis prophetas: & lapidas eos qui ad te miſſi ſunt &c̄.
Hęc loquutum Chriſtum non de prophetis legis uete⸗
ris : ſed de Apoſtolis: exponit Ioannes Chryſoſtomus:
homilia in Mattheum ſeptuageſimaquinta: ac ita dicit:
Significat iis uerbis Chriſtus Apoſtolos : & eos qui cū
Apoſtolis: & poſt Apoſtolos fuerunt: ex quibus mul⸗
ti etiam prophetabant : Quod diuus Ieronimus : lite⸗
rarum ſydus : clarius erga hęc uerba Chriſti immora⸗
tus interpretat̄,dicitℷ, Simul hic obſerua,iuxta Apo⸗
ſtolū ſcribentē,uaria eſſe dona diſcipulorū Chriſti,Ali⸗
os prophetas qui uentura p̄dicent,alios ſapientes, qui
nouerunt qn̄ debeant proferre ſermonē, alios ſcribas,
in lege doctiſſimos,Ex quibus lapidatus eſt Stephan9:
Paulus occiſus,crucifixus Petrus, flagellati in actibus
Apoſtolorū apoſtoli,& perſequuti eos ſunt de ciuitate
in ciuitatem,expellentes de Iudęa, ut ad gentiū populū
tranſmigrarēt.His uerbis Ieronymus clariſſime, ut Ste
phanū, ita & Paulū & Petrū Ieroſolymis paſſos decla⸗
rat.Et ne cuius teſtimoniū deſyderet̄,Nicolai Lyrę ho⸗
rū Chriſti uerboꝛū interpretationem ſubnectamus, Ex
eis occidetis.exponit Lyra,ſicut Iacobū fratrē Ioannis
Actuū xii.& Stephanū Actuū ſeptimo,& multos alios.

E iii

Et crucifigetis, ut Petrū & Andream fratrē eius, & multos alios, flagellabitis. sicut Paulū & Sylam, ut Actuū
sedecimo, & secūda ad Corintheos xi. tradit, Quis cō-
tra hęc firmissima testimonia uel hiscere deinceps poterit? quis reclamare? quis nō modo Ieronimū, Chrisosto
mum Nicolaū Lyranū, sed & Christū mendacii arguere
poterit? Cū ipsemet apud Lucā eadem repetens uerba,
de Petro, Andrea, & aliis quibusdā Apostolis, ea sese lo
quutū designat, inquiens, Dico aūt uobis amicis meis,
ne terreamini ab his qui occidūt corpus: & post hęc nō
habēt amplius quid faciant, Ostendā aūt uobis quē ti-
meatis, Timete eū, qui postq̄m occiderit. habet potesta
tem mittere in gehennā. Pręterea dicit Christus. Ierosolymis & non Romę, a scribis & phariseis, & non ab im-
peratoribus Romanis occidendos suos Apostolos. q̄-
uis non negem quosdam & extra Ierusalem fuisse inter-
emptos.

℘Persuasio duodeuigesima.

Videre mihi uideor satis prolixe eoꝗ me subneruas
se opinionē, qui Petrum ac romanū episcopū celebra-
rent, & hoc noīe Romanis Pontificibus nihil nō tribu-
unt, dum in summi Apostolorū principis (ut aiunt ipī)
locū suffecti sint, hancꝗ desultoriā potestatē: ceu p manus sibi tradant, At uero si quis roget, quó hęc falsissi-
ma persuasio in ecclesiam obrepserit, dicā compendio,
Si alia quoꝗ nō minus nociua, quoꝗ recens est adhuc
memoria, negligentia tempoꝗ rata habent, ut nihilomi
nus pro articulis fidei reponant, quáquá & historico-
rum de his taceant libri, & Christi dogmata, uelut ex di-
ametro cum eis decertent, solo tamē ecclesię prętextu,

non minus q̃ʒ quęuis alie, ſine quibus hominibus ſalus
non cõtingit, crędi pręcipiunt. Quibus ſi quiſpiam bo
no ſertuʒ teſtimonio occurrere uoluerit, ęque hereticus
habetur, q̃m qui in legem Chriſti fuerit impius. Quid
ergo de tam remotis ac perturbatiſſimis temporibus,
Romanę Curię palpones, circa Petri Romã, aduētum,
paſſionē, & pontificatũ cõfingere nõ poterant? Putas
ue eccleſiam quã egenus cõſtituit Chriſtus, quã omniũ
facile pauperrimi auxere Apoſtoli, opibus ditari opor-
tere: unum in ea cęteris omnibus dominari, immo eccle
ſiam non aliud q̃m tyrrannidē fieri debere? Ecquis hoc
dixerit? At uero hodie ſolenne id habet, hoc glorioſum
putatur, ut unius arbitrio oĩa fiant, circa unum ſuma &
caput reipublicę Chriſtianę cõſiſtat: unius iuſſu aut in-
iuſſu ſingula gerant : ex unius nutu cuncta pendeant,
Quod ſi quis minus reuerenter hos eccleſię proceres
inceſſerit, ſi corripuerit, ſi annuere noluerit: cõtinuo fre
munt claſſica: undelibet plebs Chriſtiana conclamatur
ad arma capeſſenda, ad omnes Chriſtianos principes
id aiunt pertinere: ne expolietur Chriſtus : neue iacturã
patiatur eccleſia : dum aliquot annui cenſus denarii eis
decreuerint: omnia ſurſum ac deorſũ uerſare non ueren
tur: ac tot Chriſtianorum fędam dilacerationem & ſtu-
pendam perniciem: interim ne pili quidē faciunt. Adeo
tyrannis hęc Romanę Curię iſtac pernicioſa opinione
inualuit: dum primatum mediante Petro ſupra omnes
alias eccleſias ſeſe acceppiſſe iactitat: & Romanus Pontifex uniuerſalis eccleſię catholicę epiſcopus cenſetur,
repugnantibus omnibus oĩm ferme libris : uoce ipſius
met Chriſti: & ritu ac exemplo primitiuę Eccleſię: Cũqʒ

recens adhuc fit memoria : qñ hęc tyrannis exordium
fumpferit:Nonne tñ inueniunt plericp:qui id perpetuo
fuiffe fcribant:id probent:pro eocp ad aras ufcp : quod
folet dici:digladientur ? Quibus non aliter quã folius
Chrifti uerbis paffim uulgus crędit,Preterea.Syluēftrū
a Conftantino Impatore honeftis muneribus donatū,
in fedecp imperatoria repofitū,quis hoc hodie e popu-
lo non credit ? refiftentibus omnibus hiftoriographis,
eorūcp cõmentitias bullarū nugas fortiffimis rationibus,doctiffimifcp uiris reprobantibus , Quãtū tñ ueritatē promoueant,apud hanc futilē plebeculam pfeudo
facerdotū pręftigiis delufam,in propatulo eft oibus,cū
nõ minus reuerenter in has opiniones.q̃ʒ in Chrifti uer
ba iurent ipfi, Nõ difficile eft exinde:diuinare,q̃ntū illis
,pcliue fuerit,quę hodie de Petro feruntur, confingere,
cū eorū temporū nullam certam habeamus hiftoriam,
pręter cõmentitias illas aliquot de Petro & Paulo paffiones,quę adeo fibi nõ conftant, ut oñibus etiã tacen
tibus,ipfe fe fatis cõfutent, prefertim quę Grecorū lin-
guagio cõfcriptę funt,Quod uel folum argumento effe
poffit,eas falfiffimas effe,cū hęc natio ab oñibus paffim fcriptoribus in hiftoria mendacii accufet,̃ Iuuenale
dicente,Quicquid audet Gręcia mendax in hiftoria, Et
alibi non fine ioco mendacē gręculū noiat . Et breuiter
nemo miretur hoc apertiffimū mendaciū fuos patro-
nos habere,cum nõ defint etiã,qui Tufciam patrimoni
um Petri appellent , qua uoce nunq̃m delirius dici aut
cogitari aliquid potuit , Et Plinius haud ignobilis author,Nullum tam impudens mendatium inueniri dicit,
quod tefte careret.

¶Altera libelli particula.
proloquium.

Solet interdum fieri lector mi , ut dum uegeto femi-
ne agrũ cõlpergimus , ni fimul nociua quęꝗ radicitus
extrahamus,urenda filix fubnafcēs, fementis pariat iacturā,Quod dum hic timemus , ne quidā cauilli animũ
tuũ torquētes, noftris iis perfuafionibus minus te crę-
dere permittāt. Alteram libello particulam addidimus,
In qua cũ feptē quibufdam Romanēfiũ cauillis,manus
cõferamus,de eis dignis rationibus(fi fors fauerit)prę
dam ablaturi.proinde interim Romanũ quenpiā,obe-
fis faucibus ac uentre ꝑminulo , imaginem fycophan-
tam,qui fic more fuo nobis inftet.

¶primus cauillus.

Quod in perfuafione dictũ eft quarta.improbius dictũ eft q̃ ut credi debeat . Paulus eĩ dũ binā fuā uerfus
Ierofolymā ꝑegrinatiõe,in ea quę ad Galathas eft epi
ftola cõmemorat,in q̃tuordecim annis poft conuerfio-
nem fuā,utranꝗ fuiffe factā intellexiffe uolut.t,& nõ in
feptē & decē annis,ut tua fert opinio,Idꝗ Nicolai Lyrę teftimonio cõfirmat , Trienniũ eĩ quo ante paulus
Ierofolymā uenerat,in fubfequentibus q̃tuordecim annis, ꝗbus fęcundario illac cũ Tito & Barnaba ꝑrexerat
abforbet,Ita Nicolao uerba pauli exponente,Deinde
poft quatuordecim annos,uidelicet a cõuerfiõe fua, af-
fumpto Tito & Barnaba &c̄. Et fic Petrus quotuorde-
cim illis annis ꝑterlabentibus Romā diuertere poterat.

Refponfio

Bella Lyrę,nifi a tot bonis authorib9, quibus ne ma-
tellā dignus erat ipfe porrigere diffentiret,crederet ex-

F

positio : sed quia nõ ausim dicere:an ullũ habeat qui in
hoc sibi cõsentiat:rationabilius tot celeberrimi sequen-
di sunt interptes:q̃m hic unus:& quidẽ ignobilior: Qui
isthoc spero aucupabat sibi g̃ram:si stulte ab aliis dissen
tiret oĩbus. Et qua cõtra inerme & imbellem : frequen-
tia militiẽ nõ solet desyderari : quẽ unus probate forti-
tudinis uir:uel euiscerare possit:unicũ Ieronimũ tot Ly
ranis anteponendũ: contra hunc ꝑducã : Qui epistolã
ad Galathas exponens: hos septemdecim annos nõ semel repetit. In principio fidei:inquit:in transitu:Paulus
Apostolos uidet:post annos:ut ipse ait:decẽ & septem:
plene cũ eis loquit̃ & se humiliat: & ne forte in uacuum
aut curreret aut cucurrisset:inquirit.Et inferius, Contu
lit euangeliũ cum Apostolis:nõ ꝗ Paulus timuerit:ne p
decẽ & septem annos falsum in gentibus euangelicũ p̃-
dicasset : sed ut ostenderet preccisoribus suis non se in
uacuũ currere aut cucurrisse:sicut putauerunt ignoran-
tes: Hẽc Ieronimi uerba:quibus manifeste q̃ntum Lyra
deliret ostenditur.

❡ Secundus Cauillus.

Quid ni credit̃ Petro apl̃oꝝ primati:qui e Roma epi
stolã quã Catholicã dicũt scribens:se Romẽ fuisse ꝓpri
is exprimit uerbis? Salutat uos inquit Ecclesia : quẽ est
in Babilone collecta: Quãtũ piaculũ dissentire a Ieroni
mo & Lyrano: quoꝝ neuter Romã p hãc Babilonẽ nõ
interptat̃: Ieronimus in libro uirorũ illustriũ:Lyranus
aũt hẽc uerba Petri explanans : Dicit enim uterꝗ Romam figuraliter nomine Babylonis designari.

Responsio.

Duplicē eſſe Babylonē a Coſmographis didicimus
Vnã in Aſſiria: quã Babilo ſapientiſſimus Medi filius
condidit: uel ſi Herodoto credimus Semiramis. Alteram: quę Ægipciaca dicitur:non procul ab Ægipto di-
ſtans:de qua meminerunt: Stephanus:Strabo & Ptho
lomeus: Et recentiorũ Lodouicus Cęlius:in Antiquita
tibus:& Raphael Volateranus in ſua Geographia,& q
dam alii. Strabo tñ plus in Arabia q̃m prouinciis Ægipti hanc eſſe ſitã oſtendit, unde Arabum lingua Chayrum illam uocant, quę uox non aliud eis deſignat q̃m
ſi Babylonē noſtrates dixerint, Et ſic perſuaſiſſimũ eſt
Petrũ ex hac Babylone:uel ſi quem arabũ oblectat dictio, Chayro, epiſtolam ſuã ſcripſiſſe, Qui in Iudea &
contermineis undiq̃ circũ & circa, regionibus Chriſti
nomen diuulgabat, Iudea aũt, ut Ieronimus uult, con-
finem ſibi habet utranq̃ Arabiam: hoc eſt & Arabiam
petream & Arabiam deſertam, Ab oriente enim habet Arabiam Petream,& iuxta hanc ad meridiem, tan-
git Arabiam deſertam, Et Apoſtolus hoc teſtatur quo-
q̃ dicens, Syna mons eſt in Arabia: quę coniuncta
eſt ei quę nunc dicitur Ieruſalem, Quas ob res in eis
collimitaneis Ieroſolymę prouinciis Petrũ prędicaſſe
Chriſtũ, & ex Chayro ad diſperſos e Ponto, Galatia,
Capadocia, Aſya, Bythinia, Chriſti fideles epiſtolam
ſcripſiſſe,hoc iam quis neget? Atq̃ eo modo uerba Petri, Salutat uos eccleſia, quę eſt in Babylone collecta,
intelligenda ſunt. At ſinamus pręterea ſuis figuris lude-
re Lyranum. Quia ſicut, inquit, Babylon fuit ciuitas
maxima, & ydolatrię dedita, ſicut patet in Danyele,
Sic Roma poſtea fuit ex ſimili opere. Sed quid de

F ii

ea Babylóne, cuius mentio apud Danyelé agit, Deus
per Ieremiã loquit dicens, Egredimini de medio Babylonis popule meus, ut faluet unufquifcp animã fuam ab
ira furoris dñi? Sed nunquid etiã eodem tropo cęteras
noui teftamenti fcripturas patiet interptari Lyranus?
qd certe neceſſe eſt. Quid de hac Babylone, hoc eſt Ro
ma:purpurata & uerſuta, ut Ieronymi utar uerbo : me-
retrice, Ioannes in Apocalypſi loquat, ſimul audiat, Ce
cidit, cecidit Babylon magna, & facta eſt habitatio de-
moniorũ & cuſtodia oĩs ſpiritus immundi, & cuſtodia
oĩs uolucris ĩmundę & odibilis, Quia de uino irę forni
cationis eius biberunt oés gentes, & Reges terrę cũ illa fornicati ſunt, Et mercatores terrę, de uirtute delitia-
rũ eius diuites facti ſunt. Mercatores hic noĩat de quibus loquit Petrus, Erunt in uobis magiſtri mendaces,
qui in auaritia fictis uerbis de uobis negotiabunt, Poſt
hęc Ioannes. Et audiui aliã uocem dicentē, Exite de illa
popule meus, & ne participes ſitis delictorũ eius, & de
plagis eoꝶ ne accipiatis, qm̃ peruenerunt peccata eius
uſcp ad cœlũ, & recordatus eſt dñus iniquitatũ eius; Ecce quid eis ſua figurata afferat interprętatio, ut oĩbus
ſcilicet a Romana Curia impune liceat deficere: Ecquid
ergo nos culpamur Boemi? O utinã oés pari modo ab
hac, noſtro ducti exemplo, deficerent Babylone, quo
fortaſſe a ſua impietate reſipiſceret citius, O uere typũ
geſſit Romanę Curię, occidentalis Babylonis, illa non
modo propheticis, ſed etiã gentiliũ literis damnata Babylon, Cui indultũ ac licitũ fuerat, ut plutarchi repetã
uerba, pſallere ſcorta alere: caupone indulgere, ſinuoſis
tunicis amiciri, pudicitiã proſtituere; An nõ ęquat mo-

do,imo etiã superat Roma ueriſſima Babylon,iſta oĩaʔ
Nonne & corpis & rerum ſacraꝛ caſtitatē impudenti9
pſtituit,q̃m uel illic munditiem corpis impudentiſſimę
fœminęʔ Apud illas em̃ quę ex fedo coitu prouenerat,
Veneri ſacra fuit ſtipes, hic qd̃ rerũ ſacratiſſimaꝛ affert
pſtitutio:Chriſto acceptũ ferri dicitʔ:Sed ne hoc loci in
Babylonē Romanenſem pluribus inueham,aliq̃ntiſper
me cohibebo,nam hęc alias pertinent.

    ❡Cauillus Tercius.

    Si nihil aliud,hoc profecto ſolũ,magno eſſet argu⸗
mento,Petrũ Romę añ priorē etiã Pauli illac aduentũ
fuiſſe,q̷ dũ e Ieroſolymis, ut Lucas in Actis apoſtolo⸗
rũ tradit,militibus comitatus, Romã uinctus duceret,
occurrerunt ei fratres ad Appii forũ,Quibus uiſis,gra⸗
tias deo egit ille , Nam quo monitore in Chriſtũ credi⸗
diſſent,ſi tunc Petrus Romę abfuerit.

    Reſponſio.

    Chriſtianos protinus poſt Chriſti paſſionē,& non
dumtaxat Paulo illac ueniente Romę fuiſſe, Oroſius,
Tertulianus, Platina, immo Chriſtianorũ hoſtis Sueto
nius Tranquillus teſtant.Oroſius em̃ libro ſeptimo ad
hunc modũ ſcribit,Poſtq̃m paſſus eſt dominus Iheſus.
Chriſtus , atꝗ a mortuis reſurrexit , & diſcipulos ſuos
ad p̃dicandũ miſit . Pilatus pręſes Paleſtinę prouincię
ad Tyberiũ imperatorē, atꝗ ad Senatũ retulit, de paſ⸗
ſione & reſurrectione Chriſti: cõſequentibuſꝗ uirtuti⸗
bus:quę uel p ipſum factę fuerant:uel per diſcipulos ei9
in noĩe eius fiebant,Et de eo q̷ certatim creſcente pluri
morũ fide: deus crederet: Tyberius ergo : cũ ſuffragio
magni fauoris retulit ad Senatũ: ut Chriſtus deus habe

                        F iii

retur:Senatus indignatione motus.q̃ non ſibi prius ſe∕
cundũ morem delatũ eſt, ut de ſuſcipiendo cultu prius
ipſe decerneret,cõſecrationẽ Chriſti recuſauit,edicto q̃
cõſtituit,exterminandos eſſe ex urbe Chriſtianos.pre∕
cipue cũ & Seianus prefectus Tiberii ſuſcipiendę reli∕
gioni obſtinatiſſime contradiceret : Tiberius tñ edicto
accuſatoribus Chriſtianorũ morte cominatus eſt, De
quo Tertulianus in Apologetico aduerſus getiles,mo
deſtius aliquanto loquit̃, Tyberius inquit, cuius tem∕
pore nomen Chriſtianũ in ſeculũ introiuit, aut nuncia∕
tũ ſibi ex Syria paleſtinaq̃,illic ueritate illius diuinita∕
tis reuelarat,detulit ad ſenatũ, cũ prerogatiua ſuffragii
ſui,ſenatus.quia non ipſe probauerat.reſpuit. Ceſar in
ſententia manſit, comminatus periculũ accuſatoribus
Chriſtianorũ, Omitto dicere: quid ſcribant Suetonius
& platina.hic in Chriſti,ille uero in Tyberii uita, Qui∕
bus ſatis inſinuat̃, tutam fuiſſe a Tyberii temporibus
ad Neronis uſq̃ imperium, & ſub eius imperio aduſq̃
pauli aduentũ,Chriſtianam Romę religionem, Tertu∕
liano adſtipulãte his uerbis, Conſulite cõmentarios ue
ſtros: illic reperietis primũ Nerone in hanc ſectam Cę∕
ſariano gladio ferociſſe.Quare nullus mirari debeat:tot
fratres Romę fuiſſe,qui Paulo ueniẽti occurrerint:Qm̃
gliſcente etiam illic pietate: ordinatione ſpirituſſancti:
nec preſbiteri illis defuerant:uti Narciſſus:Andronic9:
Iulias:& ceteri:quatenus nihil opus habuerint petri p̃∕
ſentiam deſyderaſſe:Quos deinde Paulus quoq̃ ipſe tũ
per epiſtolam faciendorũ admonuerat: tũ preſentialiter
inuiſerat: ut iam abunde in priori noſtri libelli particula
ſingula hęc indicauimus.

ℂ Cauillus Quartus.

Quibus ea res magis cōperta fieri debuit: atqʒ difci‑
pulis Apoftolicis : & qui proxime uiguerunt poft Apo
ftolos:At illi hoc nobis indubitato prodidere: Petrum
& Paulū Romę paffos fuiffe : Quorū unius: uidelicet:
Lini: Timotheū falutauerat nomine:Apoftolus dicens:
Salutāt te Eubolus & Prudēs & Linus : Alterius aūt in
actis apoftolicis celebrať memoria: inquiente Luca:
Quidā uero uiri adherentes Paulo : crędiderūt:in qui‑
bus & Dyonifius Areopagita: & mulier nomine Dema
ris:& alii cū eis:Pręterea Egefippus:qui Aniceti decimi
poft Petrū Romani pontificis tpe Romam aduenerat:
in laudibus fidei Chriftianę uerfatus: eiufce paffionis
Petri & Pauli meminit.

Refponfio.

Si mihi ñl aliud effet : quatenus probem paffiones
illas Petri & Pauli:ab eorum difcipulis non fuiffe cō‑
fcriptas : diuerfitatem illam & difcrepantiam quę illic
reperitur : firmiffimę probationis loco poncrem : Sed
quia funt mihi pleraqʒ multa ad perditam hāc fufpicio‑
nem tollendam:illius ne meminero quidem:Perfuafum
eft doctis omnibus:nō modo difcipulis apoftolicis:fed
& ipfis apoftolis adhuc fuperuiuentibus hanc iniuriam
fępius factam fuiffe:ut multa corū fub nomine:Chriftia
nę profeffioni repugnantia:in publicū ederent:Nomi
ne enim Pauli:ut origenes teftis eft:ad Teffaloniceos:
a pfeudo apoftolis quo facilius decipent:porrecta fuit
epľa : Quos apoftolus re tandem compta : propria ad
eofdem data epiftola admonet his prope uerbis : Non
cito moneamini inquit a ueftro fenfu : neqʒ terreamini:

neqʒ per ſpiritũ neqʒ per ſermonẽ:neqʒ per epiſtolã tan⁄
q̃m per nos miſſam:Et Ieronimus uiſione Þauli & Te⁄
clę ac baptiſati Leonis fabulã:ſub noíe Pauli:a quodam
Aſię p̃ſbitero:fuiſſe editã ſcribit:Quod ipſemet poſtea,
Tertuliano teſte:ſe fœciſſe Þauli amore confeſſus eſt.
Clemẽtis itẽ:cuius apͭus ad Colloſſenſes ſcribens men
tionẽ facit:multis erroribus hęretici reſperſerũt libros:
Quorũ quidã Eunomii hereſim ſapiunt:Nam diſputat
quodã in libro filiũ dei ex nullis extantibus creatũ . Itẽ
demones nõ uolũtatis malitiã fęciſſe , ſed creaturã eos
eſſe diuerſę q̃litatis ab aliis productam : Et longe plu⁄
res alii inibi reperiunͭ errores : Rurſum Dioniſii cuiuſ⁄
dam Alexandrini epiſcopi: uſqʒ adeo deprauati ſunt li⁄
bri: ut eius authoritate Arrianorũ hereſis : filiũ dei non
eiuſdẽ ſubſtantięeſſe cũ patre:auſa ſit cõfirmare.Orige⁄
nis nõdum mortui:tot iã ſubditiciis erroribus ſcatebãt
libri:ut ſępiuſcule hanc iniuriã deploraſſe legaͭ:Et Ruf
finus in Apologia pro Origene:De hęreticoꝛ inquit te
meritate: ut crędi iſtud ſcęlus facile poſſit:illa res maxi⁄
mũ credulitatis pręſtat exemplũ:q̨ abſtinere impias ma
nus:etiã a ſacroſanctis quidẽ euangelii uocibus nõ po⁄
tuerunt : Apoſtolorũ uero uel actus:uel epͭas : qualiter
polluerint:qualiter corroſerint:qualiter in oñibus ma⁄
cularint:uel addendo impia : uel auferẽdo quę pia ſunt:
ſi quís uult plenius ſcire: ex his libris Tertuliani : quos
aduerſus Marcionẽ ſcripſit: pleniſſime recognoſcet: Et
alibi inquit:Peruerſi homines aſſertione dogmatũ ſuo⁄
rũ:ſub uirorũ ſanctoꝛ noíe:tanq̃m facilius credenda in
ſeruerunt ea:quę ipſi nec ſenſiſſe:nec ſcripſiſſe crędendi
ſunt:Et ideo Origenes homilia uigeſimaſexta ſup Mat

theo dicit: Oportet caute cōsiderare:ut nec oīa secreta
q̄ ferunt in noīe sanctorū suscipiamus:Quantū ad Dyo
nisiū Areopagitā attinet : nulla est cūctatio:qn passio il
la Petri & Pauli ei adscripta non sit subdititia:Probāt
eī & Lauren.Val. & Erasmus Rother,in annotationi-
bus:libros qui sub noīe eius circumferunt:falso ei attri
butos:Vt sunt de Cęlesti Ierarchia:deTheologica Ierar
chia:de diuinis nominibus:& cęteri:Nondū eī Ecclesia: cuius tempe uiguerat ille:tantā nouerat Ceremoni-
arū turbā:quanta in eis libris tradit. De cętero aūt Petri & Pauli sub nomine Lyni euulgatę passiones: tantū
habent permixtę sibi falsitatis:ut in multis non modo
Christo & Paulinis literis: sed & Petri ipsius cōtradicāt
sermonibus: Quod equidem nisi me prolixitas arceret:
promptū esset ostendere : Persuadeo tñ mihi gręculum
quempiā:ut Iuuenalis utar uerbo:mendacē:& lenonem
potius aliquē:q̄m Lynum has passiones cōmentū fuis-
se:Qui Paulinam ad Timotheū epistolam olfęcerit magis aliquando q̄z intellexerit: Nam cū mendacem me-
moré esse oporteat:ille obliuione sua:ingenue se mentitum ostendit: Arbitror eū legisse aliqñ Paulū his uerbis
Timotheū ad sese allectantē: Festina ad me uenire cito:
Demas enim me reliquit diligens hoc sęculum : & abiit
Tessalonicam:Crescens in Galatiā:Titus in Dalmaciā:
Lucas est mecū solus : Qui quidem impostor:nō habés
perspectū: unde Apostolus epistolam ad Timotheū mi
serit : & ubi se locorū expectaturū dixerit : & ubi Titus
ac Crescens recedentes Apostolum relinquerint:passio
nem Pauli ad hunc modū exorditur: Cū uenisset Romam Lucas a Galatia;& Titus a Dalmacia;& expecta-

G

uerunt Paulũ in urbe, Quos cũ adueniens Paulus uidiſ
ſet,letatus eſt ualde , & conduxit ſibi extra urbẽ horreũ
publicũ,hẹc uerba illius:In quibus apoſtoli primũ ob
litus eſt dicentis.Crẹſcens abiit in Galatiã:Lucas mecũ
ſolus eſt: Nã prẹpoſtere Lucam dicit rediiſſe e Galatia:
quo nunq; abierat ipſe , ſed indiuiduus Apoſtoli fue
rat miniſter, Et Apoſtolus Creſcẽtem dixit petiiſſe Ga
latiam, Proinde credibilius fuiſſet ſi eundem redeuntẽ
Galatiã hic leno poſuiſſet,Poſt hẹc ſubinfert: Expecta
uerunt Paulum in urbe , quaſi Paulus e carcere quopiã
recedere potuerit , & nõ aduentũ Timothei ac Marci,
quos optauerat ante hiemẽ ad ſe uenire expectauerit,
Quõ ergo uenerat Romã,unde nõ receſſerat? Aut quõ
Lucas & Titus expectaſſent aduẽturũ Apſm quẽ in car
cere detineri ſciuerant? nimirũ cum Galatiam & Dalma
tiã proficiſcentes illic eum reliquerint,Vlterius ſcribit,
Et conduxit ſibi horreũ publicũ,ubi cũ iis & aliis fratri
b9 de uerbo uitẹ tractaret:cẹpitq; interea corrigere mul
titudinẽ maximã: & adiiciebant per eũ fidei multẹ ani
mẹ,operante dei gratia,ita ut per totam urbẽ ſonus prẹ
dicationis & ſanctitatis eius fieret:& exiret fama p uni
uerſam regionẽ de illo, hẹc ipſe . Sed Paulus diuerſum
quiddam in epiſtolạ ſua dicit,det miſericordiã dñs One
ſiphori domui, quia ſẹpe me refrigerauit , & cathenam
meã non erubuit,ſed cũ Romã ueniſſet: ſollicite me q ſi
uit & inuenit,Cõfer uerba Pauli ac Lenonis huius, hic
inquit,conduxit ſibi horreũ publicũ. Ille Oneſiphorus
cathenam meã non erubuit:niſi forte cũ cathena ex ali
quo carcere Romã Paulus profugerit : qua ſe liberare
nõ poterat. Hic dicit q fama nõ modo per urbẽ,ſed &

per oēm regionē undiqȝ de eo ferebaꞇ,& concurſus ho
minū ad eū fiebat: Ille uero Oneſiphoꝝ dicit ſollicite ſe
quęſiuiſſe:ac uix tandē inter cathenas inueniſſe,mirū qȝ
fama quę de Paulo uolitabat, illac eū non perduxerit,
Atqȝ in hunc mundū totam illā paſſione & alteram Pe
tri poſſem ſuppilare, ſed ꝓprii uoluminis hoc iam eſſet
negotiū.Hęc eȝ pauca ideo refello : ut maximū eorum
oſtendā mendaciū,qui paſſiones has cōmentitias,& in
certo authore natas,in Linū tranſſundunt. Non eȝ tā
rudis fuerat Linus, qui tunc Paulo adherebat, cū epi╯
ſtolā adTimotheū ſcripſerat,ut ſtatim dictorum obliui
ſceret,imo cōfunderet uerba Paulina,& diuerſa ſcripſe
rit ab eo,Qd idem ſentirē & de Egeſippo. Qualiter eȝ
homo ille poſt multa tpa Romā ueniens, hiſtorię ſerua
re potuiſſet uetitatē?Qui neqȝ rei geſtę aderat ipſe:neqȝ
Roma ille tempeſtate de eorū paſſionibus quicꝗm ſibi
conſcia erat,Si quidē multis poſt Egeſippū tempori╯
bus,fabulam hanc fuiſſe certum eſt.

℄Cauillus Quintus.

At eccleſia Romana,uerba ex paſſione Lini, qué tu
lenonem potius aliqué ꝗm Linumfuiſſe blaſphemas,
deprompta annuatim decantat,id neutiquam factura,
ſi eam non legittime deſcriptā ſcierit,Inter cętera in paſ
ſione Petri & hęc ponuntur uerba, Vt aūt portā ciuita
tis uoluit egredi Petrus, uidit ſibi Chriſtū occurrere, &
adorans eū ait, Dñe quo uadis ? reſpondit ei Chriſtus,
Romā uenio iterū crucifigi,Et ait ad eū Petrus.Dñe ite
rū crucifigeris, Et dixit ad eū dñus, Etiā,iterū crucifi╯
gar.Petrus aūt dixit;domine reuertar & ſequar te:Et his
dictis;dominus aſcendit in cęlū;Petrus aūt proſequtus

est eū multo intuitu: atqȝ dulcissimis lachrimis: Et quo
id magis factū crędatur: hactenus extat ibi loci ex edifi
catum sacellū;ubi hęc habita sunt uerba.

    Responsio.

Bene habet:ꝗ uniuersalis Ecclesia sancta,prophanū
hoc mendaciū;contra Christū;contra Paulū;immo cō/
tra ipsummet Petrū ac fidem catholicā non decantat:
Orientales enim ecclesię : quod sat scio : & multi etiam
in occidente fideliū;hanc uocem non recipiunt;Roma/
nam uero ecclesiam: hęc mendatia approbare;profite/
ri: decantare quid prohibet ? quę mendaciis est alioqui
refertissima potuit ne discipulus Apostolicus hęc por/
tenta horrendissima toto cętui fideliū scribere : ut iam
Christus Petro occursurus tunc e cęlis descenderit : Et
tanꝗm Petrus Christi uerbis admonit9 rursum Romā
sese recępit fratribus ea ꝗ euenerant nunciaturus;Quid
Petrus enim hac fabula apud eos promouisset non in/
telligo: ꝗm ut pro seductore & mendacę habet ab om/
nibus.Qui quondā ad Iudeos de Christo loquutus: ut
Actuū habętur tertio;dixerat; Oportet quidē cęlū Ihe/
sum Christū suscipere:usqȝ in tempora restitutiōis om/
nium quę loqutus est deus per os'sanctorū suorū a se/
culo prophetarū . Quō tunc ergo cęlū;terris Christum
reddiderat ante consumationē omniū,quę circa diē iu/
dicii primū est futura, dicentibus etiam Angelis ad eos
qui intuebant Christū in nube pergętę ad cęlū,Hic Ihe
sus qui assumptus est a uobis in cęlū sic ueniet: quéad/
modū uidistis eū euntem in cęlū . Quod explanat Mat/
theus de aduentu eiusdē ad iuditiū,Videbunt,inquit,fi
liū;hominis ueientē in nubibus cęli, cū uirtute multa

& maieſtate,Queadmodũ eñ in nube aſcenderat:ſic in
nube ad iudicandũ reueniet, Ecce q̃m incõueniat crede
re,ut unq̃m Chriſtus in ea perſona, qua a nube corre-
ptus in cęlũ deuolauit,in terras deſcenderit, Sed reuera
ad diem iudicii:primũ a fidelibus expeċtatur rediturus:
Vt ad eam ſententiã pſalmiſta quoq̃ alludit, Dixit do
minus dño meo:ſede a dextris meis:donec ponã inimi-
cos tuos:ſcabellũ pedum tuoɤ,Vnde nunq̃m adhuc p-
ſonaliter deſcendiſſe credit́ : ut alicui ſanċtoɤ in terris
apparuerit,Emuero in cęlis ſemper apparere dignatus
eſt:& abinde ad eos & loqui, Stephanus eñ intendens
in cęlum uidit gloriã dei:& Iheſum ſtantē & dextris uirtutis dei:Et Þaulũ appropinq̃ntē Damaſco ſubito cir-
cumfulſit lux de cęlo, Qui cadens in terrã audiuit uocē
dicentē ſibi: Saule Saule quid me perſequeris: Qui tre-
mens ac ſtupēs dixit,Quis es domine?Et ille: Ego ſum
Iheſus Nazarenus quē tu perſequeris: Quod ille de ſua
conuerſione mirifica:tũ illic cum Iudeos alloquit́ Aċtu
um xxii.tum ubi apud Agrippã & Feſtum þſidem Aċtu
um xxvi • data ei ſeſe defendendi copia propriis uerbis
atteſtatur, Cum irē inquit Damaſcũ:cum poteſtate & p
miſſu principũ ſacerdotũ,die media in, uia, uidi, rex de
cęlo ſupra ſplendorē ſolis circũfulſiſſe me lumen:Et Þe
tro olim:an gentibus þdicandum ſit euangeliũ halluci-
nanti:nõ quidē perſonaliter Chriſtus apparuit:ſed in ex
taſim raptum,ne quid cõmune diceret ac imundũ,edo-
cuit,Et nuſquã prorſus poſt aſenſionē ſuã alicui ſanċto
rum apparuiſſe?in eo habitu,quo poſt reſurreċtionē ſu
am per dies quadraginta conuerſatus eſt cũ diſcipulis,
conueſcebat́ & loquębatur eis de regno dei Chriſtum

                                   H

in facra fcriptura legimus:imo nęc aliqñ appariturū pri
us q̄m dies iudicii uenerit credim9, fide catholica Chri
ftiana inftructi,Quantū flagitiū ergo, tanta contra legē
dei mēdatiog̃ fimulachra difcipulo apoftolico attribue
re:quib9 bonū ille uirtutis fpecimen de fcfe prębuerat:
eorūcʒ doctrinā pulchre percalluit.Poffem hic & de fa﹣
cello quod in huius mendacii robur extructū eft,nō ni﹣
hil dicere:& probare copiofe:nullū facellū nec aliq̄m ba
fylicam ad aliquot annog̃ centurias Romę & locis ei
adiacentibus exedificatā fuiffe,fed Chriftianos in late﹣
bris & fpeluncis fubterraneis conuenire folitos: uel ad
mortem domini anunciandam uel hymnis & orationi﹣
bus : Chrifti fuffragium & diuinam gratiam fibi deme﹣
rendam.

       ❰ Sextus cauillus.

Marcus euangelifta Petri difcipulus:a pręceptore ad
monitus Romę fcripfit Euangeliū.Quod Petrus dū au
diuit & approbauit,ecclefię ad legendū authoritate fua
edidit,Vt & Clemens libro informationū fcripfit,& Ie﹣
ronimus de uiris illuftribus meminit.De quo Petrus in
fua epiftola loquitur,Salutat uos Marcus filius meus,
Qui poft confcriptū tandē euangeliū Ægiptum perre﹣
xit.& primus Alexandrię Chriftum annūcians , illis ec﹣
clefiam conftituit, exanclatifcʒ laboribus , Neroniani
imperii anno octauo uita functus eft, De cuius conuer
fatione apud Alexandriam,Philo quocʒ Iudęus librum
concinnauit.

       Refponfio.
Qui Clementi adfcribunt́ libri,minus eft tutū eis cre

dere. qm̃ cotũ quidam ſuppoſititii ſunt ac falſo Clemen
ti adſcripti. quidã uero magna ex parte deprauati ac er
roribus infecti. ut iam antea probauimus, Itacჳ ſciendũ
cჳ in noui teſtamẽti libris, duos Marci cognomine fuiſ
ſe inſignitos inuenimus, quorũ prior dicebat Ioannes
Marcus. Et de hoc legit actuũ xiii . Qd̃ Paulo cũ Bar
naba Anthiochiẹ inter Prophetas,& Chriſti nomis do
ctores exeunte, poſteacჳm uiſum eſt ſpirituſancto, ut ad
opus miniſterii ſegregarent ſeniores impoſitis ſup eos
manibus in miniſteriũ eos confirmarunt. Qui ᵖfecti in
Seleutiam, uenerunt tandẽ in Cyprũ inſulã, & Salami
nam eiuſdem inſulẹ urbem Chriſtum per Sinagogas an
nunciantes . Quibus erat adiunctus & hic Ioannes qui
cognominabat Marcus, non reprobus quidem mini
ſterio, Poſtãm aũt peruenerunt Paphũ, urbem in Cy
pro inſula ſitam, & inde nauigare uellent Pamphiliam,
iamdictus Ioannes Marcus rennuit, ᵖficiſci cũ eis, ſed e
conuerſo rediit Ieroſolymam,& poſt hac Antiochiam.
Quo aſcendẽtibus poſt aliqua tempum interualla Pau
lo & Barnaba, & aliãndiu Chriſtũ illis docentibus di
xit ad Barnabã Paulus. Reuertentes uiſitemus fratres p
uniuerſas ciuitates in qbus ᵖdicauimus uerbũ dñi:quõ
ſe habeant Act.xv. Barnabas uero ſecũ uolebat aſſume
re & Ioannẽ cognomento Marcũ, qui pridẽ iam ab eis
deſciuerat, Sed Paulus hunc rogatum habuit,ne id fa
ceret: eo cჳ non coũeniat eum deinceps in munus euan
gelicum reaſſumi : qui antea ab eis defecerat. Et per
gentes Pamphiliam relinquens, diſceſſit Ieroſolymam:
Et hinc orta eſt inter eos diſſenſio, ita ut alterutrũ ſe
pararentur. Nam Barnabas aſſumpto Marco perrexit

Cyprū, & Paulus electo Syla recępit se Syriā & Cylici
am, Qui quidē Marcus, Barnaba ob nomen Christi in
Cypro impiiffime trucidato:ꝗ Ægiptū tandē iter occu
pauerit:nemo it inficias:Cū Philomagni nominis scri∕
ptor : in Alexandria urbe Ægipti prope ostiū Nyli sita,
Christi nomē ipsum annunciasse prodat : Et Petrus ex
Chayro:hoc est Babylone: quā Stephanus & Ptolome
us in Ægipto sitam esse tradunt epistolā scribens ipsius
meminit:Salutat uos inquiēs Marcus filius meus, Cre∕
dibile est enim hunc Marcū Petro familiarem fuisse, cū
Alexandria nō procul a Chayro distet: Et de hoc Mar∕
co multa figmenta reperiunt: Primo ꝗ dū credideritᐧin
Christum amputasset sibi pollicē: ut sacerdotio repro∕
bus efficeret : Deinde ꝗ Romę scripserit euangeliū ad
uota Petri:quod protinus falsum est:Nuspiam em hūc
Marcū.perinde ut nec Petrū in libris Canonicis Romę
aliqñ fuisse inuenimus. Et scriptorū uarietas mendaciū
hoc declarat . Ieronimus em Clemētis authoritate scri∕
bit Marcū rogatū a fribus Christi euangeliū scripsisse,
Alii uero e quoꝝ numero & Platina nō ignobilis est hi∕
storicus,tradunt,ꝗ Petrus Romanoꝝ precibus mot9:
Marco qui ad hāc rē uidebat ydoneus,euangelii cōscri
bendi negotium iniunxerit: Quē omnes uelut ex cōpo
sito,octauo anno Neronis obiisse.Alexandrięꝗ sepul∕
tum fuisse scribunt:Veꝝ enimuero hos decepit eoꝝ in∕
discretio.Nō em aliū Marcum inter Apostoleꝝ discipu
los fuisse crediderant, & ideo quicquid de utroꝗ legit:
ad unum falso retulerunt,Alter nāꝗ fuerat Marcus, no
mine Aristarch9 qui coopator & discipulus fuerat Pau
li,de quo ipse in priori captiuitate sua,qua biennio Ro

mę a Nerone detenebať, ad Philemoné fcribens men- tionem facit, Salutāt te Marcus Ariftarchus Demas & Lucas adiutores mei. Deniqʒ ubi iam fecundario in ma nus deuenit Neroni, & ingrauefcente ętate ac laborib9 cófectus, diem obitus accelerare uidens, Timotheoqʒ e carcere fcribens, eiufdé Marci iteɪ ũ meminit: Feftina ad me uenire cito, Lucas eɪñ mecum folus eft, Marcũ itaqʒ affume & adduc tecũ, eft eɪñ mihi utilis in minifterio. Pe nulā quá reliqui Troade Apud Carpũ, ueniés affer te- cũ, & libros. maxime auté & membranas, Quod Iaco- bus ille Stapulenfis, nó oɪm deterrimus Apɭicus inter- pres. pulcherrime exponit inquiens: Lucā fecũ habebat Apɭus. Marcũ aũt mandat obnixe, & membranas quę apud Carpũ erant deferri. Sed ad quid nā? ɪifi ut Lucę & Marco, electis a fpiritufancto diuinis fcribis, eas re- linquerent ad reponendũ fanctũ euangeliũ, Quid apti- us his uerbis dici poterat q̃ɪn quod Marcus Ariftarch9 & nó Ioannes Marcus facrũ euangeliũ cófcripferit: qui facile Neronis imperii annos fuperauit, Cũ apɭus circi- ter tredecimũ eiufdem imperii annũ, epiftolā hanc fcri- bés, eũ fibi a Timotheo adduci poftulat, Necʒ idem, ne qué id moreť, Ariftarchus & Ioannes apud Hebreos fo nat, Ariftarchus eɪñ perinde hebreis fignificat: ac fi di- cas fufcitans coronam, Ioannes uero gratia dñi, Ex his euidentiffime patet, fabulā effe quod de Petro & Mar- co quidam fcriptitant.

⁋ Cauillus Septimus.

Philo Iudęus, uir literarũ pollétiffimus. fub C. Caligu la a gente fua Romā miffarius factus dũ nonnihil picli- tareť fecunda uice fub Claudii imperio illac remiffus,

H iii

cū Petro Apoſtolo de nōnullis contulit rebus: & tam
arctiſſimas ſecū iniit amicicias,ut tandē,quotięs modo
licuit in libris ſuis Chriſtianos honeſtis traduxerit lau⸗
dibus:Et in Ioannis Marci preconiis: pleno libro uerſa
ret ut Ieronimus in libro de uiris illuſtribus ͵pdidit.

Reſponſio.

Has nenias uel ſolus riſus potis ſit explodere: Qui
nam Philo Iudeus ſub Claudii imperio: Petrū Romę
conuenire poterat: quē nunq̃m etiā Romę fuiſſe tot iā
rationibus pſuaſimus: Siquidē Paulus in fine imperii
Claudii Romanos literis ſuis fidei ac uirtutū admonēs:
& oés preſbiteros ſeniores & muneris euangelici coad
iutores:tñ etiā quoſdā plebeos ſalutans,ſolius Petri ne
tantillū quidē meminit:Tandem quarto Neroniani im⸗
perii anno Romā perductus, Petrū illic non inuenit, &
biennio ibi exiſtens nullā eccleſiam eius ſalutat nomie,
Lucas ad quartū uſq⁊ Neronis annū hiſtoriam Apoſto
licā Romę ſcribens,Petri nullam mentionē facit, Pau⸗
lus decem pręter labentibus annis, ſęcundario Romę
captiuatus nullū Petri pręſidiū ſenſit , ſed ab omnibus
fere deſtitutus , rem euāgelicam cū uno Luca tractauit,
ſin uero ea ratione Philo Chriſtianos laudaſſe putat,
q̄ cū Petro inierit amicitiā, ego in Iudęa potius id con
tigiſſe crędiderim , ubi Petrus Chriſtū p̄dicando ętatē
ſuā cōſumpſit, & mortem inibi paſſus eſt, Aut nūquid
ſolus Iudeorū Philo Chriſti nomē dignis Encomiis ex⸗
tulerit?Ioſephus eñ,qui nō cōmemorat alicubi Petrū
uel uidiſſe. uel amicitias ſecū pactū fuiſſe,tñ adeo hone
ſtam Chriſti mentionem in ſuis de antiquitatibus fę⸗
cit libris,ut interim mirum uideatur,c tam peruicaciſſi⸗

ma gente, aliquē reperiri potuiſſe, qui tanto laudis prę
conio Chriſtū extulerit, ſed quid mirū Ioſepū talia de
Chriſto dixiſſe, cū & demonū legiones Chriſtū p̄dicare
cogerentur ꞉ Cuius & nos ueritatē & multa diſcrimina
perductā nunc defendimus, ſceleraꝗ & errores occidē
talis Babylonis patefacimus, pręmia immarceſcibilis
coronę ipſius benignitate dubio ꝓcul adepturi.

Finit libellus bifariam diuiſus, viii. kalendas
Decembres, Anno Virginei partus.
M. D. XX.

BIBLIOGRAPHY

1. ABBREVIATIONS

Act. Ap. Apocr.   *Acta Apostolorum Apocrypha* (ed. R. A. Lipsius and M. Bonnet, Leipzig, 1891). Photomechanical reprint, Hildesheim and New York, 1972.

Allen   P. S. Allen: *Opus Epistolorum Desiderii Erasmi* (Oxford, 1906–1947)

ARG   *Archiv für Reformationsgeschichte* (ed. W. Friedensburg, Leipzig).

CCath.   *Corpus Catholicorum* (ed. W. Neuss, Münster).

ComViat   *Communio Viatorum. A Theological Quarterly* (Ecumenical Institute of the Comenius Faculty, Prague).

CR   *Corpus Reformatorum* (ed. G. C. Bretschneider, Brunswick).

Knihopis   *Knihopis českých a slovenských tisku od doby nejstarší až do konce XVIII století* (ed. Z. V. Tobolka and F. Horák, Prague, 1925–1967) (National Bibliography of Books printed in Czech and Slovak up to 1800).

MPL   J. P. Migne: *Patrologiae cursus completus, series latina.*

MPG   J. P. Migne: *Patrologiae cursus completus, series graeca.*

NAKG   *Nederlands Archief voor Kerkgeschiedenis (Nieuwe serie)* (Leiden).

NThT   *Nederlands Theologisch Tijdschrift* (The Hague).

TG   *Tijdschrift voor Geschiedenis* (Groningen).

WA   *Weimarer Ausgabe (D. Martin Luthers Werke. Kritische Gesamtausgabe).*

ZKG   *Zeitschrift für Kirchengeschichte* (Stuttgart, Berlin, Cologne and Mainz).

ZThK   *Zeitschrift für Theologie und Kirche* (Tübingen).

2. SOURCES

Editions of texts and works in which texts are integrally included. The editions of the *Petrum Roman non venisse* are separately listed and discussed in the Appendix.

Balduinus, F.: *Optati Afri, Milevitani episcopi, libri sex de schismate Donatistarum adversus Parmenianum. Cum praefatione F. Balduini* (Paris, 1563).

Basnage, Jacques: *Histoire de l'Église depuis Jésus-Christ jusqu'à présent* (Rotterdam, 1699).

Basnage, Samuel: *Annales politico-ecclesiastici, annorum 645 a Caesare Augusto ad Phocam usque* (Rotterdam, 1706).

Bellarmine, Robert: *Disputationes de controversiis christianae fidei adversus huius temporis haereticos (editio tertia,* Ingolstadt, 1590).

Brieger, T.: *Quellen und Forschungen zur Geschichte der Reformation,* I: *Aleander und Luther* (Gotha, 1884).

Buddensieg, Rudolf: *John Wiclif's Polemical Works in Latin,* II (including *De Christo et suo Adversario Antichristo*) (London, 1883).

Calvin, John: *Institutio religionis christianae (CR* XXXI/XXXII).

——: *Commentarius in epistolas catholicas (Epistola Petri Apostoli prior) (CR* LXXXIII).

Chamierus, Daniel: *Panstratiae Catholicae, tomus secundus* (Geneva, 1626).

Cochlaeus, John: *Responsio Johannis Cochlei in Epistolam cuiusdam Lutherani* (Stuttgart, 1524).

——: *De Petro et Roma adversus Velenum Lutheranum libri quatuor, Johannis Cochlaei, artium et sacrae Theologiae professoris egregii atque ecclesiae divae virginis Frankfordien Decani* (Cologne, 1525).

——: *Von der Donation des Keysers Constantini, und von Bepstlichem gewalt. Grundtlicher bericht aus alten bewerten Lerern und Historien. Auch etwas vom Laurentio Valla, vom Cypriano, vom Ireneo, Hieronym, etc.*, (Cologne, 1537).

——: *Assertio pro Hieronymo Emsero, contra Lutherum De XXV annis S. Petri in Ecclesia Romana* (Ingolstadt, 1545).

Cortese, Gregorio: *Gregorii Cortesii Mutinensis s.r. ecclesiae presb. Cardinalis. Epistolarum familiarium liber.* (Venice. 1573). This includes: *Tractatus, Adversus negantem Petrum Apost. Romae fuisse.*

Dietenberger, Johannes: *Ob Sant Peter zu Rom sey gewesen. Antword Doctor Jo. Cochlei. Auff Martin Luth. disputation, ob Sant Peter zu Rom sey gewesen. Durch Doct. Johann. Dieten. vertütscht* (Strasbourg, 1524).

Faber, Johannes: *Malleus in haeresim lutheranam* (ed. A. Naegele) *CCath.* 23/24.

Ferguson, W. K.: *Opuscula Erasmi* (A Supplement to the *Opera Omnia*) (The Hague, 1933).

Fisher, John: *Convulsio calumniarum Ulrichi Veleni Minhoniensis, quibus Petrum nunquam Romae fuisse cavillatur, per Joannem Rossensem Episcopum, academiae cantabrigiensis cancellarium. Petrus fuit Romae* (Antwerp, 1522) Included in: *Joannis Fisherii Opera Omnia* (Farnborough, 1967; a photomechanical reprint from the edition of "Wirceburgi", 1597).

Flacius Illyricus, M.: *Historia certaminum inter Romanos Episcopos et sextam Carthaginensem synodum, Africanasque Ecclesias, de primatu seu potestate Pape, bona fide ex authenticis monumentis collecta* (Basle, 1554).

——: *Contra Commentitium primatum papae* (Basle, 1554; Regensburg, 1567).

——: *Verissima et ultissima legenda aut Historia de S. Petri Episcopatu vel Papatu* (Regensburg, 1567).

——: *Ecclesiastica historia, integram ecclesiae Christi ideam, quantum ad locum* (Cent. I) (Basle, 1559).

Franck, Sebastian: *Chronica, tytboeck en gheschietbibel* (1595) (no place of publication —but The Hague).

Friedensburg, W.: *Beiträge zum Briefwechsel der katholischen Gelehrten Deutschlands im Reformationszeitalter*; ZKG XVIII (1897).

Goedeke, Karl: *Pamphilus Gengenbach* (Hannover, 1856) (photomechanical reprint: Amsterdam, 1966).

Goldast, Melchior: *Monarchiae S. Romani Imperii sive Tractatum de iurisdictione imperiali seu regia et pontificia seu sacerdotali* (*tomi* II and III) (Frankfurt, 1618).

Goll, Jaroslav: *Quellen und Untersuchungen zur Geschichte der Böhmischen Brüder* (Prague, 1878).

Grotius, Hugo: *Opera Omnia Theologica* (3 vols) (Amsterdam, 1679).

Harrison Thomson, S.: *Magistri Johannis Hus, Tractatus de Ecclesia* (Cambridge, Mass., 1956).

Hessus, Simon: *Apologia Simonis Hessus adversus D. Rossensem Episcopum Anglicanum super concertatione eius cum Ulrico Veleno. An Petrus fuerit Romae. Et quid de primatu Romani pontificis sit censendum* (Basle, 1523).

Hottingerus, Joh. Henr.: *Historiae Ecclesiasticae Novi Testamenti seculi XVI. Pars II: Continens Historiam Reformationis* (ed. Joh. Henr. Hambergeri, 1665).

Kalivoda, R. and A. Kolesnyk: *Das Hussitische Denken im Lichte seiner Quellen* (Berlin, 1969).

Kaminsky, H.: *Master Nicholas of Dresden. The Old Color and the New* (Philadelphia, 1965).

Komenský, J. A.: *Retuňk proti Antikristu a svodum jeho* . In *Dílo Jana Amose Komen-*

ského, II (Prague, 1971).

Krasonický, Vavřinec: *Odporové, že svaty Petr nedržel stolice papežské v Rimě. Psani panu Ždarskému a on panu Hasištejnskému* (Manuscript in Prague, original 1500, copy—beginning of seventeenth century).

Lindanus, William: *Panoplia evangelica, sive de verbo Dei evangelico libri quinque* (Cologne, 1560).

——: *Tabulae grassantium passim haeresium* (Antwerp, 1562).

Lipsius, R. A. and M. Bonnet: *Acta Apostolorum Apocrypha* (Leipzig, 1891) (photomechanical reprint: Hildesheim and New York, 1972).

Luther, Martin: *Auf das überchristlich, übergeistlich und überkünstlich Buch Bocks Emsers zu Leipzig Antwort. Darin auch Murnarrs seines Gesellen gedacht wird.* (1521), *WA* 7.

——: *Zwo schöne und tröstliche predigt* (1546), *WA* 51.

——: *Wider das Bapstum zu Rom vom Teuffel gestifft* (1545), *WA* 54.

——: in addition to the above, quotations from *WA*, *Briefwechsel*, 2 and *WA*, *Tischreden*, 3.

Martini Lydius, Joh.: *Scriptores duo anglici, coaetanei ac conterranei. De vitis Pontificum Romanorum. Videlicet: Robertus Barns et Johannes Baleus* (Leiden, 1615).

Murner, Thomas: *Von den babstenthum* (1520). In *Deutsche Schriften* (Vol. VII), ed. Franz Schultz (Berlin, 1918–1931).

Marsilio of Padua: *Der Verteidiger des Friedens (Defensor pacis), bearbeitet und eingeleitet von Horst Kusch* (Berlin, 1958).

Migne, J. P.: *Patrologiae cursus completus. Series latina et graeca.*

Pighius, Albertus: *Hierarchiae ecclesiasticae assertio* (Cologne, 1538).

Polanus, Amandus: *Amandi Polani a Polansdorf. Partitiones theologicae juxta naturalis methodi leges conformatae duobus libris, quorum primus est de fide, alter de bonis operibus* (Basle, 1590).

——: *Sylloges thesium theologicarum disputationibus Roberti Bellarmini praecipue oppositarum* (Basle, 1597).

Reedijk, Cornelis: *The Poems of Desiderius Erasmus* (Leiden, 1956).

Revius, James: *Historia Pontificum Romanorum, contracta, et compendio perducta usque ad annum aerae Christianae* MDCXXXII (Amsterdam, 1632).

Salmasius, Claudius: *Librorum de primatu papae, pars prima (cum apparatu)* (Leiden, 1645).

Sanders, Nicholas: *De visibili Monarchia Ecclesiae libri octo* (Louvain, 1571).

Spanheim (filius), Friedrich: *Dissertationum Historici Argumenti Quaterni* (Leiden, 1679).

——: *Opera (tomus secundus)* (Leiden, 1703).

Thomas Aquinas: *Summa Theologica.* In *Sancti Thomae Aquinatis Opera Omnia, iussu impensaque Leonis XIII* (Rome, 1888).

——: *Quaestiones quodlibetales (cum introductione R. P. Mandonnet, O.P.)* (Paris, 1926).

Valla, Lorenzo: *De falso credita et ementita Constantini donatione Declamatio.* In *Laurentii Vallae Opera* (Basle, 1540) (a photomechanical reprint of this edition in *Laurentius Valla, Opera Omnia. Con una premessa di Eugenio Garin*, Turin, 1962).

Veluanus, John Anastasius: *Der Leeken Wechwyser.* In *Bibliotheca Reformatoria Neerlandica* (Vol. IV), ed. S. Cramer and F. Pijper (The Hague, 1906).

Welzig, Werner: *Erasmus von Rotterdam. Ausgewählte Schriften.* I, *Epistola ad Paulum Volzium. Enchiridion militis christiani* (Darmstadt, 1967). Another edition of the *Enchiridion militis christiani: ex officia Joannis Maire* (Leiden, 1641).

Wyclif, John: *De Christo et suo adversario Antichristo*, ed. R. Buddensieg (Gotha, 1880).

——: *De antichristo*, ed. J. Loserth (London, 1896) (photomechanical reprint London, 1966).

———: *Tractatus de potestate pape*, ed. J. Loserth (London, 1907) (photomechanical reprint, London 1966).

3. STUDIES

Allen, P. S.: *The Age of Erasmus* (Oxford, 1914).
———: *The Correspondence of an Early Printing House* (Glasgow, 1932).
Bainton, Roland: *Erasmus, Reformer zwischen den Fronten* (Göttingen, 1972).
Bakhuizen van den Brink, J. N.: *Traditio in de reformatie en het Katholicisme in de zestiende eeuw* (Amsterdam, 1952).
Bannenberg, G. P. J.: *Organisatie en bestuur van de middeleeuwse universiteit* (Nijmegen, 1953).
Bartoš, F. M.: *Zapadlé dílko bratrské vědy*. In *Vestnik kralovské ceské spolecnosti nauk* 1925 (Prague, 1926).
———: *Cusanus and the Hussite Bishop M. Lupač. ComViat*, 1962 - 1.
———: *Erasmus und die böhmische Reformation. ComViat*. 1958 - 1/2.
———: *Apologie de M. Jean Huss contre son apologiste. ComViat*. 1965 - 1.
———: *Réponse à la réponse de Paul de Vooght. ComViat*. 1966 - 3.
———: *Das Auftreten Luthers und die Unität der böhmischen Brüder*, ARG XXXI (1934).
Bäumer, Remigius: *Die Auseinandersetzungen über die römische Petrustradition in den ersten Jahrzehnten der Reformationszeit*. In *Römische Quartalschrift für christliche Altertumskunde und für Kirchengeschichte* 57 (1962) (also *Festschrift für Engelbert Kirschbaum* ,S.J.).
Baur, F. C.: *Paulus, der Apostel Jesu Christi* (2nd. edn.) (Leipzig, 1866).
Benrath, G. A.: *Wyclif und Hus. ZThK*, 1965.
Benzing, Joseph: *Der Buchdruck des 16. Jahrhunderts im deutschen Sprachgebiet* (Leipzig 1936).
—: *Die Buchdrucker des 16. und 17. Jahrhunderts im deutschen Sprachgebiet* (Wiesbaden, 1963).
———: *Buchdruckerlexikon des 16. Jahrhunderts* (Frankfurt a.M., 1951).
Berkhof, H.: *Christus, de zin der geschiedenis* (Nijkerk, II 1958).
Betts, R. R.: *English and Czech Influences on the Hussite Movement*. In *Transactions of the Royal Historical Society* (1939).
———: *The Regulae Veteris et Novi Testamenti of Matěj z Janova*. In *Journal of Theological Studies* (1931).
Bienert, W.: *Luther über die Petrus-in-Rom-Tradition*. In *Theologische Jahrbücher*, [8]. (Halle, 1940).
Boeren, P. C.: *Nieuw contact tussen grieks-romeinse wereld en Christendom*. In *Cultuurgeschiedenis van het Christendom* (Amsterdam and Brussels, II 1957).
Bohatcová, Mirjam: *Počatky publikační činnosti jednoty bratrské* (Prague, 1962).
Bouyer, Louis: *Autour d'Érasme* (Paris, 1955).
Brock, Peter: *The Political and Social Doctrines of the Unity of Czech Brethren* (The Hague, 1957).
Bruin, C. C. de: *Opmerkingen over de inspiratiebronnen van de moderne devotie*. In *Het land van Cuyk, kerkelijk en politiek verleden* (Cuyk, 1971).
Chadwyck, Owen: *JohnCassian. A Study in Primitive Monasticism* (Cambridge, 1950).
Clemen, Otto: *Beiträge zur Lutherforschung. ZKG* 36, 1916.
———: *Das Pseudonym Symon Hessus*. In *Zentralblatt für Bibliothekswesen* (1900).
———: *Flugschriften aus den ersten Jahren der Reformation*, III (Halle, 1906/1911).
Cullmann, Oscar: *Petrus. Jünger – Apostel – Märtyrer* (Zürich, II 1960).
Dankbaar, W. F.: *Op de grens der reformatie: de rechtvaardigingsleer van Jacques Lefèvre d'Étaples. NThT* 1953/1954.
Döllinger, Ignaz: *Die Papstfabeln des Mittelalters* (Munich, II 1890) (photomechanical reprint 1970).

——: *Das Papsttum* (Munich, 1891) (photomechanical reprint, 1969).

Eck, Johannes: *Epistola de ratione studiorum suorum* (ed. J. Metzler, S.J.) *CCath.* 2.

Enders, E. L.: *Luthers Briefwechsel*, III (Stuttgart, 1889)

——: *Luther und Emser. Ihre Streitschriften aus dem Jahre* 1521 (Halle, 1891).

Erbes, C.: *Petrus nicht in Rom, sondern in Jerusalem gestorben. ZKG* 22, 1901.

Faulenbach, Heiner: *Die Struktur der Theologie des Amandus Polanus von Polansdorf* (Zürich, 1967).

Frank, Karl Suso: *Vita apostolica. Ansätze zur apostolischen Lebensform in der alten Kirche, ZKG* 82, 1971.

Fruin, R.: *Het voorspel van den tachtigjarigen oorlog* (Amsterdam, 1859/1860).

Gindely, A.: *Geschichte der Böhmischen Brüder* ,I (Osnabrück, 1861). (photomechanical reprint, 1968).

Hak, H. J.: *Marsilio Ficino* (Amsterdam, 1934).

——: *De humanistische waardering van de H. Schrift in het bijzonder bij Marsilio Ficino en Faber Stapulensis, NAKG,* 29, 1937.

Hardt, Herm. von der: *Antiqua literarum monumenta. Autographa Lutheri aliorum que celebrium virorum ab A. 1517 usque A. 1546* (3 vols.) (Brunswick, 1691).

Harnack, A.: *Die Chronologie der altchristlichen Literatur bis Eusebius* (3 vols) (Leipzig, 1893–1904).

Harrison Thomson, S.: *Luther and Bohemia. ARG* 44, 1953.

——: *Pre-Hussite Heresy in Bohemia.* In *English Historical Review,* 1933.

Heussi, Karl: *Die Römische Petrustradition in kritischer Sicht* (Tübingen, 1955).

Imbart de la Tour, P.: *Les origines de la Réforme,* II: *L'église catholique, la crise et la renaissance* (Melun, II, 1944).

Jakoubek, Jan and Arne Novák: *Geschichte der čechischen Litteratur* (Leipzig, II 1913).

Jedin, H.: *Studien über die Schriftstellertätigkeit Albert Pigges* (Münster, 1931).

Jednota Bratrská 1457–1957 (commemorative collection) (Prague, 1957) (including contributions from Říčan, Bartoš, Molnár and Čapek).

Joachimson, P.: *Gregor Heimburg,* I (Munich, 1889), II (Munich, 1891).

Jonge, H. J. de: *The Study in the New Testament,* in *Leiden University in The Seventeenth Century,* Leiden, 1975.

Kaminsky, Howard: *A History of the Hussite Revolution* (Berkeley and Los Angeles, 1967).

Klink, J. L.: *Het Petrustype in het Nieuwe Testament en de oudchristelijke letterkunde* (Leiden, 1947).

Klomps, C. H.: *Kirche, Freiheit und Gesetz bei dem Franziskanertheologen Kaspar Schatzgeyer* (Bonn, 1959).

Knight, W. S. N.: *The Life and Works of Hugo Grotius* (London, 1925).

Knihopis českých a slovenských tisku od doby nejstarší až do konce XVIII století, ed. Z. V. Tobolka and F. Horak (Prague, 1925–1967).

Kristeller, Paul O.: *Die Philosophie des Marsilio Ficino* (Frankfurt a.M., 1972).

Kronenberg, M. E.: *Een onjuiste toeschrijving in de Nederlandse Bibliographie van 1500–1540.* In *Het Boek,* 13 (1924).

Kuczynski, A.: *Thesaurus libellorum historiam reformationis illustrantium* (Leipzig, 1870–1874).

Lagarde, Georges de: *La naissance de l'esprit laique au déclin du moyen âge,* III: *Le Defensor pacis* (Louvain and Paris, 1970).

Lecler, Joseph: *Histoire de la tolérance au siècle de la Réforme* (2 vols) (Paris, 1955).

Leff, Gordon: *Heresy in the Later Middle Ages* (Manchester, 1967).

Liber Decanorum Facultatis Philosophicae Universitatis Pragensis (1367–1585), *Pars* III. In *Monumenta Historica Universitatis Carolo-Ferdinandeae Pragensis* (Prague, 1832).

Lindeboom, J.: *Stiefkinderen van het Christendom* (The Hague, 1929).

Loserth, Johann: *Hus und Wiclif. Zur Genesis der hussitischen Lehre* (Munich and Berlin, II 1925).

Lubac S. J., Henri de: *Exégèse médiévale. Les quatre sens de l'Écriture.* (4 vols.) (Paris, 1959–1964).

Lübke, Anton: *Nikolaus von Kues. Kirchenfürst zwischen Mittelalter und Neuzeit* (Munich, 1968).

Lucian: The Loeb Classical Library (8 vols). Vol. VI (ed. K. Kilburn) (London, 1959).

Luchsinger, Friedrich: *Der Basler Buchdruck als Vermittler italienischen Geistes* (1470–1529) (Basle, 1953).

Macek, Josef: *Die Hussitenbewegung in Böhmen* (Prague, II 1958).

——: *Die Hussitische Revolutionäre Bewegung* (Berlin, 1958).

Martin, P.: *Saint Pierre, sa venue et son martyre à Rome.* In *Revue des questions historiques* (Paris, 1874).

Marxsen, Willi: *Einleitung in das Neue Testament* (Gütersloh, 1963).

McConica, James K.: *Erasmus and the "Julius": A Humanist Reflects on the Church.* In *The Pursuit of Holiness in Late Medieval and Renaissance Religion* (ed. C. Trinkaus and H. A. Oberman) (Leiden, 1974).

Meier, Eugen, et al.: *Andreas Cratander—ein Basler Drucker und Verleger der Reformationszeit* (Basle, 1966).

Melles, G.: *Albertus Pighius en zijn strijd met Calvijn over het liberum arbitrium* (Kampen, 1973).

Meyer, Eduard: *Ursprung und Anfänge des Christentums*, III (Berlin and Stuttgart, 1923).

Mirbt, C.: *Quellen zur Geschichte des Papsttums und des Römischen Katholizismus* (Tübingen, III 1924).

Molnár, Amadeo: *Recent Literature on Wyclif's Theology. ComViat.* 1962 - 2.

——: *Le mouvement préhussite et la fin des temps. ComViat.* 1958 - 1.

——: *Luc de Prague à Constantinople. ComViat.* 1961 - 2.

——: *Voyage d'Italie. ComViat.* 1962 - 1.

——: *Das Erziehungswesen der Brüder. ComViat.* 1964 - 2.

——: *"Probacio preceptorum minorum" de Martin Lupač. ComViat.* 1966 - 1/2.

Müller, Joseph T: *Geschichte der Böhmischen Brüder* (Herrnhut, 1922).

Munck, Johannes: *Paulus und die Heilsgeschichte* (Copenhagen, 1954).

Nauwelaerts, M. A.: *Erasmus* (Bussum, 1969).

Nijhoff, W. and M. E. Kronenberg: *Nederlandsche Bibliographie van 1500 tot 1540* (The Hague, 1923).

Oberman, H. A.: *Forerunners of the Reformation* (London, 1967).

——: *"De praedestinatione et praescientia." An anonymous 14th Century Treatise on Predestination and Justification, NAKG* 43, 1960.

Olsen, Glenn: *The Idea of the Ecclesia Primitiva in the Writings of the Twelfth Century Canonist.* In *Traditio. Studies in Ancient and Medieval History, Thought and Religion* (New York, 1969).

Panzer, G. W.: *Annales typographici ab artis inventae origine ad annum* 1500 *(contin. ad a.* 1536*)* (Nuremberg, 1793–1803).

Paulus, Nikolaus: *Die deutschen Dominikaner im Kampfe gegen Luther* (Freiburg, 1903).

Peschke, Erhard: *Die Bedeutung Wiclefs für die Theologie der Böhmen, ZKG,* 54, 1935.

——: *Die Böhmischen Brüder im Urteil ihrer Zeit* (Stuttgart, 1964).

Pfister, Rudolf: *Kirchengeschichte der Schweiz*, II: *Von der Reformation bis zum zweiten Villmerger Krieg* (Zürich, 1974).

Polman, Pontien: *L'Élément historique dans la controverse religieuse du XVIe siècle* (Gembloux, 1932).

Posthumus Meyjes, E. J. W.: *Jacobus Revius*, zijn leven en werken (Utrecht, 1895).
Posthumus Meyjes, G. H. M.: *Jean Gerson, zijn kerkpolitiek en ecclesiologie* (The Hague, 1963).
——: *De controverse tussen Petrus en Paulus* (The Hague, 1967).
Potthast, August: *Wegweiser durch die Geschichtswerke des europäischen Mittelalters (Von 375–1500)* (Berlin, 1862).
Pražak, Emil: *Oldřich Velenský a cesta českého humanismu k světovosti*. In *Ceska Literatura* (Prague, 1966).
Preuss, Hans: *Die Vorstellungen vom Antichrist im späteren Mittelalter, bei Luther und in der konfessionellen Polemik* (Leipzig, 1906).
Renaudet, Augustin: *Préréforme et humanisme à Paris pendant les premières guerres d'Italie* (1494–1517) (Paris, ɪɪ 1953).
——: *Humanisme et Renaissance* (Geneva, 1958).
Renkewitz, Heinz, et. al.: *Die Brüder-Unität* (Stuttgart, 1967).
Reusch, F. H.: *Der Index der verbotenen Bücher*, I (Bonn, 1883).
Říčan, Rudolf: *Das Reich Gottes in den böhmischen Ländern* (Stuttgart, 1957).
——: *Die Böhmischen Brüder* (Berlin and Prague, 1958).
——: *Die tschechische Reformation und Erasmus*. ComViat. 1973 - 3.
Rice, Eugene F.: *The Humanist Idea of Christian Antiquity: Lefèvre d'Étaples and his Circle*. In *Studies in the Renaissance*, IX, 1962.
Rigaux, Béda, O. F. M.: *L'Antéchrist et l'Opposition au Royaume Messianique dans l'Ancien et le Nouveau Testament* (Gembloux and Paris, 1932).
Ritter, Gerhard: *Studien zur Spätscholastik*, II: *Via antiqua und via moderna auf den deutschen Universitäten des XV. Jahrhunderts*. In *Sitzungsberichte der Heidelberger Akademie der Wissenschaften*, 1922.
Rocholl, R.: *Der Platonismus der Renaissancezeit*. ZKG 13, 1893.
Safrai, S. and M. Stern et al.: *The Jewish People in the First Century. Historical Geography, Political History, Social, Cultural and Religious Life and Institutions*, I (Assen, 1974).
Schlier, Heinrich: *Vom Antichrist*. In *Theologische Aufsätze. Karl Barth zum 50. Geburtstag* (Munich, 1936).
Schottenloher, K.: *Bibliographie zur deutschen Geschichte im Zeitalter der Glaubensspaltung, 1517–1585* (Leipzig, 1933–1940).
Seeberg, Reinhold: *Lehrbuch der Dogmengeschichte*, III (Berlin, 1930) (photomechanical reprint, 1959).
Spahn, Martin: *Johannes Cochläus* (Berlin, 1898).
Spinka, Matthew: *John Hus' Concept of the Church* (Princeton, 1966).
Staehelin, Ernst: *Amandus Polanus von Polansdorf* (Basle, 1955).
Stockmeier, Peter: *Causa Reformationis und Alte Kirche*. In *Von Konstanz nach Trient Festgabe für August Franzen* (Munich, 1972).
Strauß, D. F.: *Ulrich von Hutten* (3 vols) (Leipzig, 1858).
Tecklenburg Johns, Christa: *Luthers Konzilsidee in ihrer historischen Bedingtheit und ihrem reformatorischen Neuansatz* (Berlin, 1966).
Tierney, Brian: *Foundations of the Conciliar Theory* (Cambridge, 1955).
Valesius, Henricus (Henri de Valois): *Historiae Ecclesiasticae Scriptores Graeci* (Amsterdam, 1695).
Veesenmeyer, G.: *Von des Ulrich Velenus Schrift, daß Petrus nie nach Rom gekommen sey*. In *Sammlung von Aufsätzen zur Erläuterung der Kirchen-, Literatur-, Münz- und Sittengeschichte* (Ulm, 1827).
Vermaseren, B. A.: *Nieuwe studies over Wyclif en Hus*. TG 76, 1963.
Volf, Josef: *Geschichte de Buchdrucks in Böhmen und Mähren bis 1848* (Weimar, 1928).
Vooght, Paul de: *Hussiana* (Louvain, 1960).
——: *Jean Huss, tel qu'en lui-même (Réponse à Monsieur Bartos)*. ComViat. 1965 - 4.

——: *La notion d'Église-assemblée des prédestiné dans la théologie hussite primitive.* *ComViat.* 1970 - 3/4.

Wedever, Herman: *Johannes Dietenberger, 1475–1535. Sein Leben und Werken* (Freiburg, 1888).

Weller, Emil: *Wörterbuch der Pseudonymen* (Leipzig, 1856).

——: *Repertorium typographicum* (Leipzig, 1864).

Werner, Ernst: *Der Kirchenbegriff bei Jan Hus, Jakoubek von Mies, Jan Želivský und den linken Taboriten.* In *Sitzungberichte der deutschen Akademie der Wissenschaften zu Berlin* (1967).

Wernle, Paul: *Die Renaissance des Christentums im 16. Jahrhundert* (Tübingen, 1904).

Winter, Eduard: *Frühhumanismus. Seine Entwicklung in Böhmen* (Berlin, 1964).

INDEX OF PERSONS

Names of persons occurring very frequently in the New Testament are not included in this index.

INDEX OF SUBJECTS